DEFENDING THE ARTERIES OF REBELLION

Confederate Naval Operations
in the Mississippi River Valley, 1861-1865

Neil P. Chatelain

SB

Savas Beatie
California

Library of Congress Cataloging-in-Publication Data

Names: Chatelain, Neil, author.
Title: Defending the arteries of rebellion : Confederate naval operations
  in the Mississippi River Valley, 1861-1865 / Neil Chatelain.
Other titles: Confederate naval operations in the Mississippi River Valley,
  1861-1865
Description: El Dorado Hills, CA : Savas Beatie, LLC, [2020] | Includes
  bibliographical references and index. | Summary: "Defending the Arteries
  of Rebellion analyzes efforts by the Confederacy to maintain control of
  its key internal waterways across the Mississippi River Valley. It
  examines how numerous organizations, from the Confederate Navy, Marines,
  Revenue Service, Army, River Defense Fleet, state naval forces,
  privateers, and civilian craft, struggled to cooperate and defend the
  Mississippi River and its many tributary and distributary waterways,
  facing issues of command, supply, and overwhelming enemy forces. It also
  highlights how river warfare is a juggling act of constant maneuver,
  static fortifications, and the lingering question of where to mass
  forces to face the enemy"-- Provided by publisher.
Identifiers: LCCN 2020007691 | ISBN 9781611215106 (hardcover) | ISBN
  9781611215113 (ebook)
Subjects: LCSH: Mississippi River Valley--History--Civil War,
  1861-1865--Campaigns. | Mississippi River Valley--History--Civil War,
  1861-1865--Riverine operations. | Confederate States of America.
  Navy--History. | United States--History--Civil War,
  1861-1865--Campaigns. | United States--History--Civil War,
  1861-1865--Naval operations.
Classification: LCC E470.8 .C64 2020 | DDC 973.7/57--dc23
LC record available at https://lccn.loc.gov/2020007691

First Edition, First Printing

Savas Beatie
989 Governor Drive, Suite 102
El Dorado Hills, CA 95762
916-941-6896 / sales@savasbeatie.com / www.savasbeatie.com

All of our titles are available at special discount rates for bulk purchases in the United States. Contact us for information.

Proudly published, printed, and warehoused in the United States of America.

For my wife Brittany.
Thanks for your continued support in all that I do.

Table of Contents

List of Maps

Photos and illustrations have been placed
throughout the text for the convenience of the reader.

ACKNOWLEDGMENTS

THERE were many people who went to great lengths to provide assistance to me in my investigation for this book. Conducting research can be a tedious and difficult process. Without the help of librarians and researchers across the country, I could not have completed my work. There are far too many individuals to list here, but I want to thank some of the archives and institutions.

I found great help at the Williams Research Center of the Historic New Orleans Collection, the Howard-Tilden Memorial Library at Tulane University, and Earl K. Long Library at the University of New Orleans. Across the rest of Louisiana, I must thank those at the Louisiana State University libraries and employed at the Young Sanders Center in Franklin, Louisiana.

Across the rest of the country I am indebted to the McCain Library of the University of Southern Mississippi, the Dolph Briscoe Center for American History at the University of Texas at Austin, the library and museum of the United States Naval Academy, as well as the research centers and libraries at the University of Alabama, the University of Houston, and the University of North Carolina at Chapel Hill. Finally, the outstanding staff at the National Archives in Washington D.C. were excellent.

Additionally, I need to thank Dr. Terry L. Jones, Dr. Henry Robertson, and Gary McQuarrie, who all took an early look at the manuscript and provided great feedback and suggestions. Finally, I need to also thank the wonderful team at Savas Beatie, including Managing Director Theodore P. Savas, who accepted my manuscript, and my editor, Dana Lombardy. Both looked over my drafts numerous times and offered excellent comments, critiques, and challenges. Your efforts have made the book a much better analysis and working with you all has been a pleasure.

Most importantly, I would have accomplished nothing if it were not for the assistance, persistence, and support from my wife Brittany. Thank you for putting up with my conversations, questions, and the many long hours I spent researching and writing.

LIST OF ABBREVIATIONS USED IN NOTES

B&L	Battles and Leaders of the Civil War
New Orleans Ship Register	Ship Register and Enrollments of New Orleans, Louisiana. 6 Vols. Baton Rouge, Louisiana: LSU Press, 1941-1942.
Confederate Officers	Officers of the Confederate States Navy, 1861-1865, (Washington D.C., Government Printing Office, 1898).
DANFS	Dictionary of American Naval Fighting Ships.
OR	The War or the Rebellion: A Compilation of the Official Records of the Union and Confederate Armies.
ORN	Official Records of the Union and Confederate Navies in the War of the Rebellion.
Subject File	Subject File of the Confederate States Navy (Records Group 45), National Archives Building, Washington, DC.
Vessel Papers	Confederate Vessel Papers: Papers Pertaining to Vessels Involved with the Confederate States of America (War Department Collection of Confederate Records, Records Group 109), National Archives Building, Washington, DC.

GLOSSARY OF TERMS

Vessel Types & Weapons

Please note that some of the naval vessels mentioned in this study used a mix of different forms of protection, depending on what materials were available.

Casemate Ironclad	Ironclad vessel using a fully enclosed protective shield, complete with roof and often running most of the length of a ship, as the main deck for cannon.
Cottonclad	Vessel using bales of cotton as protection against enemy fire, often to shield paddle wheels and exposed walking-beam engines on river steamers.

Floating Battery	Immobile craft, typically anchored in place, and used as a platform for firing heavy artillery. Variants included types with partial casemates, batteries built on barges, and batteries converted from semi-submersible dry-docks.
Ironclad	Vessel using iron plates against enemy fire, typically several inches thick. Often railroad iron rails were bolted on to form protection when iron plates were unavailable or could not be manufactured.
Monitor	Name given to the Union's ironclads with round, iron-plated revolving turrets housing heavy guns. Several Monitor classes were employed by the Union Navy, including double and triple turret variants and smaller Mississippi River versions.
Mortar Boat	Vessel whose primary weapon was a large mortar, capable of firing shells in a high arc over fortifications and at targets beyond a line of sight.
Privateer	Vessel privately owned and, possessing a letter of marque and reprisal, authorized to attack the merchant and naval vessels of a designated enemy. Captured enemy ships could be condemned and sold in a prize court, with the privateer's crew and investors receiving the profits.
Ram	Vessel with a metal ram placed on its bow used to smash into enemy ships, creating a large hole to force it to sink.
Revenue Cutter	Small vessels operated by either the United States Revenue Marine or Confederate States Revenue Service. Their purpose was to collect taxes on imports and exports in port cities. Revenue cutters augmented naval forces of both sides.
Semi-Submersible	Vessel that could partially submerge for a time to limit its exposure to enemy fire.
Steamer	Vessel that used steam engines as a means of propulsion. The engine turned a screw propeller under the hull or paddle wheels typically located on the vessel's stern or along either side.
Submarine	Vessel that could completely submerge for extended periods of time.
Timberclad	Vessel that used wooden logs or thick wooden structures as protection against enemy small arms fire.
Tinclad	Vessel that used thin sheet metal as protection against enemy small arms fire.
Torpedo Boat	Small steam craft with an explosive device ("torpedo") at the end of a long spar placed over its bow.
Torpedo	An underwater explosive detonated by contact or from shore by wire connection. Known as a "mine" today.

Organizations

C.S. Army	The Confederate States Army operated warships and supply vessels throughout the Mississippi River Valley, independently and in tandem with ships of the Confederate States Navy.
C.S. Marine Corps	The Confederate States Marine Corps augmented naval crews at sea or at shore establishments and fortifications.
C.S. Navy	The Confederate States Navy operated warships throughout the Mississippi River Valley, including the Confederate Mississippi River Squadron under Commodore George N. Hollins, and smaller squadrons on the Yazoo and Red rivers.
C.S. Revenue Service	Organization of the Confederate Department of the Treasury that operated revenue cutters at New Orleans and other port cities with the purpose of collecting taxes on imports and exports. Often the vessels augmented Confederate naval forces.
Louisiana Navy	Vessels purchased, re-purposed, and outfitted by the state of Louisiana to serve as warships on the inland rivers.
River Defense Fleet	Confederate organization consisting of 14 seized river steamers re-purposed to serve as rams. They were operated by the Confederate Army and manned by civilian contractors.
U.S. Marine Corps	The United States Marine Corps augmented naval crews at sea or stationed at shore establishments and fortifications.
U.S. Mississippi River Squadron	Naval squadron of the United States operating along the entire length of the Mississippi River.
U.S. Revenue Marine	Organization of the Union Department of the Treasury that operated revenue cutters at port cities with the purpose of collecting taxes on imports and exports. Often the vessels augmented United States naval forces.
U.S. Ram Fleet	Collection of river steamers purchased and re-purposed as rams for use by the Union naval forces on the Mississippi River.
U.S. Western Gunboat Flotilla	Collection of ironclads/timberclads manned by Union naval personnel operating under the jurisdiction of the US Army in conjunction with advances down the Mississippi River. Transferred in October 1862 to the Navy, becoming the Mississippi River Squadron.
Western Gulf Blockading Squadron	Union naval squadron responsible for maintaining the blockade of the Confederacy from the port of Mobile, Alabama to the Texas-Mexico border. It was also responsible for Union naval operations on the Mississippi River from its mouth, through the city of New Orleans, to the confluence of the Mississippi River, Red River, and Atchafalaya River.

Introduction

On April 12, 1861, Confederate military forces under the command of General Pierre G.T. Beauregard opened fire on Fort Sumter, the United States Army fortification located at the entrance to the harbor of Charleston, South Carolina. The fort withstood a continuous bombardment until April 14, when Major Robert Anderson surrendered his besieged force. Hostilities between the United States and the newly organizing Confederacy, labeled as rebels by Union leadership, began. Many in both the United and Confederate States believed that the conflict would be short, relatively bloodless, and end in complete victory for their respective side. Few realized that it would take years of fighting, billions of dollars, and hundreds of thousands of lives before the United States was fully restored.

Brevet Lieutenant General Winfield Scott, commander of all army forces in the United States when the war began, was one of those who thought it would be a long war. Commanding the U.S. Army since the Mexican War and holding a general's commission since the War of 1812, Scott was recognized as America's top military mind. In the weeks after the fall of Fort Sumter, he developed a plan he believed could end the war with less bloodshed, even if it took years to accomplish. Scott wanted to encourage Union sympathizers and reconciliation through economic pressure.

The first part of Scott's strategy was a physical blockade of Confederate ports. The blockade was declared by President Abraham Lincoln five days after Fort Sumter surrendered. Without easy access to foreign trade, the Confederacy was hard pressed to supply its military needs, because of its limited industrial base and few railroads that connected less than a dozen Southern manufacturing cities.

The second part of Scott's plan was to seize control of the Mississippi River and tributaries using a large expeditionary force consisting of both naval ships and land forces to occupy the port cities of the western rivers. Federal control of the Mississippi divided the Confederacy in two, separating all of Texas and Arkansas, most of Louisiana, and all of the Indian and Arizona Territories from the rest of the Southern nation. This also cut the Confederacy's communication to the outside world via Mexico, and denied supplies and military forces in the western part of the Confederacy from reaching the eastern half of the country. Scott's proposed "Anaconda Plan" was ridiculed by some newspapers and politicians as too slow.

Ultimately, however, President Abraham Lincoln adopted the plan, in practice if not in name.

This book focuses on the campaigns for the vital western rivers and the role played by Confederate naval forces.

The Mississippi River and its tributaries comprise the largest waterway in North America. It was first settled and farmed by indigenous people as early as 4000 BCE. European explorers discovered the river, the French claiming the Mississippi and all of its tributary waters in the 17th Century. The river later served as a border between British and Spanish colonies in the west before the United States expanded its control into the area in the early 19th Century. By 1860, the Mississippi River was the great internal highway of the United States. Crops and livestock shipped down the river to New Orleans while immigrants, slaves, and imports flowed into the United States via the port city. When the Southern states seceded, leaders on both sides recognized that control of the Mississippi River and its tributaries was essential to success.

The blockade took years to gradually weaken the Confederacy. It took Federal forces less than a year after Fort Sumter to regain control of the Ohio River and most of the Mississippi River, including the South's largest and richest city New Orleans. Complete Union control of the "Father of Waters" came with the capture of Vicksburg, Mississippi, and Port Hudson, Louisiana, in July 1863. It required nearly two more years to secure its tributaries.

This study concentrates on Lincoln's strategic aim to control the Mississippi River and Confederate defensive measures to thwart the Federal goal. It examines the context, scope, means, and performance of Confederate naval and army forces in defending the Mississippi River and its tributaries.

Much was written about the Union conquest of the Mississippi River. The famous campaigns for control of the fortified towns of Vicksburg, Mississippi and Port Hudson, Louisiana, seen as the capstone of Union efforts on the river, are the most prevalent. Also important are the chronicles about the United States Navy's effort to build a riverine force that assisted in these campaigns. Often analyzed was the Union campaign for control of New Orleans and the mouth of the Mississippi River. Finally are the accounts of the Red River campaign of 1864 and the failures by Union military commanders to gain control of northwestern Louisiana. These four elements are almost always viewed from the perspective of Union forces and seem to downplay efforts by the Confederacy to provide a naval defense of North America's largest and most important waterway.

The first attempt to document the actions of Confederate naval forces on the western waters was done by a former Confederate naval officer, J. Thomas Scharf.

His book, published in 1887, devoted seven chapters to narratives about the internal waters of the Southern states. Often, Scharf took first-hand accounts from his former associates and merged them into one story. Overall, it serves as a good baseline of sequencing events and actions related to the Confederate Navy as a whole.

The Official Records of the Union and Confederate Navies in the War of the Rebellion was published in the years following Scharf's book and added volumes of documents, firsthand accounts, battlefield reports, and other collections regarding the Confederate Navy; several whole volumes were devoted to operations on the western waters. This compilation however, does not tell a cohesive story. Instead the *Official Naval Records* is a collection of documents that must be carefully explored to determine what actually occurred. Furthermore, there is a serious lack of documents from Confederate viewpoints as many naval documents were destroyed during the evacuation of Richmond, Virginia in 1865.

The next great attempt to chronicle the naval operations on the Mississippi River was done by Fletcher Pratt in 1956. His book, *Civil War on the Western Waters*, was the first full narrative of the naval war on the Mississippi River and its tributaries. Pratt's work outlined the course of the war on these rivers, but its shortcomings were a lack of adequate source documentation and small errors in describing ship construction, commissioning, and conversion. Other works, such as Jack Coombe's *Thunder Along the Mississippi*, published in 1996, sought to retell the tale of the river battles for control of the Mississippi River. Coombe's effort in particular relied on accounts from the Union perspective. Furthermore, since it was a story about the control of only the Mississippi River, the tale abruptly ends with the siege and capture of Vicksburg. Actions of the Confederacy were presented in reaction to Union endeavors. The most recent book on Civil War naval operations as a whole was by its most preeminent historian. James McPherson's 2012 *War on the Waters* highlights the river campaigns and their importance to the Union's war efforts, though he likewise follows Pratt and Coombe by largely downplaying Confederate naval efforts in this theatre as reactionary and unorganized.

Two recent works made attempts to highlight Confederate naval operations. Raimondo Luraghi's *History of the Confederate Navy*, published in English in 1996, provided an excellent overview of the Confederate Navy as a whole. Chapters are devoted to naval operations on the Mississippi River, efforts to build both a conventional and ironclad force on the river, and later efforts to do so on tributary waterways. Overall, Luraghi's work remains an impressive accounting of Confederate naval actions in the Civil War. R. Thomas Campbell's *Confederate Naval Forces on Western Waters*, published in 2005, was the first attempt to describe the

Confederate naval defense of the Mississippi River and its tributaries. Campbell's work was an engaging tale of this defense, covering issues related to forming a navy at New Orleans, the ironclad construction programs on the river and tributaries, the battles for control of the river, and the struggle for control of each tributary. Campbell's work provided the first detailed examination of Confederate naval forces on the Mississippi River. However, it did not address the Confederate defense of Mississippi Sound and Lake Pontchartrain, or operations on the upper Mississippi River and tributaries by the Confederate Army in 1864 and 1865. Nonetheless, his book set the standard for research and knowledge of Confederate naval operations in this area.

Two books that documented the campaigns for New Orleans include Chester Hearn's *The Capture of New Orleans 1862* published in 1995 and Charles Dufour's *The Night the War Was Lost* published in 1960. Other regional works include Donald Frazier's 1996-2020 quadrille about the war in Louisiana and Texas, and Edward McCaul's 2014 book *To Retain Command of the Mississippi* about the river battles for control of Memphis. These studies provide a breadth of detail regarding local operations, but sometimes neglect Confederate naval operations.

Defending the Arteries of Rebellion closely examines overall naval defense by the Confederacy for the Mississippi River and its tributaries. From the very beginning of hostilities, the Confederate States of America attempted to create a navy to protect its territory along its internal waterways. This defense included mobile armies operating near the Mississippi River, static fortifications at key points, and naval ships operating in conjunction with those fortifications and armies or on their own.

This study focuses on the Confederate Navy, but not exclusively. For example, the siege of Vicksburg is examined, but land operations in that campaign are already available in great detail in other published sources. The Confederate Navy was just one part of the naval defense that evolved. The Confederate Army usually worked with, and sometimes against, their naval counterparts to crew and operate ships, especially when naval personnel were short-staffed or unavailable. Most notably, soldiers of the local garrison at Vicksburg manned artillery on the ironclad *Arkansas* in the summer of 1862, serving directly under naval officers. Also, the Confederate River Defense Fleet established in 1862 was manned by civilian contractors and officially a part of the Confederate Army. Members of the Confederate Marine Corps and Revenue Service also rendered support when they were available and operating in the area. Some civilians established their own private naval elements, particularly at New Orleans through privateers. Individual states also created a naval defense, most notably Louisiana's efforts to build a small naval fleet in the spring of 1862.

Besides operating ships, construction and refit programs, supply systems, fortification building and expansion, ground operations, and irregular actions also were important elements in the Confederacy's defensive efforts. From large shipbuilding and supply centers in New Orleans, Louisiana and Memphis, Tennessee, to small, uninhabited areas along the Yazoo River and Bayou Teche, the Confederacy struggled to build modern warships intended to challenge Union hegemony of the river valley. Just as soldiers manned the ships when required, Confederate naval personnel contributed to the ground defense of military installations when there was a need for men and a shortage of ships in the area. Finally, there were a series of irregular exploits. These ranged in size and scale from the first successful use of underwater mines (called torpedoes), boarding enemy ships, and experimentation with submarines and torpedo boats. It was an amazing amount of inventive and improvised activities while under wartime stress and confusing and sometimes egotistical military and civilian leadership.

Defending the Arteries of Rebellion is divided into four major parts. Chapters one through three focus on efforts by the Confederate Navy and other organizations to create a naval presence on the Mississippi River; primarily on building, and equipping ships for use, particularly the first phase of ironclad construction in the fall of 1861. Chapters four through six cover the 1862 naval battles for control of the Mississippi River's upper and lower extremities such as the siege of Island Number Ten and the campaigns for control of Memphis, Tennessee, and New Orleans. Chapters seven through ten examine the final operations for control of the Mississippi River, including the year-long struggle for Vicksburg. This third part analyzes operations in southern Louisiana for control of Bayou Teche and the Atchafalaya River in 1863, contest for control of the Yazoo River in 1863 and 1864, and the second phase of Confederate river ironclad construction on these tributaries. The final part of the book, consisting of chapters eleven and twelve, discuss the actions by Confederate naval forces on the tributaries of the Mississippi River, most notably, the defense of the Red River to the end of the war.

These four parts are followed by summaries, analysis, conclusions, and insights into how the Confederacy learned quickly to defend its rivers for more than three years using impromptu construction, innovations, and ad hoc forces.

CHAPTER ONE

Building Defenses
on the Lower Mississippi River

T HE establishment of the Confederate States of America in February 1861 was a momentous event, and the delegates at the convention in Montgomery, Alabama, suspected their actions would likely result in war. They declared their independence and drafted a constitution, but the United States government under President James Buchannan refused to act in any meaningful way and took pains to avoid any official acknowledgment of the new government organized in Montgomery.

Incoming president Abraham Lincoln was staunchly against the secessionist movement, and the provisional congress of the Confederacy took measures to establish a national defense. The framework of an army was instituted first. Shortly thereafter on February 21, 1861, a navy was established. Provisional President Jefferson Davis appointed Stephen Mallory to serve as his naval secretary.

Mallory had many connections to the United States Navy before the war began. A native of Key West, Florida, his many political experiences would prove beneficial in the coming struggle. As a Florida Senator, Mallory served on the committee on naval affairs for a decade, learning how a navy operated and acted, as well as learning how politics blended with military matters in the higher echelons of the government. Mallory's lasting achievement while on the committee was the establishment of a retirement board that evaluated aging naval officers to make determinations whether they should be forcibly retired. There being no provision for mandatory retirement from the navy at that time, officers gained higher rank

Stephen Mallory, Confederate Secretary of the Navy. *Library of Congress*

and position through a seniority system that quickly swelled the senior ranks with aging and infirm officers, some of whom were in constant service for forty years or more. The new board helped make room for younger and more energetic officers.

As expected, many senior naval officers resented Mallory for his proposals while younger ambitious officers praised him for giving them the chance to both prove themselves in positions of responsibility and gain promotion, something that the new secretary would remember as the Confederate Navy was organized. Mallory's expertise proved invaluable to the Confederacy as it struggled to maintain its tenuous hold on independence.

With no actual naval force at his disposal, Mallory quickly went to work organizing his department and establishing an overall naval strategy. The only tangible asset was a plethora of naval officers who already resigned from the service of the United States, with more doing so each week. Ultimately 373 officers resigned or were dismissed form the United States Navy, approximately one-fourth of the service's total. These officers were eager to serve, but in February 1861 there were no ships to assign them to and there were no major naval yards or facilities that could build or repair warships. (Norfolk, Virginia was not available until the state seceded in May.)

The rush of officers to Mallory's office proved so great in early 1861 that he was directing many to join the army as artillery officers. However, things began to change as the new naval department established its policies and looked at a long-term strategy for the coming war. The Confederacy needed ships to defend its ports and Mallory looked immediately to New Orleans, Louisiana, as the best place to acquire them. This was because New Orleans was the only city in February 1861 in the new Confederacy that possessed "great workshops where machinery of the most powerful kind could be built" along the skilled craftsmen "capable of building ships in wood or iron, casting heavy guns, or making small arms."[1]

In addition, it was also the Confederacy's largest city and most productive port, boasting 33 steamship companies in 1860. Other civilian ports including Charleston, South Carolina, and Mobile, Alabama, with smaller privately owned repair and maintenance facilities, but nothing on the scale of New Orleans. In fact, only one naval yard at Pensacola, Florida, fell into Confederate hands before the firing on Fort Sumter, but it was rendered useless because Union soldiers held the fortifications outside the harbor, blockading the port city. In short, Mallory placed

---

1 Charles W. Read, "Reminiscences of the Confederate Navy," *Southern Historical Society Papers* 52 vols. (1876), 1:331.

his early hopes on building a naval force in the only city he knew was capable of bringing his goals into realities.[2]

Origins of a Naval Force at New Orleans

Funding was approved in March 1861 by the Confederate Congress for ten gunboats that were to be purchased or built and Mallory wasted no time in dispatching officials to find ships. Three officers, Captain Lawrence Rousseau, Commander Ebenezer Ferrand, and Lieutenant Robert Chapman, were dispatched to New Orleans with the task of finding civilian steamships that held promise for conversion into warships. Together, the trio of officers possessed nearly a century of combined naval experience. Rousseau was one of the most senior officers in the fledgling Confederate Navy. Having joined the United States Navy in 1809, it was believed that his fifty years of naval service would help in choosing civilian ships that held promise for potential conversion. In the midst of the secession crisis, Rousseau resigned from the United States Navy, casting his lot with the South. Commander Ferrand was equally experienced in naval affairs, having joined the United States Navy in 1823 and serving diligently until late January 1861, when he too resigned. Lieutenant Chapman, the most junior of the three, still boasted fourteen years of naval service.

Ship after ship was inspected by the trio, but deficiencies were found in every civilian vessel they examined. Rousseau forwarded his findings to Mallory. By the time they reached the Confederate government offices in Montgomery, Alabama, however, events intensified the situation. Confederate forces fired on Fort Sumter on the morning of April 12 and the garrison soon after surrendered. Both sides began their escalation to full-scale war. President Abraham Lincoln called for 75,000 volunteers to end the rebellion and, on April 19, declared a blockade of Southern ports. With war begun, Mallory took a closer look at the reports forwarded by Rousseau. Even with deficiencies, any ship capable must be seriously considered for use.[3]

Mallory needed to establish a naval strategy that would both protect the Confederacy and counter the Union blockade. What developed initially was a

2 David D. Porter, "The Opening of the Lower Mississippi," in *Battles and Leaders of the Civil War* (New York, 1887), 2:22. Hereafter Cited as *B&L*.

3 *Official Records of the Union and Confederate Navies in the War of the Rebellion*, 31 vols. (Washington, D.C.: Government Printing Office, 1880-1901), vol. 4, ser. 1, 156-157. All references are to Series 1 unless otherwise noted. Hereafter cited as *ORN* 4:156-157.

two-pronged approach: keep the supply lines open by circumventing the blockade, plus dispatching cruisers to sea that would wage a war against the commerce of the United States. Added to this was President Jefferson Davis's call for privateers. In response to Lincoln's call for troops to suppress the rebellion, Davis issued calls for issuing letters of marque and reprisal. It was hoped that privateers would benefit the weaker Confederacy, as it had done for the United States in both the War of 1812 and the Revolution against the British.

Mallory realized he must acquire whatever ships could be armed to form local makeshift raiders in each major port city. Originally this force was designed with the view of breaking the Union blockade, but it evolved into a defensive fleet-in-being tasked with protecting the ports and waterways of the Confederacy until purpose-built ships constructed in Europe could be purchased and sent across the Atlantic Ocean to break Lincoln's blockade.

To execute both the offensive raiding and the defensive protection parts of his strategy, Mallory relied on Rousseau's reports. Though the ships Rousseau found each had their own deficiencies, the Confederacy must make do with what was available. Instructions were sent to Rousseau to immediately begin purchasing ships and to commence the process of converting them for military purposes.

Another senior officer was with Mallory going over Rousseau's findings. Raphael Semmes, known as "old beeswax" by those familiar with him because of his impeccable moustache, was a celebrated and aggressive sailor whose pre-war reputation would only grow as the conflict continued. He joined the United States Navy in 1826 and commanded the USS *Somers* in the Mexican War before practicing law in Mobile. Semmes was among the first to gain a commission into the Confederate Navy in February 1861, with the rank of commander, and he was anxious to get to sea.

Originally, Semmes was dispatched to acquire weapons from Northern states, but after Fort Sumter was captured, Semmes returned empty handed. One morning after returning, Semmes was sitting in Mallory's office when the two began looking over Rousseau's reports. Semmes found the report on one ship, a small merchant steamer, and turned to Mallory. "Give me that ship; I think I can make her answer the purpose." Mallory agreed and Cmdr. Semmes left Montgomery for New Orleans to assume command of his vessel.[4]

---

4 Raphael Semmes, *Memoirs of Service Afloat: During the War Between the States* (Baltimore, MD, 1868), 93-94.

Rousseau initially purchased two vessels from among the list he forwarded to Mallory. Cmdr. Semmes's vessel was the *Habana*, a Caribbean merchant that transported goods between New Orleans and Cuba. Its most recent voyage took the vessel from Havana back to the Mississippi River, where it arrived on March 18, just as Rousseau's board was commencing its work.

Rousseau's report noted that the *Habana* fit many requirements needed: it was a screw propelled steamer, augmented by three masts for sail-power, with a low-pressure engine capable of steaming up to ten knots. Its one major drawback was limited storage space for coal, leaving the ship with only five days of fuel for steaming. Additionally, with a draft of about 12 feet, the ship was restricted from entering many of the Confederacy's shallow ports. Semmes believed that such deficiencies could be overcome and on April 20, 1861, Rousseau paid $65,000 (US or equivalent Confederate scrip) for the *Habana*. Two days later, he ordered First Lieutenant Joseph Fry, a Virginian with twenty years of naval experience, to begin outfitting her at the Crescent dry-dock in Algiers, just across the river from New Orleans. The vessel, once in Confederate service, would be renamed the *Sumter*, after the Confederate victory at Fort Sumter. Fry oversaw operations until Semmes arrived from Montgomery and took personal charge of the conversion.[5]

The cargo vessel *Marquis de la Habana* also showed initial promise for conversion to a warship. This vessel had a colorful past. Originally built in Philadelphia in 1859, the ship was used by Admiral Thomas Marin's naval forces siding with General Miguel Miramon's conservative movement in the Mexican Reform War. Most notably, the vessel was involved in the battle of Anton Lizardo, where it was disabled and captured by the USS *Saratoga*. Taken to New Orleans as a prize, the ship, along with the simultaneously captured *Miramon*, were classified as "pirates upon the high seas." The pair of ships were sold at auction and converted back into merchant steamers.

The *Marquis de la Habana* made one run between New Orleans and Havana before the firing on Fort Sumter. Inspected by Rousseau and his board, the ship appeared to fit the requirements needed for a man-of-war. Powered by both a screw propeller and three masts, it was believed that the steamer might serve

---

5 "Arrived Yesterday," *New Orleans* [LA] *Daily Crescent*, Mar. 19, 1861; Ibid; "Navy of the Confederacy," *Dallas* [TX] *Herald*, May 22, 1861; "The Steamers Star of the West and Habana," *Baltimore* [MD] *Daily Exchange*, Apr. 24, 1861; Captain Laurence Rousseau, "Purchase Order for Habana and Marquis de la Habana," Apr. 20, 1861, *Subject File for the Confederate States Navy, 1861-1865.* (National Archives Microfilm Publication M1091, Records Group 45, National Archives Building, Washington D.C.), Subject File AC: Construction. Hereafter cited as *Subject File*, AC, NA.

First Lieutenant Thomas B. Huger, CSN.

Naval History and Heritage Command

adequately as a raider. With a draft of 14 feet however, it was even more restricted from Confederate ports, but it was believed that such limitations were acceptable for raiding at sea. The biggest drawback was the ship's engines, which were known to have been unreliable when the vessel was operating under Adm. Marin's command. Nonetheless, it was believed that a good engineering department could compensate for such a deficiency. Additionally, Lt. Robert Chapman, one of Rousseau's board members, was the officer in charge of the prize crew onboard, bringing it to New Orleans after its capture. In late April, on Chapman's urging, Rousseau purchased the ship for $53,500. It was immediately brought to the shipyard of John Hughes in Algiers for conversion and was renamed the *McRae*.[6]

Mallory dispatched the best naval officers available to man and outfit these ships. Commander Raphael Semmes was given free range to select the officers that would serve with him on the *Sumter*. He selected First Lieutenant John M. Kell, a Georgia native with twenty years of naval experience, including service in the Mexican War, as his executive officer. Lieutenant Robert Chapman made a request to join the crew and he was detached from Rousseau's inspection board. First Lieutenants John M. Stribling and William E. Evans, both South Carolinians with over thirty years of naval experience between them, completed the list of Semmes's senior officers.[7]

6 James M. Morgan, "The Pioneer Ironclad," *United States Naval Institute Proceedings* (1917), No. 10. 43:2277; Neil P Chatelain, *Fought Like Devils: The Confederate Gunboat McRae* (Bloomington, IN, 2014), 2-7; "Talk on Change," *New Orleans* [LA] *Daily Crescent*, Jun. 28, 1861.; Captain Lawrence Rousseau, "Purchase Order for Habana and Marquis de la Habana, Apr. 20, 1861, *Subject File*, AC, NA.

7 United States Naval War Records Office. *Register of Officers of the Confederate States Navy 1861-1865* (Washington D.C., 1931), 33, 56, 106, 189. Hereafter cited as *Confederate Navy Register*.

To command the *McRae*, Mallory selected 1Lt. Thomas B. Huger, another South Carolinian. Huger was a twenty-six-year veteran of the United States Navy with service off the coast of Veracruz during the Mexican War. He was the husband of Marianne Meade, sister of future Union General George Meade, who died in 1857, leaving Thomas a widower with five children. Lieutenant Huger was present at the bombardment of Fort Sumter, commanding a battery of guns on Morris Island.

Ordered to New Orleans as Huger's executive officer was 1Lt. Alexander F. Warley. Another South Carolinian, Warley served in the United States Navy since 1840. Like Huger, Warley was present at the bombardment of Fort Sumter, commanding batteries at the Dahlgren Channel. First Lieutenants John Eggleston and John R. Dunnington, both naval academy graduates, were likewise ordered to the *McRae*.[8]

Both the *Sumter* and the *McRae* were, in Mallory's view, envisioned as commerce raiders. They remained at sea and attacked Union shipping, making the war costlier to the United States and hopefully removing support for the war from New England merchants. Furthermore, the two ships' presence abroad might add legitimacy to the fledgling Confederacy in the eyes of international governments. It was Mallory's object that they serve this purpose until ships specially constructed in Europe could be acquired to expand the Confederate raiding.

After purchasing the pair, Mallory dispatched a report to President Davis, updating him on activities in New Orleans. Mallory, like Rousseau, was unhappy with the tiny new navy, writing that "agents of the department have thus far purchased but two [steamers], which combine the requisite qualities. These, the *Sumter*, and the *McRae*, are being fitted as cruisers and will go to sea at the earliest practicable moment." In May 1861, the public learned of the acquisition of the two ships when newspapers printed word of their purchase and outfitting by the government.[9]

Other ships soon joined the *Sumter* and the *McRae* in the conversion process. When Louisiana first seceded, the United States revenue cutters *Robert McClelland* and *Washington* were seized along the New Orleans wharves. Captain John G. Breshwood, a native of Norfolk, Virginia, was in command of the *Robert McClelland*.

---

8 "Bombardment of Fort Sumter," *Keowee* [SC] *Courior*, May 18, 1861; Chatelain, *Fought Like Devils*, 10-11; *Confederate Navy Register*, 53, 54, 204.

9 "Report of Secretary Mallory" *ORN*, ser. 2, 2: 52; "Message from Jefferson Davis," *Shreveport* [LA] *Daily News*, May 11, 1861.

He, along with his two lieutenants, S.B. Caldwell and Thomas Fister, voluntarily surrendered the ship to Louisiana officials. All three men received appointments in the Confederate Revenue Service and were assigned back to the cutter, renamed *Pickens*.

For surrendering the ship, the men were summarily dismissed from the United States Revenue Marine, precursor to the Coast Guard, by U.S. Secretary of the Treasury John A. Dix. The revenue cutter *Washington* was likewise seized in Louisiana's secession and turned over to the Confederacy. Limited visits by journalists and dignitaries were allowed and on one a journalist was quick to note numerous ships "which are being fitted up with great rapidity and completeness." Revenue cutters maintained a stockpile of arms and typically held one or two cannon for defense and the pair of cutters seized in New Orleans were no exception.

The *Pickens* began patrolling the lower Mississippi River as part of the Confederate Navy; the *Washington*, smaller and lightly armed with only one small cannon, was kept at New Orleans collecting revenues on incoming ships and blockade runners.[10]

A curious addition to these improvised naval forces soon made its appearance in New Orleans. Recently captured in Texas while attempting to transport Union soldiers from isolated forts there, the *Star of the West* was taken to the Crescent City as one of the Confederacy's first prizes of war. The steamer was famous for its failed relief expedition of Fort Sumter, made in January 1861, which was repulsed by cadets from the Citadel Military Academy. Due to its nature as a passenger ship, capable of housing 1000 guests, it was purchased by Rousseau and outfitted as a receiving ship.

Placed in command of the renamed *Saint Philip* was Acting Midshipman William V. Comstock, a twenty-year-old Louisiana native with four years of naval experience. Comstock was described by the press as "very gentlemanly, affable, and courteous—an ornament to the service and an honor to our glorious little Pelican State." By May 1861, there were some 175 sailors onboard the *Saint Philip*, training and working on other ships, preparing them for active service. The entire

---

10 John Adams Dix, *Memoirs of John Adams Dix*, (New York, 1883), 1:376; "Our Little Navy," *The Shreveport* [LA] *Weekly News*, Jun. 3, 1861.

crew of the *Sumter* joined them, there being inadequate berthing space onboard Semmes's raider for the 114 crewmen while its conversion was being undertaken.[11]

Birth of the Confederate Marine Corps

When the Confederate Congress created the navy department, they likewise established the Confederate States Marine Corps. The marines, just like their counterparts in the United States, were organized to man shore installations, serve as gunners and security onboard ships, repel boarders, board enemy ships, and serve as shore parties from ships. Officers were organized in Montgomery in March 1861 and Capt. A.C. Van Benthuysen, a military veteran who previously served with Garibaldi in the Italian Revolutions, was ordered to New Orleans to establish a recruitment center. Joining him was Capt. George Holmes, a Maine-born veteran of the United States Marine Corps.[12]

New Orleans soon expanded to become the center for marine recruiting for the entire Confederacy. By April 23, 1861, Capt. Van Benthuysen enlisted 95 marines in the New Orleans area. They were organized and designated as Company B, Confederate States Marine Corps and ordered to Pensacola, Florida, for active field service. Capt. Van Benthuysen accompanied them, but soon after returned to New Orleans to maintain recruiting efforts. These proved fruitful and by the end of May, he transferred another 150 marines to Pensacola; these were combined with Company B to form a makeshift battalion. His efforts faced competition from the army, navy, militia, and privateers for available manpower. To assist in the recruiting efforts, bounties of up to $50 were offered to potential recruits. By the end of 1861, the marines recruited in New Orleans served as the nucleus of the entire corps, with many of the noncommissioned officers promoted throughout the war being taken from the cadre of those early recruits from New Orleans.[13]

---

11 "The Confederate Navy," *New Orleans* [LA] *Daily Crescent*, May 27, 1861; Confederate States of America War Department, *Proceedings of the Court of Inquiry Relative to the Fall of New Orleans* (Richmond, VA, 1864), 123 (hereafter cited as *Court of Inquiry*).

12 "Departure of Marines," *New Orleans* [LA] *Daily Crescent* (New Orleans, LA), Apr. 24, 1861; Stephen Mallory to A.C. Van Benthuysen, Mar. 30, 1861, A.C. Van Benthuysen Papers, Louisiana Historical Association Collection, Tulane University.

13 Ralph W. Donnelly, *The Confederate States Marine Corps: The Rebel Leathernecks* (Shippensburg, PA, 1989), 16-17; Stephen Mallory to A.C. Van Benthuysen," Apr. 29, 1861, A.C. Van Benthuysen Papers; Michael E. Krivdo, "Confederate Marine Corps Recruiting in New Orleans and Marine Activities in the First Year of the Civil War," *Louisiana History* (Fall 2007), No. 4, 40:464; *Confederate*

Though most marines recruited in New Orleans were dispatched to Pensacola, many were called back to Louisiana. Both Cmdr. Raphael Semmes and 1Lt. Thomas Huger wanted marines for their ships and Secretary Mallory ordered the marines in Pensacola to dispatch detachments for each ship. First Lieutenant Becket Howell, brother-in-law to President Jefferson Davis and veteran of the United States Marine Corps, led a detachment of twenty men to report to Cmdr. Semmes to serve as the CSS *Sumter's* marine guard. First Lieutenant Richard Henderson, son of Brevet Brigadier General Archibald Henderson, the "Grand Old Man of the [U.S.] Marine Corps," was ordered to the CSS *McRae* with a detachment of 24 marines. Henderson and his men reported for duty on June 17, 1861.

These shipboard marines were often called on to fill a variety of roles. One United States marine of the time period described daily life in his diary: "one day (or rather one hour) he is a soldier—the next a sailor; and when the ship is going through the process of coaling, he may be found upon the coal whip and be denominated a coal heaver." The detachments ordered to the *Sumter* and the *McRae* were the first Confederate marines joining a ship's complement. Stephen Mallory and his Commandant of the Marine Corps, Colonel Lloyd J. Beall, continued their focus of recruiting efforts in southern Louisiana. It is estimated that by the end of 1861, some 80 percent of all Confederate marines were recruited in the New Orleans area.[14]

More Ship Inspections and Conversions

While the *Sumter* and *McRae* were being outfitted for sea, Rousseau continued his efforts inspecting vessels in search of those that could meet the requirements of naval service. On April 22, Rousseau inspected the *Florida*, a mail packet that plied the waters between Mobile and New Orleans. Despite using two paddle wheels for propulsion instead of a screw propeller, he found the vessel acceptable for coastal operations and ordered its purchase. It was outfitted on Lake Pontchartrain, just north of the Crescent City with two small boats and four artillery pieces added to prepare the ship for battle in coastal waters. The vessel's draft of just six feet

---

States of America, *Journal of the Congress of the Confederate States of America* (Washington D.C., 1904-1905) 5:184 (hereafter cited as *Confederate Congress Journal*).

14 "The Yankee Note-Book Continued," *Galveston* [TX] *Tri-Weekly News*, Oct. 1, 1863; Henry O. Gusley, *The Southern Journey of a Civil War Marine: The Illustrated Note-Book of Henry O. Gusley* (Austin, TX, 2006) 45.

allowed it to operate very close to land in relative safety and to move between the many small ports in coastal Mississippi and Louisiana. First Lieutenant Charles W. Hays, an Alabamian with over twenty years of naval experience, was placed in command of the *Florida*.

Additionally, Rousseau inspected the steamer *Yankee* on May 9. Built in 1849 in Cincinnati and operating since on the Mississippi River as a tug, the *Yankee* was a reliable vessel that became a gunboat for protecting the Mississippi River. It already proved useful to river operations when it transported Louisiana militia to Fort Saint Philip in January after Louisiana Governor Thomas O. Moore ordered federal installations in the state seized. Renamed the CSS *Jackson*, the ship was entrusted to 1Lt. Washington Gwathmey, an Englishman turned Virginia resident who joined the United States Navy in 1832.[15]

Outfitting so many ships simultaneously proved more difficult than originally anticipated. There were nine dry-docks in Algiers when the war began, the largest collection being part of the shipyard owned and operated by John Hughes. Though New Orleans was a major port, the declaration of a blockade by the United States caused many foreign ships to flee the city. Additionally, many sailors were either flocking to join the army or to join a privateer. As a result, Confederate naval authorities encountered difficulties finding sailors to operate their ships. Many experienced seamen were not familiar with the requirements of men-of-war and the officers in the New Orleans area struggled to both acquire and train sailors.

The lack of experience proved catastrophic almost immediately. Tragedy struck the CSS *Sumter* on May 17. A small boat under the charge of Midshipman John H. Holden, a twenty-year-old native of Tennessee, was transporting an anchor when it capsized. The swift current of the river proved too much and four men, including the young Holden, drowned. Two months later on July 20 the *McRae* suffered a loss when recently enlisted Irishman James Keen fell off of a yardarm and fractured his skull on the wharf, dying instantly. As a result of these accidents, training was increased for all sailors in the city, with officers promoting a heightened state of safety and readiness.[16]

Raphael Semmes initially believed that fitting out his ship would be relatively easy. Reality proved otherwise as he struggled for months to prepare the *Sumter* for

15 "Payment Receipt for CSS Florida," Sept. 29, 1861, *Subject File*, AC, NA; "Payment Receipt for CSS Florida," Aug. 30, 1861, *Subject File*, BG, NA.

16 John Kell, *Recollections of a Naval Life* (Washington, 1900), 146; Semmes, *Memoirs of Service Afloat*, 102-103; "Fatal Fall," *New Orleans* [LA] *Daily True Delta* (New Orleans, LA), Jun. 21, 1861.

sea. Besides finding a crew, Semmes had to alter the *Sumter* into a cannon armed raider.

Semmes recalled the first time he set eyes on the ship after arriving in New Orleans on the morning of April 22. Though the passenger liner would need plenty of work, Semmes found himself pleased with the ship. "Her lines were very easy, and graceful," he later recalled, "and she had a sort of saucy air about her." Within ten days the ship was sent to the Crescent dry-dock in Algiers and shipyard workers began the process of removing the upper cabins, strengthening the decks to support heavy cannon, refurbishing and adding new sails and rigging, installing a new main mast, and contracting for the required supplies needed to keep a ship at sea for an extended period of time.

Though New Orleans had several shipyards, they were not accustomed to outfitting men-of-war. Additionally, since the city lacked an organized naval station, naval agents scoured for supplies like competitive companies bidding for a contract, resulting in several instances where one ship would place bids for supplies against another. "Everything had to be improvised, from the manufacture of a water-tank, to the 'kids and cans' of the berth-deck messes, and from a gun-carriage to a friction-primer." Semmes's executive officer, Lt. John Kell surmised that such improvisations "consumed much more time than we anticipated."[17]

Most important were the cannon that would change a vessel into a warship. The *Sumter* was redesigned to be armed with five cannon, four 32-pounders in broadside and one 8-inch gun on a pivot amidships. The 8-inch gun was sent from the defenses of Charleston, but the remainder of the guns needed to be found elsewhere.

Fortunately for the Confederacy, Virginia, North Carolina, Tennessee, and Arkansas seceded after President Lincoln called for volunteers to suppress the Confederate rebellion. With the secession of Virginia came the Gosport Navy Yard in Norfolk, the best naval installation in the South. It possessed hundreds of cannon, a large dry-dock, and warehouses full of supplies that Mallory's department desperately needed.

Semmes placed a request for cannon and four 32-pounders were dispatched from Virginia. Delays continued, however, due to the not always reliable rail transportation network. When the cannon finally arrived, they lacked carriages and Semmes contracted with the firm of John Roy, who was also constructing gun

---

17 Semmes, *Memoirs of Service Afloat*, 96, 98; "Payment Receipt for CSS Sumter," Jun. 13, 1861, *Subject File*, AS, NA; Kell, *Recollections of a Naval Life*, 146; John Roy, Diary, May 16, 1861, Louisiana Historical Association Collection, Howard-Tilton Memorial Library, Tulane University.

CSS *McRae. Naval History and Heritage Command and Photographic History of the Civil War*

carriages for the army, to meet his needs. After the guns were finally installed, Semmes next turned to gunpowder. Secessionists captured the United States military arsenal at Baton Rouge, Louisiana, intact in January 1861. Over 300 barrels of powder were seized and a portion was dispatched downriver.[18]

Preparations on the *McRae* were just as tedious. Lieutenant Huger's ship was considered the most formidable of Rousseau's original pair, but it faced many of the same challenges the *Sumter* did. The hull was painted black to make the ship seem more imposing and it would be more heavily armed; six 32-pounders from the Gosport Navy Yard in Norfolk were dispatched for the vessel. One 9-inch Dahlgren gun and one 24-pounder brass rifle, both mounted on pivots so they could be rotated and fired from either side of the ship, were also added to the vessel's armament. The Dahlgren gun was reinforced with two wrought-iron bands, allowing greater charges of powder to be used for added range and force.

Huger and his executive officer, Lt. Alexander Warley, worked tirelessly to organize a crew and get to sea. By June, some 120 officers and men joined the ship's complement. "You must not be surprised to hear of the *McRae* taking prizes," one sailor wrote home, pointing out the eagerness of the crew to reach the open ocean

18 Semmes, *Memoirs of Service Afloat*, 99; John Roy, Diary, May 28 and 31, 1861; "Payment Receipt for CSS Sumter," Jun. 15, 1861, *Subject File*, BA, NA.

and get to work. The greatest struggle for the *McRae* was preparing the engines, boilers, and six furnaces for sustained use. The chronic engine problems that plagued the vessel off the coast of Mexico the previous year remained and extra engineers were assigned to the ship to ensure it would be ready for a sustained cruise.[19]

The citizens of Louisiana were proud of the ongoing work at the wharves of New Orleans and Algiers. The *McRae* "is an excellent sea-boat, and is being thoroughly overhauled and strengthened in every part," printed one newspaper, "and will doubtless, under the command of her very efficient officers prove a no mean acquisition to our little navy." Furthermore, the shipyard workers of the city toiled to finish preparing the ships for service. Onboard the *Sumter*, "as many workmen as could be employed were cutting away the light passenger cabins, strengthening decks for supporting the battery."[20]

Mallory's Plans for the *Sumter* and *McRae*

Besides the senior officers commanding the ships, few knew how Mallory intended to employ the vessels being outfitted in New Orleans. A lack of knowledge did not halt speculation and rumors ranged from steaming on the open ocean to attacking up the Mississippi River. One Union newspaper editorialized that the *Sumter* and the *McRae* would be dispatched to Memphis. These thoughts echoed General Gideon Pillow, commanding troops in Tennessee, who wrote to the Confederate secretary of war, demanding that "if the President has not yet ordered the *McRae* up, let it be done as promptly as possible."

Crewmembers were unaware of where their ships were destined, though they too joined in the speculation. John H. Dent, an engineer onboard the *McRae*, ventured a logical guess to his father: "I can't imagine where we will go but I suppose we will try and sink the blockade."[21]

19 John H. Dent, Jr. to John H. Dent, Jun. 25, 1861, John Horry Dent, Jr., Letters, University Libraries Division of Special Collections, The University of Alabama; "Payment Estimate for CSS McRae," May 16, 1861, *Subject File*, AD, NA; "Payment Receipt for CSS McRae," Jul. 25, 1861, *Subject File*, BG, NA; "Payment Receipt for CSS McRae," Jun. 17, 1861, *Subject File*, EB, NA.

20 "The Confederate Navy," *New Orleans* [LA] *Daily Crescent*, May 27, 1861; Kell, *Recollections of a Naval Life*, 146.

21 "Report of Major General Pillow," *ORN* 20:789; "The Latest News by Telegraph," *Hartford* [CT] *Daily Courant*, Jun. 20, 1861; John H. Dent, Jr. to John H. Dent, Jun. 25, 1861, John Horry Dent, Jr. Letters.

Mallory wanted the armed tug *Jackson* to defend the lower Mississippi while the *Sumter* and *McRae* went to sea as raiders. Just as the two others, the *Jackson* was armed as quickly as possible. Conversions were underway for the smaller vessel to mount two 32-pounders and special gun carriages reinforced by a rail iron chassis were fabricated to add stability to the cannon.

Meanwhile, Semmes and Huger knew their deployments entailed facing Union blockading ships; Lt. Warley of the *McRae* boasted to a fellow officer that "we would sink all of Lincoln's ships by fire if we could not take them into port."

The United States Navy did not sit idly by while the Confederacy organized its new naval forces. In May, the USS *Brooklyn* started the blockade of the Mississippi River and began patrols at its entrances from the Gulf of Mexico, bringing the war to the New Orleans area firsthand.[22]

The CSS *Sumter* was the first ship completed and deemed ready for service. Raphael Semmes hoisted the Confederate flag on June 1, 1861, and conducted several days of trials before bringing the *Sumter* downriver in preparation to run the blockade. Semmes admitted to Stephen Mallory that his crew was "nearly all green," and still in need of extensive training, but he did not want to remain in Louisiana waters any longer.[23] On June 30, the *Sumter* made a daring escape from the Head of the Passes, humiliating the USS *Brooklyn* in the process. Commander Semmes was the first naval officer to fly the new Confederate flag at sea, leaving New Orleans behind for the remainder of the war. In the next seven months of cruising, he would capture 18 merchants and steam from the Caribbean to Europe.

The *McRae* was commissioned in July, but developed engine problems on its initial trials. Further complications developed while steaming to Baton Rouge to receive ammunition and powder. One engineer commented in a letter home that the *McRae* "had the misfortune to break or crack two of the wheels which drives the propeller shaft."[24] Several weeks were needed to complete a repair, time that neither Lt. Huger nor Secretary Mallory wanted to waste.

While the *Sumter* was intended to raid on the open ocean, the same was not true of the *McRae*. With commerce raiding as its cover, Mallory intended to send the vessel to England on a secret mission. Lieutenant Huger received sensitive dispatches that he was to deliver to Confederate agents in London. In them were instructions to purchase 10,000 rifles, 200 tons of gunpowder, and anything else of

22 John H. Dent, Jr. to John H. Dent, 6 Jul. 1861, Ibid; John Roy, Diary, Jun. 18, 1861.

23 "Letter from Commander Raphael Semmes," *ORN* 1: 615.

24 John H. Dent, Jr. to John H. Dent, 21 Jul. 1861, John Horry Dent, Jr., Letters.

value that could be crammed onto the ship. Once loaded, Huger was ordered to steam the *McRae* back to the Confederacy, protecting a convoy of merchant ships that were supposed to be organized in England, and attack any enemy merchant ships encountered on the journey.

To prepare for such work, extra speaking trumpets and a plethora of hand and leg irons were supplied to keep potential prisoners locked up, a new set of sails was furnished to help give chase (or escape) on ocean voyages, and wrought iron bulwarks were constructed to protect the engine and boiler rooms from enemy shells. Commerce raiding was very appealing to the officers. One boasted that "all that our officers wish is to capture and burn every thing that we cannot take."[25]

The secret plan did not transpire. On the trials following the repairs to the *McRae's* propeller shaft, more problems developed when "lugs in the driving wheels tore out." The ship turned back upriver for yet more repairs. By the time these were completed, the Union blockade tightened and Huger's secret mission was cancelled. Instead, the *McRae* was reclassified as a river gunboat to augment the tug CSS *Jackson*, still being refitted.

Conversion of the *Jackson* went more smoothly; many of the city's contractors learned valuable lessons outfitting the *Sumter* and *McRae*. With Lt. Huger protecting the southern portions of the Mississippi River with the *McRae* and augmented by the revenue cutters *Pickens* and *Washington*, it was deemed necessary to do the same further upriver and once completed, Lieutenant Gwathmey brought the *Jackson* north to Tennessee, arriving in late August.

The CSS *Saint Philip* remained at New Orleans as a receiving ship. A small hospital was added to the ship so that naval personnel could be cared for onboard. By the end of the summer of 1861, the Confederate Navy had working ships in New Orleans. With no government shipyard, no supplies, and little money, Mallory's officers acquired several vessels and prepared them for battle, albeit improvised. Confederate naval aspirations were to test the blockade of the Mississippi River, and attempt to clear the Gulf of Mexico of Union ships.[26]

---

25 John H. Dent, Jr. to John H. Dent, Jul. 21, 1861 and August 3, 1861, John Horry Dent, Jr., Letters; "Letter from Secretary Mallory," *ORN*, Ser. 2, 2: 81-82; "Sail Contract for CSS McRae," May 1, 1861, *Subject File*, AD, NA; "Payment Receipt for CSS McRae," Jun. 28, 1861, *Subject File*, EM, NA.

26 John H. Dent, Jr. to John H. Dent, Aug. 10, 1861, John Horry Dent, Jr., Letters; John Roy, Diary, May 29, 1861.

The New Orleans Privateers

The Confederate Navy was not the only organization working along the wharves of New Orleans. After the bombardment and surrender of Fort Sumter, President Abraham Lincoln declared a blockade of ports in Texas, Louisiana, Mississippi, Alabama, Florida, Georgia, and South Carolina. After the secession of North Carolina and Virginia, the blockade was extended to include those states as well.

Jefferson Davis, in response, issued a call for privateers through letters of marque and reprisal. Davis's move was a traditional one for smaller powers when facing larger foes. The United States made the same decision in the American Revolution and the War of 1812 against Great Britain. Recently, however, Europeans sought to eliminate the practice of privateers. Representatives gathered in Paris in 1856 and issued a declaration that made the use of privateers illegal to the signatories. The Declaration of Paris would not affect the coming conflict in America. This was because the United States initially refused to sign the declaration and the European powers would not let them try to do so as to benefit after the fact. Foreign powers did attempt to pressure both sides into respecting the declaration and Secretary of the Navy Stephen Mallory agreed that the Confederacy would "hold ourselves responsible to for[eign] governments for the tortuous conduct of our privateers."[27]

Some of the wealthy and elite in New Orleans answered Davis's call for privateers. There was money to be made, after all. A privateer, after receiving its letter of marque and reprisal, was allowed to attack enemy ships, both merchant and men-of-war. Each ship captured by a privateer was subject to condemnation by a prize court. After that, captured ships and cargo were available for sale to the highest bidder. The profits would then be split between the privateer's financial backers and crew. Additional prize money was offered by the Confederate government for those that were willing to attack and capture a Union gunboat.

Though the potential for prize money was enticing, it was split between many different authorities. Backlogs in the judicial system caused both court and port fees to quickly accrue. Auction fees would also be paid after a ship's capture was approved by the admiralty court. Only after the auction was complete and all fees

---

27 Stephen R. Mallory Diary, Jul. 25, 1861, vol. 1, Southern Historical Collection, The Wilson Library, University of North Carolina at Chapel Hill; "The Declaration of Paris, 1856," *The American Journal of International Law* (1907), No. 2. Supplement: Official Documents, 1:89-90.

were paid was prize money distributed. In theory, this distribution was divided evenly between the owners of the vessel and the crew. Often, there were many owners backing finances of a ship. One New Orleans privateer, the *Calhoun*, was owned in part by eight backers split in eleven parts, and prize money first went to them before sailors saw anything for their efforts. Against potential profit was the cost of supplying and operating a vessel at sea. For many sailors the lure of prize money resulted in little or nothing.[28]

The call for privateers spread across the Confederacy's major ports. New Orleans quickly bustled with activity as prominent citizens worked to organize and prepare privateers for sea. Advertisements were placed in local newspapers calling for adventurous and industrious seamen to join with the promise of a share of any prize money earned in captures.

The first privateer to gain notoriety was the *Calhoun*. She was formerly the steamer *Cuba*, New York built and operating on the river since 1851. Her captain, John Wilson, recruited 150 citizens of New Orleans and procured five small cannon—more akin to army field artillery than naval guns—to arm his small 500 ton vessel: a pair of six-pounders, one 18-pounder, and two 23-pounders. The weapons would not be able to compete against a Union warship but was enough to force unarmed merchants to submit.

The *Calhoun's* letter of marque was approved on May 15, 1861, just five weeks after President Davis issued his call for privateers, and Capt. Wilson wasted no time in proceeding to sea. The very next day, it captured the first Union merchant ship taken in the war, the *Ocean Eagle*. Captain Wilson sent it upriver with a small prize crew and the assistance of a nearby towboat while he patrolled the mouth of the Mississippi River. Two days later Wilson's crew struck again, capturing the schooner *Ella* and the merchant ship *Milan*. Crowds lined the riverbank of New Orleans as Wilson took the two captures in tow upriver for adjudication.

The *Calhoun* was just getting started. After a few days resupplying in New Orleans, Capt. Wilson again got underway for the Gulf of Mexico. He shortly caught three New England whalers, the schooners *John Adams*, in the charge of Master C.B. Averall, and *Mermaid*, commanded by a man named Soper, along with the brig *Panama*, in the care of Master Powell, about 90 miles out from the entrance to the Mississippi River. Captured on the same day, the three whalers were transporting 215 barrels of valuable whale oil. Taking his three prizes, Wilson

---

28 *Ship Register and Enrollments of New Orleans, Louisiana* (Baton Rouge, Louisiana, 1942). 6:42. Hereafter cited as *New Orleans Ship Register*.

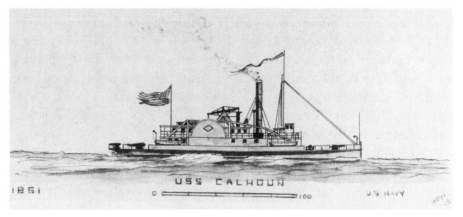

The privateer *Calhoun*.
Naval History and Heritage Command and Erik Heyl, Early American Steamers, Vol. 3.

steamed back up the Mississippi River for New Orleans. Fortunately for the privateers, they did so just in time, as the Union gunboat *Brooklyn* arrived in view and missed intercepting the *Calhoun* by mere hours. The Union gunboat then began the official blockade of the Mississippi River.[29]

The six captured ships were brought before the New Orleans district court for adjudication. The Confederacy, just like the United States, declared that district courts would serve as admiralty courts regarding captured prizes. The judge spent two months reviewing Capt. Wilson's cases before ruling that the *Calhoun's* six captures were legitimate. The prizes and their contents were placed at auction and sold on July 27, 1861. At times, cargo was just as valuable in auctions as the ships themselves and some 1,500 sacks of salt that were onboard the captured *Milan* were sold at $1.56 per sack. The whale oil was also sold at a handsome price, with final bidding at the auction bringing $30,400 for Wilson, his benefactors, and his crew, a handsome profit indeed.[30]

While the admiralty court was deciding the fate of the captured six ships, another judge was reviewing a more immediate concern brought forth by their capture. Among the 63 crewmen captured on the three whaling vessels were eight free Negro sailors. It was not uncommon for runaway slaves to escape and sign onto whaling vessels, where they typically remained safely out of reach of bounty hunters. Upon first sighting the freedmen, the *Calhoun's* crew presumed they were

29 "Arrival of Prizes," The *Carrolton* [LA] *Sun*, May 29, 1861.

30 "Sale of the Privateers' Prizes," *New Orleans* [LA] *Daily Crescent*, Jul. 29, 1861.

indeed escaped slaves and they were immediately locked away in the New Orleans police station until their status could be clarified. Messages were dispatched to Judah Benjamin, then the Confederacy's attorney general, for instructions but he stated that such a matter as to their fate should be dealt with at the level of the Louisiana court system.

For fear of disrupting potential future prisoner exchanges, the courts did nothing and the eight remained locked up for over a month. It was only after the Confederacy passed national regulations for dealing with captured civilian sailors from the United States that they were finally released, to the disappointment of many in Louisiana and to the surprise of the sailors themselves, who believed their destiny was the slave auction block.[31]

The *Calhoun* was just the first privateer operating out of New Orleans. As Capt. Wilson took his ship into the gulf for its initial voyage, another privateer was also searching for Union merchant ships. The *Music*, owned and captained by Thomas McLellan, received its letter of marque on the same day as the *Calhoun*. A smaller vessel that displaced only 273 tons, the *Music* mustered a crew of 100 sailors and volunteers to man its pair of six-pounders. Entering the Gulf of Mexico, McLellan overhauled and seized the *John H. Jarvis*—full of salt—on the same day that the *Calhoun* seized the *Ocean Eagle*, doing so "in the name of Jefferson Davis."[32]

The next day, McLellan teamed up with another privateer for yet another capture. A well-known river towboat, the *Ivy* was under the charge of N.B. Baker. His letter of marque was dated May 16, and he rushed to crew his small steamer. It soon reached its complement of 60 men to help man its single 15-pounder cannon and steamed downriver.

Being a towboat, the *Ivy* was not easily distinguishable as a privateer and Baker planned on using this to his advantage. Baker and McLellan devised a plan to trick a passing Union merchant they sighted on the horizon. The *Ivy* approached the merchant, which proved to be the *Marshall*, and offered to provide its services as a towboat. The captain of the *Marshall* agreed and his ship was towed up the Mississippi River. From there, the *Music* appeared and its men boarded the *Marshall*, which was easily overwhelmed and brought to New Orleans. The *John H. Jarvis* and *Marshall* were brought before the admiralty court, condemned, and sold at auction for a combined $50,000. The *Ivy's* career as a privateer was not over; she later

---

31 William M. Robinson, *The Confederate Privateers* (New Haven, CT, 1928), 40-41; "What Shall Be Done With Them?" *New Orleans* [LA] *Daily Crescent*, May 30, 1861.

32 Robinson, *The Confederate Privateers*, 42.

captured the *Enoch Train* and the *Sarah E. Pettigrew*, before being used as a scout ship at the Head of the Passes for the CSS *Sumter* a short while later.

Other ships applied for letters of marque from New Orleans, but failed to accomplish anything noteworthy. The *W. H. Webb* received its privateer commission in May 1861, but acted only as a troop transport on the river through 1861 and into 1862; her captain, Joseph Leach, never got the *Webb* into the open waters of the Gulf of Mexico. The *J.O. Nixon* was outfitted by Capt. Wilson of the *Calhoun* in July 1861 but made no captures. The *Mocking Bird, Matilda, Isabella*, and *Governor A. Mouton*, all received letters of marque in June 1861, but none ever got to sea, with owners either running out of money while outfitting or abandoning the projects due to the tightening blockade of the river.

The most interesting venture put forth by privateer backers involved the small tug *Enoch Train*. Not to be confused with one of the prizes of the *Ivy* sharing the same name, the *Enoch Train* was a tug in New Orleans at the outbreak of hostilities. Captain John Stevenson converted her into an ironclad ram, intending to steam down the Mississippi River against Union warships.

After the ship was completed, it was seized by the Confederate Navy, prematurely ending its privateer career. Like the *Enoch Train*, three other privateers—the *Calhoun, Ivy*, and *Music*—were eventually purchased by and incorporated into the Confederate Navy to augment river defenses. The only other privateer of note in the New Orleans area was the *Pioneer*, a submarine built in Bayou Saint John and operated on Lake Pontchartrain. It reportedly sank a test target and received a privateer's commission but was never used in battle. The engineers behind creating the *Pioneer* relocated to Mobile and later Charleston where they continued to build submarines, including the *H.L. Hunley*, the first submarine to sink an enemy ship in battle.

New Orleans Becomes a Military City

In addition to the ongoing naval preparations, southern Louisiana hummed with army-related activity as Major General David Twiggs worked to build and strengthen existing fortifications and train soldiers. The entrance to the Mississippi River was first fortified by the Spanish in 1746. Spanish and British forces clashed there during the American Revolution and the United States defended the area from British incursion during the War of 1812. The United States built another fort there in 1822-1823 named after 1812 war hero Andrew Jackson. Twiggs strengthened Forts Jackson and Saint Philip, located 75 miles downriver from New Orleans at a strategically located turn in the river. Fort Saint Philip was built by the

Spanish and used by the Americans to defeat a British fleet in 1814. Since then, well over $200,000 was spent modernizing and maintaining the old Spanish fort, now mounting fifty-two cannon. After the War of 1812, Fort Jackson, larger and mounting nearly one hundred cannon, was constructed on the opposite side of the river at a cost of nearly one million dollars. Any Union ships advancing up the river must pass directly under the guns of these two fortifications.[33]

Besides these two main forts, there were three smaller secondary positions that protected the approaches of southern Louisiana. Fort Pike, mounting 41 cannon, was designed to protect Lake Borgne and its approaches to New Orleans from the east. 10 miles northeast from there, Fort Macomb's guns protected other approaches to New Orleans via Lake Borgne and Lake Pontchartrain. Fort Livingston was constructed to protect the approaches through Barataria Bay to the southwest of the city. These old United States fortifications were strengthened by General Twiggs, who also began work on an interior set of fortifications designed to serve as a last defense of New Orleans.

Immediately downriver from the city was the Chalmette Battery, augmented by the McGehee Battery on the western bank of the river. The Chalmette Battery was located on the site of General Andrew Jackson's victory over British forces in 1815 and mounted 10 guns. The McGehee Battery was lightly armed and supported the position at Chalmette. Upriver from New Orleans was Fort John Morgan. This line of breastworks was designed to hold back a Union land attack coming from the north and west, with a few guns aimed at the river to stop approaching ships.

In addition to the fortifications, there were several training camps erected in and around the city. Camp Benjamin, named to honor Louisiana resident and Confederate cabinet member Judah P. Benjamin, was north of the city on the Pontchartrain Railroad. The Metairie horse racecourse was converted into a training camp for new recruits. Camp Lewis was erected to train militia on the site of present-day Audubon Park. These camps augmented the Jackson Barracks, continuously housing soldiers in the New Orleans area since the War of 1812.[34]

Twiggs recruited men for the defense of southern Louisiana and New Orleans, being the Confederacy's most populous city, was called upon to supply a large proportion of the volunteers. The state militia was strengthened and by the end of

---

33 "New Orleans," *Harper's Weekly*, May 10, 1862.

34 Codman Parkerson, *New Orleans: America's Most Fortified City* (New Orleans, LA, 1990), 60-105, *passim*; U.S. Ship Portsmouth Log, May 9, 1862, Williams Research Center, The Historic New Orleans Collection.

1861 numbered 26,000 men, 15,000 of whom were garrisoned or drilling in the New Orleans area. Many volunteer regiments also formed for service in the Confederacy's provisional army. By the spring of 1862, the greater New Orleans area was protected by eleven infantry regiments, five infantry battalions, one heavy artillery regiment, and seven batteries of artillery, all of which mustered for three years of service. This force of some 10,000 trained volunteers formed the backbone of army defenses for New Orleans. When combined with the local militia, there were, theoretically, some 25,000 soldiers prepared to defend the city.

The Confederate Regular Army also used New Orleans as a recruitment pool. One infantry company and one artillery battery of regular soldiers enlisted in New Orleans in 1861 and added to the city's defenses. Besides this, at least 10 other Louisiana state regiments were organized and trained in the New Orleans area before being dispatched north, where they were serving in Kentucky and Virginia along the Confederacy's northern borders.

In early October 1861, General Twiggs grew ill and was relieved at his own request. Following a lengthy debate, Twiggs's immediate subordinate was tapped to fill the replacement. That man was Major General Mansfield Lovell. Questions over his qualifications were focused on his loyalties. Lovell was considered a northerner, a native of Washington D.C. who graduated from West Point and served in the Mexican War. His family had a robust military history and his father served as the first surgeon general of the United States Army. Lovell left the U.S. Army in 1854, helping to organize John Quitman's filibuster expedition to Cuba before working in New York City until the war began. He ignored the skepticism and doubts of his loyalty and brought a professional attitude to New Orleans, working tirelessly to strengthen its defenses, with a belief in a unity of command.[35]

Upon assuming command, Lovell made a tour of all fortifications, determined to improve them. He dispatched ordnance officers to Virginia and Florida to find newer cannon for the forts. Lovell also placed log obstructions on the Mississippi River both above and below the city. The logs were anchored in the river by heavy chains, positioned between Fort Jackson and Fort Saint Philip. They were deemed quite formidable "because of the swift current down and the slowness of the ships below, which together, would prevent [Union ships] from striking it a blow of sufficient power to break through." A small gap, directly under the guns of the nearby forts, was left to allow Confederate ships to pass. Another log barrier was constructed upriver from New Orleans at Fort John Morgan. More log barriers

35 Stephen R. Mallory Diary, Sept. 14, 1861, Vol. 1.

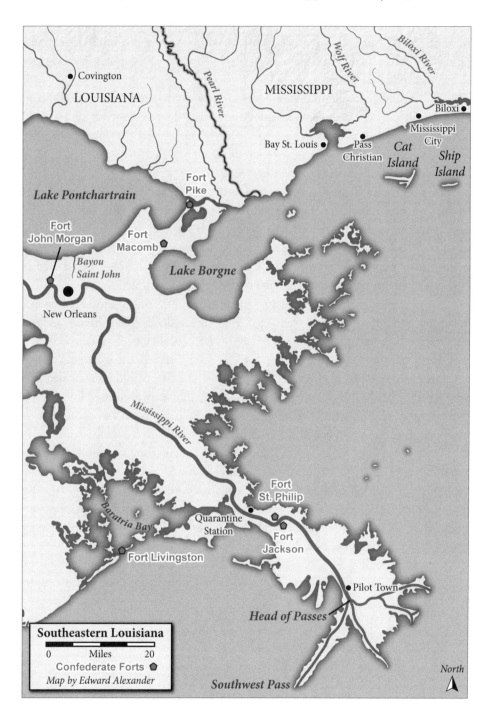

Covington

LOUISIANA

Pearl River

Wolf River

Biloxi River

MISSISSIPPI

Biloxi ●

Bay St. Louis ●

Pass
Christian

*Cat
Island*

Mississippi
City

*Ship
Island*

Fort
Pike

Lake Pontchartrain

Fort
John Morgan

Fort
Macomb

*Bayou
Saint John*

Lake Borgne

New Orleans

Mississippi River

Baratria Bay

Quarantine
Station

Fort
St. Philip

Fort
Jackson

Fort Livingston

Pilot Town ●

Head of Passes

Southeastern Louisiana

0   Miles   20

Confederate Forts ⬠

Map by Edward Alexander

Southwest Pass

North

were proposed further upriver to protect Memphis using floating batteries and rafts anchored in place, but a lack of available supplies and funding forced their abandonment in the planning stages.[36]

Unfortunately, a buildup of river mud and a swift current threatened to destroy his main barrier at Forts Jackson and Saint Philip. Lovell sent for his brother, William S. Lovell, to provide a close inspection of the barrier. The younger brother was a graduate of the United States Naval Academy who made numerous cruises off of Africa, South America, and the Arctic before resigning his commission in 1858 and becoming a cotton planter in Mississippi. William also held a connection to the Quitman family, having married the daughter of John Quitman. With his naval experience combined with the loyalty of being the commanding general's brother, William, who was at the moment in Pensacola in charge of its harbor police force, was a good candidate to both provide a detailed inspection of the log barrier and ensure things were handled to the general's satisfaction.[37]

The younger Lovell, a major of artillery, made a survey of the barrier and found it lacking and "very much broken up." He quickly determined to recreate the barrier, this time using ships instead of logs. Lovell commandeered old schooners that were "anchored across the river, in line abreast, between the forts, and chains and lines were passed from vessel to vessel."[38] The use of old ships instead of wooden logs made the obstruction more formidable in preventing Union ships from passing. The elder brother was pleased with William Lovell's work and saw to his army promotion as a lieutenant colonel.

The city of New Orleans was also becoming a center of military production. By the summer of 1861, "a laboratory was established in New Orleans, and authority given for the casting of heavy cannon, construction of gun carriages, and the manufacture of projectiles and ordnance equipments of all kinds."[39] Three powder works were also created in the city and by early 1862 New Orleans was producing over 5,000 pounds of gunpowder daily.

---

36 Alfred Thayer Mahan, *The Gulf and Inland Waters* (New York, 1883), 70-71; John Roy, Diary, May 1, 1861; "Anonymous Letter," Jul. 3, 1861, Anonymous Confederate Letter, Louisiana and Lower Mississippi Valley Collections, Louisiana State University Libraries, Baton Rouge, LA.

37 Neil P. Chatelain, "William S. Lovell: Confederate Army Riverine Expert," *Civil War Navy–The Magazine* (Winter 2019), No. 3, 6:17-18.

38 *Court of Inquiry*, 67; Read, "Reminiscences of the Confederate Navy," 341.

39 Jefferson Davis, *The Rise and Fall of the Confederate Government*, (New York, 1881), 2:213.

Additionally, an old hospital was commandeered by the army, with half being used to treat sick soldiers and the remainder being converted, apparently without much thought, into an ammunition factory. Four major iron works and foundries in the city were converted for manufacturing guns and naval supplies. The Southern Shoe Factory hired more workers and was soon making 250 pairs of boots daily. Though the blockade caused a considerable downturn in the city's economy, New Orleans' industry remained busy to meet the needs of the Confederate military.

Cooperation at Ship Island

The buildup of military infrastructure made New Orleans an even more crucial target for Union ambitions. Recognizing this, the city's civilian and military leadership worked diligently to bolster the defenses of the lower Mississippi River and prevent Union incursions at its mouth and in the many lakes and bayous that covered southern Louisiana. In 1861, the largest and most coordinated of these defensive activities was the Confederate occupation and fortification of Ship Island, strategically located off the coast of Mississippi. The operation materialized in the summer after Union blockading ships began dispatching steam launches into the sounds and inlets of coastal Louisiana and Mississippi. Lawrence Rousseau and General David Twiggs both saw these small incursions as a serious threat and formed an expedition to take care of the situation. They turned to 1Lt. Alexander Warley, a former lieutenant in the United States Navy who resigned on Christmas Eve in 1860 after his native state of South Carolina seceded. After participating in the capture of Fort Sumter, he was ordered to New Orleans as the executive officer of the CSS *McRae*, which was still undergoing final preparations for sea in early July.

Warley was approached by Capt. Edward Higgins, an old friend and former naval officer who was then serving in the 1st Louisiana Heavy Artillery Regiment. It was he who proposed to David Twiggs the clearing the Mississippi Sound of Union launches and occupation of Ship Island. At first Warley was reluctant to assist; Lt. Thomas Huger, his commanding officer, was out of town on business and he did not want to act without permission. Higgins insisted that the men would only be needed for two days and Warley finally acquiesced, gathering a large part of the crew from the *McRae* and augmenting them with some recently arrived marines from Pensacola. The force of some 80 sailors and 55 marines boarded two steamers, the *Oregon* and the *J.D. Swain*, in Lake Pontchartrain just north of New Orleans and they charted a course for the Mississippi coast.[40]

---

40 "Alexander F. Warley Papers," *Subject File*, HJ, NA.

The two ships departed Lake Pontchartrain on July 5, 1861 for Bay Saint Louis, a small coastal Mississippi town. Arriving there, the sailors spent the rest of the day loading their two steamers with sandbags and cotton bales to offer protection against rifle and artillery fire. Departing at 9:00 am the next morning, they began the search for Union launches. No enemy craft were sighted on the horizon and after a day of fruitless searching, Higgins proposed landing on Ship Island and fortifying the position. Warley eagerly responded that he "was in for it" and a landing was made at 4:00 pm on the afternoon of July 6.[41]

Being the only safe deep-water anchorage between New Orleans and Mobile, Ship Island was strategically located as the best staging and supply point for Union forces in the eastern Gulf of Mexico. Higgins wanted to fortify the island to prevent the Union Navy from using the island as a staging point for an invasion up the Mississippi River. Aware of its strategic value, the United States began work on a permanent fort there in 1857, work that remained incomplete during the secession crisis.

After their initial landing, Warley's men unloaded sandbags and cannon and dug earthworks to withstand an enemy attack. The group brought one 32-pounder cannon, one eight-inch cannon, and two howitzers from New Orleans. A lookout was placed in the lighthouse to keep watch on the horizon. This was fortunate, for two ships were quickly sighted. They proved to be small fishing boats and after an inspection by the crew of the *Oregon*, the fishermen were released. Work continued into the evening, but Warley's contingent was not prepared to provide a permanent garrison because most of the sailors and marines were crewmembers of the CSS *McRae* loaned to the army. As his sailors constructed fortifications, Warley dispatched Capt. Higgins and the two ships back to New Orleans with requests for replacements to garrison the island.[42]

For three days, the sailors fortified Ship Island. Warley split the artillery, placing two guns in the still incomplete fort and two in sand earthworks on the beach. The biggest worry was the limited supply of available powder and shells. Taking a small towboat, Midn. Sardine Stone travelled back to Bay Saint Louis to plead with local army commanders. They responded with the requested supplies, as well as additional manpower. A militia detachment of 75 men returned with Stone as an immediate reinforcement, bringing the total number of personnel on the island to just over 200.

41 Ibid.

42 Chatelain, *Fought Like Devils*, 20-22.

On the evening of July 8, the lookout in Ship Island's lighthouse spotted a Union gunboat on the horizon. The enemy ship, which proved to be the USS *Massachusetts* under the command of Cdr. Melancton Smith, closed and anchored within a mile of Warley's guns for the night. At dawn, Warley ordered Midn. Charles W. Read to open fire on the Union ship with the 8-inch cannon, doing so while the officers of the *Massachusetts* were gathered for breakfast.[43]

Commander Smith ordered his guns manned and surveyed the Confederate positions, looking through his glass, finding "3 secession flags, 39 tents, and 4 batteries in process of erection, the materials used in construction being bales of cotton and sand bags." The artillery exchange was short and, after about an hour, Smith withdrew the *Massachusetts* out of range, with only minor damage "cutting up the rigging somewhat." Overall, Warley's men fired some 26 shots while Smith's gunners replied with seventeen "which sank in the sand" ineffectually.[44] There was only one casualty in the exchange, a Confederate who suffered a slight leg injury.

While Warley's men exchanged shots with the *Massachusetts*, Capt. Higgins was collecting reinforcements. The *Oregon* and *J.D. Swain* arrived in New Orleans on the morning of July 7 and Higgins secured the cooperation of Lieutenant Colonel Henry W. Allen, a Louisiana lawyer and politician, with a contingent of 400 men from the 4th Louisiana Infantry Regiment. A day later, the *Oregon* and the steamer *Gray Cloud* were loaded with men, ammunition, and supplies and departed for Ship Island, arriving several hours after the exchange of cannon fire. They docked and immediately began to offload men and supplies.

As Allen's men were disembarking, the *Massachusetts* again appeared with "the intention of shelling the working party." Warley's sailors opened fire once again and the ship withdrew after replying with one symbolic shell in defiance. The Confederates completed offloading reinforcements and Lt. Col. Allen relieved Warley as commander of Ship Island that evening. Warley and his men, with the exception of one midshipman who remained behind as a temporary advisor, boarded the *Oregon* and the "tired and sandy crowd turned cityward [sic]" to finish outfitting the CSS *McRae*.[45] Higgins praised Warley and his sailors in his

---

43 "The Engagement at Ship Island," *Baltimore* [MD] *Sun*, Jul. 26, 1861; "Alexander F. Warley Papers," *Subject File*, HJ, NA.

44 "Report of Commander Smith," *ORN* 16:581; "The Engagement at Ship Island," *Baltimore* [MD] *Sun*, Jul. 26, 1861; "A Naval Brush at Ship Island," The *Shreveport* [LA] *Weekly News*, Jul. 22, 1861; Read, "Reminiscences of the Confederate States Navy," 333.

45 "Report of Lieutenant Warley," *The War of the Rebellion: A Compilation of the Official Records of the Union and Confederate Armies*, 128 Vols. (Washington, DC, 1880-1901), Ser. 1, 53:709. All references

after-action report, noting this first instance of Confederate joint military operations, even if largely improvised, as a great success.

Four days after Lieutenant Colonel Allen assumed command, the *Massachusetts* made another appearance, this time anchoring about three miles from Ship Island. Allen wanted to entice Cmdr. Smith into a trap. As Smith noted in a report to his superior, "the *Oregon* and *Arrow*, were discovered under full steam, heading for this vessel."[46] Allen tried to use the two ships as bait to lure the *Massachusetts* into the range of his land batteries. The ploy did not work and Smith opened fire on the two Confederate ships with his long-range guns. As they retreated, the *Massachusetts* did not pursue. Lieutenant Colonel Allen's plan failed and this second engagement between Cmdr. Smith and the defenders of the island ended with no damage on either side.

Back in New Orleans, General Twiggs recognized that armed gunboats were needed to support Ship Island, lest the *Massachusetts* and other Union ships harass and assault the island at their leisure. He wrote to the secretary of war in early August requesting "a force of efficient gun-boats to co-operate with the Ship Island fort. I would respectfully recommend that such a force be stationed in Mississippi Sound with the least possible delay."[47] A small force of gunboats was indeed ordered constructed in New Orleans specifically for service in this coastal region, but it would be months before they were ready. The best that could be offered immediately was the promise of more reinforcements to garrison the island. By the end of August, Lt. Col. Allen had four companies of the 4th Louisiana Infantry Regiment, two companies of the Confederate Regular Army, and one independent company called the Washington Light Infantry manning 13 heavy guns.

In early September, 1861, Col. Johnson Duncan, commanding officer of the 1st Louisiana Heavy Artillery, was ordered to assume command of Ship Island and conduct a survey of its defense. Duncan was not impressed. "The fort on Ship Island," he concluded, "is wholly incapable of resisting a combined land and water attack like that which the enemy threatens." Duncan further claimed that "however much they may be strengthened, they can still be starved into submission without firing a single shot," concluding "the occupation of the island is objectless." Major

---

are to Series 1 unless otherwise noted. Hereafter cited as *OR*, 53:709; "Alexander F. Warley Papers," *Subject File*, HJ, NA.

46 "Report of Commander Smith," *ORN*, Ser. 1, Vol. 16, 602.

47 "Letter of Major General David Twiggs to Leroy P. Walker," *OR*, 53:720.

Martin L. Smith, who accompanied Duncan in his survey, wanted to maintain the position, but noted that if the island were to be evacuated, "the proper defense of the sound is a question to be taken in connection with the gunboat force that is or will be available."[48]

Senior officials did not wait long to analyze Duncan's and Smith's reports and on September 13, Maj. Gen. Twiggs ordered the island evacuated. (Twiggs resigned the next month due to health concerns.) Colonel Duncan disabled the lighthouse and began evacuating the garrison, reporting "all the guns, carriages, equipments, implements, &c., ammunition, commissary, and quartermaster's stores, engineer's tools, and all other public and private property" taken off the island by the *Oregon*.[49] The evacuation was completed on the morning of September 16, 1861.

Union forces wasted no time and quickly occupied the island. The same day that the Confederates left, Cmdr. Melancton Smith ordered the USS *Massachusetts*, accompanied by the USS *Preble* and the USS *Marion*, to land parties on the island. The landing force took possession of "thirteen shanties and building still standing, a large quantity of lumber, some iron, and 36 head of cattle." Commander Smith also found a note from Lt. Col. Allen addressed to him offering "our best wish for your health and happiness" but assuring Smith that "before the war closes . . . we may meet face to face in closer quarters."[50]

Colonel Duncan argued that the island should be abandoned and gunboats instead used to defend Mississippi Sound. However, no such a force yet existed. By the time Confederate gunboats were available for use, they were insufficient to contest control of the coastline of Mississippi and Louisiana or challenge Union control of Ship Island. By the end of 1861, the island became a staging area for the invasion of southern Louisiana with thousands of Union soldiers massed there for a planned assault up the Mississippi River to capture New Orleans.

---

48 "Letter of Colonel Johnson Duncan," *OR*, 6:733; "Letter of Major Martin L. Smith," *OR*, 6:736.

49 "Report of Colonel Johnson Duncan," *OR*, 53:740; "Note from General Samuel Cooper," *OR*, 6:738.

50 "Report of Commander Smith," *ORN*, 16: 678; "Note from Lieutenant Colonel Henry W. Allen to Commander Smith," *ORN*, 16:679.

CHAPTER TWO

Initial Movements and Counters

Kentucky's Neutrality Challenged

AT the start of the war, Union leadership was adamant about acquiring gunboats to both protect against Confederate incursions up the Mississippi River and to commence Federal campaigns downriver. By the end of the summer of 1861, Cmdr. John Rodgers purchased and outfitted three gunboats, the USS *Tyler*, USS *Lexington*, and USS *Conestoga*. They served as the first line of defense for the strategic town of Cairo, Illinois and began scouting out Confederate defenses further downriver.

Confederate officials were aware of these gunboats and others under construction and dispatched the newly commissioned CSS *Jackson* upriver to offset their presence. Under the command of 1Lt. Washington Gwathmey, an English born veteran of the United States Navy, the *Jackson* was a small, fast, and improvised gunboat armed with a pair of eight-inch guns. Though lightly armed and hastily fabricated, Gwathmey had orders to back up land batteries being constructed in Tennessee to safeguard the Confederacy's control of the upper Mississippi River Valley.

Major General Leonidas Polk, a West Point graduate, veteran of the Mexican War, and the Episcopal Bishop of Louisiana, commanded Confederate forces in western Tennessee. A personal friend of Jefferson Davis, Polk was tasked with defending the Mississippi River from Union raids; he recognized that the *Jackson* would not be able to single-handedly withstand a Union armada. Land defenses were needed, but Polk was restricted as to where he could operate.

Kentucky declared neutrality on May 16 and both the Union and Confederate governments initially honored that for fear of pushing the state to the other side.

Polk wanted to fortify the Kentucky riverbank towns of Columbus and Hickman, which were well suited to construct fortifications and post cannon, before local Union commanders could attempt to do the same.

In early September, Brigadier General Ulysses Grant's Union Army encamped at Belmont, Missouri, on the opposite side of the Mississippi River from Columbus, with the goal of establishing a base for further operations downriver into Confederate territory. Commander John Rodgers joined Grant's force with the USS *Tyler* and USS *Lexington*. Together, they technically maintained Kentucky's neutrality by occupying the Missouri side of the riverbank. Polk, not wishing to be outmaneuvered, had discretionary orders to protect the area and took it upon himself to occupy Columbus and Hickman on September 3, 1861. He ordered Brig. Gen. Gideon J. Pillow, the senior general of Tennessee's state militia and fellow Mexican War veteran, to advance his forces from New Madrid, Missouri, to Columbus. Polk explained his reasoning in a letter to the governor of Tennessee, where he claimed the movements were "in consequence of the armed position of the enemy, who had posted himself with cannon and intrenchments [sic] opposite Columbus."[1] Pillow's forces landed at Hickman on September 3 and began to construct batteries on the shore. Most of the Confederates marched for Columbus.

Union forces were quick to respond. With the Confederacy making the first violation of Kentucky's attempted neutrality, Cmdr. John Rodgers reasoned that he could now advance his gunboats downriver to Hickman and disperse Confederate transports and Pillow's men before they could fortify their positions. They left Belmont on the morning of September 4, proceeding downriver. Fortunately for the Confederates, the CSS *Jackson* recently loaded coal in Memphis and steamed upriver. It arrived at Hickman on September 3 and joined in helping to transport Pillow's Confederates ashore. Though neither side expected a naval skirmish, the stage was set for the first naval engagement on the upper portions of the Mississippi River as Rodgers's two gunboats steamed downriver.

James Tomb, a Florida native serving on the *Jackson* as an engineer officer, described the scene on September 4: "There was a small company of artillery on the shore with a small Napoleon rifle. They took position just above the town, and when the two Yankee gunboats came in sight, we moved out from the bank into

---

1 "Letter from Major General Polk," *OR*, 4:180.

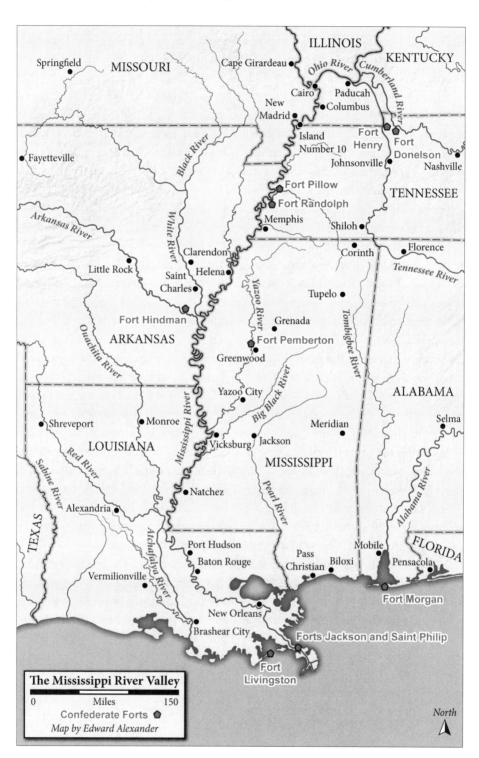

ILLINOIS

KENTUCKY

Springfield   MISSOURI   Cape Girardeau   *Ohio River*   *Cumberland River*

Cairo   Paducah

New Madrid   Columbus

Black River

Island Number 10   Fort Henry   Fort Donelson

Fayetteville   Johnsonville   Nashville

White River

Fort Pillow   TENNESSEE

Fort Randolph

Arkansas River   Memphis   Shiloh

Clarendon   Corinth   Florence

Little Rock   Helena   *Tennessee River*

Saint Charles

Tupelo

Fort Hindman   *Yazoo River*   Grenada

ARKANSAS   Fort Pemberton   *Tombigbee River*

Greenwood

Ouachita River   Yazoo City   *Big Black River*   ALABAMA

Shreveport   Monroe   Meridian   Selma

LOUISIANA   *Mississippi River*   Vicksburg   Jackson

Red River   MISSISSIPPI   *Alabama River*

Natchez   *Pearl River*

Sabine River   Alexandria

TEXAS

Port Hudson   Mobile   FLORIDA

Baton Rouge   Pass Christian   Biloxi   Pensacola

Vermilionville   *Atchafalya River*   Fort Morgan

New Orleans   Forts Jackson and Saint Philip

Brashear City

Fort Livingston

The Mississippi River Valley

0   Miles   150

Confederate Forts ⬠

Map by Edward Alexander

North

the river, and headed for them."[2] When the Union ships were in range, 1Lt. Gwathmey ordered his forward gun to open fire.

The *Tyler* and *Lexington* came about in the river so that they faced upstream and opened fire using their stern guns. The move was a cautious one, allowing for a quick escape upriver should the battle turn against them. The Confederates on the riverbank quickly joined in the duel and "when three or four shots had been exchanged, a battery on shore fired several guns." After firing some 20 rounds at the *Jackson* and the Confederate shore battery, Rodgers noticed his ships losing to the river current, which was pulling them toward the Confederate positions; fearing being dragged under the Confederate guns, he ordered a withdrawal upriver. During the retreat, Rodgers's ships were harassed by Pillow's main body of infantry, still marching to Columbus. Rodgers lobbed a few shells at the Confederates, causing no damage, before continuing to Cairo, Illinois. The Union infantry at Belmont likewise withdrew upriver, leaving Columbus in Confederate hands and Belmont unoccupied.

The entire engagement was a bloodless affair. The *Jackson* moved upriver and moored along the riverbank at Columbus just before nightfall. Expecting the Union ships to return, 1Lt. Gwathmey positioned his ship to be ready to fight come morning, with both guns pointed upriver and the ship ready to get underway at a moment's notice.[3]

As expected, the *Lexington* and *Conestoga* returned on September 5, with each ship firing once on the *Jackson*. Prepared and waiting, Gwathmey's sailors responded and the two Union ships again withdrew upriver unscathed. General Pillow now fortified the bluffs just outside Columbus, bringing up several heavy guns to strengthen the defenses from both naval and land assault. With large cannon overlooking the river at Columbus, the *Jackson* was no longer deemed essential and was sent back to New Orleans.

Union forces swiftly responded to the Confederate incursion into Kentucky. While Rodgers surveyed the Confederate occupation of Columbus on September 5, Gen. Grant's forces seized the town of Paducah, Kentucky, on the presumption of protecting Kentucky's neutrality and to ensure that strategic position was denied to Polk's Confederates. Within a month Columbus and several other key positions on the river were fortified, becoming major obstacles to Union forces attempting

2 R. Thomas Campbell, ed., *Engineer in Gray: Memoirs of Chief Engineer James H. Tomb* (Jefferson, NC, 2005), 21.

3 "Report of Commander Rodgers," *ORN*, 22:309; Campbell, *Engineer in Gray*, 22.

to advance down the Mississippi River. The fortifications impressed one sailor who boasted that Columbus "can never be taken" because of the guns mounted in "natural fortifications."[4]

A direct challenge against Columbus came only once in the ensuing months. Gen. Grant led an attack against Belmont, Missouri, just opposite the river from Columbus, on November 7, 1861. The ensuing battle was chaotic and indecisive. Union forces advanced and captured Confederate camps outside of Belmont before being driven back by reinforcements sent across the river by the unarmed river steamers *Prince*, *Charm*, *Hill*, and *Kentucky*. After the Battle of Belmont, Confederate efforts to fortify Columbus were increased and the position soon became, in the eyes of many, impregnable.

The Confederate advance to Hickman and Columbus was seen as a violation of Kentucky's neutrality and the state sided with the Union. Though thousands of Kentucky's citizens would serve on both sides in the war, the majority would side with the United States. Additionally, most of Kentucky remained in Union hands for the entire war, giving the United States complete control of the Ohio River. Polk claimed Columbus as the first major bastion to defend the Mississippi River for the Confederacy, but his imprudent action resulted in serious negative strategic consequences and was regarded as a major blunder.[5]

A New Naval Commander at New Orleans

While the *Jackson* fought at Columbus, work continued in New Orleans as Capt. Rousseau searched for additional ships. Some of the easiest acquisitions proved to be several corsairs operating out of New Orleans. The first privateers that found their way into the Confederate Navy were the *Calhoun* and *Ivy*.

The *Calhoun* was spacious and loud. Propelled by two paddle wheels and with one small mast, it was not ideally suited for naval service. Rousseau and others in New Orleans, however, used whatever was available and the ship proved its worth by capturing several enemy merchants. The *Ivy* was better suited for this work and became one of the Confederacy's most active vessels. A third privateer, the small and lightly armed *Music*, also joined the C.S. naval service later in the year.

---

4 John H. Dent, Jr. to John H. Dent, Dec. 4, 1861, John Horry Dent, Jr., Letters; E.B. Long, "The Paducah Affair: Bloodless Action that Altered the Civil War in the Mississippi Valley," *The Register of the Kentucky Historical Society* (October 1972), 70:162-264.

5 Robert D. Whitesell, "Military and Naval Activity Between Cairo and Columbus," *The Register of the Kentucky Historical Society* (April 1963), 61:112-114.

Commodore George N. Hollins, CSN.

Naval History and Heritage Command

Besides these privateers, Rousseau made contracts to convert river steamboats, strengthening the decks to handle the weight of cannon. The first of these was the *Livingston*. Built in the shipyard of John Hughes in 1861, Rousseau purchased the new vessel, keeping it in the shipyard to be strengthened. However, it took several months to complete the conversion and cost an additional $80,000. Another alteration took place onboard the *Tuscarora*, purchased from the Southern Steamship Company operating out of New Orleans. The *Tuscarora* was lightly armed, with only one 32-pounder and one eight-inch Columbiad.[6] Even if vessels did not meet the requirements of warships, the Confederate Navy continued to purchase and outfit them, reasoning that any ship was better than none.

Some disagreed with this improvisation method, believing it was a waste of time, limited funds, and scarce resources better suited for more focused projects. Prominent officials and politicians proclaimed in newspapers that the river fleet being built in New Orleans was small and would be unable to win a full-scale battle. Others blamed Rousseau's age—he was born in 1790—claiming he was infirm and could not handle situations aggressively. Secretary Mallory bowed to the pressure of such claims and relieved Rousseau.

However, there were only a few high-ranking Confederate naval officers with the experience of handling a fleet of ships. In the end, Mallory tasked George N. Hollins as the replacement. Hollins was slightly younger than Rousseau. Born in 1799, he served in the United States Navy since 1814. He was captured by the British in the War of 1812 and held as a prisoner of war, later fought Algerian pirates, participated in the Mexican War, and commanded the USS *Cyane* when it

6 "Payment Receipt for CSS Livingston," Jan. 10, 1862, *Subject File*, AC, NA.

bombarded the Nicaraguan coast in 1854. When the Civil War began, Hollins was in command of the USS *Susquehanna*, operating in the Mediterranean Sea. Attempting to resign his commission in June 1861, Hollins, who was described by a fellow officer as "a man of decided character" was instead dismissed from the naval service. He soon found a commission as a captain waiting for him in the Confederate Navy.

Hollins's first actions of the war were to capture several Union merchants in the Chesapeake Bay. The seizures got his name in the newspapers and attracted the attention of Stephen Mallory. In July, Hollins was summoned to Richmond where Mallory promoted him to the rank of commodore and ordered him to New Orleans to assume command of all naval forces operating on the Mississippi River and coastal Louisiana. Hollins was in New Orleans by the first week of August 1861. It was hoped that he would use the same aggressive actions on the river that he showed off Virginia.[7]

Contesting the Mouth of the Mississippi River

While the two navies skirmished upriver near Columbus, Union forces made forays into the mouth of the Mississippi River, testing the strength of Confederate defenses. The blockade was growing tighter with each passing day as more Union ships arrived in the Gulf of Mexico to join expanding patrols. With more ships, Union officers became more aggressive. At the time, most of the Confederate Navy in New Orleans was undergoing conversions in shipyards and there were only a few vessels serviceable and ready for action. Only two vessels, the revenue cutter *Pickens* and the former corsair *Ivy*, were available to contest Union sorties and protect blockade runners.

The *Ivy* was recently acquired by the Confederate Navy. The former privateer could no longer escape into the Gulf due to the increased effectiveness of the Federal blockade. She was a side-wheel steamer that was armed with four cannon, including a prized long-range eight-inch English-made Whitworth rifled gun. In command was Lt. Joseph Fry, a career naval officer from Florida whose naval service dated to 1841. He resigned from the United States Navy in February 1861 and received a commission in the Confederate Navy the following month.

---

7 Morgan, "The Pioneer Ironclad," 2278; George N. Hollins, "Autobiography of Commodore George Nicholas Hollins, C.S.A.," *Maryland Historical Magazine* (1939), No. 3. 34:232, 235, 238; John Roy Diary, Aug. 8, 1861.

Fry first served as the Confederate Navy's lighthouse inspector and briefly supervised the conversion of the *Sumter* before overseeing the *Ivy's* time-consuming conversion. To make up for the limited amount of skilled shipyard workers in the city, thanks in part to the many conversion projects, slaves were leased from local plantations to assist in refurbishing the *Ivy's* sail plan. Once completed, the vessel was sent downriver tasked to "keep a lookout on the motions of the enemy, and to report them from day to day."[8]

The Mississippi River bends and turns through southeast Louisiana and splits up at the Head of Passes. From there, water streams into the Gulf of Mexico through several passes. The most commonly traversed pass was the Southwest Pass, but the South Pass and the Pass à Loutre were also navigable by most ships that drew less than ten feet of water. A small telegraph and pilot station at Pilot Town in the Head of Passes facilitated movement of traffic upriver. Federal naval commanders thought correctly that by taking and holding the Head of Passes, a blockade of New Orleans and the Mississippi River became immensely easier than maintaining ships at each individual pass.

Throughout the summer and fall of 1861, as the blockade of the Mississippi River tightened, Union forays up the river increased. The first was made by the USS *Powhatan*, commanded by Lt. David D. Porter. Assigned to blockade the Southwest Pass, Porter saw both the CSS *Sumter* and CSS *Ivy* anchored in the Head of Passes in early July and he wanted to take action before the ships could escape and prowl the Gulf of Mexico.

Porter's plan was complicated and daring. In the night, a picked crew would steam in a small launch to the telegraph station at the Head of Passes and capture it. When the *Ivy* docked alongside the station the next morning, the small Union crew lying in wait would seize the Confederate vessel and, depending on circumstances, attack the *Sumter* or steam upriver to New Orleans in the hope of destroying the CSS *Saint Philip*. The Federal sailors steamed into the river undetected and managed to reach the telegraph station. A vigilant Confederate sentry detected the sailors as they landed and spread the alarm. With surprise gone, Porter's men temporarily disabled the telegraph before abandoning their plan and returning to the *Powhatan*.

Another incursion was made on September 20 by the USS *Water Witch*, a smaller and more lightly armed blockader. Believing that the Confederates were

---

8 Jeanie Mort Walker, *Life of Captain Fry: The Cuban Martyr* (Hartford, CT, 1875), 143-144; "Payment Receipt for CSS Ivy," Oct. 23, 1861, *Subject File*, AC, NA; "Payment Receipt for CSS Ivy," Nov. 2, 1861, *Subject File*, AS, NA. "Payiment Receipt for CSS Ivy," Aug. 31, 1861, *Subject* File, BG, NA.

erecting batteries along the riverbank, the *Water Witch* entered the river with orders to locate and destroy the positions. The *Ivy* took notice of the advance and Captain Fry ordered his ship underway, taking in tow the revenue cutter *Pickens*, also anchored at the Head of Passes. The Confederate ships withdrew to Fort Jackson as the *Water Witch* fired 23 shots at them. Left on its own, the *Water Witch* shelled the riverbank for several hours before withdrawing that evening back to the Gulf of Mexico, tailed by the *Ivy* "at a very respectful distance," until the Confederate ship reoccupied its position from that morning.[9]

By early October, four Union warships were blockading the entrances to the Mississippi River. This small squadron was under the command of Capt. John Pope, a career naval officer whose service dated back to 1816. Pope ordered his ships into the Mississippi River, believing a permanent naval presence was needed in the Head of Passes. The *Water Witch's* scouting mission of the previous month helped to confirm that the remainder of Pope's ships could safely cross the river bar—an elevated section of sediment that raised the bottom level of the river. People in New Orleans took notice of this encroachment, with one newspaper broadcasting that several Union ships "are lying at anchor a short distance above the Head of the Passes."[10] Captain Pope's intentions were to unify the blockade of the river and build a small fortification at the Head of Passes where supplies could be stored for the blockading ships. It was easier to blockade the Head of Passes than post ships at every individual outlet into the Gulf.

It took several days for the Union ships to cross the bar and assemble in the Head of Passes. The USS *Richmond*, flagship for the small flotilla, with the assistance of a tow provided by the USS *Water Witch*, succeeded in crossing the bar of the Southwest Pass in the afternoon of September 28 and Capt. John Pope anchored his ship at Pilot Town. The USS *Vincennes* joined Pope on October 2 and Capt. William McKean, commanding the blockade of the entire Gulf of Mexico, also dispatched the *Preble* to the Head of Passes to bolster the position. Onboard the *Richmond* was 1Lt. Walter McFarland, a United States Army officer in the Corps of Engineers. His job was to look for potential sites for permanent fortifications and supply stations. McFarland discovered a location where a battery could be erected. Lumber was unloaded in preparation for construction.

9 "Report of Lieutenant Winslow," *ORN*, 16: 683; "Important from the Head of the Passes," *Shreveport* [LA] *Daily News*, Sept. 28, 1861.

10 "Increase of the Federal Force in the Mississippi," *New Orleans* [LA] *Bulletin*, Oct. 3, 1861; Charles F. Gunther, *Two Years Before the Paddlewheel: Charles F. Gunther, Mississippi River Confederate*, Ed. by Bruce S. Allardice and Wayne L. Wolf (Buffalo Gap, TX, 2012), 141.

The Confederates were aware of Pope's incursion. The *Ivy* initially kept watch on Union movements, keeping several miles out of range of Federal guns. On the afternoon of October 9, Lt. Fry steamed toward the Union ships and opened fire. Fry's eight-inch Whitworth rifled gun had a greater range than any of the Union cannon and Pope was unable to return fire while his ships remained at anchor.

Pope sent a dispatch to his superior Capt. McKean expressing concern that "we are entirely at the mercy of the enemy" and that his flagship could be captured or destroyed "by a pitiful little steamer mounting only one gun." McKean received the note and began talks with U.S. Army officers at Fort Pickens, in Pensacola harbor, to borrow several heavy pieces of artillery to protect his ships. McKean obtained two guns, one 30-pounder and one 12-pounder Parrot gun for use in the Head of Passes fortification, but the Confederates took action before they could be installed. Lieutenant Fry observed the arrival of the Union guns from the deck of the *Ivy* and steamed upriver to give notice to senior officers in New Orleans.[11]

The Iron Turtle Joins the Confederate Fleet

In New Orleans, Cmdre. Hollins developed a plan of action to hopefully clear the river of the growing Union presence. It was a gamble that required the use of all of the ships at his disposal. The plan was to launch a surprise attack against Pope's flotilla in the early morning and drive it into the Gulf of Mexico in confusion. It was risky, especially since none of the ships at his disposal were designed as warships.

As Hollins planned his attack, one ship in particular stood out. It looked rather odd, being described as an iron turtle, a floating cigar, and a whale in the water. This was the *Enoch Train*, a strong tug built as an icebreaker in 1855. The *Enoch Train* was purchased by John Stevenson, a prominent New Orleans river captain who was also secretary of the New Orleans Pilots' Benevolent Association. As the war began, Stevenson approached Stephen Mallory and Jefferson Davis, proposing to buy and convert New Orleans tugs by armoring them "to make them comparatively safe against the heaviest guns" and adding a ram to "render them capable of sinking by collision the heaviest vessels ever built." Davis and Mallory ignored the proposal and Stevenson determined to make a try of it on his own. In May 1861, he began raising $100,000 in subscriptions from the wealthy of New Orleans so that his ship could be converted into an ironclad ram. Renamed the

---

11 "Report of Captain Pope," *ORN*, 16:697, 699-700; "Abstract Log of USS Water Witch," *ORN*, 16:724.

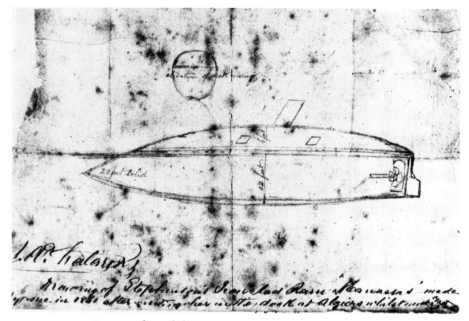

Diagram of Ironclad *Manassas*. Naval History and Heritage Command

Manassas in honor of the Confederate victory earlier in the summer of 1861, it was hoped by its investors that the vessel could produce great results.[12]

Stevenson intended to take the *Manassas* to sea as a privateer, but first it had to undergo a great transformation. Its upper works were cut away before reinforcing the deck in one inch of iron plating. The iron was taken from local railroad reserves and was dovetailed into each other to increase strength. The conversion took place in the Louisiana Dry-Dock Number Two of John Hughes and Company in Algiers, just opposite the Mississippi River from New Orleans.

A single old 64-pounder cannon was fixed on the bow, protruding from a gun port; the entire ship maneuvered to aim it. The real power, however, was in the iron ram fixed to the bow. The ram itself was "made of the best cast iron" and "firmly secured by means of heavy wrought bolts." The ship's redesign ensured that the hull "projected only two feet above the water, and her plated top was convex causing cannon shot to glance off harmlessly." It included an ingenious design that could "eject a shower of scalding water and a cloud of blinding and suffocating

12 "Privateer Manassas Articles of Agreement," Sept. 12, 1861, Subject File, SP, NA; Gunther, *Two Years Before the Paddlewheel*, 168, 179; "Report of John A Stevenson," *OR*, Ser. 4, 1, Part 1:347.

steam over the curved iron deck, making it slippery and untenable." This would help prevent enemy boarding parties from successfully gaining a foothold on the vessel.

The conversion was completed in August and the *Enoch Train* made a successful test run in the Mississippi River. With work on his vessel completed, Stevenson gathered "a loud-mouthed set of toughs" to serve as a crew and trained them in several trials up and down the river at the city. He then applied for a letter of marque. While waiting, the ship was anchored at Algiers, just opposite Jackson Square in New Orleans.[13]

Hollins wanted to add Stevenson's ship to his small makeshift squadron and sent a note politely asking for his cooperation. Stevenson, unwilling to abandon his privateering venture, replied that the Commodore "did not have men enough to take her."[14] An enraged Hollins ordered the ship seized, turning to 1Lt. Thomas B. Huger and the CSS *McRae*. With his crew at quarters, Huger brought the *McRae* alongside the iron turtle. His executive officer, 1Lt. Alexander F. Warley, took a boat commanded by Midn. James Morgan and a party of eight armed men to board the *Enoch Train* and take formal possession of the craft, by force if necessary.

Stevenson did not intend to give up his ironclad without a fight and when Warley's boat arrived alongside, they found the crew "lined up on the turtleback, swearing that they would kill the first man who attempted to board." Unfazed, Warley climbed a ladder onto the ship and the privateer crew "ceased their defiant billingsgate and stood on the turtleback in speechless, as well as, helpless amazement." Several of the crew went below but Warley and a small contingent of sailors followed them and drove them back up to the main deck. The *McRae's* sailors then "drove them ashore, some of them jumping overboard and swimming for it."[15] Thus, the Confederate Navy ingloriously seized its first ironclad ram.

Warley gathered the remaining crew and declared his authority as the new commanding officer, telling them their promises for prize money would no longer be honored. This speech "created much dissatisfaction" and 14 more crewmen went ashore. With them went Captain Stevenson, who fumingly vowed to never cooperate with the Confederate Navy again. Among those who remained with the

13 "The Wrought Iron Prow," *Charleston* [SC] *Mercury*, Apr. 9, 1862; *Dictionary of American Naval Fighting Ships*, 8 Vols. (Navy Department, 1959-1991), 2:546. Hereafter cited as *DANFS* 2:546; Robinson, *The Confederate Privateers*, 157; Morgan, "The Pioneer Ironclad," 2277.

14 James M. Morgan, *Recollections of a Rebel Reefer* (New York, 1917), 55.

15 Ibid; Morgan, "The Pioneer Ironclad," 2278.

First Lieutenant Alexander F. Warley, CSN.

Battles and Leaders of the Civil War

confiscated ironclad were its chief engineer and two mates. Warley received volunteers from the *McRae, Jackson, Ivy,* and *Calhoun* to bring the complement of the *Manassas* back to its full strength of 36 men. He personally remained in command of the vessel as it would take a daring officer to command and Warley "was just that sort of fellow."[16]

With the *Manassas* bolstering his forces Hollins steamed downriver, anchoring his squadron alongside Fort Jackson on October 11. There they waited until nightfall. All his available naval resources were mustered for this attack.

The flagship was the spacious but loud *Calhoun,* under the nominal command of 1Lt. Jonathan H. Carter, a North Carolinian who served in the United States Navy since 1840 and only left that service following the attack on Fort Sumter. The *Calhoun* was armed with five cannon. The CSS *Ivy,* Hollins's scouting ship, joined the group at Fort Jackson, providing valuable intelligence of Union positions. The CSS *McRae,* mounting eight guns and commanded by the able Thomas Huger, was the most heavily armed ship available. Also present was the CSS *Jackson,* just returned from its skirmishing in Kentucky. The revenue cutter *Pickens* likewise added its weight to the squadron. Finally, there was the recently converted CSS *Tuscarora,* armed with one 32-pounder and one eight-inch carronade. The unarmed tug *Watson* rounded out the squadron, there to provide support. Added to all of this was the armored ram *Manassas.*

Hollins's plan was simple, but incredibly risky. The *Manassas* would steam ahead of the squadron in the early morning fog with the objective of breaking through the Union perimeter and ramming the largest Union warship at the Head

---

16 Robinson, *The Confederate Privateers,* 158; John E. Hart to Mrs. John E. Hart, Nov. 26, 1861, John E. Hart Letters, Special Collections and Archives, United States Naval Academy; "Privateer Manassas Articles of Agreement," Sept. 12, 1861, *Subject File,* SP, NA.

of Passes. Warley would then launch a rocket to signal success. Upon seeing the signal, the Confederate squadron would release several fire rafts downriver to create a panic amongst the Union ships. Hollins himself described these fire rafts, writing after the war that he "placed chains from the bows of the two barges so that when the steamers struck the enemy's ships the flat boats would swing round, by the force of the tide & laying on each side, set her on fire & completely destroy her"[17] Hollins's squadron would then close and open fire, either sinking or forcing the Union ships out of the Head of Passes. To help keep the element of surprise—and to protect their exposed engineering machinery—the *Jackson* and *Calhoun* would steam a mile behind the rest of the squadron so that the Union sailors would not hear their loud engines. The *Pickens* likewise remained behind the main group because of its lack of any engines whatsoever, which severely restricted its maneuverability in the battle.

With the plan finalized, preparations for the attack advanced. "We are going on a grand expedition tonight to attack Lincolns [sic] men-of-war now anchored at the Head of the Passes," boasted one engineer onboard the *McRae*.[18] At midnight the moon set, leaving the night dark, and Hollins ordered his ships to weigh anchor and slowly proceeded downriver.

Hollins's plan had one big hurdle to overcome. His seven ships mounted a total of 22 cannon. The Union squadron consisted of fewer ships, just four, but their total of 55 guns was more than double the Confederate firepower. Captain Pope's flagship, the USS *Richmond*, alone mounted 22 guns. His remaining ships were the USS *Vincennes*, mounting 19 guns, the USS *Preble*, mounting 10 guns, and the USS *Water Witch*, mounting four guns. In fact, Pope believed his ships were in no danger of attack at all, despite the previous harassment by the *Ivy*.

Pope ordered his ships to re-coal in the night and placed no advance picket boat up the river to warn of an enemy approach. The most advanced picket was a few sentries onboard the schooner *Frolic*, a recently captured blockade runner, anchored just a few hundred yards upriver of the *Richmond* and the *Preble*. Pope's oversight played into Hollins's plan. Though he had fewer cannon, several of the guns in the Confederate squadron had a longer range and Hollins intended to use this advantage and the *Manassas's* ram to good effect to overcome the Federal squadron's greater strength.

17 Hollins, "Autobiography," 240.

18 John H. Dent, Jr. to John H. Dent, Oct 10, 1861, John Horry Dent, Jr., Letters.

The Battle of the Head of Passes

The *Manassas* steamed quietly toward the Head of Passes with Acting Master Charles Austin at the helm and J. Stevens Mason, the privateer pilot that Captain Stevenson hired, assisting. Warley planned to steam slowly until he sighted the Union ships, when he would order his chief engineer, William H. Hardy, to ensure that "tar, tallow, and sulphur that had been held in reserve for this moment were thrown into the furnace."[19] This combination would quickly increase the heat in the boilers and boost the speed of the *Manassas* for the final strike.

The *Manassas* steamed past the picket schooner *Frolic* and the USS *Preble* and Warley raised speed for the final blow. The commanding officer of the *Preble*, Cmdr. H. French, was awoken by the night watch. Making his way to the quarterdeck, he saw the *Manassas* "not 20 yards distant from our quarter, moving with great velocity toward the bow of the *Richmond*." French immediately hoisted a red light to warn Pope. Warley ordered his engines to full power, not seeing the signal from the *Preble*, and "huge clouds of the densest, blackest smoke rolled up" from the iron turtle's smokestacks as Hardy's concoction was thrown into the furnaces.[20]

At the last moment, sailors onboard the *Richmond* noticed French's red light. Lookouts began scanning the water and spotted something in the darkness. The call to man the guns was hurriedly passed by the officer of the deck. They managed to open fire, but by then it was too late; the *Manassas* was too close and the shells passed clear over. At 3:40 am on October 12, the CSS *Manassas* successfully rammed the USS *Richmond* and the Battle of the Head of Passes was on.

Warley's ironclad was steaming at 10 knots when the blow struck, smashing "a hole five inches in diameter in her hull," mostly below the waterline. The damage could have been much worse however. Alongside the *Richmond* was the *Joseph H. Toone*, a schooner recently captured as a blockade-runner and being used as a supply ship to transfer coal. The *Manassas's* ram struck between the two vessels and broke the *Toone* loose, deflecting much of the force that would have been directed into the *Richmond*. The force of the blow was, however, enough to fracture the ram, and one

---

19 Robinson, *The Confederate Privateers*, 158.

20 "Report of Commander French," *ORN*, 16:712.

Battle of the Head of Passes.

Naval History and Heritage Command and Harper's Weekly

third of the ram's prow fell into the water as the *Manassas* backed from the collision.[21]

Lieutenant Warley immediately ordered Acting Master Sardine Stone, a young volunteer borrowed from the CSS *McRae*, to launch the signal rocket. Stone made his way to the weather deck and lit the rocket. In his excitement "he burned his hand, dropping the stick, and the rocket went sizzling down into the hold," burning the hand of Petty Officer John McGadock.[22] Panic briefly struck the sailors below, with the belief that the rocket was an enemy shell. Warley calmed the crew while Stone regained his composure and launched a second rocket into the air.

Seeing the signal rocket, Hollins passed the order to release the three fire rafts, which were "braced apart from each other by timbers and secured together by a chain cable." The timbers and cables separated the rafts and allowed them to snag against the hull of an enemy ship, engulfing it from both sides with fire. The unarmed tug *Watson*, which was towing the rafts for the fleet, released the tow and *Jackson* and *Pickens* guided the rafts downriver; concurrently, the bulk of the Confederate squadron opened fire with their cannon. An engineer onboard the CSS *Jackson* wrote that the rafts "went down the river all in a blaze, and made a most

21 "Washington, Oct. 25," *Gallipolis* [OH] *Journal*, Oct. 21, 1861; "The Battle of the Passes: The Enemy's Account," *New Orleans* [LA] *Daily Picayune*, Oct. 15, 1861; "The Wrought Iron Prow," *Charleston* [SC] *Mercury*, Apr. 9, 1862.

22 Robinson, *The Confederate Privateers*, 160; "The Battle of Southwest Pass," *New Orleans* [LA] *Daily Crescent*, Oct. 21, 1861.

magnificent sight to us, who were behind her," taking comfort in the belief that "to the Yankees it must have been the reverse."

One raft approached the *Preble* while the ship was weighing anchor. Cmdr. French ordered his anchor chain slipped and abandoned to speedily maneuver away from the raft, which closed to within 150 yards. The desperate act worked and the *Preble* barely evaded the rafts; all three drifted with the river current onto the western bank, "where they consumed themselves without having done damage to anything else," but creating a widespread panic nonetheless.[23]

Hollins's plan was working despite mixed results. The *Manassas* struck with surprise, but its ram was damaged. The fire rafts all missed their targets, although they did cause expected fright and confusion among the Union naval officers. "It was a terrible shock the *Bull Run* [*Manassas*] gave them," exclaimed one officer in the fleet. Another officer gleefully commented home that "it was a beautiful sight to see" the Union squadron in such a panic.[24] Onboard the *Richmond*, Capt. Pope ordered his ships to weigh anchor, abandon the Head of Passes, and make their way into the Gulf of Mexico via the Southwest Pass. The spreading fear had the potential to cause disaster.

The *McRae*, *Ivy*, and *Tuscarora* closed and opened fire, adding to the chaos. As these ships' guns fired, Warley struggled to get the *Manassas* under way again. After ramming the *Richmond*, a loose cable from the Union flagship "slipped over the bow of the *Manassas* and mowed off her little smokestacks even with the turtleback." While struggling to back off the *Richmond*, Pope's guns fired on the ironclad, striking true three times. One shot made a small dent in the armored deck while another "broke the flagstaff, and a third took off one of the smokestacks." The third shot actually slammed into the remaining smokestack and smashed it against the vent of the first smokestack that was carried away by the *Richmond's* cable. With both her smokestacks gone and the vents blocked, the ironclad quickly filled with smoke. Warley ordered his crew to the main deck to prevent suffocation, but Chief Engineer Hardy grabbed an axe and cut away the wreckage blocking the vents while Acting Master Austin held him steady.[25]

---

23 "Particulars of the Naval Combat at the Head of the Passes," *Shreveport* [LA] *Daily News*, Oct. 18, 1861; Campbell, *Engineer in Gray*, 24; Morgan, "The Pioneer Ironclad," 2280.

24 John H. Dent, Jr. to John H. Dent, Oct. 15, 1861; John H. Dent, Jr. to John H. Dent, Oct. 27, 1861, John Horry Dent, Jr., Letters.

25 Morgan, *Recollections*, 56; "Particulars of the Naval Combat at the Head of the Passes," *Shreveport* [LA] *Daily News*, Oct. 18, 1861; Robinson, *The Confederate Privateers*, 160.

Even after the smoke cleared out and the crew returned below, the *Manassas* was still not able to maneuver. Charles Read, the sailing master onboard the *McRae*, noticed the *Manassas* along the riverbank, later writing that the effects of the ramming caused her to have "entangled her propellers, disabled her engines, and carried away her smokestacks." Warley painstakingly guided the *Manassas* toward the riverbank where the ship ran aground. As the rest of the Confederate squadron moved downriver to engage the enemy, Lt. Fry ordered the *Ivy* to briefly halt to tow the ironclad to safety, but in attempting to do so the ship "parted two lines in trying to get her off."[26] In the disorder of maneuvering around the disabled ironclad, the *Tuscarora* also ran aground.

As the Union squadron retreated, disaster struck it as the USS *Richmond* and the USS *Vincennes* both ran aground at the bar of the Southwest Pass. The *Preble* also grounded briefly, but her sailors "after two or three smart rolls worked herself over [the bar]." The *Water Witch* managed to escape over the bar without injury, with the *Frolic* in tow.

The Confederate ships quickly realized what happened to the two larger Union vessels and immediately concentrated their fire on them. The *McRae* targeted the *Richmond*, firing its nine-inch pivot gun "from a very respectable distance," steaming in circles to throw off the aim of Union gunners and maintain its relative position. Lieutenant Fry passed orders and the CSS *Ivy*, "made a dash for the helpless *Vincennes*, and, taking up a position under her stem, commenced to throw thirty-two-pound shells, from her one little smooth-bore gun, into the sloop-of-war's cabin windows." Lieutenant Fry's report corroborates that the *Ivy* steamed the closest to the Union ships, closing "within easy range of the enemy, and firing so as to take perfect aim at him [the USS *Vincennes*], my shell exploded alongside of his smokestack."[27] The *Richmond* fired on the *Ivy* to protect the grounded *Vincennes* and Fry withdrew after several near misses covered the sailors on his main deck with water.

The firing continued through dawn and into the morning. Confederate Colonel Johnson Duncan, in command of Fort Jackson upriver, sent a telegram to New Orleans, claiming, "the broadsides are almost incessant."

Captain Pope was in a bad predicament. Two of his ships were aground, including his own flagship. Fortunately, the USS *Richmond* settled in the mud with

26 Read, "Reminiscences of the Confederate Navy," 335; Walker, *Life of Captain Fry*, 146.

27 "Report of Commander French," *ORN*, 16:713; Morgan, *Recollections*, 57; Walker, *Life of Captain Fry*, 148.

her broadside facing up the Southwest Pass, allowing the ship to aim most of its guns at the Confederates. The USS *Vincennes*, however, was not so fortunate. Her sailors had only two guns that could aim down the pass. In a desperate attempt to break free, sailors on the *Vincennes* "hove overboard the rest of her armament, with her chains, anchors, etc., to lighten her."

Previously, the *Richmond* sent a message to the *Vincennes* through signal flags informing her commanding officer that Pope insisted that *Vincennes* break free and retreat into the Gulf of Mexico. Commander Robert Handy, the captain of the *Vincennes*, and a man described by fellow officers as "an old idiot" who was "incapable of anything," misinterpreted the order.[28] Instead of an order to retreat, he interpreted it as an order to abandon his ship in the mud. Just after throwing his guns overboard, Handy ordered his men into the ship's boats. He lit a slow match to the powder magazine so that the ship would not fall into enemy hands.

Captain Pope was preoccupied with trying to get the *Richmond* free of the bar and was unaware that the *Vincennes* was abandoned until Handy boarded the *Richmond* with his ship's flag tied around his waist. Pope demanded an explanation and when Handy stated that he was following the orders to abandon received by the signal flag hoist, Pope became infuriated, immediately ordering Handy and his crew back to the *Vincennes* and to lighten her until the ship could escape. Fortunately for the Union sailors, the slow match was of poor quality and did not reach the powder magazine before sailors returned and extinguished it.

The Confederate squadron maintained its distance as it fired into the two grounded enemy ships. The gunners on the *Richmond* were not ready to give up and continued to return fire whenever possible. Several shots passed over the *McRae* and *Tuscarora* rather closely and by 10 am, Cmdr. Hollins determined that his ships could do no further damage to the enemy squadron; he gave the order to withdraw.

His reasoning had merit; the Union squadron still outgunned his reduced force by a wide margin and the *Manassas* was temporarily out of action and needed repairs. In addition, three miles beyond the mouth of the Southwest Pass was the USS *Santee*, a sailing frigate of 50 guns whose draft was too deep to enter the river. If Hollins continued to press the fight, he would enter the range of the *Santee's* guns

28 "A Naval Brush with the Enemy at the Head of the Passes," *New Orleans* [LA] *Daily Picayune*, Oct. 12, 1861; "The Attack on Our Squadron at the Mouth of the Mississippi," *Harper's Weekly*, Nov. 9, 1861; John E. Hart to Mrs. John E. Hart, Nov. 26, 1861, John E. Hart Letters.

as she was "under a cloud of canvas, sailing back and forth like a caged lion," eager to join in the battle.[29]

Instead of continuing a fight in daylight against more numerous guns, the commodore declared victory after driving the Union ships out of the Head of Passes and ordered his squadron to return to Fort Jackson. Before heading upriver, however, the Confederates burned the wood put aside for the construction of the Union fort. They also took the abandoned *Joseph H. Toone*, with 15 tons of coal still onboard, upriver as a prize. The Union Army transport *McClellan*, carrying the guns intended for the prospective fort, joined the Union squadron in the afternoon of October 12, too late to influence the outcome of the brief but intense struggle. The Battle of the Head of Passes was over.

Lieutenant Joseph Fry, commanding the *Ivy*, had his clerk count the number of shots each ship fired in the battle, noting in his report that the *Richmond* fired 117 times, the *Vincennes* fired 16 shots, the *Water Witch* fired 18 shots, the *McRae* fired 23 shots, the *Ivy* fired 26 shots, and the *Tuscarora* fired six shots.

The *McRae* was the first ship sighted at Fort Jackson around 12:30 that afternoon. Within an hour, two more gunboats came within view, one of them towing the captured *Toone*. After the *Calhoun* anchored at the forts, Hollins immediately telegraphed his success to New Orleans, cabling that all of the Union ships were forced "aground on the Southwest bar, except for the sloop-of-war *Preble*, which I sunk." It was an overstatement contradicted by the Union commanders whose own reports appeared in northern newspapers challenging that Hollins's "report of a 'complete success,' is manifestly untrue."[30]

After sending his telegraph to New Orleans, the commodore wrote out a more detailed report sent to the navy department in Richmond and dispatched it to New Orleans under the care of Midn. James Morgan. Hollins then took stock of the situation, resupplying his ships and assessing damage.

Commodore Hollins's plan to free the Head of Passes from Union control worked. Through surprise and daring, his night attack startled the Union squadron into abandoning its position in great haste. The Federal fortification in the Head of Passes was never built and the *Joseph H. Toone* and the supplies onboard the barge were captured. At first glance, the battle appeared to be a significant Confederate victory. The strategic situation, however, was not changed.

---

29 Morgan, *Recollections*, 57.

30 "Gallant Attack on the Blockaders," *New Orleans* [LA] *Daily Picayune*, Oct. 13, 1861; "Thingamajigs," *White Cloud* [KS] *Chief*, Oct. 31 1861.

Pope's ships retreated, giving the Confederates the tactical victory, but the Federal blockade of the Mississippi River was still effective. Union warships simply blocked each pass individually, depriving Hollins of his ultimate goal of opening the Gulf to Confederate blockade-runners. The Confederate ships caused some minor damage to the USS *Richmond*; one shell burst in the captain's cabin and another destroy a small boat, but neither side reported any casualties in the fighting.

Midn. James Morgan travelled upriver, reaching the wharves of New Orleans at 3:00 pm on October 13. Hollins himself arrived with the *Calhoun* that night at midnight; a crowd gathered to meet him and "sent up a hearty shout" in celebration. Despite the unbroken Federal blockade, southern newspapers printed special editions, proclaiming the "glorious news," and declaring that the "expedition had been entirely successful."

The next morning, the damaged *Manassas* arrived at the city and was immediately dry-docked for repairs. One young New Orleans girl took stock in the victory: "thus have the insolent blockaders and invaders received another most signal rebuke for their insane attempt to subjugate this free and indomitable people." Another Southern woman ambitiously wrote in her diary "Hollins of the navy has broken the blockade of New Orleans . . . without the least damage to himself and men." "Henceforth the name of Hollins will be mentioned with pride throughout the broad extent of the Southern Confederacy," proclaimed one newspaper. Citizens across the state agreed. Within a few days, Louisiana's legislature unanimously voted a resolution of thanks for Hollins and his sailors while the citizens of New Orleans presented him with a pennant and a flag, the canton of which was emblazoned with an "anchor . . . surrounded by a circle of eleven stars." One man wrote gladly to a friend on the front line in Kentucky that "Hollins withdrew and returned to the city, well satisfied with his achievements."[31]

Following the battle, described as "Pope's Run" in several newspapers, Capt. John Pope was relieved of his command. Flag Officer McKean clearly understood the failure of his officers during the battle, writing that "the more I hear and learn of the facts, the more disgraceful does it appear." Commander Handy was also relieved of command; his executive officer angrily wrote a letter home claiming that

31 "The Naval Victory at New Orleans," *Wilmington* [NC] *Journal*, Oct 24, 1861; "Naval Triumph in the Passes," *Daily Picayune*, Oct 13, 1861; Elliott Ashkenazi, ed., *The Civil War Diary of Clara Solomon: Growing Up In New Orleans 1861-1862* (Baton Rouge, LA, 1995), 194; Judith W. McGuire, *Diary of a Southern Refugee, During the War* (New York, 1868), 68-69; "The Great Naval Victory," *New Orleans* [LA] *Daily Crescent*, Oct 14, 1861; "The Compliment to Com. Hollins," *New Orleans* [LA] *Daily Crescent*, Oct 22, 1861; E. C. Hermann, ed., *Battle-Fields of the South* (New York, 1864), 181.

"if Old Handy had not have compelled us to leave the ship, we would have been mentioned with a great deal of credit."

Union sailors quickly develop "ram fever" and the next night, the *Richmond* thought the *Manassas* was returning, throwing everyone into another panic about "'Rams' and all other infernal machines." McKean wrote to the navy department that he planned to recapture the Head of Passes, even sending the USS *Water Witch* and the recently arrived USS *South Carolina* upriver as far as the Head of Passes on October 17 to reconnoiter. There the two Union ships met the CSS *Jackson* and CSS *Ivy*, exchanging a few shots, "but owing to the long range, without marked effect." Confederate officials recalled that the shots "fell thickly around our steamers" without result.[32] After a brief exchange of fire, the two Union ships withdrew back into the Gulf of Mexico, satisfied that the Head of Passes remained well defended by the Confederate Navy.

McKean was likewise relieved from his post before he could take any major action to reclaim the position or his reputation. It was a very embarrassing loss for Union commanders, with one admiral writing after the war that Hollins's surprise attack was "the most ridiculous affair that ever took place in the American Navy." In the end, it supplied the people of New Orleans a victory of raised morale and increased confidence in their little improvised navy, while simultaneously lowering the morale of the Union blockaders. "I am in tolerably good health," claimed one blockading officer, "but very low in spirit."[33] Nonetheless the blockade remained in force and the Confederate victory at the Head of Passes achieved no tangible permanent results. In fact, the little victory might have increased Confederate spirits and confidence too much, leading to an aura of invincibility just as Union forces were concentrating for a larger assault in their direction.

---

32 "Report of Flag Officer McKean," *ORN*, 16:705; John E. Hart to Mrs. John E. Hart, Nov 26, 1861, John E. Hart Letters; "Report of Flag Officer McKean," *ORN*, 16:707; "Another Skirmish at the Passes," *Washington Evening Star*, Nov 6 1861; Robert M. Oxley, "The Civil War Gulf Blockade: The Unpublished Journal of a U.S. Navy Warrant Officer Aboard the USS Vincennes, 1861-1864," *International Journal of Naval History* (April 2002), No. 1, 1:5.

33 David D. Porter, *The Naval History of the Civil War* (New York, 1886), 91; John E. Hart to Mrs. John E. Hart, Nov 26, 1861, John E. Hart Letters.

CHAPTER THREE

Strengthening the Confederate Navy
on the Mississippi River

Ironclad Construction on the Mississippi

CONFEDERATE Secretary of the Navy Stephen Mallory and the officers under his charge strived to forge the nucleus of a regular navy at New Orleans, but much more was needed. As 1861 drew to a close, it was clear that the United States would not abandon the conflict. As a result, Confederate officials made preparations for a protracted war.

The main objective of the new Confederate Navy was breaking the Federal blockade. To do this, Mallory needed ironclad warships capable of defeating the more numerous wooden Union warships. Work was already in progress across the Confederacy on local armored vessels, most notably in Norfolk, Virginia where the former USS *Merrimack* was being converted into a powerful ironclad that would gain notoriety under the name *Virginia*.

Hampton Roads, Virginia was not the only place where Mallory desired ironclads for defense. He wanted powerful armored warships built on the Mississippi River to provide Confederate dominance of the vital strategic inland waterway. Others were of the same mind.

In the summer of 1861, Mallory received an ambitious plan. In late August, two brothers, Asa and Nelson Tift, wrote to Mallory with a proposal to build at New Orleans a 4,000-ton armored behemoth mounting 20 cannon behind a sloped casemate shielded by 3.5-inch armor. The finished ship, which they promised to deliver by December 15, 1861, would be christened the *Mississippi*. Mallory enthusiastically embraced the idea and the Tift brothers, who offered to work for free, received official approval by the end of August. The two brothers then journeyed to New Orleans where they could begin the construction process. What made their model so promising was their recognition of the lack of professional shipbuilders in the Confederacy. By using a simple design, traditional carpenters and smiths could be used to work on the vessel.[1]

Mallory approved a second ironclad design for New Orleans in mid-September. What became the *Louisiana* was proposed by Kentucky shipbuilder E.C. Murray. Smaller than the Tift brothers' design, only displacing 1,400 tons and mounting 16 guns, the *Louisiana* resembled the larger ironclad by having a similar armored casemate. It had two propellers plus a central paddle wheel for propulsion.

These two ironclads were optimistically expected to sweep aside the Union blockading squadron in the Gulf of Mexico. However, there were numerous difficulties building these ships, the first of which was a lack of facilities to construct them. Though New Orleans had numerous shipyards and dry-docks across the river at Algiers, few builders possessed the knowledge to construct ironclads. Only the John Hughes shipyard had some experience and that was in converting the tug *Enoch Train* into the armored ram *Manassas*. That was a much smaller project of conversion compared to a new construction from the keel up.

A site was chosen at Jefferson City, just upriver from New Orleans where the two ironclads began to take shape at adjacent yards. After gathering the needed lumber, the keel for the Louisiana was laid in mid-October. Murray purchased the old river steamer *Ingomar* with the intention of removing its four engines and two drive shafts for installation in the *Louisiana*. The remaining drive shafts needed were obtained from Kirk and Company in New Orleans, but they had to first build a steam hammer large enough to construct them.

To assist the builders, Mallory dispatched Joseph Pierce to New Orleans. An accomplished shipbuilder, Pierce was the master ship carpenter at the Gosport Navy Yard in Norfolk, Virginia, before the war. After Virginia seceded, he was appointed the acting chief naval constructor for the Confederate Navy and helped to design the plans to convert the USS *Merrimack* into an ironclad. By the summer of 1861, Pierce was the most senior and experienced shipbuilder in the

---

1 Stephen R Mallory Diary, Sept. 1, 1861, Vol. 1.; John Roy Diary, Sept. 20, 1861; George M. Brooke Jr., ed., "Brooke Journal," Jul. 30, 1861, *Ironclads and Big Guns of the Confederacy: The Journal and Letters of John M. Brooke* (Columbia, SC, 2002), 91.

Confederacy and Mallory asked him to oversee what many considered the most important construction projects, those of the two ironclads at New Orleans. Pierce took to his duties with concentrated effort, analyzing drawings and models and helping the designers ensure their plans were practical before assisting with procuring needed supplies and labor.

Procuring supplies proved challenging. Murray turned to the Clark Rolling Mill of New Orleans for the needed iron. This quantity proved inadequate and Murray took an additional five hundred tons of rail iron "sequestered by the Government." Once the iron was in hand, workers went on strike for better wages, delaying the project for days in Murray's race against time. Despite these setbacks, work continued through the winter of 1861 until the *Louisiana* was launched on February 6, 1862, afloat but still missing her iron armor, cannons, and engines.[2]

Work on the Tift brothers' much larger ironclad was slower and faced even more challenges. Since the Tift brothers had little shipbuilding experience, Mallory instructed Joseph Pierce to assist them as deputy constructor for the program. Pierce did so with a passion. The keel for the *Mississippi* was laid in mid-October and Pierce performed a miracle in getting the hull completed in 110 days, an unheard-of timeframe for a vessel so large. This included a four-day strike by carpenters in mid-November that only concluded when they received an increase in wages from three to four dollars a day.

The *Mississippi* needed engines and the Tift brothers scoured Louisiana for suitable machinery. First turning to Leeds and Company of New Orleans, the brothers were told that Leeds could not complete the order. Jackson and Company was next approached and they laid out specifications for the construction of "three engines, 36 inches in diameter, and 2-foot stroke shelf valves, three propellers, 11 feet in diameter, with cast (or if wrought-iron can be had, to be paid in difference) iron shafts" along with eleven boilers.[3] The machinery was expected to be delivered January 31, 1862.

Besides the engines, the *Mississippi* also needed drive shafts and Ward and Company in Nashville was contracted to fabricate them. They quickly retracted their offer, citing a lack of available materials. John Clark and Company in New Orleans promised to produce them, but only after they first manufactured the tools needed to do so. They could not deliver the drive shafts until February 1862 at the

2 "Testimony of Mr. Murray," *ORN*, Ser. 2, 1:754; William N. Still Jr., *Confederate Shipbuilding* (Columbia, SC, 1969), 72-73.

3 "Jackson and Company to Secretary Mallory," *ORN*, Ser. 2, 1:572.

earliest. The main central shaft, however, was too large to construct in the Confederacy. An old steamer, the *Glen Cove*, was gutted for her shaft and brought to the Tredegar Iron Works in Richmond, Virginia in late-January 1862 but was not completed until March 24.

For armor plate, the Tift brothers turned to the rolling mill of Schofield and Markham in Atlanta, Georgia to produce 100 tons of armor plating; production commenced in December 1861. The *Mississippi* was launched on April 19, lacking armor plating, and with its shafts not yet connected to its propellers. The iron rudder was contracted for with Leeds and Company in New Orleans, who delivered the piece on April 25. The limited manufacturing capability of the Confederacy was clearly hindering progress as companies strained to either fill orders or to even produce prerequisite materials needed to manufacture needed machinery.

Iron plating had to be procured from Atlanta, but only after the mills fabricated equipment capable of producing what was required. Getting the iron to New Orleans required extra time because supplies and troop transportation for Confederate Army commanders took precedence on railroads in their areas of control. The main shipment of iron for the *Mississippi* did not arrive until April 1862. When it came time for assembling and installing the iron castings of the *Mississippi*, the Tift brothers found that available shipyard labor was not sufficient and they drafted three-hundred slaves from neighboring plantations, who "worked as a night gang" in an attempt at keeping the work on schedule.[4]

The two New Orleans ironclad programs were classified by Secretary Mallory as some of the navy department's most important work. No effort was spared in getting the *Louisiana* and *Mississippi* ready for service. Jefferson Davis knew about the obstacles that were being overcome in the city. "They had to prepare a shipyard," the President noted, "procure lumber from a distance, have the foundries and rolling-mills adapted to such iron work as could be done in the city."

The greatest concern was a lack of immediate funding from the treasury department; Mallory regularly wrote asking for funds to pay shipyard workers and procure needed materials, but there were often shortfalls that caused still more delays. The question on everyone's minds was whether the vessels would be ready

---

4 *Court of Inquiry*, 111.

before Union forces began their campaigns in the spring of 1862. Each delay cost the Confederate dearly in this race against time.[5]

While ironclad construction in New Orleans was better known, there was also a program to provide for the defense of the upper portions of the Mississippi River as well. These efforts were centered in Memphis, Tennessee, an important river port that was the only other city besides New Orleans on the river that had shipyards and construction facilities available for the Confederacy. Also, like New Orleans, the port of Memphis had never constructed such warships and the carpenters and mechanics there had to improvise.

Memphis entrepreneur John T. Shirley was introduced to Mallory in August 1861, proposing to build two ironclads there. On August 23, 1861, the same week the Tift brothers received approval, the Confederate Congress approved $160,000 for construction of two ironclads in Memphis. Shirley optimistically promised delivery of the two ships by Christmas of 1861. The only fear at first was that efforts in Memphis would compete with those in New Orleans for available materials and skilled laborers.

Shirley's two ironclads were different from the *Louisiana* and *Mississippi*. Their design was smaller, displacing only 800 tons each, and mounted fewer guns, between eight and ten each. This ensured they could safely steam through the upper portions of the Mississippi River. Both ships, however, retained a large armored casemate, just like the vessels on the lower river. The two Memphis ironclads were similar to each other in design and construction and each was fitted with a powerful ram at the bow, just as the smaller *Manassas* had been.

Unsurprisingly, work proceeded slowly. Lack of materials and skilled workers caused delays, which were compounded by competition between New Orleans, Memphis, and at times even Norfolk, vying for contracts from the same firms. Mallory cautioned Jefferson Davis that the ironclad projects "progress very slowly" due to a lack of available labor, which was being augmented where possible by local slaves.[6]

The delays were so great that Gen. Pierre G.T. Beauregard, second in command of Confederate forces west of the Appalachian Mountains, dispatched

---

5 Davis, *Rise and Fall*, 1:209; Stephen Mallory to C.G. Memminger, Feb. 22, 1862, *Letters Received by the Confederate Secretary of the Treasury 1861-1865* (National Archives Microfilm Publication M499, Records Group 365), National Archives Building, Washington DC.

6 Stephen Mallory to Jefferson Davis, Jan. 15, 1862, *Letters Received by the Confederate Secretary of War 1861-1865* (National Archives Microfilm Publication M437, Records Group 109), National Archives Building, Washington DC.

an aide to Memphis to determine the cause. He reported to Beauregard that the vessels would not be ready before April 1862. As a result, Shirley virtually abandoned one of his hulls, christened the *Tennessee*, to focus on the more complete hull known as the *Arkansas*. It was another race against time as Union forces were preparing for their spring campaigns in Kentucky and Missouri. The question was whether the *Arkansas* could be ready in time to meet the Union ships gathering upriver.

Work began to convert another vessel, the *Eastport*, into an ironclad on the Tennessee River. The *Eastport*, however, was captured by Union gunboats before it could be clad in iron. The ship was then taken to Cairo, Illinois where it was fully converted and entered the Union Navy in late 1862. This would serve as an object lesson for the Confederate Navy, which never again allowed one of its ironclads to be captured while still undergoing construction or conversion. Additionally, at Nashville, the Confederate Navy purchased four vessels: the *Hilman* for $40,000, the *James Johnson* for $35,000, the *James Woods* for $40,000, and the *B.M. Runyan*, for $25,000. Each of these ships were traditional side wheelers built in Indiana. Entrusted to the care of Lt. Isaac N. Brown, the four ships began to undergo conversion into gunboats in January of 1862.[7]

By the end of 1861, the Confederacy had an emerging river-borne ironclad fleet, with four ironclads being constructed on the Mississippi River and a fifth on the Tennessee River, plus the little *Manassas*. An astounding amount of money, manpower, and resources were used, but many believed that once these ironclads were completed, they would be a powerful deterrent to the large Federal fleet and, backed up with the host of wooden craft already in operation, could protect the Confederate stretch of the Mississippi River while simultaneously providing the weapons to break the Union blockade.

Hollins Bolsters His Defenses

As work continued on the river ironclads, Cmdre. Hollins was busy strengthening the traditional wooden steamers at his disposal. He was determined to pay any cost and use any method to acquire or build ships to add to his growing squadron. Though many thought Hollins was squandering money just as they thought Rousseau had, even at the expense of the ironclad programs, Hollins believed that with more ships at his disposal, the better he could oppose the United

---

7 "Report of Secretary Mallory", *ORN*, 22:812; *DANFS*, 2:538.

States Navy when it began full campaigns on the river. His victory at the Head of Passes convinced many the value of these converted wooden ships and Hollins's good judgment.

Hollins reorganized his squadron of ships at New Orleans. Several of his ships rotated through dry-docks following the Battle of the Head of Passes, undergoing repairs needed to keep them operational, utilizing rented slaves to augment crews or assist in work when needed. Hollins shifted his pennant from the *Calhoun* to the *McRae*, making that his flagship. Additionally, Hollins took on two aides. Midn. James Morgan was a young 16-year-old serving on the *McRae*. A Louisiana native who left the U.S. Naval Academy when his state seceded, Morgan helped transfer weapons and gunpowder from New Orleans to Pensacola at the start of the war before joining the *McRae* in Baton Rouge while the ship was receiving its own ordnance supplies from the Louisiana State Arsenal. The commodore also took on Ramon S. Sanchez as his clerk and secretary. Sanchez was a coxswain and clerk on the CSS *Jackson* while it was operating upriver in September. Upon returning downriver, Lt. Gwathmey, in command of the converted tug, personally recommended Sanchez to Hollins.[8]

Determined efforts in New Orleans continued to convert river steamers into gunboats and by early 1862, more ships were added to Hollins's squadron. On Lake Pontchartrain, the *Florida* was converted in the summer of 1861 and the *Oregon* transferred supplies from New Orleans to Ship Island on the Mississippi coast. Another steamer was purchased in July and finished its conversion in early September. Named the *Pamlico*, the vessel was similar in size and construction to the *Florida*. Using two side-wheels for propulsion and armed with three eight-inch smoothbores and one 6.4-inch Brooke rifled cannon, the small 65-man crew was entrusted to 1Lt. William G. Dozier, a 33-year-old with 11 years of naval experience. Assigned as Dozier's executive officer was John G. Blackwood, a South Carolinian with previous service in the United States Revenue Marine. Later in the year, Hollins contracted with ship constructor John Hughes to build two more steamers. To be constructed on Bayou Saint John, just north of New Orleans, these two ships provided naval support for operations on Lake Pontchartrain and the Mississippi coastline.[9]

---

8 "Payment Summary for CSS Manassas," Nov. 1861, *Subject File*, AC, NA; "Payment Receipt for CSS Manassas," Nov. 20, 1861, *Subject File*, AC, NA; "Payment Summary for CSS Ivy," Oct. 23, 1861, *Subject File*, AC, NA.

9 *DANFS*, 2:554.

With a small flotilla growing on Lake Pontchartrain, and more ships under construction there, Hollins also focused his attention on steamers to operate on the Mississippi River. The rising wooden naval force, however, was not without detractors. At a time when shipyard workers were striking and the Tift brothers were scavenging for resources to build their ironclads, Hollins continued to funnel time, money, and resources into construction and conversion of wooden gunboats. Capt. William C. Whittle was appointed to command the New Orleans Naval Station with oversight on ship construction projects in the city. Joseph Pierce supervised the work on the two armored vessels. Thus, Hollins might have believed that there was no major issue with the ironclad construction program in New Orleans and that he could concentrate on acquiring his wooden ships as quickly as possible. Furthermore, many of his wooden conversions were underway when work on the ironclads began and he did not feel that the wooden conversions should be halted midway.

Work continued on procuring and converting river steamers and by early 1862, five more were added to his squadron. The *Ed Howard* was built in Indiana in 1852. By mid-1861, she was inspected and found acceptable for naval operations. Upon the recommendation of Gen. Leonidas Polk, who wanted the ship for service on the upper river, Hollins paid $8,000 for the vessel and brought it to the Algiers shipyards where she was stripped to a "mere shell."[10] Small by weight, at just 390 tons displacement, the vessel's draft of less than six feet made it useful for river operations. Built without a mast, the *Ed Howard* was propelled solely by steam propulsion. Renamed the CSS *General Polk*, after Leonidas Polk, the ship was armed with seven guns and placed in commission in early November 1861. First Lieutenant Jonathan H. Carter, a North Carolinian who joined the United States Navy in 1840, was placed in command at the request of Gen. Polk, who found him to possess a "knowledge of our [the army's] wants and how to meet them." The conversion was not without difficulties as First Assistant Engineer John Lawson, who was initially appointed as the ship's chief engineer, unexpectedly resigned within two weeks of joining the vessel, adding to the problems.[11]

The outfitting of the *General Polk* showed how Confederate officials and military commanders used their limited resources. Carter wanted to outfit his ship

10 Ibid, 524.

11 "Letter from General Polk," *OR*, 3:708; *New Orleans Ship Register*, 5:73; *Confederate Navy Register*, 31; "Appointment of 1st Assistant Engineer Lawson," Nov. 1, 1861, *Subject File*, NN, NA; "Resignation of 1st Assistant Engineer Lawson," Nov. 18, 1861, *Subject File*, NN, NA; "Resignation Approval of 1st Assistant Engineer Lawson," Nov. 26, 1861, *Subject File*, NN, NA.

with modern rifled cannon, but none were available. Instead, old 32-pounder smoothbores were manually rifled in Memphis. Before these guns could be mounted Carter had to manufacture carriages to hold them. Although it was primarily a wooden craft, Carter installed bars of iron on the bow and stern to protect against glancing shots and enemy small arms.

Junior officers were also needed and Carter implored senior commanders to send experienced midshipmen to him. Outfitting was slow due to the summer rains that daily plague southern Louisiana, but overall Carter was pleased with the ship and desired to get it into active service. As with other ship building projects, local slaves were leased to perform manual labor on the city's dry-docks; one owner received $500 for the lease of five slaves for just two months of work. In two months, over $9,000 in parts were purchased, more than what was paid for the ship itself, to reconfigure and outfit the *General Polk* for war.[12]

Another vessel purchased in mid-1861 was the *Grosse Tete*, a steamer built in Indiana in the 1850's. Drawing seven feet of water and without masts, it would likewise serve adequately in river operations, though her two side-wheels were not as desirable as a screw propeller. Renamed the *Maurepas*, after the lake in southern Louisiana, the vessel was entrusted to 1Lt. Joseph Fry. Fry was shifted from the small and fast *Ivy*, leaving it under the command of 1Lt. William L. Bradford, an Alabamian with a decade of naval experience. The *Ivy* remained near the Head of Passes for the remainder of 1861, firing on Union incursions several times, including on the USS *Niagara* and one of its cutters in early November. Armed with five guns, the *Maurepas* was placed in commission in early 1862.[13]

Hollins continued his search for any vessel that might prove useful. He found the *Livingston*, a towboat under construction in one of the John Hughes dry-docks in early 1861. With a length of 180 feet, a beam of 40 feet, and a draft of nine feet six inches, the *Livingston* was comparable to other vessels of that class. The boat was purchased by the navy department in November 1861 and Hollins ordered a crew to oversee its final construction. Assigned to command was 1Lt. Francis B. Renshaw, a Pennsylvanian who married a Pensacola woman. Renshaw served in the United States Navy from 1828 before resigning in January 1861. Lieutenant Renshaw oversaw the completion of the *Livingston*, which included an overhaul of

---

12 "First Lieutenant Carter to Major General Polk," Aug. 29, 1861, *Subject File*, AC, NA; "First Lieutenant Carter to Major General Polk," Sept. 19, 1861, *Subject File*, AC, NA; "Payment Receipt of CSS General Polk," Nov. 7, 1861, *Subject File*, AC, NA.

13 *New Orleans Ship Register*, 5:100; *DANFS*, 2:547.

engineering machinery and deck spaces, along with the installation of her armament consisting of two 30-pounders and four shell guns. The *Livingston* was commissioned in late-January 1862 but proved to be slower than originally advertised; one young naval officer in New Orleans sarcastically noted that "she was so slow that her crew facetiously complained that when she was going downstream at full speed they could not sleep on account of the noise made by the drift logs catching up with her and bumping against her stern."[14]

The *Lizzie Simmons* was another Indiana-built steamer that Hollins obtained. Inspected and purchased in October 1861 and renamed the CSS *Pontchartrain*, it was another standard Mississippi River steamer. The *Pontchartrain* held no masts and was propelled by two side-wheels. Armed with seven guns, including at least one eight-inch smoothbore based on the French Paixhan model built at the Leeds foundry in New Orleans and two 32-pounders, the *Pontchartrain* was entrusted to 1Lt. John Dunnington, a Kentuckian with over 20 years of naval experience who was reassigned from the CSS *McRae*. Dunnington then commanded the CSS *Tuscarora* until that vessel was destroyed by fire in November 1861. He assumed command of the *Pontchartrain* and supervised its conversion. This conversion, however, took some time and the *Pontchartrain* was not ready for naval service until March 1862.[15]

Another vessel finalizing construction in late 1861 was the *Slidell*. Supposedly armed with eight guns, not much is known about this craft except that it was constructed at New Orleans in 1861. This steamer had four engineering officers assigned to operate its equipment, along with two acting masters to command the deck crew. Ready for service about January 1862, the *Slidell* was brought up the Mississippi River, possibly serving as a transport, before disappearing from the records. There is a reference claiming it sunk on the Tennessee River in February 1863.[16]

Besides the conversion of river steamers, Cmdre. Hollins began working on other, less traditional, naval craft. Taking lessons learned in the Crimean War the decade before, the idea was to take any available dry-docks at New Orleans and convert them into floating batteries. Essentially towable fortresses, these anchored and blocked a part of the Mississippi River while providing gunfire support to land

---

14 *DANFS*, 2:544; *Confederate Navy Register*, 163; Morgan, *Recollections*, 61; "Payment Summary for CSS Livingston," Feb. 11, 1861, *Subject File*, AC, NA.

15 *New Orleans Ship Register*, 6:174; *DANFS*, 2:558.

16 "Payment Receipt for CSS Slidell," Jan. 25, 1861, *Subject File*, AC, NA; *DANFS*, 2:567.

Union Newspaper Portrayal of the Floating Battery *New Orleans.*

Philadelphia [PA] *Inquirer, April 11, 1862*

installations. In the latter part of 1861, the plan was approved and two dry-docks, the Atlantic dry-dock and the Gulf Line dry-dock, were purchased. Great confidence must have been foreseen in these proposed floating batteries because the government spared no expense to acquire them; the Atlantic dock, first constructed in 1850, was bought from owner James Martin for $50,000 and the Gulf Line cost $38,000. Work began to convert the Atlantic dock at Algiers in August, 1861, but the final purchase of the Gulf Line dock was not finalized until December, delaying the commencement of work on that conversion.[17]

Dubbed the *New Orleans* and the *Memphis* respectively, the converted dry-docks were each designed with a wooden casemate sloped to one side, providing the men onboard with some protection against enemy fire. Furthermore, they were augmented with hoses connected to pumps that would allow the crew to repel boarders by scalding them with boiling water or to flood the shell lockers and powder magazine in an emergency; steam gauges and feeders from the boilers were installed to ensure such actions could be used when needed.

With the delay in purchasing what would become the *Memphis*, all work was focused on completing the *New Orleans*, which was commissioned on October 14, 1861. Work progressed slowly on the battery *Memphis* due to supply limitations, but more than $2,000 was spent in April 1862 alone on outfitting the battery. This was a case of too little too late however, as the *Memphis* was still loading its guns and lacking a crew when New Orleans fell to Union forces at the end of that month.

17 "Sale Announcement of Atlantic Dry-Dock," Aug. 20, 1861, *Subject File*, PD, NA; "Payment Receipt of Atlantic Dry-Dock," Sept. 9, 1861, *Subject File*, PD, NA; "Payment Receipt of Gulf Line Dry-Dock," Dec. 21, 1861, *Subject File*, PD, NA; William H. Seymour, *The Story of Algiers: Now Fifth District of New Orleans, The Past and the Present* (Algiers, Louisiana, 1896), 57.

Designed to mount 20 guns total, 17 eight-inch cannon, one nine-inch gun, and two rifled 32-pounders, the *New Orleans* was an imposing craft. When commissioned, it was placed under the command of Lt. Samuel W. Averett. A Virginian and 1859 graduate of the United States Naval Academy, Averett served with distinction on the CSS *Jackson*, prompting his assignment to command the floating battery. After being converted, the *New Orleans* lay alongside Bienville Street, visited by thousands of the Crescent City while awaiting orders to move to the front lines.[18]

Since the *New Orleans* had no berthing facilities and no engine power, a tender was required for the crew to live on and to tow the battery wherever it was needed. Confederate officials purchased the side-wheel steamer *Red Rover* on November 7, 1861, for a price of $30,000 to serve in this capacity. Built in Missouri in 1859, the *Red Rover* displaced 786 tons, and was entrusted to 1Lt. John J. Guthrie, a native of North Carolina and resident of Virginia. Guthrie joined the United States Navy in 1834 and served in the Mexican War. Except for a few engineers permanently assigned to the *Red Rover*, most of its crew was shared with the *New Orleans* when needed and the tender rarely left the side of the floating battery once the two were joined together.[19]

Though Hollins focused his efforts in New Orleans itself, he did not limit himself strictly to the New Orleans area. Though ships were now being readied on both the Mississippi River and Lake Pontchartrain, Hollins saw the need for more ships to protect other approaches to the river and inland waterways. Thus entered the *Mobile*, a Philadelphia built steamer constructed in 1860. Seized in Berwick Bay, near Brashear City, Louisiana—modern day Morgan City—at the start of the war, the Confederate Navy was able to later acquire the vessel on a $5,000 lien. Assigned to command the vessel was 1Lt. Francis E. Shepperd, a North Carolinian and naval veteran whose father once served in the United States Congress. Ready for service through a local shipyard owned by John Hughes in October 1861, the vessel was small, displacing only 283 tons, but was armed with five guns: three 32-pounder smoothbores, one rifled 32-pounder, and one eight-inch smoothbore. The mission

---

18 *DANFS*, 2:549, 552; *Confederate Navy Register*, 6-7; "The New Orleans Floating Battery – Louisiana to the Rescue," *Yorkville* [SC] *Enquirer*, Dec. 5, 1861; "Payment Receipt for CSS Memphis," Nov. 20, 1861, *Subject File*, AC, NA; "Payment Receipt for CSS Memphis," Apr. 1, 1861, *Subject File*, AC, NA; "Payment Receipt for CSS Memphis," Feb. 8, 1861, *Subject File*, EB, NA; "Payment Receipt for CSS New Orleans," Nov. 20, 1861, *Subject File*, EB, NA; "Sale Announcement of Atlantic Dry-Dock," Aug. 20, 1861, *Subject File*, PD, NA.

19 *DANFS*, 2:560; *Confederate Navy Register*, 77.

of the *Mobile* was to protect the approaches to the Atchafalaya River and Berwick Bay, defending the blockade-running port of Brashear City, which was linked by rail to New Orleans.[20]

Construction and conversion projects continued as opportunities arose. In February 1862, the Algiers shipyard owned by James Martin began construction on "two heavy steam rams to carry four guns each." These were envisioned as gunboats to patrol the upper Mississippi River, the Cumberland River, and the Tennessee River and reinforce the ironclads being constructed at Memphis. Unfortunately, the vessels were just being started when New Orleans fell to Union forces at the beginning of May.

To bolster the ironclad program a second wave of such rams were contracted for. These were planned as reinforcements for the *Louisiana* and *Mississippi* ironclads to secure dominance of the Mississippi River and Gulf of Mexico, and were designed as "ironclad steam gunboats, with iron prows as rams." Yet another ironclad, designed as a "double propeller iron-plated gun boat" was contracted for service protecting Lake Pontchartrain.[21]

These armored ships, first contracted in March of 1862, were under the direction of shipbuilder James Watson. As with the Martin gunboats, these were never completed due to the fall of the Crescent City. A fascinating what-if to consider is what these six ironclads—the *Louisiana*, *Mississippi*, *Manassas*, and the three contracted with James Watson—might have accomplished if the Confederacy had a few more months and the resources to complete them.

Ship construction and conversion were not the only naval preparations in New Orleans. At the start of the war, a small naval laboratory was established in the Crescent City and by the end of 1861 fully operational. Acting Master W.A. Robbins commanded the facility, which was located on the river at Elysian Fields Avenue. Robbins, who was described as "an active, energetic officer, and well calculated to conduct the laboratory on an economical scale," was assisted by Acting Gunners David G. McComb and G.H. Merrifield, and a civilian pyrotechnic expert by the name of Mr. H.D. Lassinot. Employing 69 civilians, the laboratory manufactured fuses, lights, friction primers, cartridges, and tackles.

---

20 *DANFS*, 2:550; *Confederate Navy Register*, 177; "Payment Receipt for CSS Mobile," Nov. 2, 1861, *Subject File*, EB, NA.

21 "Report of Secretary Mallory," *ORN*, Ser. 2, 2 150; "Testimony of Mr. Martin," *ORN*, Ser. 2, 1:502; "Contract for Bayou Saint John Ironclad," Mar. 2, 1862, *Subject File*, AC, NA.

Most notably, ammunition made at the laboratory was done by women, and preference in employment was given "to the wives and daughters of the sailors" of Hollins's squadron. Some 100,000 shells were ordered by the Confederate government, but testing proved them too unstable for use in shipboard cannon. Many were shipped to Atlanta for storage and use by the army. Other shells and small arms ammunition were contracted for with Leeds and Company, who began production immediately and commenced delivery of the ammunition, as well as fuses and other accessories needed, beginning in the latter half of 1861.[22]

Artillery procurement for warships was vital. Hollins and his ordnance officer, Lt. Beverly Kennon, worked hard to produce guns. However, the process of manufacturing cannon was complex and those produced were not wholly satisfactory and up to Kennon's standards. Several foundries and iron works attempted to manufacture cannon, including a dozen 12-pounders at the Leeds Foundry, seven 32-pounders at the Bujac Foundry, and three nine-inch Columbiads by Bennet and Lurges Company. A dozen of these guns were rejected for not passing inspection or failing tests; the remaining 10 were incorporated into both the naval and land defenses of New Orleans. Furthermore, Leeds and Company was contracted to gather materials and construct naval carriages for at least a score of 32-pounders; by ordering in bulk, naval officials managed to obtain a discounted price of $350 per carriage.[23]

Hollins expanded the naval laboratory in New Orleans, and quickly accrued a debt of almost $500,000 in financing its construction and outfitting. These expenditures were made without authorization from the navy department and upon hearing of the unapproved expenses, Stephen Mallory became furious. Lieutenant Robert D. Minor, chief of the bureau of ordinance and hydrography, was dispatched to New Orleans to audit Hollins's squadron. The Confederate Congress passed a special appropriation to pay for everything and the New Orleans Naval Station ordnance officer, Lt. Beverly Kennon, was removed from his position and ordered to Richmond, Virginia in disgrace. Upon arriving there, Kennon resigned from the naval service. Lieutenant Minor was kept at New Orleans to assume duties as Hollins's ordnance officer and he increased the naval

22 "Report of Lieutenant Minor," *ORN*, Ser. 2, 1:777; *Leeds and Company Papers*. (National Archives Microfilm Publication M346, Records Group 109), National Archives Building, Washington DC.

23 "Testimony of Lieutenant Kennon," *ORN*, Ser. 2, 1:561; *Jackson and Company Papers*. (National Archives Microfilm Publication M346, Records Group 109), National Archives Building, Washington DC.

laboratory production facilities in the city while striving to keep within his remaining budget.[24]

Shifting to an Upriver Defense

While work continued on the river ironclads, other more conventional methods were being used to strengthen the defenses of the Mississippi. At the beginning of 1862, Confederate naval officials decided to focus most of their available strength in Kentucky. For much of the latter half of 1861, Gen. Leonidas Polk repeatedly pleaded for ships to bolster his position in western Kentucky and Tennessee. On February 19, 1862, Polk's requests were heeded when Cmdre. George Hollins was ordered to bring his ships upriver with orders "cooperate with military forces" at Columbus.[25]

Learning of the Union successes at Forts Henry (captured on February 6) and Donelson (February 16), Stephen Mallory and Jefferson Davis both believed that a major attack on the river would soon come from Federal forces gathering in Cairo, Illinois, and Saint Louis, Missouri. Davis and his top military advisors believed that Forts Jackson and Saint Philip, combined with the ironclads then under construction in New Orleans, were sufficient to defend the mouth of the Mississippi. Furthermore, after Hollins's victory at the Head of Passes in October, the Union blockaders had not made any major ventures into the river and it was deemed safe to begin drawing forces upriver in anticipation of the coming spring campaign.

Already operating at Columbus was an army gunboat, the *Grampus*, a 352-ton sternwheeler and former towboat. Captain Marsh Miller commanded the vessel, which was armed with two 12-pounder bronze Napoleon field guns. His instructions were to serve as a scouting and transport ferry for Confederate soldiers at Columbus.[26]

Hollins anticipated his order north and began sending ships upriver in late 1861, with others joining in January and February of the next year. There is some conjecture as to when each Confederate ship made the journey upriver. Reports are

---

24 "Testimony of Lieutenant Minor," *ORN*, Ser. 2, 1:778-779; "Resignation Approval of Lieutenant Kennon," Dec. 10, 1861, *Subject File*, NN, NA.

25 "Telegram from Stephen Mallory," *ORN*, 22:824; "Letter from Major General Leonidas Polk," *ORN*, 22:794; "Letter from Stephen Mallory," *ORN*, Ser. 2, 1:518.

26 *DANFS*, 2:529.

contradictory and some officers were vague in this regard. Nonetheless, it is possible to draw a fairly accurate picture of how and when Commodore Hollins's ships proceeded to Columbus.

The first to move was the CSS *General Polk*. The ship left New Orleans on November 10, 1861, soon after being commissioned, moving upriver against the current at a decent speed and making stops at Vicksburg, Mississippi, and Memphis, Tennessee, before anchoring off of Columbus on November 20. Following the *General Polk*, the CSS *Ivy* and the floating battery *New Orleans* were next sent upriver. The floating battery's tender, the *Red Rover* left New Orleans on November 25 and it rendezvoused with the *New Orleans* at Columbia, Arkansas, relieving the *Ivy* of its tow. From there, the two vessels made their way to Columbus, anchoring at the fortifications there on December 11, 1861. A nearby house, originally used as a temporary hospital, was commandeered to accommodate the officers of the floating battery.[27]

The CSS *Tuscarora* left New Orleans following the battle of the Head of Passes. Disaster struck before it arrived in Kentucky when, on November 23, 1861, an uncontrolled fire started in the boilers as the ship was passing Helena, Arkansas. It quickly spread. The pilot beached the vessel and the captain ordered it abandoned, but not before elements of the crew made efforts to throw the ship's gunpowder supply overboard. Before all of the shells were cast overboard, the fire reached them and they began exploding. The remainder of the crew hastily abandoned ship as explosions continued, engulfing the vessel, damaging parts of the nearby Harbert plantation's slave quarters, and throwing the ship's flag into a burning tree. The entire crew managed to escape to the riverbank without serious injuries, but the ship was lost. No one ever discovered the cause of the blaze. The crew proceeded to Memphis, except for Acting Master George E. Brown and six men, who remained at the wreck to salvage what they could. [28]

To replace the *Tuscarora*, Hollins dispatched the CSS *Livingston*, carrying a load of coal to keep the squadron supplied upriver. In February, Hollins, accompanied by 1Lt. Thomas B. Huger of the *McRae*, journeyed upriver by rail to assume personal command of the ships gathering in Kentucky. He ordered the CSS *McRae*, left in the care of its executive officer Lt. Charles W. Read, to join him at Columbus,

27 Robert J. Freeman, "Journal of Medical and Surgical Practice on board of the CS Steamer Genl Polk," 10-20 November 1861, *Confederate States of America. Medical Records*, McCain Library and Archives, The University of Southern Mississippi; *DANFS*, 2:560; "Memorandum Extract from Guthrie Papers," *ORN*, Ser. 22:800; "Captain J.J. Guthrie Papers," *Subject File*, HA, NA.

28 "Burning of the C.S. Gunboat Tuscarora," *ORN*, 22:804.

Kentucky. The *McRae* left about the same time Hollins and Huger departed by rail, arriving upriver at the end of February. The CSS *Maurepas* also made the journey separately, arriving by early March. Finally, when the CSS *Pontchartrain* was commissioned in March, Lt. John Dunnington brought his ship upriver as well.[29]

The journey of the *McRae* was not easy. The ship left New Orleans and stopped at Baton Rouge, Louisiana; Vicksburg, Mississippi; and Memphis, Tennessee, before finally arriving at Columbus. At each stop, locals lined the riverbank to cheer and catch a glimpse of a warship of the new Confederate Navy, victor of the Battle of Head of Passes. However, unseen by the cheering crowds was the vessel's flaw.

The *McRae's* weak engines struggled to overcome the strong current. On several occasions, the ship steamed into the riverbank "bumping into a mud bank and lying helpless" in an effort to build up enough steam pressure for the engines to propel the ship further. This occurred once on a stretch of the riverbank of some distinction, the plantation of President Jefferson Davis. One sailor onboard commented "for this heroic performance, it is needless to say, none of us were promoted, and we lay ingloriously stuck in the mud until we were pulled off by a towboat."[30]

With the transfer of Cmdre. Hollins and most of his squadron upriver and despite the confidence of most citizens due to recent victories, some in New Orleans grew anxious about its defenses. General Lovell, commander of the forts and army units around New Orleans, begged the commodore to leave some ships behind. The United States Navy made no forays into the Mississippi River following the Battle of the Head of Passes in October. However, there were grumblings in the Crescent City that unless ships remained to protect the entrance of the river, Union craft would quickly return. The navy department disagreed, reasoning that if such occurred, Forts Jackson and Saint Philip could stop any advance.

To appease Lovell, Hollins left behind a token force. The revenue cutters *Pickens* and *Washington*, though only sail-powered and used mainly to collect taxes from blockade runners, were still in the area with full crews to man their guns. Alongside the wharves of the city remained the *Saint Philip*, still serving as a

29 "Testimony of Commodore Hollins," Ibid, Ser. 2, 1:516.

30 Morgan, *Recollections*, 62.

receiving ship and hospital, though for a time it was envisioned as a blockade runner carrying arms from Cuba.[31]

There were also six small steam launches at the city for communications that also transferred supplies. On Lake Pontchartrain remained the *Pamlico*, *Oregon*, and *Florida*. Additionally, two more ships, the *Bienville* and *Carondelet*, finalized their construction along Bayou Saint John and joined these small steamers in protecting coastal Louisiana and Mississippi. Finally, guarding the approaches to the river itself and patrolling the Head of Passes was the cigar shaped ironclad *Manassas*, the small converted towboat *Jackson*, and the former privateer *Calhoun*. It was hoped that this force, augmented by army fortifications, was sufficient to defend the Louisiana coastline, at least until the ironclads the *Louisiana* and *Mississippi* were completed.

The *Manassas*, *Jackson*, and *Calhoun* were active at the Head of Passes to discourage advances by Union blockaders. However, two of the ships did not remain there for long. In January, the *Calhoun* was reclassified as an armed blockade runner and steamed out of the river for Cuba with 651 bales of cotton. The cotton was sold in Havana and the *Calhoun* was reloaded with cases of gunpowder equaling a total of 500 barrels, along with "arms, ball cartridges, percussion caps, bar steel, quicksilver," and a Confederate commissioner returning to the southern states. On January 23, 1862, while making the return trip, she was spotted about five miles from the entrance of the Southwest Pass of the Mississippi River by the USS *Colorado* and a chase commenced. Unable to escape, the *Calhoun's* crew abandoned the vessel and set it afire, taking to their small boats and rowing into the river to avoid capture. Union sailors scrambled onboard the burning *Calhoun*, extinguished the flames, and surveyed their prize. Finding it a useful hull with little permanent damage, the vessel was brought to Ship Island where it was repaired, armed, and manned, becoming the *USS Calhoun*. General Mansfield Lovell, upon hearing of the *Calhoun's* capture, sent a note to the Confederate secretary of war, lamenting that the ship "will prove a great pest on the coast."[32]

With the loss of the *Calhoun*, only the iron turtle *Manassas* and the lightly armed *Jackson* remained guarding the Head of Passes. After the battle there, the *Manassas* was brought back to New Orleans for repairs and an overhaul. Her 64-pounder was replaced with a 32-pounder carronade and her cast iron ram, partially shattered off in the battle, was replaced with one made of wrought iron. The work was

---

31 "Telegram from Stephen Mallory," *ORN*, Ser. 2, 1:518.

32 "Report of Major General Lovell," Ibid, 17:75; "Report of Captain Bailey," Ibid, 17:72-74.

completed following the recommendation of First Assistant Engineer James Loper, the chief naval engineer in New Orleans, who closely inspected the *Manassas* after the battle, noting each deficiency and issue. Additions and alterations were also made to the ship to ensure it fully met military specifications and numerous sections of the iron plating were replaced.

Through January and February, Lt. Alexander Warley and his small crew of 36 sailors made several forays into the Head of Passes to watch for Union ships. One such mission occurred on January 1, 1862, with the *Manassas*, described by a blockading officer as "cigar shaped, with a shield deck, and heavy guns in the extremities," anchored at the lighthouse marking the entrance to Pass à Loutre. Watching the *Manassas* from outside the pass were the USS *Kingfisher* and USS *Mississippi*. After being anchored there for several hours, rumors falsely circulated on the blockaders that the ironclad ran aground. The ship was fine and at 11:30 that morning, Lieutenant Warley sent a boat loaded with 10 men to the lighthouse, where they burned the house of L. M. Chester, keeper of the light. After doing so the *Manassas* raised anchor and steamed back into the Head of Passes.[33]

Captain Thomas Selfridge onboard the USS *Mississippi* kept watch throughout the day and believed that the burning of the light keeper's house was a warning to prepare for further action, speculating that the *Manassas* would reappear that night for an attack on the blockading fleet. Not wanting to repeat the embarrassment of the battle last October, he made careful preparations in anticipation of a Confederate attack: "I anchored with a short scope, ready to slip in a moment; the guns were cast loose and everything prepared for action; no hammocks were below, one watch lying at their quarters and the other on the berth deck; a most vigilant lookout was kept and I was up and on the alert."[34] The preparations proved for naught as Warley had no intention of launching another attack, resulting only in a sleepless night for Selfridge and his crew.

The *Manassas*, however, did not remain in the area for much longer. Confident that the Union blockading fleet was not planning offensive forays into the river, Lt. Warley was ordered to bring his small ironclad upriver to reinforce Cmdr. Hollins's forces in Missouri and Kentucky. After receiving a brief docking period fortifying iron plating and resupplying, the *Manassas* left the lower river in March and

---

33 "Report of Captain Selfridge," Ibid, 17:30; "Abstract Log of USS Kingfisher," *ORN*, 17:33; "The Wrought Iron Prow" *Charleston* [SC] *Mercury*, Apr. 9, 1862; "Payment Summary for CSS Manassas," Oct. 1861, *Subject File*, AC, NA.

34 "Report of Captain Selfridge," Ibid, 32.

proceeded upriver to Memphis, leaving only the CSS *Jackson* to guard the Head of Passes. However, on its way upriver, the *Manassas* hit an underwater snag and ran aground, forcing it to remain at Memphis undergoing repairs. Nonetheless, its presence in Memphis was noted and caused anxiety amongst local Union commanders.[35]

Speculation abounded that the growing Confederate naval presence in Kentucky was a precursor to a major offensive up the Mississippi River. The success of Cmdre. Hollins at the Head of Passes the previous October only added to the perceived strength of the squadron. A Nashville newspaper conjectured that the naval squadron would unite with Gen. Albert S. Johnston's army in Kentucky, the combined host then advancing to force "military movements on a grand scale, involving great strategy and important battle." Other Confederate reporters boasted "the Federals are more apprehensive of an attack from us than we from them, owing to our preparations in this place, and the sudden appearance of Commodore Hollins' fleet." Even Jefferson Davis expected an offensive, though he left the particulars to Gen. Johnston.

The Confederates, however, were not preparing any kind of offensive. Instead, the ships were sent upriver to defend the area against Union ships known to be under construction in Cairo, Illinois, and Saint Louis, Missouri. An engineer on the Confederate flagship wrote to his father that they "expect an attack at Columbus hourly" by the Cairo-based Union flotilla.[36]

The River Defense Fleet is Born

The people of New Orleans grew apprehensive about the lack of naval forces protecting their city. Two riverboat captains were particularly troubled and they determined to take action on their own. James E. Montgomery and J. H. Townsend, both long-time Mississippi River captains, approached government officials with a plan to seize and arm river boats for use in protecting the Mississippi River. The two received support from congressmen whose districts lay next to the river, as well as from Maj. Gen. Leonidas Polk in command of the defenses at

---

35 "Payment Receipt for CSS Manassas," Feb. 24, 1862, Subject File, AC, NA; "Letter of Flag Officer Foote," *ORN*, 22:673.

36 "Our Bowling Green Correspondence," *Nashville* [TN] *Union and American*, Nov. 26, 1861; "From Columbus" *The Athens* [TN] *Post*, Dec. 20, 1861; John H. Dent, Jr. to John H. Dent, November 26, 1861, John Horry Dent, Jr., Letter; Jefferson Davis to Albert S. Johnston," Mar. 12, 1862, *The Papers of Jefferson Davis*, 14 Vols. (Baton Rouge, LA, 2003), 8:92-94.

Columbus. Newly appointed Secretary of War Judah Benjamin, another Louisiana resident and the former Confederate attorney general, approved the plan and issued orders in January 1862 to Maj. Gen. Mansfield Lovell to seize 14 river steamboats "intended for service on the rivers, and will be composed of the steamboatmen [sic] of the Western waters."[37]

Known as the River Defense Fleet, these ships operated officially as part of the army, with the crews composed of contracted civilians. To emphasize their separation from the navy, nine of the vessels were renamed to honor army leaders.

It was initially hoped that Thomas P. Leathers, an experienced river steamboat captain, would command. Leathers, however, declined the offer and the River Defense Fleet fell into the hands of the man who first proposed it, Captain James Edward Montgomery, who was tasked with overseeing the acquisition, conversion, and direction of the ships. Montgomery was a native of Kentucky, born there in 1817. Before the war, he operated a mail packet service on the Ohio River before moving to New Orleans and continuing his trade as a river captain on the Mississippi. His expertise was considered so great on the river that a young Samuel Clemens (the future Mark Twain) worked for him before the war. The future author described Montgomery as "always a cool man; nothing could disturb his serenity." Montgomery likely owed his position in command to his personal friendships with both and Judah Benjamin and the Confederate president.[38]

It was left to Gen. Lovell to determine what vessels to confiscate and he turned to naval officers, as well as his younger brother William, to help him inspect and classify appropriate craft. Though 14 vessels were authorized for purchase, Lovell and his team inspected at least two-dozen. Of those 24, 14 ships were chosen for the River Defense Fleet, two more were purchased by the state of Louisiana, and the remaining eight were purchased by the Confederate government and converted into blockade-runners.

Appointed to oversee the River Defense Fleet conversions was William S. Lovell, younger brother to the general and now a lieutenant colonel. Colonel Lovell supervised the hull transformations, crew training, and the supply of each ship in the River Defense Fleet. As a result of his efforts, one of the vessels was renamed the *Colonel Lovell*, making him one of the first graduates of the United States Naval Academy to have a ship named in their honor.

---

37 "Letter from Judah P. Benjamin to Major General Mansfield Lovell," Jan. 19, 1861; *OR*, 6:811.

38 Mark Twain, *Life on the Mississippi* (Boston, 1883), 487; S.A. Cunningham, "The Last Roll, Commodore J.E. Montgomery," *Confederate Veteran* (September 1902), 10:416-417.

James E. Montgomery. *Confederate Veteran*

The eight vessels that became blockade runners were the *Atlantic, Austin, Florida, Magnolia, Tennessee, Texas, Victoria,* and *William G. Hewes.* These eight were all owned by the Charles Morgan Steamship Company, with three of them operating on the Texas line and the remainder operating as trade ships along the river and the Gulf of Mexico. Of the eight ships, four were eventually captured by the U.S. Navy and commissioned into that service, one was burned after it ran aground on a cotton run, two were unable to escape the blockade and remained operating in auxiliary roles on the Mississippi, and one has no record following its seizure.[39]

The origins of many of the 14 vessels that became the River Defense Fleet is limited or unknown, but extensive records were kept by the Confederate military afterwards. The *Colonel Lovell* was the Cincinnati-built *Hercules,* which operated as part of the Ocean Towing Company of Louisiana since 1843. The ship was entrusted to Captain J.C. Delancy. The *Defiance* was also Cincinnati-built; it previously was part of Charles Morgan's Southern Steamship Company but was now commanded by Captain Joseph D. McCoy. The *General Bragg* was formerly the *Mexico,* another vessel in Charles Morgan's steamship line that plied the trade between New Orleans, Mexico, and Panama. She was built in New York in 1850, possessed three masts, and was propelled by both steam and sail power. The vessel was known for its speed. "She runs like a Grayhound" one observer noted, and "was steady and quiet and swift as a Sword-fish." Captain W. H. H. Leonard was

39 *DANFS,* 2:501-502, 520, 545-546, 574-575, 578, 581-582; "George Hollins to William Nixon," Oct. 19, 1861, Subject File, NN, NA; "Testimony of Lieutenant Kennon," *ORN,* Ser. 2, 1:528; "Report of Captain Craven," *ORN,* 17:138-140; "Report of Acting Rear Admiral Lee," *ORN,* 9:291.

River Defense Fleet Ship *General Sterling Price*. Naval History and Heritage Command

placed in command of the *General Bragg*, assisted by First Officer David Davis and Chief Engineer John Porter.[40]

The *General Sumter* was originally known as the *Junius Beebe*, a steamer built in Algiers in 1853 that displaced 524 tons. The ship was part of Charles Morgan's Steamship Company until the start of the war when the state of Louisiana acquired and used her until Captain Montgomery inspected the ship for conversion. The *Sumter* was entrusted to Captain W. W. Lamb. The vessel had the distinction of having a second captain onboard as well. Something of a local celebrity, Jefferson Davis Howell joined the crew in New Orleans. As the younger brother of Varina Howell Davis, young Jefferson had a close tie with his brother-in-law the president of the Confederacy.[41]

The *General Sterling Price* was originally the *Laurent Millaudon*. Built in Cincinnati in 1856, the ship was comparable in size to the *General Sumter* and was entrusted to Captain J. H. Townsend. Nothing is known about the *General Beauregard* before Montgomery selected the vessel, but the ship was led by Captain J. H. Hunt, who

40 M. Jeff Thompson, *The Civil War Reminiscences of General M. Jeff Thompson* (Dayton, OH, 1988), ed. by Donald J. Stanton, Goodwin F. Bernquist, and Paul C. Bowers, 157; *DANFS*, 2:510, 514, 522-523, 525; *New Orleans Ship Register*, 5:64, 146, vol. 6, 124; J. Thomas Scharf, *History of the Confederate States Navy* (New York, 1887), 252.

41 *DANFS*, 2:525; Scharf, 252. United States Naval War Records Office, *Officers of the Confederate States Navy, 1861-1865*, (Washington DC, 1898), 157. Hereafter cited as *Confederate Officers*.

was assisted by First Officer Robert D. Court and Chief Engineer Joseph Swift. The *General Breckinridge* similarly has no background history, but she was entrusted to Captain James B. Smith. The *Breckinridge's* first officer was Richard Ranger and the chief engineer was Charles E. Whitmore, an Ohio native who previously served onboard the CSS *Ivy* before resigning from the Confederate Navy in January 1862.

The *General Earl Van Dorn* was commanded by Captain Isaac D. Fulkerson, a career river captain who earlier served with the Confederate Army in Missouri. John W. Jordan served as his first officer, while the former tugboat *General Lovell* was commanded by Captain Burdett Paris, a 41-year-old Mississippi native turned river pilot. The *General M. Jeff Thompson* was another side-wheel steamer that was commanded by Captain John H. Burke.[42]

The *Resolute* was a side-wheeler tug that Montgomery placed under the command of Captain Isaac Hooper. The *Stonewall Jackson* was another side-wheeler and was entrusted to Captain George M. Phillips, a river captain who commanded an army transport in the Mexican War. Another side-wheeler, the *Warrior*, was commanded by none other than Captain John A. Stevenson. After his *Manassas* ironclad ram was seized, and still holding a grudge against the Confederate Navy, Stevenson continued to look for a way to make money by striking at the Union blockade; he saw the potential of Montgomery's River Defense Fleet and wanted to be a part of the venture. The *Little Rebel* rounded out the list of 14 accepted ships and served as Montgomery's personal flagship. Propelled by a screw, the small 159-ton vessel was originally the *R. E. And A. N. Watson*, built in Pennsylvania. Montgomery was assisted by the ship's captain, T. White Fowler, the first officer, Alonzo J. Hawthorne, and the chief engineer, David Hall.[43]

It was noted in Gen. Lovell's order that the 14 vessels could be seized without compensation, but the Confederate government did eventually pay, just as in the case of when the navy department compensated Captain Stevenson after the *Manassas* was appropriated. Following their initial inspections, a board of six men, including Captain Stevenson and Chief Constructor John L. Porter (no relation to the *General Bragg's* chief engineer), convened and determined that the vessels were collectively worth $900,000. The Confederacy purchased them for $563,000 and they were converted into rams at the Algiers shipyards.[44]

---

42 DANFS, 2:523, 525; *New Orleans Ship Register*, 5:151; Scharf, 252; *Confederate Officers*, 155-156.

43 *DANFS*, 2:543, 561, 569, 580. *Confederate Officers*, 157.

44 Scharf, *History of the Confederate Navy*, 250.

To crew the ships, Montgomery, Townsend, and Stevenson sought out men who worked on the river, either on the steamers moving goods up or down the waterway or on the wharves and shipyards along its banks. Each of the 14 ships needed a crew of about 40 men, creating a demand for nearly 600 sailors. Several were former sailors in Hollins's squadron while others transferred from the army. Many were crewmen on the steamers before they were seized and retained employment on them.

Each ship was crewed similarly with a captain and two senior officers. Each engineering department was led by a chief engineer with two or three assistant engineers. On at least seven of the ships a surgeon was assigned. A carpenter, gunner, and one or two experienced river pilots rounded out the senior personnel onboard each vessel of the River Defense Fleet. Coal heavers and water tenders assisted the engineers operating the machinery. Each captain had some flexibility in determining positions for each sailor and what those positions were called; in an effort to sound more intimidating, several of the ships called their deckhands marines. Others stuck with the traditional terminology of seaman. Two cooks and two stewards, along with several youths serving as cabin boys rounded out each crew.[45]

To quickly obtain men to serve with the River Defense Fleet, higher pay was offered than they received for similar work in the navy. Deck hands in the Confederate Navy were paid a monthly wage of less than $20, but the River Defense Fleet offered $25. Engineering personnel were paid between $30 and $35 while petty officers, cooks, and stewards could make $50 or more while the most pay that enlisted sailors in the Union and Confederate navies earned was $45. This attracted men who once might have served on privateers to seek prize money, but impeded recruitment efforts by Hollins's officers looking for men to operate the New Orleans ironclads nearing completion.[46]

Work began immediately on the ships brought to the shipyards in Algiers for conversion. The 14 ships were reinforced for ramming "by placing a 4-inch oak sheath with a 1-inch iron covering on [each] bow, and by installing double pine bulkheads filled with compressed cotton bales" to protect engineering machinery.

---

45 For an example of the use of such rank positions, see "Shipping Articles of Confederate Steamer Defiance," *Confederate Vessel Papers: Papers Pertaining to Vessels Involved with the Confederate States of America* (War Department Collection of Confederate Records, Records Group 109), National Archives Building, Washington, DC. Hereafter cited as *Vessel Papers*.

46 "Pay Roll of Confederate Steamer Resolute," *Vessel Papers*.

Colonel William S. Lovell oversaw the changes and virtually no assistance was provided by the navy in outfitting and equipping the ships.

A supply of cannon, mostly 32-pounders, was provided by Gen. Lovell with one or two mounted on each ship. Additionally, the senior Lovell "furnished them ammunition and small-arms, and established a system of signals" for communication. Additional cannon shells were furnished by contract with Leeds and Company of New Orleans. The guns, however, were seen as secondary. The use of the *Manassas* at the Head of Passes convinced Montgomery that rams could be most effective if commanded by daring and skillful men.[47]

The ships began entering the Algiers shipyards in February. Some in New Orleans, particularly naval officers, believed that converting these lightly armed and small steamers was a waste of the limited pool of workers, sailors, and supplies that could be better used completing the ironclads or servicing Confederate ships already in operation. However, the army persisted.

The final cost proved exorbitant. By mid-April, army agents spent over $800,000 outfitting, coaling, and provisioning the 14 ships—that was in addition to the initial $563,000 purchase price—and even more money was allocated to pay the promised wages for the crews. This was well over the $1,000,000 that the Confederate Congress allotted for river defenses in January of 1862. Like the navy's purchases, the army ran well over budget.[48]

As work continued on the vessels of the River Defense Fleet, questions arose as to just how they should be employed. The war department wanted to send the ships upriver to augment the defenses of Tennessee, Kentucky, and Missouri. Louisiana politicians lobbied that the ships remain on the lower river protecting New Orleans, claiming that until the ironclads *Louisiana* and *Mississippi* were ready, there was no other naval defense of the city. After all, the idea of forming such a fleet was done because New Orleans felt threatened.

General Mansfield Lovell intended to follow the orders of the war department and send the ships upriver, but an unforeseen event soon changed his mind. The chain and log barrier between Forts Jackson and Saint Philip broke apart after winter snows melted and flooded the Mississippi River. The loss of this barrier created a major breach in New Orleans's defenses and Lovell sought to replace it with another barrier built of sunken wooden ships chained together. Lovell

---

47 *DANFS*, 2:525; Court of Inquiry, 68; "Payment Receipt for Artillery Ammunition," Apr. 3, 1862, *Leeds and Company Papers*.

48 Scharf, *History of the Confederate Navy*, 250-251; "An Act of Congress," ORN, 22:814.

believed that this barrier was a vital part of the defense of the lower river, which would force approaching enemy ships to slow down under the guns of Forts Jackson and Saint Philip. Until it could be replaced, Lovell made the decision to keep some of the River Defense Fleet at New Orleans as an emergency protection force. He dispatched a message to commanders in Tennessee explaining that the ships would stay, at least until the barrier was replaced, because if Union naval forces advanced from the Gulf, the Mississippi was "now open to them if they pass the lower forts."[49] Ultimately, six ships stayed behind while eight moved upriver as soon as their conversions were completed.

While the ships were being converted, the captains in charge of each found that while trying to train their improvised crews the men were not inclined to follow military discipline. One of Lovell's aides overseeing the conversion of the vessels noted that the river steamers possessed "no discipline, no organization, but little or no drill of the crews."[50] To remedy this situation, Lt. Col. William S. Lovell dispatched a 32-pounder cannon to the shipyards specifically for the River Defense Fleet sailors to train on. Lovell furthermore employed a retired naval gunner to oversee the installation of the heavy cannon onto the vessels of the River Defense Fleet and to train the sailors how to fire them. The training cannon, however, remained largely unused.

Work continued into March on the 14 ships. The first of them, the *Defiance*, was completed on March 10 and sent out of John Hughes's shipyards. After that, each week witnessed more fully converted ships. The *Stonewall Jackson* and *Warrior* left the shipyards on March 16 and the *General Sterling Price*, *General Bragg*, and *General Van Dorn* all left New Orleans for the upper Mississippi River on March 25. The *Resolute* left the shipyard on March 31, followed by the *General Beauregard* on April 5. Two more ships, the *General M. Jeff Thompson* and *Little Rebel*, left New Orleans on April 11, followed by the *General Sumter* and *Colonel Lovell* on April 17. The final two ships, the *General Lovell* and *General Breckinridge*, left the New Orleans shipyards on April 22 and were sent downriver to bolster the defenses of Forts Jackson and Saint Philip.[51]

49 "Letter from General Lovell," *OR*, 6:648.

50 *Court of Inquiry*, 70.

51 "Payment Receipt for River Steamer Defiance," Mar. 1, 1862, *John Hughes and Company Papers*. (National Archives Microfilm Publication M346, Records Group 109), National Archives Building, Washington DC.

Major General Mansfield Lovell, CSA.
Library of Congress

Back in New Orleans General Lovell had reservations about using these vessels in battle and after a short time working with their captains, his suspicions were reinforced. He sent a message to the secretary of war that "the river pilots (Montgomery and Townsend), who are at the head of the fleet, are men of limited ideas—no system and no administrative capacity whatever."[52] Nonetheless, Lovell followed his orders and continued to oversee their outfitting.

The six ships held at New Orleans were the *Defiance, Resolute, Stonewall Jackson, Warrior, General Lovell,* and *General Breckinridge.* Placed under the overall command of Captain John Stevenson, these six were used to bolster the defenses of Forts Jackson and Saint Philip in April when Union forces advanced against the city. The remaining eight were sent upriver under command of Captain Montgomery to join with Hollins's naval squadron and army forces operating in Tennessee and Missouri.

It is possible to track the movements of the River Defense Fleet ships upriver to a certain extent, thanks to the log kept by Louis F. Delesdernier, a Texas native onboard the *General Price.* The *General Price, General Bragg,* and *General Van Dorn* all left New Orleans on March 25. They travelled independently, with the *Bragg* and *Van Dorn* leaving during the day and the *Price* that night. The *Price* continued upriver alone, passing the Red River, on the morning of March 28. The ship spent an hour and a half alongside Vicksburg on March 29. The *Price,* along with the *General Van Dorn,* apparently was still in need of armor, but none could be found at Vicksburg.

Continuing upriver, the *Price* arrived at Eunice, Arkansas on March 31. Not finding any surplus iron, the crew spent several days tearing up three miles of

52 Scharf, *History of the Confederate Navy,* 251.

railroad tracks for use, a sad but often repeated act of destroying communications and supply lines to protect ships for battle. Leaving Eunice fully loaded with railroad iron, the *Price* then proceeded to Memphis, arriving in the afternoon of April 3. The *Bragg* arrived the day before and the *Van Dorn* joined them only an hour after the *Price* moored on the riverbank. The three ships were then sent up the river to rendezvous with Confederate forces at Fort Pillow. The remaining five River Defense Fleet ships sent upriver to join them arrived by the end of April.[53]

Louisiana's Independent Navy

As the River Defense Fleet vessels were converting to warships in the New Orleans shipyards, the state of Louisiana looked to increase the naval defense of New Orleans on its own. In January of 1862, the state legislature passed bills appropriating $2.5 million for naval defenses. What became the Louisiana State Navy emerged alongside Montgomery's River Defense Fleet.[54]

Mansfield Lovell inspected 24 ships for the River Defense Fleet, but only took possession of 14. Two vessels examined, but initially not selected, were the *Charles Morgan* and the *Galveston*. Both, like several of Montgomery's ships, belonged to Charles Morgan's Southern Steamship Company. The governor of Louisiana, at Gen. Lovell's recommendation and wishing to further augment his state's defense using the legislature's appropriations, issued orders in March 1862 to purchase and outfit these two vessels. The *Charles Morgan* was a side-wheel steamer built in New York in 1854, possessing a walking beam engine and a schooner rig. The ship was renamed the *Governor Moore*, after the current governor of the state. The *Galveston* was another river steamer built in New York in 1857. Displacing 945 tons, the ship held three masts as well as side-wheels for propulsion. The *Galveston* was originally inspected by Capt. Rousseau in June 1861 for use as a gunboat, but he found it "too cramped for mounting guns." It was renamed the *General Quitman*, named for former Mississippi governor and Mexican War general, John A. Quitman.[55]

Governor Thomas Moore turned to two men to command his ships. Lieutenant Beverly Kennon was a Virginian and veteran of both the Union and

---

53 Ibid, 252.

54 Adolphus Oliver to Daniel Ruggles, Jan. 3, 1862, *Adolphus Oliver Letters*, MSS 2281, Louisiana and Lower Mississippi Valley Collections, Louisiana State University Libraries, Baton Rouge, LA.

55 Beverly Kennon, "Fighting Farragut Below New Orleans," *B&L*, 2:77; *DANFS*, 2:524; *New Orleans Ship Register*, 5:44, 98.

Confederate navies. After being removed as Cmdre. Hollins's ordnance officer in late 1861, Kennon resigned his commission in disgrace, determined to "engage in privateering on my own book." Governor Moore personally asked Kennon to volunteer and assigned him to command the ship named after the governor. Additionally, based in large part to his naval experience, Kennon acted as the commander of Louisiana's tiny naval force. The *General Quitman's* captain was Captain Alexander Grant, who was "the same class as the commanders of the River Defense Fleet," being a river captain with no military training and a member of the Plaquemine Steamboat Association. Grant, though not possessing any military training, desired to serve the Confederacy, formerly assisting Raphael Semmes when he "carried dispatches from the Confederate raider *Sumter*" into New Orleans in 1861.[56]

The two ships were hurriedly converted for war use. Overseeing the process was Lt. Col. W. S. Lovell, brother to the commanding general, who brought them to the ever-crowded Algiers shipyards to add to his workload for conversion. The younger Lovell brother probably chose the ship names, for he was married to the daughter of John A. Quitman and likely wished to honor his father-in-law. "I had the whole charge of these two steamers," Lovell wrote, and "all that was done by the State was to pay the bills approved by me." One Union officer described them as "sea going steamers, whose bows were shod with iron like those of the River Defense Fleet and their engines protected with cotton." In addition, they were prepared by being "reinforced for ramming by two strips of flat railroad iron at the waterline, strapped and bolted into place, with pine lumber and cotton-bale barricades to protect her boilers" The cotton bulkhead barriers were considered important. One New Orleans newspaper editor's description of the *Governor Moore* was that it was "converted into a war steamer by means of cotton bulkheads." A naval officer in the city also described this outfitting, noting that the two ships contained "pine and cotton barricades to protect the more vulnerable part of their machinery."[57]

---

56 "Testimony of Lieutenant Beverly Kennon," *ORN*, Ser. 2, 1:523; Mahan, *The Gulf and inland Waters*, 67; *DANFS*, 2:518.

57 *Court of Inquiry*, 68; Second Director of the Treasury to the Secretary of War, Jul. 8, 1863, *John Hughes and Company Papers*; "Payment Receipt for Steamer Governor Moore," Apr. 19, 1862, *John Hughes and Company Papers*; Mahan, *The Gulf and Inland Waters*, 67; *DANFS*, 2:524; Terry L. Jones, ed., *The Civil War Memoirs of Captain William J. Seymour: Reminiscences of a Louisiana Tiger* (Baton Rouge, LA, 1991), 28; John Wilkinson, *The Narrative of a Blockade Runner* (New York, 1877), 14.

The *Governor Moore* of the Louisiana State Navy.

Naval History and Heritage Command and Navy Art Collection

The best description of the outfitting of these two ships was left by Lt. Beverly Kennon himself. He described that the *Governor Moore* was outfitted with "two strips of old-fashioned flat railroad iron, held in place by short straps of like kind at the top, at the water-line, and at three intermediate points. These straps extended about two feet abaft the face of the stem, on each side, where they were bolted in place." Kennon further explained the outfitting of the two ships with "boiler-houses, engines, and boilers protected by a bulkhead of cotton bales which extended from the floor of the hold to five feet or more above the spar-deck."[58] Both ships were armed with two cannon each, supplied by Gen. Mansfield Lovell from his land defenses: the *Governor Moore* with two rifled 32-pounders and the *General Quitman* with two smoothbore 32-pounders.

Finding crews to man the two ships was more difficult than converting them. Between the army and navy, blockade runners, privateers, and the River Defense Fleet, there were few sailors left in New Orleans to man Louisiana's two gunboats. In addition, most of the remaining sailors "belonged to the various volunteer companies around New Orleans" whose officers did not want to transfer them to naval service. The end result was a hodgepodge crew for both vessels. Again,

---

58 Kennon, "Fighting Farragut Below New Orleans," 77.

Kennon best describes this predicament, writing that "my officers were merchant mates, so were the quartermasters; the gunner had been to sea as a sailor on a man-of-war. My crew consisted of artillery and infantry detachments, and of longshoremen, cotton-pressers, and river boatmen." The artillerymen mentioned were members of Company G, 1st Louisiana Heavy Artillery Regiment, which was headquartered in Fort Macomb on the eastern edge of New Orleans protecting the approaches into Lake Pontchartrain.

By the end of March, Kennon recruited a total of 93 men for the *Governor Moore* while Grant succeeded in manning the *General Quitman* with a crew of about 90. Two-thirds of these men were sailors; the remaining third were the heavy artillerists. Once completed, the crews did not have time to train and instead the two vessels were immediately sent downriver to join, along with Captain John Stevenson's detachment of the River Defense Fleet, in the defenses of Forts Jackson and Saint Philip.[59]

By the early months of 1862, the Mississippi River was transformed into a string of Confederate military fortifications with naval support. Defenses stretched from the Head of Passes in the south to as far north as Columbus, Kentucky. Conversions provided improvised wooden warships with powerful ironclads under construction. Though incomplete in April, there was great confidence in the ironclad programs in both New Orleans and Memphis. Many believed that these armored ships were the key to controlling the Mississippi River.

These Confederate efforts were improvised and makeshift, but definitely a formidable presence on the river that Union forces must overcome in order to take control of the Mississippi River. The spring campaign of 1862 determined whether the young Confederacy could stop the United States invasion that was preparing to simultaneously strike both up and down the river.

59 Wilkinson, *The Narrative of a Blockade Runner*, 15; Kennon, "Fighting Farragut Below New Orleans," 89; Neil P. Chatelain, "Pelican Gunboats: The Louisiana State Navy and the Defense of Confederate New Orleans," *Journal of America's Military Past* (Spring/Summer 2015), 40:11.

CHAPTER FOUR

The Campaign for the
Upper Mississippi River

Union Winter Strikes

THE Confederate military did not have long to wait for the Federal campaigns to commence. Through the fall and winter of 1861, Union commanders built up their land and naval resources. The initial offensive began in February 1862, aiming to push down the Mississippi River and remove Confederate controlled areas in Kentucky. The first main defense on the Mississippi River to be overcome was Columbus, heavily fortified since Maj. Gen. Leonidas Polk's men occupied it in early September 1861. Directly across the river, Confederates successfully repulsed Union forces under Ulysses Grant at the Battle of Belmont on November 7, 1861. By the end of the year, Polk amassed 12,000 men to defend the area with several of Cmdre. Hollins's ships in support.

Before the 1862 land campaign began, naval forces scouted each other's positions. The first skirmish occurred on November 30, 1861 when three Union gunboats approached the Confederate positions at Columbus on "one of their usual voyages of discovery." In response, the CSS *General Polk*, the small army gunboat *Grampus*, and the CSS *Ivy* raised steam to challenge the Union advance. Facing an equal number of ships of unknown strength, the Union flotilla withdrew back upriver under the protection of Fort Holt, which fired several shots at the Confederate ships before they likewise withdrew back to Columbus, content at keeping the Union ships at bay.

Another skirmish occurred on January 7, 1862 when Union ships again approached Columbus. This time, the floating battery *New Orleans*, recently arrived from its namesake city, lay in wait. Lieutenant Guthrie spotted the Federal ships and ordered his men to man their battle stations before he "sunk the dock" for maximum protection.[1] Upon seeing the floating battery ready for battle, the Union ships withdrew without firing a shot.

A third foray occurred four days later. That morning three Confederate ships, believed to be the CSS *General Polk*, the *Grampus*, and possibly the CSS *Jackson*, steamed upriver on a reconnaissance mission. Accompanying the group was the *Red Rover*, with the floating battery *New Orleans* in tow. A dense fog obscured the surrounding area and Gen. Polk wanted to know if Union forces were preparing to launch an attack against his land fortifications.

Union Gen. John McClernand's forces, occupying nearby Fort Jefferson, spotted the Confederate flotilla steaming upriver and informed Cmdr. William D. Porter on the USS *Essex*. Porter ordered his ship to weigh anchor and signaled for the USS *Saint Louis* to follow. Both were newly completed ironclads and it was their first test in battle; Porter thought it might presage an attack against Fort Jefferson. Rounding Lucas Bend, the Union ships spotted a large Confederate steamer which, as Cmdr. Porter of the *Essex* noted, sounded "her whistle the moment we were seen." This vessel was likely the *General Polk*, as it was larger than both the *Jackson* and *Grampus*. The three Confederate gunboats opened fire. Commander Porter recalled that the first shot "struck the sand-bar between us, and ricocheted within about two hundred yards of this vessel, when it burst."[2] Porter directed his ironclad to return fire, targeting the transport *Red Rover*, which immediately retreated back downriver to Columbus towing the floating battery *New Orleans*.

The USS *Saint Louis* returned fire with its rifled cannon while the USS *Essex* used its bow guns. The Confederate ships continued firing as well, "filling the whole surrounding country with the roar," but failing to hit anything.[3] After 20 minutes, the Confederates withdrew downriver, occasionally stopping to lob a shell toward the Union ironclads, continuing on and taking shelter under the land batteries of Columbus. Commander Porter, under orders to prevent an

---

1 "A River Skirmish" *New Orleans* [LA] *Daily Crescent*, Dec. 5, 1861; "Late From Cairo" *Daily Nashville* [TN] *Patriot*, Dec. 11, 1861; "Our Gunboats after the Federals—Movements of Federal Troops" *Nashville* [TN] *Union and American*, Dec. 6, 1861; "Extract of Diary of Lieutenant Guthrie," *ORN*, 22:813.

2 "The Campaign in Kentucky" *New York Times*, Jan. 20, 1862.

3 "Western Military Correspondence" *New Orleans* [LA] *Daily Crescent*, Jan. 16, 1862.

Confederate Army Gunboat *Grampus*. *Naval History and Heritage Command*

engagement with Columbus, withdrew his two ironclads upriver. No casualties were reported on either side in the skirmish.

An amusing exchange occurred after the battle when Cmdr. Porter sent a note in a small toy boat down the Mississippi River toward Confederate lines. Crewmen on the towboat and tender *Red Rover* discovered the toy and Lt. Guthrie of the *New Orleans* took the note into his possession. It was a challenge: "come out here, you cowardly rebels, and show your gunboats." The next day, Capt. Marsh J. Miller, commander of the army gunboat *Grampus*, sent a reply where he boasted that his ship would "meet the *Essex*, at any point and time." Porter, not one to be outdone, replied to Miller's note that the *Grampus* was welcome to show itself and that it would "meet with a traitor's fate—if you have the courage to stand."[4]

Despite his setback at Belmont, General Ulysses Grant was not discouraged. From his headquarters in Cairo, Illinois he gathered 15,000 soldiers and planned a joint operation with the United States Navy to capture Forts Henry and Donelson. The two forts were only 12 miles apart overland. Fort Henry protected the Tennessee River and Fort Donelson guarded the Cumberland River, both tributaries of the Ohio River that were key to control of southern Kentucky and

4 A. Angelo Brittan, "Samuel Byron Brittan, Jr., U.S.N.," *Brittan's Journal: Spiritual, Science, Literature, Art, and Inspiration* (1874), No. 3, 2:308-309.

central Tennessee. Grant's advance bypassed the Confederate positions in Kentucky.

In the first bombardment by ironclad warships against shore fortifications, Fort Henry was attacked by seven Federal gunboats under Flag Officer Andrew H. Foote on February 6, 1862. All but a small contingent of the Confederate garrison evacuated to Fort Donelson before the battle. Foote's seven warships deployed more than 50 cannon. The Confederate rear-guard surrendered to the navy after a gallant stand—its 11 guns scored over 60 hits, disabling the *Essex* and another ironclad. The loss of Fort Henry after less than two hours sent shock waves all the way to Richmond.

Grant's soldiers now marched overland and began enveloping Fort Donelson on February 12. Foote's ships arrived the next day to threaten total encirclement.

A Confederate break out might have worked at that point. Unfortunately, the commanders at the fort were disorganized and rancorous. When the attempt was finally made on February 15, it failed. At one point the defenders of Fort Donelson thought they would be relieved. Rumors spread that "Commodore Hollins with the ram, *Manassas*, and thirteen Confederate Gun-boats passed Memphis . . . on his way to our relief."[5] This was untrue, as Hollins was not ordered upriver for several days and the ships already up the Mississippi were held back to protect Columbus.

Fort Donelson surrendered on February 16. It was the largest capture of troops since the 1781 British surrender at Yorktown during the American Revolution. U.S. Grant became the northern hero "Unconditional Surrender" Grant for the terms he gave the Confederates.

Confederate military leaders learned the strengths and weaknesses of the Union ironclad flotilla operating against Forts Henry and Donelson, but that information was not shared until six months after the siege. Two Federal ironclads were disabled in the assault against Fort Henry and another two were disabled in the February 14 naval attack on for Fort Donelson that was repulsed. Brigadier General Lloyd Tilghman, commander of Fort Henry, witnessed the effectiveness of his artillery against the Union squadron. Though captured, Gen. Tilghman documented what he saw and compiled his official report while a prisoner of war. In it, he took great pains to record the actions that caused the Union ironclads to be disabled: "The weak points in all their vessels were known to us, and the cool precision of our firing developed them, showing conclusively that this class of boats, though formidable, can not stand the test of even the 32-pounders, much

5 "Fort Donelson, Feb. 13, 9 P.M." *Clarksville* [TN] *Chronicle*, Feb. 14, 1862.

less the 24-caliber rifled shot, or that of the 10-inch columbiad." He went on further to note that "the immense area, forming what may be called the roof, is in every respect vulnerable to either a plunging fire from even 32-pounders or a curved line of fire from heavy guns. In the latter case shell should be used in preference to shot."[6] Unfortunately for the Confederates, the report did not reach military leaders in Richmond until August 1862 after Tilghman was exchanged; his vital intelligence was not available to Confederate forces for the spring 1862 river campaigns.

Some of the garrison of 12,000 defenders escaped before Fort Donelson surrendered, but the remainder represented nearly half of General Albert Sidney Johnston's forces in central Tennessee. The defeat forced the Confederates to concede more than 20,000 square miles of territory in Tennessee and Kentucky without a fight.

Johnston's defensive position in central Kentucky was now untenable, and he ordered an evacuation of Bowling Green, Kentucky. Nashville, the capital of Tennessee, was evacuated on February 23 and the four gunboats undergoing conversion there under the direction of Lt. Isaac N. Brown were burned to prevent their capture. This left most of central Tennessee open to Union invasion. It was this disaster that caused Secretary Mallory to order Cmdr. Hollins and ships of his River Defense Fleet upriver to assume personal command of the naval forces operating near Columbus. By the end of February, Hollins's squadron included the *McRae*, *Livingston*, *Maurepas*, *General Polk*, and the floating battery *New Orleans*, along with the local army gunboat *Grampus*. The *Manassas* and *Pontchartrain* were on the way and would arrive in March.

On paper, the squadron seemed impressive, but Hollins knew its limitations. With all of his available ships gathered upriver, they mounted just 49 cannon and only the *Manassas* was ironclad. The Union naval river force consisted of six ironclad vessels mounting 86 pieces of heavy artillery, backed by three wooden gunboats called timberclads, and several mortar boats. Clearly the manufacturing capability of the United States gave them the advantage, but Hollins only needed to keep his fleet intact long enough for the four ironclads at New Orleans and two at Memphis to be completed. Once they arrived, along with the River Defense Fleet ships refitting in Algiers, Hollins would have a powerful force to confront the Union naval presence on the upper river on roughly equal terms.

---

6 "Report of Brigadier General Tilghman," *ORN*, 22:560.

CSS *Manassas,* shown incorrectly with one smokestack instead of two.

Official Records of the Union and Confederate Navies in the War of the Rebellion

Gen. Grant's victory at Forts Henry and Donelson outflanked Gen. Polk's positions in western Kentucky. Polk received orders to retreat from Columbus and he did so on March 2, 1862. Hollins's naval squadron likewise withdrew downriver to New Madrid, Missouri. Flag Officer Foote's squadron and Union infantry occupied Columbus on March 4. Polk withdrew his men to Memphis, Tennessee. The first major Confederate fortification on the Mississippi River fell without a fight. It was not the last time Union commanders would use the tactic of outflanking and isolating a Confederate bastion on the Mississippi River.[7]

The Siege of New Madrid

As Gen. Grant was investing Forts Henry and Donelson, Brig. Gen. John Pope was gathering another Federal army to advance directly down the Mississippi River. Pope was a West Point graduate and veteran of the Mexican War. His plan was to move across the Missouri side of the riverbank and capture New Madrid, Missouri. From there, he would outflank and secure Island Number Ten, the next major Confederate fortification on the Mississippi River after Columbus. It was

---

7 Alexander Miller Diary, Mar. 3, 1862, MSS 296, Louisiana and Lower Mississippi Valley Collections, Louisiana State University Libraries, Baton Rouge, LA.

named so because the island was then tenth one downriver from Cairo, Illinois, at the merging point of the Mississippi and Ohio Rivers.

Pope assembled 26,000 men that he called the Army of the Mississippi for his expedition. He marched his men overland and on March 3, 1862 they arrived at the outskirts of New Madrid, just to the west of and just downriver from Island Number Ten. Facing them were approximately 3,000 Confederates commanded by Maj. Gen. John P. McCown, another graduate of West Point and Mexican War veteran. McCown's men occupied two fortifications, one on each end of New Madrid and connected with trenches. After the evacuation of Columbus, Hollins brought his squadron of ships to New Madrid. McCown hoped that they would be the key to holding this position, providing fire support to the garrison while keeping the supply and communication lines open with Island Number Ten upriver and Memphis to the south.

The area around New Madrid and Island Number Ten was a good choice for Confederates to fortify. Island Number Ten lies at a point where the Mississippi River makes a sharp turn north, forcing downriver traffic to slow and turn. From here, Confederate batteries could fire on any approaching ships. Hollins ordered the floating battery *New Orleans*, along with its tender *Red Rover*, to deploy anchored alongside the island to "command the inner channel" and add more guns to the formidable defense.

New Madrid was just a few miles downriver, but northwest, of Island Number Ten. Any Union ships that ran past the island must face Hollins's ships and New Madrid's guns as the river made yet another sharp turn south again. The weakest part of the defenses was New Madrid. It provided a good position to cover the Mississippi River, but it was exposed from the north. There was only one road leading to New Madrid used to transport supplies. Furthermore, if the town was captured by Union forces, Island Number Ten's defenses could be surrounded and besieged. This was precisely what Gen. Pope planned to accomplish and he pushed his men forward to seize the town.

Confederate officers knew of New Madrid's weakness and one senior army officer relied "much on them [Hollins's squadron] to drive the enemy back." General Leonidas Polk agreed that a Confederate naval presence was required at New Madrid, warning, "should the enemy's gunboats pass this point, New Madrid

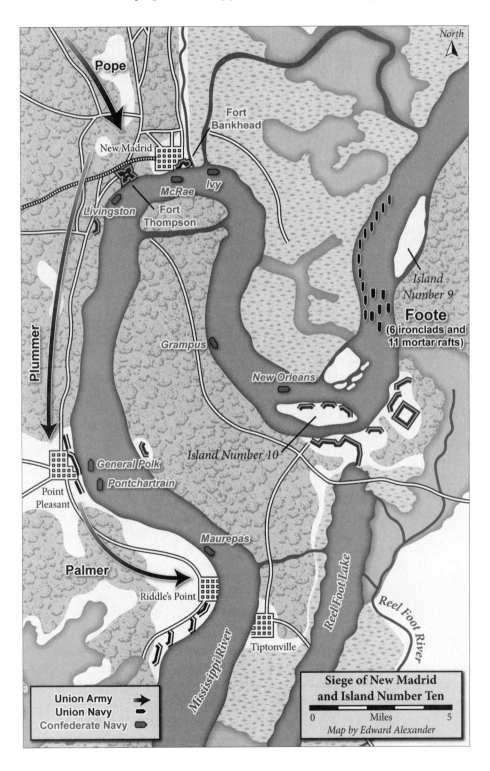

North

Pope

Fort
Bankhead

New Madrid

McRae   Ivy

Livingston   Fort
Thompson

Island
Number 9

Foote
(6 ironclads and
11 mortar rafts)

Plummer

Grampus

New Orleans

Island Number 10

General Polk

Pontchartrain

Point
Pleasant

Maurepas

Palmer

Riddle's Point

Reel Foot Lake

Reel Foot River

Tiptonville

Mississippi River

Union Army
Union Navy
Confederate Navy

Siege of New Madrid
and Island Number Ten

0   Miles   5

Map by Edward Alexander

could not be held six hours unless Commodore Hollins could defeat them."[8] The first serious test of the Confederate Navy on the Mississippi River was at hand.

As Pope's men approached New Madrid, Brig. Gen. M. Jeff Thompson of the Missouri State Guard, whose men were fighting a delaying action against Pope's advance, was seen approaching the CSS *McRae*, flagship of the Confederate squadron. "There are a hundred thousand Yankees after me and they have captured one of my guns," Thompson yelled to Hollins, "and if you don't get out of this pretty quick they will be on board of your old steamboat in less than fifteen minutes!"[9] Though his number of Federal soldiers was wrong, Thompson's report alerted the Confederates about the advancing Union soldiers. Hollins ordered his ships to prepare for battle.

Major General John McCown commanded five regiments of infantry and three batteries of artillery at New Madrid. Through 1861, his men constructed two forts, one on either side of the town. Fort Thompson, with two regiments of infantry and two companies of artillery, was on the western side while Fort Bankhead, with three regiments of infantry and one company of artillery, lay to the east. McCown personally remained in Fort Thompson while Brig. Gen. Alexander P. Stewart oversaw the defense of Fort Bankhead.

Pope's forces arrived and immediately attempted to storm the Confederate positions. This assault failed thanks in large part to Hollins's ships keeping back the Union infantry. As the Confederate ships fired their guns, officers and men in the forts cheered. Not all Confederates fought bravely this first day, however; Lt. Charles Read of the *McRae* described one interaction: "I saw [Col. Edward W.] Gant[t] when the Yankee shells first began to fall in our lines. He took the 'shell fever' quicker than any man I ever saw."[10] Gantt, an Arkansas attorney and colonel of the 12th Arkansas Regiment, was considered a drunkard who owed his position to his political connections.

After the assault of March 3 failed, Gen. Pope laid siege to the town and its fortifications, hoping the surrounded Confederate garrison would quickly surrender. He requested heavy artillery be dispatched to his position and his men began digging entrenchments to encircle New Madrid from the landside. The

8 "Captain J.J. Guthrie Papers," *Subject File*, HA, NA; Thompson, *The Civil War Reminiscences of M. Jeff Thompson*, 145; "Letter from Major General Polk," OR, 8:762.

9 Morgan, *Recollections*, 62-63; Alpheus Baker Diary, March 1, 1862, Alabama Textual Materials Collection, Alabama Department of Archives and History, Montgomery, AL.

10 Read, "Reminiscences of the Confederate States Navy," 337; Alpheus Baker Diary, Mar. 3, 1862.

artillery took time to arrive due to the muddy roads. In the meantime, Pope moved to isolate New Madrid's defenders from their base of supply.

Many believed that it was the Confederate naval squadron that saved General McCown's men on March 3. One engineer in Hollins's squadron suggested that "Pope could have taken them [New Madrid] at any time had our ships been away." Pope's own officers concurred. "Our officers are confident of an early and complete victory," one northern newspaper cautioned, only "if the enemy's gunboats are driven away." Another reporter from Baltimore commented, "the Federal officers believe that the place can easily be taken after the boats are driven off." Pope agreed with these assessments, writing that "it would not have been difficult to carry the intrenchments [sic], but it would have been attended with heavy loss, and we should not have been able to hold the place half an hour exposed to the destructive fire of the [Confederate] gunboats." An alternate plan to lay siege began and "the dirt commenced to fly while the artillery kept up a desultory fire."[11]

Hollins kept his squadron ready at all times for immediate battle. Officers remained on deck through the night and guns were pre-loaded for firing at the first sign of trouble. It was not long before Hollins's precaution was put to the test. In the predawn hours of March 5, Confederate pickets raised the alarm and soldiers ran to their entrenchments. Hollins immediately ordered his ships to open fire on the Union positions. However, no Union assault came. The false alarm was caused by nervous pickets. In any case, men in the Confederate trenches were glad the fire support came so quickly from their ships.[12]

Once the land encirclement was completed, the Army of the Mississippi expanded its siege lines by digging more trenches to isolate the Confederate fortifications. On March 6, 1862, Pope sent Brig. Gen. Joseph B. Plummer's division south to assault and capture Point Pleasant on the Missouri side of the river overlooking the only supply road available for use to McCown's men. Once Point Pleasant was in Union hands, Gen. Plummer began erecting a battery of guns to shell the Confederate ships as they lay at anchor, cutting off Confederate entrenchments from resupply.

---

11 Campbell, *Engineer in Gray*, 28; "Fighting at New Madrid, Missouri," Hartford [CT] *Daily Courant*, Mar. 10, 1862; "The War News," Baltimore [MD] Sun, Mar .8, 1862; "Report from Major General Polk," *OR*, 8:81; Morgan, *Recollections*, 64.

12 Alpheus Baker Diary, Mar. 5, 1862.

With McCown's forces besieged, it fell to the Confederate naval squadron to dislodge the Union battery at Point Pleasant. Commodore Hollins sent the CSS *Pontchartrain*, recently arrived under 1Lt. John Dunnington, and the CSS *General Polk* to investigate Union movements at Point Pleasant. The *Pontchartrain* came close against the riverbank to ascertain what was happening when "she was fired into by musketry, killing and wounding several." Among the wounded was a powder boy, just 14 years old, pierced by a musket ball. Not to be outdone, another boy sprinted up to Dunnington, and exclaimed "Captain, I will be your powder boy now!" Both the *Pontchartrain* and *General Polk* returned fire with their deck guns. "Many bottles of medicines in the dispensary were broken by the concussion of the after pivot gun," noted the *Polk's* surgeon, "and their entire contents lost."[13]

Rumors spread back at New Madrid on both sides about what was happening. Union soldiers digging trenches heard the din of "massive cannonading apparently down the river," while rumors circulated among officers in Confederate lines that the gunboats were fired upon after being lured in with the display of a white flag. One account went so far as to proclaim that the Union soldiers attracted Confederate ships closer to the riverbank by dressing as women. Another account in a Memphis newspaper speculated that Hollins "proceeded down with two gunboats … to break up the nest, which he doubtless succeeded in doing." In truth, Hollins, believing that if the Union battery at Point Pleasant was not silenced all "navigation from below will be completely cut off." His ships shelled the Point Pleasant battery on several occasions from March 7 through March 9 without result. "We had some really good tussles with them," claimed one Southern sailor, but they failed to dislodge the battery.[14]

Hollins dispatched a note to Gen. McCown summing up the situation: "The gunboats can drive them from the bank while they are firing, but they fall back out of reach and advance again as soon as the gunboats leave." Ground forces would be needed to complete the dislodgement of the Union battery at Point Pleasant, but none were available since they were all bottled up in New Madrid's defenses. As a result, the Union guns remained in place and Confederate supply ships now had to make runs past the Point Pleasant Union battery.

---

13 "Report of Major General McCown," *ORN*, 22:751; "Letter from New Madrid," *Memphis* [TN] *Daily Appeal*, Mar. 9, 1862; Robert J. Freeman, "Journal of Medical and Surgical Practice on board of the CS Steamer Genl Polk", 6 Mar. 1862, *Confederate States of America. Medical Records.*

14 Oscar L. Jackson, *The Colonel's Diary* (Sharon, PA, 1922), 46; "Point Pleasant," *Memphis* [TN] *Daily Appeal*, Mar. 9, 1862; "Report of Commodore Hollins," *ORN*, 22:835; Alpheus Baker Diary, Mar. 7 & 10, 1862; Morgan, *Recollections*, 65.

The first to do so was the *Kentucky*, the transport that assisted Confederate movements at the Battle of Belmont the previous year. The captain of the small side-wheel steamer ordered his lights extinguished and the vessel steamed upriver on the night of March 7. The Union battery sighted the transport, but much later than if it was steaming with full lighting. In the time it took the *Kentucky* to pass the Union guns, only one shot fired at it, causing no damage whatsoever. The supplies reached Confederate lines the next morning, bolstering the defense of New Madrid.[15]

With Plummer now controlling the land and river supply routes into New Madrid, Pope tried another assault on Gen. McCown's fortifications. Colonel J. L. Kirby Smith's brigade advanced into the town on March 7 and attempted to isolate the two Confederate forts from each other. Smith commanded the 43rd and 63rd Ohio Regiments, along with the 11th Battery of Ohio Light Artillery. The two regiments pushed Confederate skirmishers into New Madrid. Accompanying the soldiers was a newspaper reporter from the *Belmont Chronicle*, who related his experience. The reporter described the scene as Smith's men advanced "until we were in possession of two of the streets of the town." They continued their advance "to within 700 yards of the upper fort [Bankhead], driving the enemy infantry." Commodore Hollins was quick to react. The Union soldiers' success was short-lived as Hollins's gunboats "then opened upon us with shells and for the space of half an hour the air over our heads was literally filled with them, bursting in all directions." For many of Smith's brigade, it was their first time in combat. "The firing between them and us was pretty sharp and brisk," recalled one officer in the 63rd Ohio; "these were the first musket ball I had heard whiz. They had not the unearthly sound of rifled cannon shot, nor the death-like crashing of heavy shells."[16]

Midshipman James Morgan was Hollins's aide de camp during the siege. He remembered the *McRae* firing into the 11th Ohio Light Artillery Battery with the ship's nine-inch Dahlgren gun, describing the scene as he watched shells land amongst the Union artilleryman: "to see horses, men, and guns cavorting in the air was a most appalling sight." Just as the *McRae's* gunners reloaded to deliver another round, their gun burst with the muzzle smashing into the deck before falling

---

15 "Letter from Commodore Hollins," *OR*, 8:773; "From New Madrid," *Memphis* [TN] *Daily Appeal*, Mar. 9, 1862.

16 "Report of Brigadier General Stanley," *OR*, 8:98; "From the 48D Regiment," *Belmont* [OH] *Chronicle*, Mar. 20, 1862; Jackson, *The Colonel's Diary*, 46.

overboard. Morgan, who was near the gun as it exploded, recalled Hollins's reaction. The commodore approached his young aide and yelled out to him "Youngster, you came near getting your toes mashed!"[17]

After a few attempts to redeploy their forces to avoid enemy fire, the Ohio regiments retreated. Once again Hollins's ships held off the Union assault. Undeterred, Gen. Pope continued to expand his trenches. General McCown was concerned about Pope's March 7 attack, and he ordered his men to abandon the entrenchments between his two forts, taking cover in the protection of the fortifications but now isolated from each other. This left only the Confederate river squadron to relay messages between the two forts and bring supplies. Cut off from supplies by land and isolated inside of Forts Thompson and Bankhead, McCown's situation was desperate. Commodore Hollins and his squadron could only do so much against the Union land forces.

Besides occasional combat, the Confederate sailors also fought boredom and quarreled. One of the *McRae's* sailors, Fireman First Class George Kendricks, found a pig ashore and brought it onboard to share with his fellow engineers. He hid the pig in the engine room, but the ship's chief engineer, Samuel Brock, also saw it and ordered the pig thrown into the furnace. Second Assistant Engineer James Tomb disliked Brock and was particularly enraged when "all the pork chops that the mess had been counting on for a few days went up in smoke and smell." Added to this, Brock refused to let men read while on watch in the *McRae's* engine room. Tomb later got his revenge when, after finding one of Brock's books, he ordered Kendricks to "put this book the way the pig went, and don't be long about it either." Tomb wrote of his dislike of Brock after the war, commenting, "it would have been for the good of the service, if Brock had followed the pig and the book."[18]

Hollins ordered continuous forays ashore to scout out enemy positions and to pass communications between the now isolated Forts Thompson and Bankhead. Being the commodore's aide, Midn. James Morgan was often personally involved in these missions, making dashes into Confederate lines to relay reports from the naval forces. During one instance, an army major saw Morgan and exclaimed that it was "a damned shame to send a child into a place like this!"[19] Morgan, who attended the United States Naval Academy before Louisiana seceded, considered

17 Morgan, *Recollections*, 65.

18 Campbell, *Engineer in Gray*, 29-30.

19 Morgan, *Recollections*, 64.

himself a military professional and he grew furious at the insult; he very nearly challenged the major to a duel, but was dissuaded by his friend Lt. Charles Read back on the *McRae*.

In another instance, Morgan led a party of sailors ashore to burn a barn that was obscuring Union positions from the Confederate ships. The group was successful, but young Morgan was slightly wounded by a spent bullet that struck him in the arm. During the ensuing action, Morgan found a piano in an abandoned home and brought it to the riverbank. The *McRae's* executive officer examined the piano and found "a number of treasonable letters under the lid." Two women approached the Confederate sailors in the hope of recovering the piano, but when they learned the letters were discovered, the women ran off quickly.

In another foray ashore, the *McRae's* sailors captured two Union soldiers that became separated from their unit. They were brought onboard and interrogated by 1Lt. Thomas Huger. The two soldiers barely spoke English and it was discovered that they were recent immigrants who "had been landed one day and enlisted the next."[20]

Even by this stage in the siege, General McCown remained confident that the campaign would have a positive outcome. In a letter to his superiors, McCown praised Cmdre. Hollins's cooperation, noting that the naval commander has "given me the most hearty support in everything."[21] McCown went further, confidently boasting that any Union assaults against New Madrid would be defeated by the combination of Confederate gunboats and the artillery in his two forts. Events unforeseen by McCown, however, would drastically change the situation.

The heavy artillery that Gen. Pope requested arrived at Cairo on March 11. It took two more days to get the guns into position in front of New Madrid, and on March 13 Pope's heavy cannon opened fire on the Confederate lines. The louder din of larger guns was corroborated by a group of soldiers that recovered and inspected one of the big cannon balls. General McCown was caught by surprise, not believing that "heavy guns could be [carried] through the swamps at all."

The Federal bombardment continued through the day and when the morning fog lifted, a fire "was opened warmly" by Hollins's gunboats against the Union heavy artillery.[22] A small Union force advanced against Fort Thompson in the

20 Campbell, *Engineer in Gray*, 28, 31.

21 "Report of Major General McCown," *OR*, 8:777.

22 John Pope, *The Military Memoirs of General John Pope* (Chapel Hill, NC, 1998), 50; Alpheus Baker Diary, March 13, 1862; "Report of Brigadier General Gantt," *OR*, 8:166.

afternoon to observe the effectiveness of the heavy barrage, but they were pushed back by fire from Confederate cannon emplaced in the fort and on the CSS *Pontchartrain*. The exchange of fire lasted throughout the day but only disabled one Union 24-pounder.

Generals McCown and Stewart boarded the *McRae* at sunset and held a council of war with Cmdr. Hollins and the captains of his ships. After reviewing the situation, the group determined that an evacuation of New Madrid was required that night because "our gunboats are not sufficiently protected for such heavy metal" fired by the Union heavy artillery.[23] Both Forts Thompson and Bankhead were evacuated by Hollins's squadron and the army transports available. The ships dispatched to the two forts were: the CSS *General Polk*, CSS *Livingston*, and transport *Louisville* to Fort Thompson while the CSS *Pontchartrain*, and the army transports *De Soto*, *Winchester*, and *Ohio Belle* moved to Fort Bankhead. In case the Union guns tried to interfere, the cannon on the CSS *McRae* and CSS *Ivy* provided cover fire. Before the evacuation began, the captain of the transport *Winchester* refused to obey the order and instead withdrew his ship downriver. As a result, the mission of both the *McRae* and *Ivy* changed to assisting the evacuation at Fort Bankhead.

The embarkation from Fort Thompson was overseen by Gen. Stewart, McCown's second in command while 1Lt. Jonathan H. Carter on the *General Polk* directed the naval forces there. Most of the enlisted men and junior officers in the fort believed they were preparing to launch an attack when the order to muster came. Instead, they began loading the fort's ammunition onto the ships. "Sailors, artillerymen, and most of the infantry remaining were set to work" moving the artillery shells and gunpowder onboard the *General Polk* and *Livingston*. It began to rain, soon turning into a ferocious storm. One Confederate sailor recalled that "a darker and more disagreeable night it is hard to conceive; it rained in torrents, and our poor soldiers, covered with mud and drenched with rain, crowded on our gun-boats." One of Fort Thompson's officers agreed, later claiming that "the night became so dark that it was difficult to see, except by the flashes of lightning."[24]

Lieutenant Carter was worried that Pope's army would spot his vessels and open fire on the Confederates as they tried to leave. General McCown recalled that Carter "was hurrying them, telling them he intended to save his boats, and would

---

23 "Telegram from Major General McCown," *ORN*, 22:737.

24 J.C. Poe, ed., *The Raving Foe: The Civil War Diary of Major James T. Poe, C.S.A. and the 11th Arkansas Volunteers and a Complete List of Prisoners* (Eastland, TX, 1967), 28; Read, "Reminiscences of the Confederate States Navy," 337; "Report of Brigadier General Stewart," *OR*, 8:164.

leave them to shift for themselves if the enemy fired." The rain continued to grow worse, masking the evacuation, but "the mud and water soon became so deep as to render the road to the river next to impassable," forcing several heavy guns to be spiked and left behind.[25] After loading the ammunition, all remaining supplies that could be found were crammed onto the gunboats and the transport *Louisville.*

Work continued through the night at Fort Thompson. After all of the supplies and ammunition, Carter and Stewart loaded the garrison. This was completed at around 3 am on March 14 and the two gunboats and the transport *Louisville* departed. The CSS *Livingston* also towed off a wharf-boat that was being used as a hospital with some 100 sick and injured soldiers and their medical caretakers. The ships steamed to Tiptonville, the chosen rendezvous point down the river. Despite the heavy rain, the evacuation of Fort Thompson went smoothly and largely without incident.[26]

Evacuating Fort Bankhead was markedly different. Large 32-pounder shells were first loaded on the CSS *Pontchartrain* before it was diverted to pick up a picket guard outside of the fort, leaving only the *De Soto* and *Ohio Belle* to take the fort's men and supplies. Since the *Winchester's* captain refused to cooperate, Cmdr. Hollins directed the *McRae* and *Ivy* to assist with the transfer. Six field guns were loaded onto the *De Soto* overloading and nearly sinking it. When the fort's garrison saw the *De Soto* leaving, many panicked and rushed the ships. The *Ivy* nearly capsized from the onrush of soldiers; it was only through the resolve of her captain and several officers that order was established and the ship stabilized.

Seeing this, Lt. Read of the *McRae* determined to maintain order on his ship. As a crowd of disorganized soldiers approached the flagship, Read met them on shore. When a large soldier tried to board the ship, the *McRae's* young executive officer drew his sword which "flashed out of its scabbard and came down on the head of the mutineer, felling him to the ground."[27] The remaining soldiers then fell into ranks at Read's order and boarded the *McRae* in an orderly fashion. Just as at Fort Thompson, once the soldiers of Fort Bankhead were loaded onto the ships, they were brought downriver.

---

25 "Report of Brigadier General Stewart," *OR*, 8:164; "Report of Brigadier General Gantt," *OR*, 8:168.

26 "Report of Brigadier General Stewart," Ibid, 164-165.

27 "Report of Brigadier General Walker," Ibid, 169-170; Morgan, *Recollections*, 69; Alpheus Baker Dairy, Mar. 13, 1862.

The Confederate naval squadron and army transports moved past the Union battery at Point Pleasant without being detected and landed them several miles below at Tiptonville, Tennessee. From there, McCown marched his soldiers north where they joined the garrison at Island Number Ten. The Confederate naval forces remained at Tiptonville to monitor activity and provide support.

At dawn on March 14, Pope's men advanced into the Confederate works around New Madrid, surprised that the fortifications were abandoned. Pope wired his superior, Maj. Gen. Henry Halleck, that his men captured some "twenty-five pieces of heavy artillery . . . two batteries of field artillery; an immense quantity of fixed ammunition; several thousand small arms; hundreds of boxes of musket-cartridges; three hundred mules and horses; [and] tents for an army of 12,000 men." Union newspaper reports were more conservative in their estimates, with one claiming "the rebels evacuated both forts last night, crossing the river by means of transports during a heavy storm. They left fourteen heavy guns, a large quantity of ammunition, tents, camp equipage, several flags, about three hundred horses and mules, besides wagons, stores, [and] officers' baggage." A Confederate paper in Louisiana claimed that "everything was saved except the large guns."[28]

Island Number Ten Besieged

New Madrid was now in Union hands, leaving Island Number Ten almost totally cut off. Only a small stretch of marsh with one road to Tiptonville linked the island to its base of supply and reinforcements. Gen. McCown's men marched north from Tiptonville and augmented the defense of Island Number Ten.

Aware of the siege at New Madrid, the garrison on the island was prepared for Union ships to appear at any moment. However, no enemy ships arrived through the entire siege and the defenders used that time to improve their defensive positions.

Hollins was concerned about ammunition in his squadron. He wrote a letter to Gen. Beauregard pleading for more, citing a current shortage among his ships. He additionally passed orders to his captains to conserve ammunition and to not

28 "St. Louis, March 15," *Gallipolis* [OH] *Journal*, Mar. 20, 1862; "Important News from New Madrid: The Town in the Hands of Our Troops" *Gallipolis* [OH] *Journal*, Mar. 20, 1862; "Telegraphic," *The Semi-Weekly Shreveport* [LA] *News*, Mar. 21, 1862.

"throw it away without some return from the enemy for it." One officer estimated there was "not ammunition enough in the whole fleet for a fight of three hours."[29]

Not waiting for Beauregard's reply, Hollins dispatched Lt. Thomas Fister from the *McRae* down to Memphis, pleading for ammunition and powder from the army's arsenal there. Unable to acquire anything from the arsenal, a trainload of naval ammunition was sent from New Orleans. However, it was stopped before it reached Memphis and discarded by the rails to make room for army supplies, even though Hollins had a steamer waiting at Memphis to bring it upriver. This lack of coordination within the Confederate supply system hampered military efforts everywhere.

Manpower was likewise an issue, particularly trained engineers. Hollins ordered all but one of the engineers away from the floating battery *New Orleans* anchored at Island Number Ten, to augment the crews on his other vessels.

Before Union ships arrived to bombard Island Number Ten, the Confederates made considerable improvements. Eight separate batteries mounting 26 heavy cannon were constructed on the Tennessee shore stretching upriver for two miles across from Island Number Ten. On the island were another 23 heavy guns and four siege mortars in five additional batteries. Finally, the CSS *New Orleans* floating battery was moored along the island "so as to command the north channel."[30] Altogether there were 18 eight-inch Columbiads, six 24-pound Dahlgren guns, 13 32-pounder rifled guns, 21 32-pounder smoothbore guns, and four eight-inch mortars, 62 guns in total. Including the New Madrid garrison, the island was now manned by some 7,000 men divided into eight regiments of infantry, two squadrons of cavalry, and 11 artillery companies.

After the capture of New Madrid, Pope's men set up batteries to bombard the river while Foote's gunboats moved downriver. The Union gunboats and mortar boats arrived on March 15 and commenced their bombardment. The only Confederate response was when Capt. E. W. Rucker, in command of Battery Number One, fired on several Union transports that approached. With battle imminent, the island's leadership decided to sacrifice one of their transports, believing that "a large steamboat sunk in the slough during the night," was worth the loss of a transport.[31]

---

29 "Letter from Commodore Hollins," *ORN*, 22:738; "Letter from J.T. Trezevant," *ORN*, 22:741.

30 "Report by Captain Gray," Ibid, 748.

31 "Report by Captain Rucker," Ibid, 753; Alexander Miller Diary, March 15, 1862.

Four Federal mortar boats continued the bombardment on the 16th. They kept an incessant fire until sighting a white flag raised above Battery Number One. On inquiring the meaning of the flag, the Union sailors learned that it was a signal flag, not a flag of surrender. The Federal firing quickly recommenced, but Confederate guns remained silent.

On March 17 Foote tried a new tactic, lashing together three of his ironclads, the USS *Cincinnati*, the USS *Pittsburgh*, and the recently commissioned USS *Benton*.[32] The three vessels were placed about one mile upriver on from Battery Number One on the Tennessee side of the river with the goal of enfilading the battery to force its submission. The target of three ironclads was too tempting and this time the Confederates returned fire. Two more Union gunboats steamed downriver and added their fire to the contest.[33]

Through the day, several Confederate shots "struck the *Benton*, but, owing to the distance from which they were fired, but did little damage." Union guns, on the other hand, were having some effect on the Confederate fortifications. In the battery, 2Lt. William M. Clark was killed and seven enlisted men were wounded. Captain Rucker noted, "many shot and shell fell immediately in the rear of our guns, while others passed through the parapet, plowing up the earth and destroying much of the work." The Union ships continued to pound away at Battery Number One until 7 pm, when they retired for the evening, but the mortars continued their bombardment through the night. Two Union fieldpieces, just arrived overland from New Madrid, joined in the night bombardment, targeting the floating battery *New Orleans*, which returned fire and with "a few well-directed shots drove them off."[34] This action was repeated by the Union field artillery on the night of March 18, with similar results.

After the first couple of days of this bombardment, Confederate leaders thought that their defenses at Island Number Ten were secure and McCown was ordered to report downriver to Fort Pillow to receive several important communications in person. The island was believed to be so safe that he was ordered to take six regiments of infantry and two batteries of field artillery with

32 USS *Pittsburgh* is often spelled as *Pittsburg* thanks to the US Government standardizing the city's official spelling as Pittsburg from 1890-1911. As a result, the OR and ORN spell the city and ship as *Pittsburg*, even though it held the h at the end during the war. It is often spelled either way.

33 Alexander Miller Diary, Mar. 17, 1862.

34 Henry Walke, "The Western Flotilla at Fort Donelson, Island Number Ten, Fort Pillow and Memphis," *B&L*, 1:439; "Report by Captain Rucker," *ORN*, 22:754. "Report by Lieutenant Averett," *ORN*, 22:745.

him. These men were needed to help reinforce Gen. Albert S. Johnston's army gathering at Corinth, Mississippi for a counterattack against the Union armies in central Tennessee. They fought at the Battle of Shiloh on April 6 and 7, 1862.

McCown left Brig. Gen. L.M. Walker in command of the island's defenses until he returned on March 21. The transfer of McCown's forces to Johnston at Corinth left eight regiments defending Island Number Ten along with artillery. The island's garrison had 30 days of fresh bacon and flour, along with three months of rations. Island Number Ten was considered well defended, but many of the men there were sick. An inspector dispatched by Gen. Polk reported that 1,500 men of the garrison were too ill to fight. The local swamps affected both sides. Of Pope's 26,000 men, only 18,000 were present and fit for duty. The remainder were similarly incapacitated.

Through the bombardment, Hollins's squadron remained active. After dropping off the evacuees from New Madrid, Hollins kept his ships at anchor near Tiptonville during the day, ready to support operations as necessary. At night, the commodore sent a gunboat past New Madrid to deliver supplies and communications to Island Number Ten. The Army of the Mississippi did not allow the Confederate gunboats to pass unscathed. "Our boats have a great many [musket] balls through them," lamented one engineer after a run to the island.[35]

While Foote bombarded Island Number Ten, Gen. Pope expanded his army's position on the Missouri side of the river. He directed Brig. Gen. John M. Palmer's division to march south from New Madrid, pass through Point Pleasant's defenses, and set up masked batteries at Riddle's Point, just opposite Tiptonville. The men worked for several days to secretly set up hidden batteries to bombard the Confederate forces at Tiptonville. If successful, they might cut off the island's only line of supply.

The morning of March 18 Palmer's secret battery opened fire. The previous night, his division completed erecting a battery of three 24-pounders on the riverbank. At first light, they fired on two Confederate transports steaming upriver with supplies. The supply ships "set up a continuous whistling" to warn the Confederate squadron. Hearing it, Hollins dispatched the *McRae's* steam launch to investigate. As the launch neared, Union guns opened fire. Seeing this, Hollins ordered his squadron to close and engage. The *McRae*, *Maurepas*, *General Polk*, and *Pontchartrain* promptly weighed anchor and steamed downriver to Riddle's Point. When they got in range of the Union battery, they opened fire. "The first shell came

35 John H. Dent, Jr. to John H. Dent, Mar. 23, 1862, John Horry Dent, Jr., Letters.

from a boat directly opposite the rifle pits, passing over them and exploding just over the rear trench," recalled one soldier in the newly erected Union battery.[36]

After exchanging fire for a few minutes, Hollins directed three of his ships to round a bend in the Mississippi River just south of Riddle's Point to fire into the flank of the Union battery. After repositioning, the *McRae* opened fire with three of its guns while the other two Confederate ships followed suit, adding to the racket as well. "The fire from all the boats was continuous," remembered a soldier in the 46th Indiana Regiment covering the battery, "and left no room outside the trenches for any living thing."

The Union battery had a difficult time returning fire at the Confederates, but when they did, the gunners proved accurate. They initially targeted the CSS *Maurepas* and Lt. Joseph Fry described the effect of the Union battery, noting that his ship was "struck eight or nine times by cannon balls, and probably by thirty or forty [musket] balls. The deck has been covered with splinters; my back, also; my stove-pipe cut in two in the cabin; my table, secretary, sideboard, looking-glass frame, etc., all smashed and scratched."[37] Additionally, a small boat was cut away from the *Maurepas* and drifted downriver.

The *McRae* "ceased firing, and went a mile below to pick up the boat" while the remaining ships continued targeting the battery. Meanwhile, the Union artillery emplacement shifted its fire to the *General Polk*, which soon "received a shot between wind and water, and signalized that she was leaking badly." The *General Polk* immediately withdrew downriver to escape the Union fire, with damage to her hull. Her crew found it necessary "to resort to her pumps" to keep the ship afloat.

Though two Confederate ships were damaged, the Union gunners abandoned their position; Hollins ordered his remaining ships to withdraw. Afterwards, a Memphis newspaper reported, "the Federals attempted to plant a battery opposite this landing [at Tiptonville], but were deterred by the timely interference of Commodore Hollins, who drove them away and took their guns." The Union gunners, however, did not retreat for long and the battery continued to pester the Confederates. Hollins withdrew his ships downriver to avoid further damage to the squadron. He was heard to bark out in exasperation, "the campaign had taught him

36 Order of the Regimental Association, *History of the Forty-Sixth Regiment Indiana Volunteer Infantry: September, 1861-September, 1865*, (Logansport, IN, 1888), 23-24.

37 Ibid; Walker, *Life of Captain Fry*, 153.

Siege of Island Number Ten. Union ironclads and mortars (bottom) fire on the island. The Confederate fleet is split to the right of the island (center) and downriver around New Madrid Bend (top). *Harper's Weekly*

one thing and that was that gunboats were not fitted for chasing cavalry."[38] The Union battery at Riddle's Point was now being used against Island Number Ten just as the battery at Point Pleasant was used against New Madrid. Commodore Hollins's squadron and the army transports in the area now had to run past two enemy batteries, plus New Madrid, to bring supplies to the Confederates in Island Number Ten's defenses. Nevertheless, the nightly runs continued to keep the front-line soldiers supplied.

As Pope extended his forces south, Flag Officer Foote's gunboats continued their relentless bombardment of Island Number Ten. In the artillery exchange, the *Red Rover*, tender to the floating battery *New Orleans*, received a shell that penetrated through all her decks and caused her to leak considerably. Impatient with the bombardment, Pope suggested a daring plan on March 17: one of the gunboats should make a run past the island defenses. Pope would use it to cover a small force as it crossed the Mississippi River to capture Tiptonville, thus cutting off Island

38 Read, "Reminiscences of the Confederate States Navy," 338; "Hot Work Up the River," *Memphis* [TN] *Daily Appeal*, Mar. 20, 1862; "Tiptonville," *The Semi-Weekly Shreveport* [LA] *News*, Mar. 28, 1862; Morgan, *Recollections*, 70.

Number Ten from its last road for supplies. After several days of discussion and planning, Foote saw its merit and determined to try.

Meanwhile, Hollins squabbled with his army counterparts over their limited supplies. In late March, eight heavy cannon were delivered to Memphis. The guns, four rifles and four 32-pounder smoothbores, were intended to serve on the ironclads under construction in the local shipyards. Finding the ironclads there not near completion, Hollins prepared to send the guns downriver to New Orleans to arm the nearly completed ironclad *Louisiana*. Instead, Beauregard seized them, intending the guns for the River Defense Fleet.

When Hollins learned of this, he dispatched his son, Acting Master Frederick W. Hollins, to reclaim the guns. The younger Hollins was one of two of the commodore's sons in the squadron. The other son, George N. Hollins Jr., was an engineer attached to the floating battery *New Orleans*, who served onboard the CSS *Ivy* since January. When he demanded the guns, young Master F. W. Hollins was rejected. The commodore then sent a note to Secretary of the Navy Stephen Mallory to intercede. Mallory insisted and the guns were ordered returned. On March 21, Hollins dispatched the CSS *Ivy* to Memphis to claim the eight guns and to take them downriver to New Orleans.[39]

The siege of Island Number Ten continued, but without Gen. McCown. As word spread across the Confederacy about the loss of New Madrid, there were a growing number of critics working against the general. On March 31, McCown was replaced by Brig. Gen. William W. Mackall, a graduate of West Point and veteran of the Seminole and Mexican Wars. A Marylander, Mackall left the United States Army in June of 1861, anticipating the secession of his home state. General McCown was relieved after controversy regarding his evacuation of New Madrid, with the claim that he left behind too many supplies – mixed with the speculation that he was drunk. McCown would later be cleared of such charges and restored to active duty, but the fate of Island Number Ten was no longer in his hands.

In addition to the bombardment and planned raid to capture Tiptonville, Pope and Foote were also working to build a canal that could bypass the island, thus making its capture moot. The canal was not large enough for gunboats, but barges could fit. Once completed, Foote sent barges to New Madrid for Pope's men to use in crossing the Mississippi River. Meanwhile, his ships maintained a constant daily

39 "Appointment of Acting Master Hollins," Jan. 2, 1862, Subject File, NN, NA; "Letter from Secretary Mallory," *ORN*, 22:755-756; "Report by Commodore Hollins," *ORN*, 22:756-757.

bombardment of the Confederate defenses until he was ready to launch one of his ironclads past the island.

Pope's original idea had one ironclad steam past the Confederate position and, once safely clear, provide protection for the barges Pope planned to use to capture Tiptonville. Foote held several meetings with his captains; most were of the opinion that none of their ships could safely pass the Confederate positions. Only one man, Cmdr. Henry Walke, said it could be done and Foote tasked him to take his ironclad, the USS *Carondelet*, veteran of Forts Henry and Donelson, and make the attempt.

Commander Walke studied the Confederate fortifications closely. On April 4, he received orders to proceed that night. Walke's sailors made last minute preparations to ensure that the *Carondelet* was ready; he noted that "hawsers and chain cables were placed around the pilot-house and other vulnerable parts of the vessel, and every precaution was adopted to prevent disaster. A coal-barge laden with hay and coal was lashed to the part of the port side on which there was no iron plating, to protect the magazine."[40] Foote gave specific instructions to Walke in the event that his ship was disabled or faced capture, he was to scuttle and burn the *Carondelet* to prevent its capture.

The *Carondelet* got underway at 10 pm, after the moon set. "Dark clouds now rose rapidly over us and enveloped us in almost total darkness," recalled Cmdr. Walke as the *Carondelet* weighed anchor, "except when the sky was lighted up by the welcome flashes of vivid lightning, to show us the perilous way we were to take."[41] Walke steered his ironclad downriver and managed to get abeam of Battery Number Two before Confederate sentries realized what was happening and gunners opened fire in the rain.

Had the information been available to the gunners about the weak point of the Union ironclads that was learned at Forts Henry and Donelson, the *Carondelet* might have suffered serious damage. Instead, the Confederate artillery was largely ineffective. Adding to the land batteries, the CSS *New Orleans* joined in the firing, but the *Carondelet* managed to pass the batteries without any serious damage and without taking any casualties. Walke moored his ship alongside the Union positions at New Madrid around midnight, surprised that he made it through so quickly and undamaged.

---

40 Walke, "The Western Flotilla," 442.

41 Ibid, 443.

General Pope did not wait long to use the *Carondelet*. On April 6, several army officers boarded the ironclad and joined in a reconnaissance all the way to Tiptonville, destroying a Confederate battery of 24-pounders opposite the river from Point Pleasant before returning to New Madrid. The Federal movement was witnessed by Cmdr. Hollins and sailors onboard the CSS *McRae*. The commodore afterwards wanted to determine where the *Carondelet* was mooring at New Madrid so he might launch a surprise attack by his ships. To gather the information, Hollins dispatched Midn. James Morgan on a reconnaissance up the river in the *McRae's* steam launch.

Morgan steamed upriver, intent on locating the Union ironclad, recalled: "being of a curious turn of mind I wanted to see what was around the river bend, so kept on. As we turned the point my helmsman exclaimed, 'The *Tom Benton!*' The *Tom Benton* was the largest Union ironclad on the river and all ironclads were *Tom Bentons'* to us." Morgan, seeing the *Carondelet* raising steam, immediately turned his launch around to report its position to Hollins. Several captains in the Confederate squadron begged Hollins to attack, but "the old commodore was firm in his decision to remain inactive." "You dared to think, sir!" a worn-down Hollins chastised to the young and curious Morgan, "I will have you understand I am the only man in this fleet who is allowed to think!"[42]

Flag Officer Foote was relieved to hear of the safe passage of the *Carondelet* and he determined to repeat that success. At 2 am on April 7, the USS *Pittsburgh* successfully passed Island Number Ten's batteries, again without incident, and moored at New Madrid. It became clear that the island defense was untenable. Mackall prepared to evacuate the island, ordering most of his men to depart. Left behind as a rear guard were some artillerymen and one regiment of infantry. The rest marched to Tiptonville and from there hoped to escape under the cover of the Confederate fleet.

Mackall was at the vanguard of his column as it marched through the night of April 8. As he approached Tiptonville, the general found that his arrival "was preceded by the [Union] gunboats, and the infantry, artillery, and cavalry." Pope's men beat the Confederates to Tiptonville by mere hours and Mackall, with no other alternative, surrendered his column at 4 am. Hollins's squadron, blocked by the two Union ironclads, could do nothing but watch helplessly from a distance.

Foote's ships then advanced on Island Number Ten, facing only the small Confederate rear-guard. Lieutenant Samuel Averett saw Union infantry forces

---

42 Read, "Reminiscences of the Confederate Navy," 339; Morgan, *Recollections*, 66-67.

approaching the floating battery *New Orleans* and "opened the valves, and shortly after it went down in deep water, with all the ordinance stores and guns on board." Additionally, the transports *De Soto, Yazoo, Simonds, Ohio Belle, Admiral, Mars, Mohawk,* and *Winchester* were either sunk on the river or captured by Union forces. The army gunboat *Grampus* was also sunk and the damaged tender *Red Rover* fell into Union hands, later becoming a Union hospital ship. The island's rear guard attempted to destroy supplies, but a total of 7,000 men were captured along with "20 pieces of heavy artillery, 7000 stand of arms, and a large quantity of ammunition and provisions."[43]

The Union campaign against New Madrid and Island Number Ten was well organized and coordinated. The Confederate defenses were strong and backed by Hollins's squadron of wooden ships, but the daring passage by the *Carondelet* sealed Island Number Ten's fate. It enabled Pope's infantry to cross the river and get behind Confederate lines without interference from the Confederate Navy, which was unwilling to face the Union ironclads. What marks this campaign different from many others was the relatively low casualties suffered on both sides. Besides the final Confederate prisoners, there were fewer than 200 casualties total. The campaign was largely one of operational maneuver. Both sides proved they were capable of army-navy cooperation, that ships could safely pass fortifications, and that ironclad warships dominated their wooden opponents on the Mississippi River.

Both sides remembered these lessons as the struggle for control of the river continued. The United States used Island Number Ten as an example on how to organize future joint operations, conduct river-borne raids, and continue campaigns of maneuver against fixed positions. For the Confederacy, Island Number Ten was where the officers of the Confederate Navy's Mississippi River Squadron became veterans; a versatile and ambitious group who would launch their own counterattacks featuring ironclad vessels, marshal limited resources to bolster fortified positions, run their river steamers past Union strongholds, and combine these methods with the introduction of unconventional weapons of war.

---

43 "Report by Brigadier General Mackall," *OR*, 8:133; "Report by Captain Jackson," *OR*, 8:158; Walke, "The Western Flotilla," 446; Alexander Miller Diary, Apr. 8, 1862; Steven Louis Roca, "Presence and Precedents: The USS *Red Rover* During the American Civil War, 1861-1865," *Civil War History*, No. 2 (June 1998), 44:91-92.

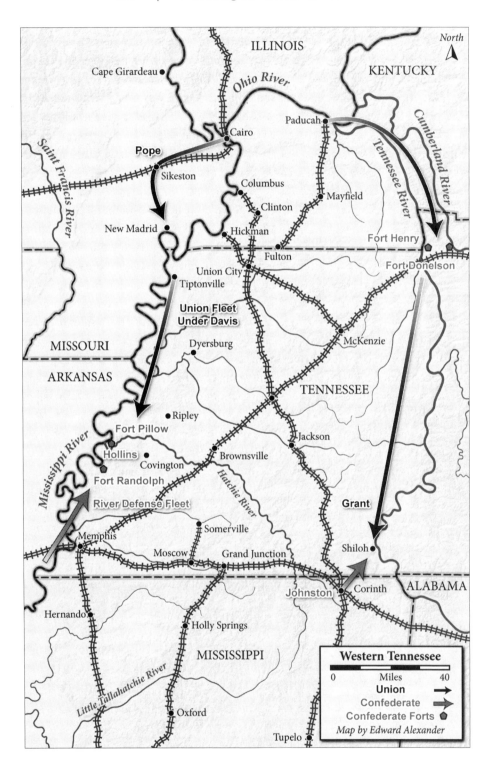

North

ILLINOIS

Cape Girardeau

KENTUCKY

Ohio River

Paducah

Cairo

Pope

Sikeston

Columbus

Mayfield

Clinton

New Madrid

Hickman

Fort Henry

Fulton

Fort Donelson

Union City

Tiptonville

Union Fleet
Under Davis

MISSOURI

Dyersburg

McKenzie

ARKANSAS

TENNESSEE

Ripley

Fort Pillow

Jackson

Hollins

Covington

Brownsville

Fort Randolph

River Defense Fleet

Grant

Somerville

Memphis

Shiloh

Moscow

Grand Junction

Johnston

Corinth

ALABAMA

Hernando

Holly Springs

MISSISSIPPI

Western Tennessee

0   Miles   40

Union

Oxford

Confederate

Confederate Forts

Map by Edward Alexander

Tupelo

Fort Pillow and Plum Point Bend

With Island Number Ten and New Madrid now in Union hands, Hollins withdrew his squadron to Fort Pillow, Tennessee, the next Confederate defensive position on the Mississippi River. Brig. Gen. John B. Villepigue, the commander there, was told to "prepare for an attack by the enemy's ironclads." Hundreds of refugees from western Tennessee attempting to escape the Union advance passed by Fort Pillow as they evacuated southward to Memphis.

In a case of civilian aid, Confederate sailors were sent ashore to investigate some cotton found on the riverbank. Lieutenant Charles W. Read, executive officer of the *McRae*, along with Third Assistant Engineers James Tomb and John H. Dent, approached a woman described as "a remarkable old lady and full of fire," who owned 200 bales of cotton, but had no way of getting out south.[44] The officers offered to purchase the cotton on behalf of the government and after the woman agreed, they burned all 200 bales. In a show of gratitude, the woman provided the sailors with several jars of preserves and four turkeys that her son just shot. The sailors on the flagship feasted on the turkeys and preserves that night in celebration.

The spring campaign had not gone well for the Confederacy. The fortifications at Columbus were viewed as impregnable and that Island Number Ten could beat back any Union assault. With their loss, people grew concerned, particularly in Memphis. As a precaution, the hull of the still incomplete ironclad *Arkansas* was inspected and then towed down the Mississippi River and brought up the Yazoo River, where construction work continued far away from Union threats. The ironclad *Tennessee*, still unable to float on its own because of work delays and scarce materials, was left at Memphis. Since it was nearer completion, efforts focused on finishing the *Arkansas*. Once it was completed, mechanics and workers would return to finish the *Tennessee*. It was not the last time that Confederate officials were forced to abandon one project to use limited resources to complete another.[45]

Fort Pillow was a strong position to defend; some considered it more even more defensible than Island Number Ten. In an effort to calm worried citizens, newspapers outlined the position in detail, one printing that at the fort "the bluff rises abruptly from the stream about a hundred feet, and at all points is very difficult of ascent except where artificial means are used. Along its base for nearly

---

44 Morgan, *Recollections*, 71; Campbell, *Engineer in Gray*, 33.

45 "Captain J.J. Guthrie Papers," *Subject File*, HA, NA.

three-fourths of a mile strong works have been constructed about twenty feet above the level of the river."[46] Guns on Union ironclads would have difficulty hitting the batteries at such a high elevation, giving hope that the fort could hold out and would not suffer the same fate as both Columbus and Island Number Ten.

Captain James Montgomery and the eight vessels of the River Defense Fleet sent upriver at Memphis were intended as reinforcements for Hollins's ships anchored at Fort Pillow. However, when Montgomery's ships arrived on April 12, 1862, Hollins's and two ships were gone.

On April 9, word arrived from Capt. William C. Whittle, commander of the New Orleans naval station, that the Crescent City faced imminent attack. Hollins requested permission from superiors in Richmond to move his ships downriver to oppose the threat at New Orleans. Hollins's reasoning was that Fort Pillow was a strong position against Federal gunboats and no Union infantry were available to encircle Fort Pillow; Pope's troops were called east to merge with the Union armies commanded by Gen. Henry Halleck, fresh off of their victory at the Battle of Shiloh.

Hollins did not wait for Mallory to respond to his request and left for New Orleans on the fast-moving CSS *Ivy*. The CSS *Jackson* also went back downriver. The commodore left 1Lt. Thomas Huger of the CSS *McRae* in command of the naval forces at Fort Pillow until Cmdr. Robert Pinckney in Memphis could come up to assume local command. Once Pinckney arrived, Huger had orders to turn over command and then take the *McRae* downriver to join Hollins at New Orleans. It was after Hollins left that Mallory's response came denying permission to move downriver. Mallory believed that the ironclads *Mississippi* and *Louisiana* were enough to stop the Union fleet approaching New Orleans, which consisted of only wooden vessels. Mallory, however, was misinformed as the two ironclads being built in Louisiana were not yet completed. Until Hollins and his ships arrived, only the *Manassas*, which recently arrived back from Memphis, and the vessels of the River Defense Fleet and Louisiana State Navy still being converted, were able to confront the Union squadron downriver.

Huger was active while he awaited Cmdr. Pinckney. On April 12, he ordered his ships to get underway and scout the Union fleet's anchorages. The River Defense Fleet, having just arrived at the fort, decided to join in the reconnaissance. Huger's ships found no enemy until "just after dark our attention was attracted by

46 "The War on the Mississippi," *Harper's Weekly*, Jun. 28, 1862.

River Defense Fleet Ship *General Bragg. Naval History and Heritage Command*

someone on shore, hailing and waving a torch."[47] The man informed Huger that Union ships were just ahead and plans were made to launch a surprise attack the next morning. Besides the *McRae*, Huger had what remained of "Hollins's fleet," including the CSS *Livingston*, CSS *General Polk*, CSS *Maurepas*, and CSS *Pontchartrain*, along with the River Defense Fleet ships *General Price*, the *General Van Dorn*, and *General Bragg*. If he could surprise the Union ships upriver, Huger believed he could cause enough damage to delay naval operations against Fort Pillow and enable more ships to join Hollins downriver to defend New Orleans.

The Confederate squadron moved off at 8:30 am to launch their surprise attack. Union scouts detected the Confederate movement and the USS *Benton* opened fire on the advancing Confederate ships. The CSS *Maurepas* "replied to her from a nine-inch Dahlgren," but neither ship suffered any damage in this opening exchange. Huger continued advancing the Confederate flotilla until they rounded a bend and, as the log of the *General Sterling Price* recorded, "the Federals now showed their whole fleet, consisting of eleven gunboats and eight mortars." Instead of a

47 Read, "Reminiscences of the Confederate Navy," 339.

surprised scattering of Union ships, the Confederates were encountering a well-prepared and vastly superior Union squadron lying in wait; Huger immediately ordered a withdrawal. The Union gunboats gave chase.

The *General Sterling Price* acted as a rear guard, firing into the pursuing ships. By 11:30 am, the Confederate ships reached Fort Pillow and alarmed the garrison. One Confederate naval officer remembered, "when we reached Fort Pillow the enemy's fleet was only three or four miles astern. The Yanks came to, above the fort a few miles, and without delay began to shell it."[48] The shelling did not last long and the Union ships withdrew upriver. They returned the next day, however, and began a regular bombardment of Fort Pillow with their mortar boats, lasting from sunrise to sunset each day attempting to shell Fort Pillow into submission.

Commander Robert Pinckney, a Marylander who left the United States Navy after Fort Sumter was fired on, relieved Huger as commander of naval forces at Fort Pillow; he established the *Livingston* as his flagship. Huger then promptly left with the *McRae* for New Orleans. Pinckney did not remain at Fort Pillow for long. He reassigned the CSS *Maurepas* and the CSS *Pontchartrain* to the White River in Arkansas, a tributary of the Mississippi, to clear away Union advances in Arkansas and to help move supplies and men. The CSS *General Polk* and CSS *Livingston* were withdrawn to Memphis to resupply and refit. This left the eight ships of the River Defense Fleet under Captain James Montgomery as the only naval support at Fort Pillow. Union scouts did not detect this. As late as April 24, 1862, Union newspapers were reporting the fort's naval defenses consisted of "fourteen gunboats and the ram *Manassas* lying off the forts, and that Captain Hollins and the *McRae* were also there."[49]

Capt. Charles H. Davis replaced Flag Officer Foote due to complications of a foot wound Foote suffered at Fort Donelson. Davis continued the bombardment of Fort Pillow into May. Davis kept most of his ships upriver each day; only one mortar boat protected by a single ironclad approached the Confederate defenses to continue the bombardment. The ships were rotated daily, allowing each one to resupply in safety while keeping the bombardment continuous, if not very effective.

On the other side, Montgomery was anxious to engage with his rams, periodically sending forays up the river to disrupt the bombardment. On May 9, he

48 Scharf, *History of the Confederate Navy*, 253; Read, "Reminiscences of the Confederate Navy," 340; Alexander Miller Diary, Apr. 8, 1862.

49 "The Situation," *New York Herald*, Apr. 24, 1862.

called a council of war with his River Defense Fleet captains. Montgomery's plan was simple: he wanted to use the rams to overwhelm the one advanced Union mortar boat and to then capture the ironclad guarding it. If successful the attack might surprise the Union squadron and cause confusion and further damage. One hopeful participant in the meeting boasted, "as there was no telegraph, we expected to surprise even Cairo and nothing then could stop us from St. Louis." Brigadier General M. Jeff Thompson of the Missouri State Guard was present at the meeting and volunteered his men to serve as improvised gunners in the fighting, augmenting the inexperienced riverboat men. Thompson was an enthusiastic supporter of the as yet untested River Defense Fleet, believing that Montgomery's ships could "defend every bend and dispute every mile of river." Not wanting to miss the action, Thompson boarded the *General Bragg*. Written instructions to explain the battle plan were distributed to each ship to help the civilian captains who "were not experienced enough in Signals to rely upon them in the smoke of Battle."[50] The instructions were clear: move upriver in a column and ram the enemy ships as they presented themselves.

In the early morning of May 10, 1862, the USS *Cincinnati* towed *Mortar Boat Sixteen* into position and at around 5 am the Union mortar began the daily bombardment of Fort Pillow. There was no indication that the day would be any different from previous ones and the crew expected to be relieved in 24 hours. Unbeknownst to the gunners manning the mortar, all eight ships of the River Defense Fleet were closing on their position. Around 6:30 am, the Confederate ships rounded Plum Point Bend in the river. The *General Bragg*, in the lead, was the first to spot the pair of advanced Union ships. Captain W. H. H. Leonard ordered Chief Engineer John Porter to increase speed as he pointed the *General Bragg* directly at the *Cincinnati*. "Every valve was opened to its uttermost," recalled Gen. M. Jeff Thompson, "and we rushed like the wind at the Iron Clads before us."[51]

Seeing the approaching Confederate ship, the ironclad crew immediately weighed anchor and manned battle stations. Within moments, gunners on the *Cincinnati* opened fire at the *General Bragg*, while other sailors fired muskets. One of the first volleys struck the *General Bragg* and caused mayhem in the engine room, where a musket ball "caromed on three sides of the room" before smashing into a cook assisting the engineers, killing him instantly. Captain Leonard was not

---

50 Alexander Miller Diary, Apr. 8, 1862; "Telegram of General Thompson," *ORN*, 23:57; Thompson, *The Civil War Reminiscences of M. Jeff Thompson*, 154-155.

51 Ibid, 156.

deterred and his *General Bragg* continued on to the *Cincinnati*, successfully ramming the Union ironclad with "a violent blow on the larboard bow."[52] One of the ironclad's guns was dismounted in the collision and the vessel began to twist in the river. Union marksmen continued to fire at point blank range, mortally wounding John Welsh, a landsman who served on the CSS *McRae* before transferring to the River Defense Fleet. Hearing the commotion downriver, the ironclads USS *Mound City* and USS *Carondelet* got underway from the Union squadron, moving to the sound of the guns.

The *Cincinnati's* marksmen continued firing at the *General Bragg* as it backed off, but most of the small arms fire "glanced off and as our starboard wheel climbed her sides" recalled one participant, "she let fly a broadside at not exceeding ten feet distance." One lucky shot "fouled a tiller tope and [the *General Bragg*] had to drift out of the action." The two ships exchanged fire so close that smoke completely obscured both ships and both appeared set afire. Captain Montgomery's ships continued their advance and the next ship in line, the General *Sterling Price* under the command of Captain J. E. Hawthorne, closed on the *Cincinnati* which could not avoid the second Confederate attacker because it was still spinning from the shock of the first blow. The *Price* rammed the *Cincinnati* on her stern, "a little starboard of midships, carrying away her rudder and stern post, disabling her." The force of this blow caused the *Cincinnati* to continue swinging around, opening the way for the *General Sumter* to ram her a third time. The *Cincinnati's* captain, Cmdr. R. N. Stembel, was severely wounded in the action and the ironclad took on water. Sailors worked to contain the damage, but it was too great and the *Cincinnati* "ran into the bank . . . and sunk in 11 feet of water."[53]

The USS *Mound City* and USS *Carondelet* steamed downriver to try and save the sinking *Cincinnati*. Once in range, they both opened fire on the *General Price* and *General Sumter*, just as those ships were ramming the *Cincinnati*. Commander H. Walke, in command of the *Carondelet*, recalled having "fired a 50-pound rifled shot … through the boilers of one of them while running into the *Cincinnati*, as they exploded immediately, and she dropped downstream." Walke's description was somewhat accurate. His gunners engaged the *General Price* and did manage to hit the Confederate ship. This shell did not explode a boiler, instead only "cutting off the

52 Ibid, 158; Scharf, *History of the Confederate Navy*, 254.

53 Thompson, *The Civil War Reminiscences of M. Jeff Thompson*, 157; "Report of Brigadier General Thompson," *ORN*, 23:57; Scharf, *History of the Confederate Navy*, 254; "Report of Lieutenant Phelps," *ORN*, 23:19.

Battle of Plum Point Bend, May 10, 1862.
*Naval History and Heritage Command and Walke's Naval Scenes and
Reminiscences of the Civil War of the United States*

supply pipes and causing her to leak."[54] Nonetheless, the *General Price*, just like the *Bragg*, was now disabled and out of the fight.

The *General Van Dorn* next made its way toward the USS *Mound City* while simultaneously engaging *Mortar Boat Sixteen* at a distance of no more than 20 yards. Gunner W. G. Kendall commanded the *Van Dorn's* single 32-pounder mounted on its bow and he directed the cannon's fire at the mortar boat with good effect. "I received two 32-pound shots through my boat" recalled Second Master T.B Gregory on the mortar boat. At the last moment, the *Mound City* turned away from the *Van Dorn* in an attempt to avoid a collision. It was too late; the *Van Dorn* successfully rammed the Union ironclad "driving in her hull about six feet, causing her to leak badly." Commander A.H. Kilty knew his ship was crippled and he directed the *Mound City* to the Arkansas side of the river where it sank along the riverbank. The *General Van Dorn* was also damaged as her captain, Isaac Fulkerson, suffered a contusion to the hand and Steward W. W. Andrews was killed when "a ball struck the end of a guard timber turned downwards," decapitating the man.[55]

The USS *Carondelet* was now the only Union ship still underway; the remainder of the Union fleet was still upriver raising steam in an effort to join the battle. The

54 "Report of Commander Walke," *ORN*, 23:15; Scharf, *History of the Confederate Navy*, 254.

55 "Report of Second Master Gregory," *ORN*, 23:16; Scharf, *History of the Confederate Navy*, 254; Thompson, *The Civil War Reminiscences of M. Jeff Thompson*, 158.

veteran gunners on the Union ironclad fired from extreme range. The ironclad's Commander Henry Walke wrote later "the upper deck of the *Carondelet* was swept with grape-shot and fragments of broken shell." The remaining four unengaged Confederate ships moved to engage the *Carondelet*, but they quickly surmised that the Union ironclads further upriver were finally getting underway and moving to shallow water for protection.

The Union ships held a smaller draft than Montgomery's rams and they could find safety from ramming in shoal water. Captain Montgomery saw this and "as our cannon were far inferior to theirs, both in number and size, I signaled our boats to fall back, which was accomplished with a coolness that deserves the highest commendation."[56] The fighting lasted most of an hour. Montgomery's captains reported about a dozen casualties in the entire squadron, with only two men killed outright and the rest slightly wounded. Landsman John Welsh, who was mortally wounded when the *General Bragg* rammed the USS *Cincinnati*, died on May 13 and was buried in the Elmwood Cemetery in Memphis, bringing the total count of Confederate dead to three.

What became known as the Battle of Plum Point Bend was a clear Confederate tactical victory. At the cost of a dozen casualties and some temporary damage to several of the River Defense Fleet's ships, two Union ironclads were rammed and sunk, a great embarrassment to the Union naval forces on the western waters. Returning to the protection of Fort Pillow, emergency repairs on the Confederate rams were carried out.

The cotton bale bulkheads proved their worth, protecting vital machinery and exposed parts of each ship, with several of the Southern vessels reporting enemy shot lodged within the dense cotton bales lining the craft. General M. Jeff Thompson recalled that for several of the ships, "the Smoke Stacks or funnels looked like huge Nut-Meg graters, and the upper works were completely riddled," but other than that, there was little damage. Montgomery was elated at his success against the United States Navy and boasted to General Pierre G.T. Beauregard, commanding all Confederate armies west of the Appalachian Mountains, that "you may rest assured . . . they will never penetrate farther down the Mississippi"[57]

However, the tactical victory failed to produce strategic benefits. Immediately after the battle, the Union mortars recommenced their firing on Fort Pillow,

---

56 Walke, "The Western Flotilla," 448; "Report of Captain Montgomery," *ORN*, 23:56.

57 "Battle of the Gunboats," *Memphis* [TN] *Daily Appeal*, May 13, 1862; Thompson, *The Civil War Reminiscences of M. Jeff Thompson*, 158; "Report of Captain Montgomery," *ORN*, 23:56-57.

negating the Confederate hopes of ending the bombardment. Within a few months, both the *Mound City* and *Cincinnati* were refloated and brought to Cairo, Illinois, where they were repaired and eventually rejoined the Union fleet. Montgomery's rams surprised the Union ships, caused temporary damage, and raised Confederate morale, but Union pressure on Fort Pillow continued unabated. In the long term, the only thing gained from the battle was a healthy respect for rams by the Union fleet.

Outflanked Again and the Loss of Memphis

The continued bombardment of Fort Pillow by the United States Navy was not the main threat to Confederate control of the region. Union officers proposed sending gunboats past the fort to engage the Confederate ships in a surprise attack, much like what occurred at Island Number Ten. But with no land force available to invest the fort directly, the scheme was deemed impractical. Most Federal soldiers were sent east to join Maj. Gen. Henry Halleck's army. Halleck was leading a force of 100,000 men, the combined armies of Generals Don Carlos Buell, Ulysses Grant, and John Pope. Their objective was Corinth, Mississippi, a major rail junction between the Mobile & Ohio and the Memphis & Charleston railroads. Defending Corinth was Gen. Pierre G.T. Beauregard's battered Confederate army from Shiloh. He was greatly outnumbered by the approaching Union host.

Fort Pillow's main drawback was that of any fixed fortification: it relied on resupply from nearby areas to maintain its garrison. Holding Corinth was key to maintaining Fort Pillow. The fort received its supplies and reinforcements through Corinth, which was connected by rail to the interior of the Confederacy. Unfortunately for Gen. Villepigue and his Fort Pillow garrison, Corinth was evacuated on May 30, 1862, by Beauregard, who felt that the entrenchments at Corinth could not hold out against a Federal force more than twice his army's size. This prompted Gen. Villepigue to likewise abandon Fort Pillow on June 4.

For the second time in the 1862 spring campaign, Confederate fortifications were outflanked and fell to Union forces. About 600 Confederate soldiers were evacuated on the steamer *Golden Age* and brought to Vicksburg, Mississippi. The remainder under Villepigue marched overland, first to Memphis, then to Grenada,

Mississippi. Beauregard withdrew his army to Tupelo, Mississippi, to regroup and resupply.[58]

With the loss of Corinth and Fort Pillow, Confederate forces remaining in western Tennessee were in danger of isolation, including the city of Memphis, which was ordered evacuated. Commander Robert F. Pinckney directed the Confederate naval squadron to steam downriver and scatter, with ships moving up each major tributary of the Mississippi to protect them from Union incursions. After covering the evacuation of Fort Pillow, the River Defense Fleet arrived at the Memphis docks on June 5, looking for coal to resupply and continue downriver. All that remained at the Memphis waterfront were a few civilian ships lying abandoned and the burning wreck of the unfinished ironclad *Tennessee*, which Pinckney ordered destroyed to keep it out of Union hands. Montgomery sent teams to the civilian steamers and confiscated their remaining coal. Besides Montgomery's ships, only Gen. M. Jeff Thompson and a few of his men remained as a rear guard for the retreating army.

Little coal was left, not enough for all of Montgomery's ships. The Union naval squadron, reinforced by the U.S. Army Ram Fleet under Col. Charles Ellet, Jr., was already at recently captured Fort Pillow making preparations to advance to Memphis. On the night of June 5, Montgomery held a council of war on the *Little Rebel*. He saw three options for the River Defense Fleet: abandon their ships and burn them to prevent capture, escaping by foot with the army; transfer all of the remaining coal and take only part of the fleet, abandoning and burning the remainder; or remaining and using what was left of their supplies in a final attack against the Union fleet. Montgomery's fellow captains each expressed their views and cast a vote; the consensus was to fight it out. Montgomery assented and ordered his ships to prepare for battle in the morning.

At dawn, Gen. Jeff Thompson boarded the *Little Rebel* and offered his few remaining soldiers to Montgomery to help augment cannon crews and serve as sharpshooters. Montgomery gladly accepted, but before the soldiers could march from their encampment at the railroad station to the docks, the Confederate ships departed. Instead, Thompson's soldiers became spectators, watching the battle from the riverbank.[59]

---

58 L. McKissick to Daniel Ruggles, Jun. 3, 1862, *William W. Hunter Papers*, Confederate States of America Records, 1856-1915, Dolph Briscoe Center for American History, The University of Texas at Austin.

59 "Report of General Thompson," *ORN*, 23:139.

The Union naval squadron advanced with its nine vessels, ready to meet any Confederate resistance; "the heavens were one solid cloud of black smoke," remembered one of Montgomery's officers, as enemy ships were seen approaching the city.[60] The Union Navy was prepared for a fight. Five ironclads, the *Benton*, *Louisville*, *Carondelet*, *Cairo*, and *Saint Louis* were arrayed in battle formation. Behind them were four of Col. Ellet's rams, the *Queen of the West*, *Monarch*, *Lancaster*, and *Switzerland* that had orders to rush forward and ram any Confederate ships that appeared. Ellet's rams were quite similar to Montgomery's, with reinforced bows and few cannon, but officially under army jurisdiction. This combined Union naval flotilla faced Montgomery's eight River Defense Fleet ships buoyed from their victory a month earlier at Plum Point Bend.

Unfortunately for Captain Montgomery and his sailors, they were unaware that Ellet's rams joined the Union fleet, a lack of information that would prove catastrophic. The *Little Rebel*, *General Sterling Price*, and *Colonel Lovell* steamed upriver in a line abreast, opening fire on the Union ships, when two Union rams, the *Queen of the West* and the *Monarch*, moved to the front of the Union squadron. Montgomery sent the *Price* and *Lovell* to engage upriver while he assessed these two new Union ships from the *Little Rebel*. The two Confederate rams steamed straight ahead at their two Union counterparts in a collision course.

Captain James C. Delancy on the *Colonel Lovell* lost his nerve at the last instant and ordered his chief engineer, Aug. R. Mann, to back the engines, trying to turn the ship. The order was issued too late and the *Queen of the West*, Col. Ellet's flagship, ran directly into the *Colonel Lovell*, almost cutting the ship in half. The *Colonel Lovell* rapidly sank "in water to her hurricane deck, in the channel of the river" with many of her crew lying dead on the decks. Montgomery dispatched his boats to assist in recovering survivors, but out of the crew of 86, only 18 men survived. Among the dead was William Cabell, "an old and well known riverman" who volunteered as the *Lovell's* pilot.[61]

The *Queen of the West* was damaged in the collision with the *Lovell*. Just as Ellet's men separated the two vessels, the *Sumter* rammed the *Queen of the West* and drove her ashore. Sharpshooters onboard the *Sumter* then opened fire on the disabled Union ram. Gunner George B. Morrell added to the fray, firing the *Sumter's* single 32-pounder. One shot hit Ellet's flagship "on the bulwarks, causing the splinters to

---

60 Scharf, *History of the Confederate Navy*, 259.

61 Ibid; "The Battle of Memphis," *Daily Nashville* [TN] *Union*, Jun. 14, 1862.

fly pretty freely."[62] In this exchange of fire, Col. Ellet was wounded in the knee. The wound proved mortal and by the end of the month, the colonel was dead.

As Ellet lay wounded, the *Monarch*, which was led by Ellet's brother Lt. Col. Alfred W. Ellet, increased speed to engage the *General Beauregard* and the *General Price* positioned on either side of the Union ship. Both Confederate ships missed ramming the *Monarch*, and instead the *General Beauregard* rammed the *General Price* "on her port side, cutting her down to the water-line, tearing off her wheel instantly." One newspaper account noted that the ramming of the *Price* was catastrophic, "leaving the boat nearly a wreck." First Officer Joseph Hawthorne directed the *General Price* toward the Arkansas side of the river and "with only one wheel left, she managed to get ashore, but too late for the crew to make their escape." Unfortunately for the Confederates, the *General Price* ran into the riverbank near where the *Queen of the West* was disabled. Seeing this, the mortally wounded Col. Ellet dispatched a detachment of sailors who took the entire crew prisoner.[63]

The Union ironclad force advanced in two lines abreast while Ellet's two rams caused mayhem, firing into the Confederate ships whenever a clear shot could be taken in the melee. As the *Beauregard* rammed her sister ship, the USS *Benton* took aim. Captain J. Henry Hart on the *Beauregard* began to back his ship off the wreck of the *General Price*, and he aimed his gun at the *Benton*, firing a 42-pound shell at the Union ironclad. The shot missed, but the *Benton's* gunners did not. A shell from the *Benton* struck the boiler of the *Beauregard*, destroying the ship in a massive explosion. Lt. S. L. Phelps, commander of the *Benton*, wrote after the battle, "some 14 of her scalded people are in our hands. How many were killed we do not know." Captain Hart, who managed to escape unscathed, gave a more defiant epitaph, writing after the battle that his ship "floated down the river about one-fourth of a mile, and sunk in twenty feet water, face to the enemy, and colors flying."[64]

Montgomery's flagship, the *Little Rebel*, was the next to engage. The ironclads were firing on the flagship and scored several hits, including a shot to her boilers. Disabled, Montgomery likewise steered "her course into the shore, where all but three [men] made their escape." Union forces quickly took possession of the abandoned ship. The *General Thompson* was also disabled by fire from the Union

62 Scharf, *History of the Confederate Navy*, 259.

63 Walke, "The Western Flotilla," 450; "The War on the Mississippi," *Harper's Weekly*. Jun. 28, 1862; Scharf, *History of the Confederate Navy*, 260; Alfred W. Ellet, "Ellet and His Steam-Rams at Memphis," *B&L*, 1:457.

64 "Report of Lieutenant Phelps," *ORN*, 23:136; Scharf, *History of the Confederate Navy*, 260.

The Battle of Memphis. *Naval History and Heritage Command*

ironclads. Her crew ran her into the riverbank and set her afire. Abandoning the vessel, the *General Thompson* blew up "with a tremendous report" after fire reached her magazine.[65] The *Sumter* was likewise disabled and forced ashore, but her crew failed to destroy the vessel as they escaped ashore. Instead, the *Sumter* fell into Union hands as a prize of war.

The *Monarch* proceeded to the wreck of the General *Beauregard* and picked up the surviving crew while the rest of the Union squadron pursued the remaining two Confederate ships: the *General Van Dorn* and the General *Bragg.* These two did not participate in the fighting and, upon seeing their sister ships beaten and destroyed, hastily turned downriver to escape. As the *General Bragg* turned, she was hit by shells from the Union ironclads that started a fire in the cotton bales that served as protection. Captain W. H. H. Leonard then steered the *Bragg* for the Arkansas shore and abandoned the ship. Union sailors boarded the burning *Bragg* and extinguished the fire before it spread to the magazine. After taking possession of the vessel and doing a quick assessment, Union sailors concluded that she was "a good deal shattered in her upper works and hull" but could be repaired. Captain Isaac Fulkerson and the *General Van Dorn* managed to escape from Union ships that pursued for several miles before giving up the chase. He took the ship downriver, nearly all the way to Vicksburg, Mississippi, confiscating coal wherever

65 Scharf, *History of the Confederate Navy*, 260; Ellet, "Ellet and His Steam-Rams at Memphis," 457.

Brigadier General M. Jeff Thompson, Missouri State Guard. *Battles and Leaders of the Civil War*

he found it. From there, he brought the *General Van Dorn* up the Yazoo River to resupply and to regroup with the CSS *General Polk*, CSS *Livingston*, and the unfinished ironclad *Arkansas*, which left Memphis after the fall of Island Number Ten.[66]

The Battle of Memphis was the first use of the United States Ram Fleet and the last time that the River Defense Fleet offered serious resistance to Union ships. After the fighting, a small Federal force from the Army of the Mississippi occupied Memphis, whose citizens were shocked by the defeat that was witnessed by hundreds lined along the riverbank. Union ships anchored at Memphis as the unfinished ironclad *Tennessee* continued to burn. Colonel Charles Ellet, Jr., however, was not able to savor his victory. His wound, at first appearing slight, festered and he died fifteen days after the battle. His younger brother, Lt. Col. Alfred W. Ellet, who commanded the ram *Monarch*, ascended to command of all of the rams eventually was promoted to brigadier general.

The Union 1862 spring campaign was a juggernaut. From February 6 to June 5, despite setbacks, Confederate naval resistance was overcome and the Confederate fortifications on the Mississippi River at Columbus, Island Number Ten, New Madrid, and Fort Pillow captured. By summer of 1862, only a few Confederate gunboats remained afloat on the upper Mississippi River and its tributaries, and those were now hiding. Union Flag Officer Charles Davis now turned his attention downriver to the last stronghold that remained in Confederate hands, Vicksburg, where he expected to meet Union ships led by Flag Officer David G. Farragut steaming up from New Orleans.

66 "Report of Flag Officer Davis," *ORN*, 23:120; Alexander Miller Diary, Jun. 6, 1862.

CHAPTER FIVE

Operations in Coastal Louisiana
and Mississippi

Six Months of Coastal Skirmishes

THE Confederate defense of the Mississippi River was not solely confined to the river itself. As the war progressed, the many tributaries of the Mississippi were used to move men and supplies. These were also potential invasion routes requiring defensive fortifications. For example, in southern Louisiana there were other water approaches to New Orleans. In the War of 1812 the British brought soldiers within a few miles of New Orleans via the Mississippi Sound.

Southwest of New Orleans, the CSS *Mobile* guarded the approaches to Brashear City via the Atchafalaya River and Berwick Bay from October 1861. South of the city, Fort Livingston guarded Barataria Bay, which could be crossed to reach New Orleans through swamps and bayous that were first used by the pirate Jean Lafitte. Forts Jackson and Saint Philip guarded the Mississippi River itself, backed up by naval forces converted in New Orleans.

Just north of New Orleans was Lake Pontchartrain, a large and fairly shallow body of water, rarely more than 10 feet deep at any point. Used by smaller vessels plying inland waterways, Lake Pontchartrain was an important water approach to the city, linked by a railroad line. Lake Pontchartrain was connected to the east to other water sources. Both the Chef Menteur Pass and the Rigolets pass connected Lake Pontchartrain to Lake Borgne, which was, like Pontchartrain, not a land locked lake. Lake Borgne was only separated from the Gulf of Mexico by several barrier islands. It was from Lake Borgne, in fact, that the British successfully landed their forces in late 1814 for their failed assault against New Orleans.

Both the United States and the Confederacy knew of these waterways and the vulnerability of New Orleans. Prior to the war, the United States constructed two fortifications: Fort Macomb guarded Chef Menteur Pass while Fort Pike blocked entrance into Lake Pontchartrain via the Rigolets. When Louisiana seceded on February 5, 1861, the state dispatched troops to occupy these fortifications. By the end of 1861, Cmdr. Hollins, who held control over both the Mississippi River and the coastline of the Gulf of Mexico to Mobile, Alabama, managed to convert and commission two gunboats, the CSS *Florida* and CSS *Pamlico*, for service in the area. Joining them was the *Oregon*, an army supply transport also armed and equipped as a gunboat. These three vessels were lightly armed with only a dozen guns total amongst them. Additionally, the army transport *Arrow* transported supplies near Ship Island and on Lake Pontchartrain in 1861, armed with a single 32-pounder. There was also the *Corypheus*, a lightly armed yacht operating as a transport for the army. To bolster this small force, two gunboats were contracted and constructed along Bayou Saint John, a tributary bayou in Lake Pontchartrain just north of New Orleans. These two vessels, the *Bienville* and *Carondelet*, were built by the shipyard company owned by John Hughes.

Through the winter of 1861 and 1862, this small flotilla fought a series of engagements against the Union blockading squadron, with actions ranging from as far away as Mobile back to coastal Louisiana in an effort to both maintain control of the coastal waterways and to protect blockade runners. The first such action occurred in late October 1861. First Lieutenant Charles W. Hays brought the CSS *Florida*, just having been commissioned on Lake Pontchartrain, to Lake Borgne. There, he was drilling his crew at their guns and observing Union blockading patterns. A blockade-runner entered Lake Borgne from Lake Pontchartrain and Hays determined to safely escort it into the Gulf of Mexico. Unfortunately, the *Florida* ran aground during the escort and the blockade-runner moved on alone; it took 36 hours for Hays and his men to break free, a mortifying start to Confederate coastal operations.

After refloating the vessel, Hays ordered it to steam to Pass Christian, Mississippi, to patrol in the direction of Ship Island. On October 19, he spotted four Union blockaders anchored at the island. Hays, who "thought it a good opportunity to try the efficiency of our guns," closed within a few miles of the island and opened fire with his 6.4-inch rifled cannon. The USS *Massachusetts* weighed anchor to give chase and the *Florida* began retreating, continuing to fire with its rifled gun. The Confederate gunners proved accurate; Cmdr. Melancton

Smith reported that a shell struck on the *Massachusetts'* starboard side "abaft the engine, 5 feet above the water line, cutting entirely through 18 planks of the main deck, carried away the table, sofas, eight sections of iron steam pipe, and exploded in the stateroom on the port side, stripping the bulkheads of four rooms, and setting fire to the vessel."

The two ships continued to exchange fire, the *Florida* retreating to shoal water while the *Massachusetts* attempted to close the distance. Suddenly, Hays's 6.4-inch rifled gun misfired and was put out of action. The chase continued until the *Massachusetts* ran out of ammunition, never scoring a hit on the Confederate ship, and withdrew back to Ship Island. Hays brought the *Florida* back to Louisiana waters, docking the vessel in Lake Pontchartrain to repair his gun and replenish his ammunition. Hays praised his crew to Hollins, proclaiming that his men "behaved in a manner worthy of the highest praise."[1]

Resupply and repair efforts were completed and the *Florida*, as well as the newly commissioned CSS *Pamlico* under Lieutenant Dozier, continued patrols in the Mississippi Sound, steaming as far as Horn Island, just east of Ship Island. While on patrol, Lieutenants Hays and Dozier formed a plan to board and capture an unsuspecting Union blockader. Taking a detachment of soldiers onboard the *Pamlico*, they carried out their plan on December 4, when Hays observed the five-gun USS *Montgomery* anchored near Horn Island Pass, on the island's eastern shore.

Their plan was simple: use the single rifled gun on each ship to disable the *Montgomery* while keeping out of range of the Union guns; once disabled, they could close and board. When within range, the two Confederate ships opened fire, with the *Florida* positioned to protect the soldiers lining the *Pamlico's* deck. Cmdr. T. D. Shaw ordered the *Montgomery's* guns to return fire, but he was out of range, observing Confederate shells "falling ahead and astern of us" while his own ineffectively "fell far short." Seeing the soldiers crowding the *Pamlico's* deck and immediately understanding the Confederate intentions, Shaw ordered his ship to weigh anchor and escape, passing instructions to burn all important documents and the ship's signal book in case of capture. The *Montgomery* managed to escape to the open sea. Confederate newspapers praised the "most valiant naval

---

1 "Report of Lieutenant Hays," *ORN*, 16:745; "Report of Commander Smith," *ORN*, 16:743; "Firing Between a Confederate Gunboat and a Federal Steamer," *New Berne* [NC] *Weekly Progress*, Oct. 29, 1861; "Report of Lieutenant Hays," *ORN*, 16:745.

engagement," some writers inaccurately claiming a break in the blockade as a result.[2]

The pair of Confederate ships then split up, the *Florida* heading to Mobile to resupply and the *Pamlico* moving west. The fighting on Mississippi Sound continued just a few days later when Lt. William Dozier spotted Union ships steaming toward Mississippi City. Docking the CSS *Pamlico* at noon on December 7, Dozier gathered what forces were available in the town to confront the Federals. He found the army gunboat *Oregon* there, loading equipment from a local powder mill for transportation to New Orleans. Captain A. L. Myers was glad to offer the assistance of his ship and Dozier assumed command of both vessels, ordering them underway. The approaching blockaders were the USS *New London* and USS *De Soto*. The two Union ships mounted a total of 14 cannon versus Dozier's two ships' eight, but two of them were rifled.

A fog set in over Mississippi City in the afternoon and the two Confederate gunboats struggled to target the blockaders while simultaneously remaining in shallow shoal water to keep the Union vessels at a distance. Dozier's plan worked; the Union ships could not close the distance to engage while the two rifled guns of the Confederates peppered them. In response, the captain of the USS *New London* "ran up the rebel flag, union down, and fired a lee gun as a challenge for them to come out and fight." The Confederates refused and the blockaders withdrew, leaving Mississippi City in Confederate hands. Captain Myers then brought the *Oregon* back to the dock to finish loading the powder mill equipment for transportation. Once loaded, the *Pamlico* provided escort all the way back into Lake Pontchartrain. The joint effort greatly increased the gunpowder production in New Orleans; within a few weeks, the city was manufacturing 5,000 pounds of powder each day.[3]

After offloading the supplies, the *Oregon* and *Pamlico* returned to Lake Borgne. There they rendezvoused with a blockade-runner and set course for the Gulf of Mexico, intending to escort the vessel to open water. The three ships neared the Gulf of Mexico on December 20, just having to sneak past Ship Island's blockading station. Alert sentries on the island spotted the ships and three blockaders weighed

2 "Report of Commander Shaw," *ORN*, 16:808; "Letter from New Orleans," *Nashville* [TN] *Union and American*, Dec. 8, 1861; "Abstract Log of USS Montgomery," *ORN*, 16:809; "The Florida on a Frolic," *Richmond* [VA] *Daily Dispatch*, Dec. 14, 1861.

3 "Abstract Log of USS New London," *ORN*, 16:811; "Abstract Log of USS De Soto," *ORN*, 16:811. "Report of Captain Myers," *ORN*, 16:811; "Talk on Change," *New Orleans* [LA] *Daily Crescent*, Dec. 14, 1861.

anchor to intercept. Unwilling to risk battle, the three Confederate ships withdrew back to Lake Borgne, providing the ever-tightening Union blockade with a small victory.[4]

Christmas Eve of 1861 saw another attempt by the *Florida* to challenge the Union blockade. After its encounter with the USS *Montgomery* in early December, Lt. Hays brought the *Florida* to Mobile to resupply. The Union blockade afterwards moved to block the ship from leaving Mobile Bay, sending several ships to keep watch. As a Christmas present to the people of Mobile, Lieutenant Hays steamed the *Florida* out toward the blockaders in challenge.

The USS *Huntsville* was a small propeller driven steamer under the command of Cmdr. Cicero Price. Armed with one 64-pounder and two-32 pounders, its mission was to blockade the Pelican Island entrance channel to Mobile Bay. The *Florida*, ready for action, cleared Mobile Bay on the morning of December 24 and closed on the *Huntsville*. Keeping inside the channel reef and close to Fort Morgan that guarded the entrance channel, the *Florida* opened fire on the *Huntsville* with its 6.4-inch rifle. Price closed and returned fire with his 64-pounder and one 32-pounder. When the 32-pounder shot fell short, he ordered its gunners to cease fire. As the ships closed distance, both ships fired their remaining guns into the melee.

The action produced a sensation in Fort Morgan as "all the forces at the fort were apparently out to witness the affair." The crew of the nearby blockader the USS *Potomac*, which drew too much water to join in the battle, watched from the topsails and masts as well. Both ships traded fire at a distance of less than two miles with little effect. The *Florida* fired about 50 shells in an hour and "a dozen or twenty other rifled projectiles struck within a cable's length of me," reported Cmdr. Price. He responded with fewer shells which likewise failed to cause damage, "though many of the shells exploded quite near" the *Florida*.[5] After an hour of firing, the *Florida* withdrew under the guns of Fort Morgan. That night, it returned to Mobile to resupply its coal and ammunition. Both ships claimed victory in the encounter. In the end though, the skirmish failed to break the blockade. Renamed the *Selma*, the *Florida* remained in Mobile Bay until it fell to Union forces in 1864.

---

4 "Log Entry," Sept. 1, 1862, *U.S. Ship Portsmouth Log.*

5 "Report of Commander Price," ORN, 17:12; "Naval Engagement," *Richmond* [VA] *Daily Dispatch*, Jan. 2, 1862.

Construction Efforts at Bayou Saint John

Following the Christmas Eve expedition of the *Florida*, military action in the Mississippi Sound slackened; Confederate officers in New Orleans waited for their gunboats under construction in Bayou Saint John to be completed while Union naval forces grew in numbers in anticipation for the upcoming campaign for New Orleans. The construction efforts in the John Hughes shipyard on Lake Pontchartrain were in full swing as 1862 dawned, though serious hurdles were overcome to complete the ships. Ample material was available for the construction of the wooden ships, but finding sufficient labor was a constant challenge throughout the New Orleans area. All male civilians were members of the local militia and were called to drill, slowing work. Shipyard owners sought exemptions for their employees from military service, but these were granted grudgingly and sparingly. Even with workers exempted from service, labor remained in short supply to complete the many contracts throughout the city.

By the start of 1862, shipyards in Algiers, Jefferson City, and Bayou Saint John were constructing or converting dozens of ships and the skilled craftsmen in the yards were overworked. Some went on strike to raise their wages from three to four dollars a day, halting work for several days. As the need for completed vessels grew, shipyard owners, including John Hughes, grew more desperate. One by one, yard owners and superintendents turned to slave labor to assist in construction efforts. A slave could be leased for $100 for one month of work, a great source of income for slaveholders. The use of slaves was expanded and crews of hundreds of slaves began to be leased for working on nightshifts, enabling shipyard work to continue around the clock. The ship contractors on Bayou Saint John also employed slave labor.[6]

Citizens of New Orleans often traveled the few miles to the Bayou Saint John docks to view the ships under construction. Acting Constructor Sidney Porter's efforts began to bear fruit. The first of the Bayou Saint John ships, named the *Carondelet*, was launched on January 25, 1862. Final preparations took another month and the vessel was officially commissioned in mid-March. First Lieutenant Washington Gwathmey was given command of the *Carondelet*. An Englishman by birth and experienced naval officer who previously commanded the CSS *Jackson*, Gwathmey struggled with a lack of funds and arms in New Orleans due to the

---

6 "Payment Receipt for CSS General Polk," Nov. 7, 1861, Subject File, AC, NA; *Court of Inquiry*, 111.

focus on completing the ironclad vessels being constructed on the Mississippi River. Furthermore, assembling a crew competed with the recently organized River Defense Fleet offering more pay and the drafting of local civilians into the militia.[7]

Only one naval 32-pounder was available to arm the *Carondelet* and Gwathmey turned to the army for assistance. Knowing the importance of holding Lake Pontchartrain and the Mississippi Sound, Maj. Gen. Mansfield Lovell, commanding the city's defenses, assisted in the fitting out of the *Carondelet*. Five 42-pounder cannon were transported to Bayou Saint John from Lovell's stockpile of artillery and gun carriages were constructed to mount them. To augment the lack of sailors, Lovell furnished soldiers to help man the cannon. Thirty volunteers were raised from the garrison of Fort Pike, consisting of detachments from the 1st Louisiana Heavy Artillery Regiment and the 22nd and 23rd Louisiana Infantry Regiments.[8]

The *Carondelet's* twin was launched in February and likewise underwent its final preparations through March. First Lieutenant Carter Poindexter, a twenty-year veteran naval officer, assumed command of the vessel and oversaw the final preparations, including installation of new sails and onloading of guns, likewise provided by Gen. Lovell's supply. The final payment for the vessel was provided on April 8, 1862 and the CSS *Bienville* was officially commissioned. Volunteers from Fort Pike brought the *Bienville* to a full complement. Lovell's cooperation went still further when he furnished a supply of gunpowder for both the *Carondelet* and *Bienville*. The naval officers on Lake Pontchartrain were delighted; Lt. Poindexter gladly told superiors in Richmond that Lovell was "always willing and anxious to assist in every way."[9]

Not everyone serving on the ships was a loyal volunteer and still others had second thoughts about serving on these makeshift gunboats. At least 11 sailors from the *Florida* deserted in Mobile in February 1862; all were apprehended by local police, who received a bounty for their efforts, and returned to their ship. Five more deserted from the CSS *Pamlico* between January and March 1862. One man,

---

7 *Court of Inquiry*, 95; *DANFS*, Vol. 2, 504; Gunther, *Two Years Before the Paddlewheel*, 203; *Confederate Navy Register*, 78; Wilkinson, *Narrative of a Blockade Runner*, 15; "Pay Roll of Confederate Steamer Resolute," *Vessel Papers*.

8 "Receipt for Gun Carriages," Jan. 9, 1862, *Jackson and Company Papers; Court of Inquiry, 95; Andrew B. Booth, Military Records of Louisiana Confederate Soldiers and Louisiana Confederate Commands*. 3 Vols. (New Orleans, Louisiana, 1920), 1:77 & 218.

9 *Court of Inquiry*, 80; See also "Payment Receipt for CSS Bienville," Apr. 8, 1862, Subject File, AC, NA; "Payment Receipt for CSS Bienville," Apr. 2, 1862, *Subject File*, AS, NA.

Seaman Samuel Sampson, was never apprehended, but the others were detained by New Orleans police, who were paid bounties for each deserter caught. Even the volunteers from Forts Pike and Macomb were not all reliable. Three privates from the 1st Louisiana Heavy Artillery Regiment deserted from the CSS *Carondelet* and were never apprehended.[10]

With the completion of the *Carondelet* and *Bienville*, Sidney Porter planned the next naval project for Lake Pontchartrain. In March 1862, Porter contracted with New Orleans constructor James Watson for an ironclad warship to serve as the flagship of the coastal Louisiana squadron. This vessel had two propellers, was protected by iron plating, and specifically designed with a small draft to operate on Lake Pontchartrain. The navy department paid Watson a $25,000 down payment for the ironclad, constructed from the keel up at the Bayou Saint John shipyard.[11]

The Union Solidifies Control of the Mississippi Sound

As Union forces began their opening movements in the campaign for New Orleans, the Confederate ships operating in Lake Pontchartrain and the Mississippi Sound were up to their usual activity. On the morning of March 25, the CSS *Pamlico* escorted the army gunboat *Oregon* out of Lake Pontchartrain. After clearing Fort Pike and entering Lake Borgne, the two ships steamed east as far a Pass Christian, Mississippi. There the *Pamlico* anchored while the *Oregon* docked alongside a wharf and unloaded a cargo of supplies. After discharging its cargo, the *Oregon* got underway and steamed east toward Ship Island with the intention of scouting out what Union blockaders were there. The *Oregon* closed to within several miles of the island when she was noticed and so returned to Pass Christian. Ordered to give chase was the USS *New London*, the blockader from the December skirmish with the *Pamlico* and *Oregon*.

The *Oregon* returned to Pass Christian by 2 pm and alerted the CSS *Pamlico* of the Union vessel giving chase. The *New London* "approached as near as practicable on account of shoal water" and fired a gun to challenge the Confederates to come out. First Lieutenant William Dozier of the *Pamlico* acknowledged the request,

10 "Payment Receipt to Mobile Police Department," February 12, 1862, *Subject File*, NZ, NA; "Payment Receipt to Frank J. Ames," Jan. 16, 1862, *Subject File*, NZ, NA; "Form of Allotment Book," *Subject File*, XA, NA; "Payment Receipt to Charles Roray," Mar. 15, 1862, *Subject File*, NZ, NA; "Payment Receipt to John Ward," Mar. 12, 1862, *Subject File*, NZ, NA; "Payment Receipt to James Morrison," Feb. 28, 1862, *Subject File*, NZ, NA; Booth, *Military Records*, 1:77, 218.

11 John Mitchell, "John Mitchell to W.R. Howell," Mar. 27, 1862, *Subject File*, AC, NA.

weighed anchor, and with the *Oregon* alongside, steamed toward the Union ship. They closed to within 2,000 yards and began to exchange fire. "Many of the enemy's shot and shell passed over us," recalled Dozier, and "many struck near our bow and stern, and some fell short." A problem soon developed regarding the *Pamlico's* guns, however. Lieutenant Dozier initially ordered Acting Gunner John Rogers to fire broadsides from his 8-inch smoothbores. After two broadsides however, they ceased fire because "only one [shell] out of six which were fired reached the enemy; the others exploded alongside the vessel, a part of one shell striking the corner of the starboard wheel-house."[12] Dozier, not trusting the defective shells for his 8-inch guns, directed Gunner Rogers to use only the 6.4-inch rifle gun.

Firing continued for nearly two hours with little effect on either side; both sides resisted closing with the enemy for fear of being outgunned, disabled, and captured. At about 4 pm, another disaster befell the *Pamlico* when a shell became jammed in the barrel of their 6.4-inch rifled gun. Unable to extract it, and leaving the *Pamlico* without any working cannon, Lt. Dozier signaled to Captain Myers on the *Oregon* to withdraw from the action. The Confederates withdrew into Pass Christian and the *New London*, unable to follow because of the ship's deeper draft, stayed on station for several hours before retiring back toward Ship Island. Lieutenant Dozier was able to finally extract the jammed shell in the pass and he then steamed west, docking in the Rigolets, near Fort Macomb, that evening.

In his report, Dozier was careful to note how his gunnery fire affected the structure of his converted vessel: "the concussion of our guns carried away the greater part of the paneling on the gun deck, also the leading chock of the wheel rope on the port side, together with nearly all the window glasses in the vessel." Besides this, he needed to replace the defective shells to be ready for the next battle. Confederate newspapers typically heralded the fight as another naval victory, with several incorrectly claiming that the USS *New London* was sunk in the fighting.[13]

The final naval action in the Mississippi Sound occurred as an act of retaliation against a flag of truce. On April 1, the local Union Army commander sent a boat flying a flag of truce to Biloxi, Mississippi, with the intention of sending ashore a little girl that was taken off the recently captured blockade-runner *Black Joker*. Upon reaching shore, the soldiers were fired upon by the local Confederate garrison, who

---

12 "Report of Lieutenant Read," ORN, 18:75; "Report of Lieutenant Dozier," ORN, 18:76.

13 "Report of Lieutenant Dozier," ORN, 18:76; "Telegraphic," *Semi-Weekly Shreveport* [LA] *News*, Apr. 1, 1862.

were unaware of the girl's presence or the mission of the soldiers. The detachment hastily withdrew away from the town.

Major General Benjamin Butler, in command of the U.S. Army forces operating in the Mississippi Sound, was furious and immediately called for a joint raid to land at Biloxi to demand an apology from the townspeople. Afterwards, the force steamed west to Pass Christian and drive out any Confederate troops in the area. Assigned to command the expedition was Maj. George C. Strong, of Gen. Butler's staff. Strong took a detachment of the 9th Connecticut Regiment and a section of light artillery, altogether some 1,200 soldiers, onboard the transport *Henry Lewis*. Escorted by the USS *New London* and the USS *John P. Jackson*, the expedition left Ship Island on April 2. Lieutenant A. Read of the *New London* was in overall command of the naval forces.

Landing at Biloxi that evening, Strong delivered the demand for an apology to the town's mayor. The mayor was quick to do so, as he was at the mercy of the 500 soldiers with Strong. The force remained at Biloxi until the evening of April 3, when the ships weighed anchor and set their course for Pass Christian. Meanwhile, Confederate forces were preparing a counterstroke. There were three companies of infantry encamped at Pass Christian and they received word of the Union operation and its intention to land against their encampments. The army requested help from Capt. William C. Whittle, commander of the New Orleans naval station and the senior officer there after Hollins moved upriver, who agreed to dispatch help. The gunboat *Pamlico* and the army gunboat *Oregon* were ordered to Pass Christian. Additionally, the recently commissioned gunboat *Carondelet*, fresh from its final outfitting in Lake Pontchartrain, was sent to bolster the Confederate forces. With some luck, the three ships might surprise the Union gunboats and transport and disable the Union vessels.[14]

The Union flotilla left Biloxi on the evening of April 3 and anchored that night off of Pass Christian intending to land soldiers ashore the next morning. The three ships dispatched by Whittle from New Orleans moved to intercept and reached Pass Christian in the early morning of April 4, just before the Federal landing operation was to commence. Lookouts spotted the three Confederate ships approaching at 4:40 am and the Union flotilla weighed anchor and moved to engage. The Confederate ships opened fire and Lt. Read ordered his two gunboats to respond. After about a half hour of exchanging fire in the darkness, a shell struck

---

14 "Report of Lieutenant Read," *ORN*, 18:100-101; "Payment Summary for CSS Carondelet," Feb. and Mar., 1862, *Subject File*, AC, NA.

the transport *Henry Lewis*, wounding one U.S. Army captain and two privates in the landing force. Lieutenant Read then ordered the *Henry Lewis* to withdraw from the action "on account of the crowded state of her decks."[15]

The exchange of artillery fire continued for another 45 minutes with slight damage suffered by both sides. The USS *John P. Jackson* was struck twice, once "on the port guard, completely cutting it in two and carrying away one of our iron sponson braces, the other splitting one of the stanchions of the gallows frame." These shots likely were fired from the 32-pounder on the CSS *Carondelet*. Both the *Oregon* and the *Carondelet* received hits to their wheels and one shot pierced the pilothouse of the *Oregon*, wounding the pilot.[16] With damage inflicted on the wheels of two ships and sighting another Union gunboat, the USS *Hatteras*, approaching to join in the fighting, the Confederate force withdrew to the west, back into Lake Borgne and Louisiana waters. With the Confederate withdrawal, the U.S. Army transport *Henry Lewis* moved into Pass Christian and landed 1,200 soldiers ashore; the landing force then cleared out the small Confederate garrison in the area. Meanwhile, the Federal navy captured the *P. C. Wallis*, a blockade-runner waiting for a chance to escape into the Gulf of Mexico, loaded with turpentine, rosin, pitch, oil, and lime.

The Confederate ships withdrew into Lake Pontchartrain, under the protection of Forts Pike and Macomb, repairing their damage with supplies dispatched from New Orleans. Confident of their ability to defeat their Confederate counterparts, the growing number of Union blockading vessels forayed farther into the Mississippi Sound. As a result, the small flotilla operating out of Lake Pontchartrain never left the confines of that lake again. It was clear that Union forces were preparing for a strike against New Orleans and commanders in the Crescent City wanted to preserve their forces for the coming battles. The result was that the Confederate gunboats *Carondelet*, *Bienville*, and *Pamlico*—along with the army gunboat transports *Arrow* and *Oregon*—waited at anchor in both the Chef Menteur and Rigolets Passes for the Union assault to commence. The main Union thrust against New Orleans, however, began elsewhere.[17]

---

15 "Report of Lieutenant Read," *ORN*, 18:100.

16 "Report of Acting Lieutenant Woodworth," Ibid, 102; "News from the Sound," *Memphis* [TN] *Daily Appeal*, Apr. 11, 1862; "Gunboat Fight in the Gulf," *Memphis* [TN] *Daily Appeal*, Apr. 15, 1862.

17 "Payment Receipt for CSS Carondelet," Apr. 24, 1862, *Subject File*, AC, NA.

CHAPTER SIX

The Campaign for New Orleans

Union Plans and Organization

PRESIDENT Abraham Lincoln and his cabinet knew how important New Orleans was to the Confederacy and they wanted to regain control over it as quickly as possible. However, there was no plan to take the city back in 1861 as crises elsewhere took priority. Commander David D. Porter changed this situation with one of his own. In November 1861, while his ship was undergoing repairs in New York, he travelled to Washington and approached Gustavus Fox, Lincoln's assistant secretary of the navy, with his plan. Fox readily approved, and Porter sought out the naval secretary. After a chance meeting with a pair of senators in the navy department's offices, who liked the idea and could provide congressional support, Porter then spoke with the secretary of the navy, Gideon Welles, and afterwards with President Lincoln. Porter's idea to seize the Confederacy's largest city was enthusiastically approved.

David Dixon Porter previously served on coastal survey details and spent the better part of 1861 helping to blockade the Mississippi River while in command of the USS *Powhatan*. Porter attempted to chase down Cmdr. Raphael Semmes and the CSS *Sumter*, but to no avail. His time on monotonous blockade duty facilitated his formulation of a plan for taking control of the mouth of the Mississippi River and capturing New Orleans.

The plan, borrowing ideas being implemented elsewhere, was similar to what was done upriver in Kentucky and Missouri, and what had recently occurred in the capture of Port Royal Sound, South Carolina, that November. Porter's proposal called for a squadron of mortar boats to move up the Mississippi River and bombard Forts Jackson and Saint Philip into submission while heavy cannon on Union warships protected the mortar craft from the Confederate naval vessels undergoing construction and conversion in the Crescent City. After the two forts surrendered, the squadron could continue upriver and force the capitulation of New Orleans. Nearly 20,000 infantry accompanied the ships to provide an occupying garrison. Once the United States flag flew over the city again, the Union Navy could then move upriver to unite with Federal ships moving down from Cairo, Illinois.

Porter's plan was approved and the navy began to muster its forces for the expedition. As early as December 1861, Union infantry were being transported to Ship Island, which was fast becoming a large naval resupply station. The island was the forward staging area for the coming campaign; exactly what Confederate leadership feared when they ordered it occupied the previous summer. The army could not provide the 20,000-man requirement; instead a total of 15,000 were assigned. The army forces were commanded by Maj. Gen. Benjamin Butler, who owed his military position to the fact that he was a leading Democrat who supported the war effort. Many Republicans, including Lincoln, saw sending Butler south as a way to get him away from the more public spotlight of the fighting in Virginia.

Porter's mortar boats were expected to silence the main Confederate fortifications within two days of commencing a bombardment. The watercraft securing the mortars must first be built from the hull up. They were described as being "from 200 to 300 tons each, of great strength and solidity, and carrying each a mortar, weighing 8 ½ tons, of thirty-nine inches length of bore, forty-three inches external and fifteen inches internal diameter, and intended to throw a 15-inch shell weighing, when unfilled, 212 lbs."[1]

Finding a naval commander was a more difficult issue. There were several candidates with ample experience at sea, but most were old and deemed too unaggressive. Though Cmdr. Porter proposed the plan, he was too junior in rank. The decision finally fell on Capt. David Farragut, a Tennessee native and Virginia resident at the start of the war, who chose to remain loyal to the Union. His service included participation in the War of 1812 and Mexican War, but because of his Southern ties some thought he was not the man for the task. Even so, Lincoln promoted him to the rank of flag officer, then the navy's highest rank given to

1 W.J. Tenney, *The Military and Naval History of the Rebellion in the United States* (New York, 1866), 191.

Flag Officer David Farragut, USN.

The National Archives

denote squadron command, and gave Farragut command of the newly organized Western Gulf Blockading Squadron. Though responsible for overseeing the blockade from the Mexican border to Florida, his main focus was to work with General Butler to seize the lower Mississippi River and New Orleans.

Farragut gathered his ships for the attack and dispatched them to Ship Island. In early April 1862, his squadron began the slow process of crossing into the Head of Passes. Altogether he had 24 warships, several of them large sea-going vessels, assembled for the campaign. Added to this were 17 mortar boats to bombard the forts. Since Cmdr. Porter devised the idea for the expedition, he commanded the mortar flotilla. Seven transports and support ships moved the infantry and supplies. The entirety of the Union force was composed of wooden craft.

Marshalling a Defense

As 1862 dawned, most of the citizens of New Orleans basked in the belief that their city was impregnable, thanks in large part to the numerous Confederate fortifications across southern Louisiana and the Confederate Navy's tactical victory in October 1861. Many of the wealthy and elite "showed little sensitiveness to the great struggle in which we were engaged. Festivity was the order of the day; balls, parties, theatres, operas, and the like, continued as if we were not in the midst of a furious war." Despite the revelry, this optimistic sentiment gradually changed. The sunken barrier blocking the Mississippi River at Forts Jackson and Saint Philip washed away. General Mansfield Lovell rebuilt the barrier with anchored ships sunk and chained together, but some within the city considered this second barrier to be a weaker version compared with the original. Nonetheless, morale in New Orleans generally remained high; one Confederate soldier later recalled, "we felt too secure."[2]

The fighting in Kentucky and Tennessee impacted the defenses of New Orleans. After the fall of Forts Henry and Donelson, along with the evacuation of Nashville and Columbus, Confederate forces were expelled from Kentucky and retreated from most of central and western Tennessee. To replace the loss of troops that surrendered at Fort Donelson and prepare for a counterstroke, Gen. Albert S. Johnston called for reinforcements. Louisiana Governor Thomas Moore reluctantly answered the call. In February and March 1862 eight infantry regiments and one infantry battalion, along with three batteries of artillery, amounting to 5,000 men were sent north to Tennessee. These men, some of the best-trained soldiers in Louisiana, joined Johnston at Corinth, Mississippi, along with several regiments from Island Number Ten, and took part in the Confederate attack at the Battle of Shiloh on April 6-7, 1862.

General Lovell did not want to send these well-trained soldiers north. Their departure made him apprehensive regarding the city's defenses and, in response, Lovell activated 10,000 members of the Louisiana militia. Lovell detailed most of them to guard camps and buildings in New Orleans, keeping his better-trained troops in more vital positions such as the outer ring of defensive forts guarding the approaches to New Orleans. To ensure that the militia actually mustered, Lovell declared martial law in New Orleans and the surrounding area. Even many shipyard workers were forced to answer the militia call, stalling work on numerous wooden gunboats. The only militiamen exempted from immediate service were those shipyard workers constructing the ironclads *Louisiana* and *Mississippi*, and they were only excused after a series of special requests by the Jefferson City shipyards.

Forts Jackson and Saint Philip were the largest fortifications in the Confederate lower Mississippi defense and Lovell placed his best men to serve as their garrisons. Fort Jackson had two companies of infantry, five companies of heavy artillery, and one battery of light artillerymen. Fort Saint Philip was manned by four companies of heavy artillery, one company of light artillery, and one

---

2 E. C. Hermann, *Battle-Fields of the South*, 182.

company of infantry from the Confederate Regular Army. Altogether, there were about 1,000 men manning the guns of the two forts.

Brigadier General Johnson K. Duncan, who recommended the evacuation of Ship Island the previous year, was in command of the outer fortifications of the defense of New Orleans. These included Forts Jackson, Saint Philip, Pike, Livingston, and Macomb. Gen. Duncan, like Lovell, was a northerner. A native of Pennsylvania, he attended West Point and participated in the Seminole War before leaving the army in 1855 to become the superintendent for construction and repairs in New Orleans. When the war began, Duncan became colonel of the 1st Louisiana Heavy Artillery Regiment and was quickly promoted by Lovell to command the outer ring of defenses in southern Louisiana.

In direct command of Forts Jackson and Saint Philip was Col. Edward Higgins. After helping to briefly secure Ship Island for the Confederacy, Higgins became the second in command of the 22nd Louisiana Regiment, with three companies manning the two forts. Higgins was promoted to colonel in early April 1862 and made his headquarters in Fort Jackson. In nominal command of the day-to-day operations of Fort Saint Philip was Capt. M. T. Squires of the 1st Louisiana Heavy Artillery. To block against a land assault on the two forts, Gen. Duncan deployed one regiment of militia to the Quarantine Station. Located a few miles upriver from Fort Saint Philip, Col. Ignatius Szymanski's 700-man Chalmette Militia Regiment was situated to keep supply lines and communications open between New Orleans and the forts.

Army forces under Gen. Duncan and Col. Higgins were not the only military forces in the area. Once word reached the city that a Union fleet was entering the river, all available naval vessels were ordered downriver in support. Lieutenant Beverly Kennon brought the two ships of Louisiana's state navy downriver and anchored them at the forts. As their conversions were completed, Captain John Stevenson brought his six vessels of the River Defense Fleet down to the forts as well. Commander John K. Mitchell, a capable naval officer, if poor manager, was placed in command of the Confederate naval craft at New Orleans. Mitchell brought downriver the CSS *Jackson* as well as the CSS *Manassas*, recently returned from its excursion upriver and just repaired after its grounding near Memphis. Kennon vowed to cooperate with Cmdr. Mitchell in preparing a defense, but Captain Stevenson, remembering the navy's seizure of his ironclad *Manassas*, swore that his six ships would answer to no naval officer, despite the pleading of Generals Lovell and Duncan.[3]

---

3 "Payment Receipt for CSS Manassas," Apr. 3, 1862, *Subject File*, AC, NA; David P. McCorkle to John M. Brooke," March 19, 1862, *Ironclads and Big Guns of the Confederacy*, 83-84.

Commodore George Hollins was upriver at Fort Pillow when he received word of the Union invasion force entering the Head of Passes. He immediately forwarded a request to proceed downriver. Assuming that his request would be granted, he boarded the CSS *Ivy*, the fastest ship in his squadron, and proceeded downriver, accompanied by his young aide, Midn. James Morgan. He left orders for the CSS *McRae*, his flagship and most powerful vessel, to join him downriver as soon as practicable.

The CSS *Ivy* landed at New Orleans and Hollins established his headquarters at the Saint Charles Hotel, dispatching Midn. Morgan to the forts to begin coordination. While steaming downriver, the commodore developed his plan of action, intending to catch the Union fleet still crossing the bar at the Head of Passes, looking to "attack the enemy's fleet of wooden ships below the forts and drive them out of the river." This plan had merit; many of the heaviest Union warships were still crossing the bar into the Mississippi River and assembling at the Head of Passes. If a daring attack was launched, Hollins believed that the surprised Union squadron would retreat into the Gulf, just as what occurred the previous October: a repeat of "Pope's Run" from the Head of Passes. Young Morgan arrived at Fort Jackson with the Union mortar bombardment already commenced. As he entered the fort to report and begin naval coordination, a shell exploded nearby, covering him in mud and "disturbing several large alligators who lashed the water furiously with their tails."[4]

Farragut's fleet began crossing the bar into the Mississippi River in late February, continuing that process for over a month. Most ships in the Union squadron expended their supply of coal in crossing the bar and it was not until mid-April that they were all resupplied. Hollins later claimed that he could have "whipped their smaller craft with my squadron, and have prevented their larger vessels from getting over it had it not been in my power to have destroyed them." Other officers were of a like mind; 1Lt. Alexander Warley, commander of the ironclad ram *Manassas*, agreed that the enemy would have a difficult time in passing the bar with Hollins's ships harassing them. Captain William C. Whittle wrote that Hollins's leadership and upriver squadron "would have greatly embarrassed, if they had not succeeded in stopping, the passage of the enemy's fleet."[5] These delaying actions might have provided enough time for the ironclad *Louisiana* to be completed. Unlike Pope the previous October, Farragut believed his ships might

---

4 Read, "Reminiscences of the Confederate States Navy," 341; Morgan, *Recollections*, 71.

5 *Court of Inquiry*, 89, 99.

be attacked at the bar. He accordingly took precautions but met no Confederate challenge. Farragut's mortar boats moved to the forts and opened fire on April 17.

In compliance with Hollins's orders, the CSS *McRae* arrived at New Orleans on April 15, 1862. As the ship steamed downriver, it passed Vicksburg where the ship's officers observed "active work going on above the hills." When the *McRae* anchored at the Crescent City, Lt. Huger ordered his executive officer, Lt. Charles W. Read, ashore to report their arrival to the commodore. By then Hollins received shocking news. Richmond relieved the commodore of his command for moving downriver without authorization. Secretary Stephen Mallory was already upset that Hollins previously spent $500,000 in late 1861, money not authorized the navy department, and this latest movement without permission was the final straw. Furthermore, it is likely that Jefferson Davis had a low opinion of the commodore's abilities, an opinion influenced by the president's brother who constantly wrote to Davis that Hollins was incompetent. Read returned to the *McRae* and, without Hollins, the ship steamed down to the forts, arriving on April 16.[6]

Both Capt. Whittle and Gen. Lovell sent telegrams to Stephen Mallory in Richmond, pleading with him to allow Hollins to remain in command, at least until the crisis facing New Orleans passed. They both found merit in Hollins's plan to "make a dash at the enemy" and wanted the chance to carry it out.[7] Even Governor Moore sent a wire to Richmond in favor of the commodore. It was not enough; Secretary Mallory ignored the pleas and Hollins left for Richmond as the bombardment by Farragut's mortars continued. The navy defended New Orleans without its commander, the man that many on the spot considered quite capable of the task, and who could coordinate with both army and local civilian leadership.

Opening Naval Gambits

Flag Officer David Farragut succeeded in getting his ships into the Mississippi River, delayed but without major incident, and he deployed to commence the bombardment of Forts Jackson and Saint Philip. On the Confederate side, Gen. Johnson Duncan made last-minute preparations of his own. Duncan needed reliable intelligence on the Union squadron. Dispatched downriver was the *Star*, a small towboat, whose mission was to tap into Union telegraph communications at

---

6 Campbell, *Engineer in Gray*, 24; Joseph E. Davis to Jefferson Davis, Apr. 20, 1862, *The Papers of Jefferson Davis*, 8:147.

7 "Testimony of Commodore Hollins," *ORN*, Ser. 2, 1:475.

the Head of the Passes. On April 9, Farragut's ships spotted the *Star* and two Union gunboats gave chase as it retreated upriver. Soldiers in Fort Jackson paused from mounting and cleaning cannon when "a brisk cannonading was heard in the direction of the Hds. Of the Passes." The little *Star* managed to reach the Confederate forts, which commenced firing at the two chasing ships. After a brief cannonade the Union gunboats returned downriver, content with temporarily halting the scouting.[8]

The Confederates continued to fortify the two forts while Duncan cabled messages to New Orleans pleading for naval reinforcements. By April 13, the Union ships were ready to proceed upriver and a detachment of officers from the department of coastal survey began to mark positions for mortar boats while a few ships fired on Fort Jackson to determine ranges for pre-marked positions. In response, Duncan dispatched a company of scouts and sharpshooters into the swamps outside the fort. They fired on the Union sailors, attempting to disrupt Farragut's preparations, but accomplished nothing more "than to tear and mutilate the branches and trunks of the gigantic live-oaks."[9]

Though the scouts caused no damage, Farragut grew worried about the possible damage that the Louisiana sharpshooters might inflict if allowed to remain in position. His warships bombarded the swamps, driving the soldiers back into Fort Jackson. Realizing that his sharpshooters could not effectively challenge Farragut's fleet of gunboats, Duncan sent them back to New Orleans as a reserve force.[10]

With the Confederate marksmen removed, Farragut steamed his squadron up from the Head of Passes and placed them in positions preselected by the coast survey. Inside the forts, soldiers noticed their arrival, with the "tall masts and upperyards of the heavy sloops of war" plainly visible to Confederate gunners.

With a bombardment now expected at any moment, Gen. Duncan ordered the first phase of his defense activated. This consisted of fire rafts, much the same as was used the previous October at the Battle of the Head of Passes by Cmdre.

8 Jones, *Memoirs*, 13; Freeman Foster Jr. to Freeman Foster, Apr. 2 & 9, 1862, *Freeman Foster Jr. Letters*, MSS 3170, Louisiana and Lower Mississippi Valley Collections, Louisiana State University Libraries, Baton Rouge, LA.

9 Jones, *Memoirs*, 14.

10 E. C. Hermann, *Yeoman in Farragut's Fleet: The Civil War Diary of Josiah Parker Higgins* (Monterey, CA, 1999), 23.

Hollins and described as "a scow loaded with tar and other combustibles."[11] Being watercraft, the rafts fell under the jurisdiction of Cmdr. John Mitchell. His standing orders from Duncan were to release the rafts downriver into the Union ships once the bulk of Farragut's squadron moved upriver. Just as the previous year, the rafts failed to do any damage, owing to the strong river current and their poor handling. However, they did cause several scares among the Union fleet over the coming days.

Three Union ships raised anchor and steamed into range of Fort Jackson's guns the morning of April 16, 1862. Once near the forts, they began the opening shelling, commencing Farragut's bombardment. Duncan ordered three of his guns to respond and after a few minutes of exchanging fire, the Union vessels withdrew downriver. This action was repeated several times throughout the day as Farragut's sailors finalized range markings against the fort. In the afternoon, two of Porter's mortar boats joined in the bombardment, adding their heavy shells against Fort Jackson for an hour and a half.

The opening bombardment did not cause any damage within the perimeter of Fort Jackson and the Confederate response was slight. In fact, Gen. Duncan grew increasingly concerned over the quality of his gunpowder, fearing that the swampy air was degrading powder already suspected of being poor quality. Thus, he conserved ammunition whenever possible and ordered another fire raft downriver. A volunteer in Fort Jackson remembered that it "drifted right among the Yankee Fleet and produced a great commotion; shots were fired into the burning mass and it was with the greatest difficulty that they prevented their mortar vessels from catching fire."[12] Several of Farragut's ships weighed anchor rather quickly to avoid the raft. Three of them opened fire and a cannon shell from the USS *Winona* smashed a large hole in the raft, which sank before it struck any of its intended targets.

John Mitchell did not sit idly and wait while Farragut's ships continued their bombardment. In the afternoon of April 17, Mitchell ordered five ships downriver, past the barrier of chained ships, to engage and disrupt the Union squadron. The force included the CSS *Jackson*, the Louisiana Navy ships *Governor Moore* and *General Quitman*, and the River Defense Fleet ships *Warrior* and *Resolute*. In a surprising display of coordination and cooperation, these ships "exchanged a few shots, with the hostile gunboats and mortar boats." The Union ships responded, led by the

11 Jones, *Memoirs*, 15; Hermann, *Yeoman in Farragut's Fleet*, 24.

12 Jones, *Memoirs*, 16.

Commander John K. Mitchell, CSN.

Naval History and Heritage Command

USS *Kineo*. The two sides exchanged fire for a while with little effect, one officer in the Union squadron penning in his diary "some of the enemy's shot reached well to our boats, while our shot mostly exploded in the air."[13] Inflicting no damage, and with the threat of becoming overwhelmed if Farragut dispatched more ships to engage them, the Confederate ships withdrew back to the protection of the forts, having shown they were willing to fight.

After the Confederate ships withdrew upriver, Mitchell released another fire raft. Once again, it failed to cause any harm, but the day's activity did convince Farragut to delay his mortar bombardment until the next day, allowing Duncan's men to continue to strengthen their defenses. Every delay was critical, for each day gained was one closer to completing the ironclad *Louisiana*. If the Confederates could hold out until the *Louisiana* was ready, then Farragut would face an ironclad ship stronger than any of his wooden vessels. Further delays might obtain the time required to finish the *Mississippi* and other ironclad ships under construction.

The Mortar Bombardment

On the morning of April 18 David D. Porter's mortars began their bombardment of Fort Jackson. Porter boasted that he could force the fort to surrender within 48 hours and the sailors on the mortar boats worked hard to achieve that goal, firing each large mortar at 10-minute intervals. Shells slammed into brick buildings of Fort Jackson and lodged deep in the swamp mud. William Seymour, a volunteer staffer, described the first casualty in the fort, a soldier "who

13 "Report of Brigadier General Johnson Duncan," *ORN*, 18:265; "Diary of Commander H.H. Bell," *ORN*, 18:692.

had narrowly escaped from being crushed by a falling shell, running away from the place laughing in great glee; but before he had run ten yards the shell exploded, throwing fragments of bricks in all directions—one of which struck this man in the back."[14] The laughing soldier died instantly.

Added to the mortars were four of Farragut's warships, firing cannon shells directly into the ramparts of Fort Jackson. Duncan's men responded from both the water battery in Fort Jackson and with guns across the river in Fort Saint Philip. Through the day Cmdr. Mitchell released more fire rafts, but they each ended in failure due to high wind extinguishing flames and redirecting them harmlessly onto the riverbank.

As shells exploded within Fort Jackson, buildings began to catch fire. Several of these were rapidly extinguished while quick-acting teams eventually contained others, but the most serious threat came at dusk when flames neared the fort's magazine. The entirety of the fort's garrison was roused out of their bombproofs to suppress the fire, utilizing wet blankets, buckets, and even a fire engine that was previously sent down from New Orleans. Through their exertions, the garrison managed to save the magazine from catching fire.

From down the river, the mortar bombardment continued into the next day and both sides began to inflict some damage. Union mortars managed to dismount seven guns in Fort Jackson, though most were remounted during the night. One Union shell even penetrated into a Confederate ammunition bombproof, but failed to explode, saving the garrison from oblivion once again. Confederate gunners struck the USS *Arletta* once and the USS *Oneida* twice. Most significantly, the mortar boat USS *Maria J. Carleton* was sunk after a direct hit by a Confederate shell. The crew abandoned the vessel quickly, with all hands saved. Sailors in the Union fleet considered it lucky that their force suffered only limited damage, believing that such luck would not hold out for long.[15]

Porter's boast proved empty that he could force the forts into surrendering within 48 hours as the bombardment proceeded into its third day. Farragut grew concerned that the mortar bombardment was having little or no tangible results and he prepared a bold and daring backup plan. Much like Flag Officer Foote did with the ironclad *Carondelet* at Island Number Ten, he wanted to push gunboats past the Confederate fortifications. Farragut, however, thought on a much larger

14 Jones, *Memoirs*, 17.

15 John Hart Diary, Apr. 20, 1862, MSS 134, Williams Research Center, The Historic New Orleans Collection.

scale, using a large part of his naval force for the passage instead of just one ship. The main obstacle to his plan was the barrier of anchored sunken ships blocking an advance up the river, but Capt. Henry Bell, Farragut's second in command, presented an idea to tackle that problem.

Using just three ships, the USS *Itasca*, USS *Pinola*, and USS *Kineo*, Capt. Bell planned to steam up the river at night and break the chains connecting the sunken ships, creating a gap large enough for Farragut's force to pass through. Farragut approved and Bell loaded his three ships with barrels of gunpowder to blow up one or two hulks. As the sunken hulks burned, the chains between them could be cut. An experimental explosive "torpedo" (mine) was also loaded onboard one of the ships. After a final inspection of previously inflicted damage on the *Kineo*, Bell decided to leave it behind; at 10 p.m., the *Itasca* and *Pinola* got underway and proceeded upriver, expecting to be quickly spotted by Confederate gunners.

Bell led the *Pinola* to the eastern-most hulk in the barrier and, after some confusion, managed to load and arm the torpedo device. Nothing happened when it was detonated; there was a fault in the wiring that rendered it useless. While the *Pinola* was offloading its torpedo, the *Itasca* steamed in between two hulks, ramming the connecting chain and severing it completely. The ship shuddered violently as it became temporarily lodged in the barrier in the middle of the river. The noise alerted both Confederate gunners rushing to man their posts and Capt. Bell, who hurried the *Pinola* to the *Itasca* to tow it to safety.

Once roused, gunners in Fort Jackson opened fire on the two Union ships. In addition, Mitchell ordered fire rafts released. Once again, the rafts proved ineffective. By dawn on April 21, the Union ships were back with the main squadron, having accomplished their mission, though not exactly as planned. Duncan in Fort Jackson and Lovell in New Orleans knew that with the chain barrier breached Union ships could bypass the forts and fall upon the supporting Confederate squadron. The result would be disastrous. To counter this, Lovell turned to Capt. William C. Whittle to order Cmdr. Charles McIntosh to bring the CSS *Louisiana* downriver to bolster the Confederate defenses.[16]

Back in the shipyards of Jefferson City, the *Louisiana* lay incomplete. Though most of her iron plate armor was installed, deficiencies remained: her guns were not mounted, the ship lacked a full crew, iron was still being installed to protect the pilothouse, and her engines were not connected to her screw propellers via drive-shafts. Nonetheless, Cmdr. McIntosh carried out his orders and the ironclad

16 John Hart Diary, Apr. 21, 1862, Ibid.

was towed downriver, arriving on the night of April 21. Before departing, a draft crew of sailors was taken from the *Pamlico*, lying on Lake Pontchartrain. Work continued as it proceeded. A few guns were mounted during the trip and soldiers from Fort Saint Philip were ordered onboard to man them. Engineers from the *McRae* also went onboard to assist in "labors upon the machinery and battery."[17] Civilian dockworkers slept in tugs alongside while working to install the engines. Would the armored Confederate vessel be ready in time?

General Duncan saw the arrival of the *Louisiana* as his opportunity to seize the initiative and wreak havoc among the Union ships while giving his gunners a respite to rebuild the battered defenses in Fort Jackson. He sent a messenger to Mitchell, asking him to place the *Louisiana* downriver of the two forts where it could fire directly into the Union squadron. Flabbergasted, Mitchell cautioned that the *Louisiana* was immobile; once there, it could not move upriver in the event Union ships approached. This disagreement grew into a tense argument between the army and navy commanders with each mortar shell fired into Fort Jackson.

Unaware of the Confederate quarrel, Farragut continued the bombardment. In the afternoon of April 22, Magazine Number Two caught fire in Fort Jackson and Duncan once again roused the garrison to extinguish the flames. Fortunately for the Confederates, the charred door to the magazine held back the flames long enough for soldiers to extinguish it. "A few more minutes of delay in putting this fire out would have proved our destruction," remembered one anxious Confederate soldier, who saw the fort's powder magazines saved a third time.[18]

While Confederate gunners fought fires, sailors from the CSS *McRae* inspected damage aboard the tugs *Belle Algrine* and *Mosher*. The two tugs were serving as tenders to the growing Confederate fleet as well as guides to tow fire rafts downriver. They were damaged while near the breached chain barrier, attempting to repair the gap made by Capt. Bell; Union gunners took notice and several near misses caused damage on each. Inspections by the *McRae's* engineers found the *Belle Algrine* "leaks badly in the bows, from two holes knocked in her," recalled one engineer on the survey team, while the *Mosher* "loosened the after-bearing of her

---

17 Wilkinson, *Narrative of a Blockade Runner*, 16; "Payment Receipt of CSS Louisiana," Apr. 21, 1862, *Subject File*, AC, NA; "Payment Receipt of CSS Louisiana," Apr. 22, 1862, *Subject File*, AD, NA; "Testimony of Commander Mitchell," *ORN*, Ser. 2, 1:465.

18 Jones, *Memoirs*, 23.

shaft."[19] After minor repairs took place that evening, the two tugs were again serviceable and continued at their posts.

As Confederate enlisted men carried out repairs both afloat and ashore, senior officers continued to argue about the ironclad *Louisiana*. On April 23, Lovell went to see Capt. Whittle in New Orleans, begging him to order the *Louisiana* to the position that Gen. Duncan requested. Whittle responded that he commanded the naval station alone and that since the ironclad was deployed, he no longer held authority over it. Distraught, Lovell then journeyed to Fort Jackson to see if he could convince Cmdr. Mitchell to move the ironclad. Once again, Mitchell refused, noting that the *Louisiana* was in no shape to fight yet, pointing to workers still atop its casemate installing armor and guns.

Farragut was either unaware of the ironclad's presence or did not think it a serious threat. He learned from a deserter what damage was being inflicted in Fort Jackson and believed that it was inconsequential. He resolved to try passing between the two forts. All through April 23, while Generals Lovell and Duncan argued with Cmdr. Mitchell, Farragut's engineers placed range marks in the river and conducted surveys of the hulk barrier, seeing if the breech in the chains was still there and if it could allow large ships to get through.

Farragut's plan was to steam 17 warships upriver in three divisions, fire at the forts in passing, and attack the makeshift Confederate squadron at point blank range. The first division of eight ships, under Capt. Theodorus Bailey, moved against Fort Saint Philip. The second division of three ships, under Farragut, followed behind. The third division of six ships under Capt. Henry Bell brought up the rear, taking Fort Jackson under fire.[20]

To prepare for the passage, Farragut ordered anchor chains "stopped up and down on the sides in the line of the engines" in an effort to create makeshift chain-mail armor protecting vital engineering machinery. Decks were hastily whitewashed so crewmembers could move about more easily in the night, loose spars were sent ashore, and five ships' masts were removed. After Farragut's fleet successfully passed the forts and broke through the defending squadron of smaller Confederate vessels, the Union warships were to proceed to New Orleans, cutting off the Confederate forts from their communications and supply depots. Porter's mortars, protected by several large warships, remained behind to continue the

---

19 "Report of Thomas Huger and Samuel Brock," *OR*, 6:538.

20 David Farragut, "Circular," Apr. 17, 1862, "General Order," Apr. 20, 1862, *Charles H.B. Caldwell Papers*, MSS 253, Williams Research Center, The Historic New Orleans Collection.

bombardment and guard against whatever remained of the Confederate squadron.[21]

General Duncan and Cmdr. Mitchell observed the increased Union activity throughout April 23. Many men, both officers and enlisted, correctly predicted an enemy dash past the forts that night. Lieutenant Charles Read, executive officer of the CSS *McRae*, paid a visit to Fort Jackson, delivering messages from the squadron to Duncan. While there, the young lieutenant met with Col. Edward Higgins. "We were both of the opinion that a move would be made on the forts the following night." Read returned to the *McRae* and prepared for the upcoming battle, including directing the anchor to be made "ready for slipping and a man stationed to unshackle it at a moment's warning." Read ordered half the crew on deck through the night, kept the engineering spaces fully manned with steam pressure built up, and the guns "cast loose and loaded with 5-section [second] shell."[22]

Similar preparations consumed most of April 23 throughout the Confederate squadron. "The naval officers were quite sure that an attempt would soon be made . . . to force the passage," penned Lt. John Wilkinson, serving as Read's counterpart onboard the ironclad *Louisiana*. First Lieutenant Alexander Warley, commanding the ironclad *Manassas*, believed that "judging from the character of the officers in the enemy's fleet, most of whom we knew—[we] believed the attack was at hand." Warley went over to the CSS *McRae* to deliver letters to his friend, 1Lt. Thomas Huger, with instructions to deliver to his family if he was killed in the battle. Ironically, Huger was just about to call on Warley for the same purpose. Upon returning to the *Manassas*, Warley was met by Captain Alexander Grant of the Louisiana gunboat *General Quitman* and by Captain Isaac Hooper of the River Defense Fleet ship *Resolute*. The three captains briefly discussed their prospects for the coming battle and to Warley's surprise, even this close to battle, Captain Hooper flatly denied that any ship of the River Defense fleet was under naval jurisdiction; he even "denied that they were under the command of Generals Lovell and Duncan, or of any one except the Secretary of War" and that his purpose at the forts was to "show naval officers how to fight."[23]

21 Tenney, *The Military and Naval History of the Rebellion in the United States*, 194; Log Entry, Apr. 13 and 19, 1862, *U.S. Ship Portsmouth Log*.

22 Read, "Reminiscences of the Confederate States Navy," 342.

23 Wilkinson, *Narrative of a Blockade Runner*, 16; A.F. Warley, "The Ram Manassas at the Passage of the New Orleans Forts," *B&L*, 2:89; *Court of Inquiry*, 79.

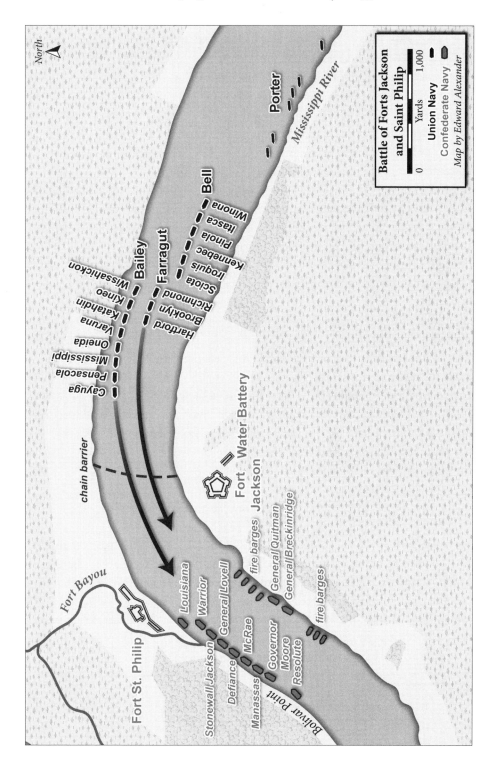

Battle of Forts Jackson and Saint Philip

Map by Edward Alexander

Lieutenant Beverly Kennon climbed the mast of the Louisiana gunboat *Governor Moore* that day and saw the Union engineers marking the river. His preparations included orders that "four sentinels were always posted on the spar-deck and wheel-houses, and a quartermaster in the pilot-house; an anchor and engine-room watch was set; the chain was unshackled and the fires were banked" as well as pre-loading and aiming both of his cannon downriver. One more attempt was made by Gen. Duncan to convince Cmdr. Mitchell to move the *Louisiana* to a more direct line of fire against Farragut's ships, but once again it was refused.[24]

Interestingly, Mitchell made no major preparations for coordinating the Confederate fleet. Though everyone believed a major Federal attack was imminent, Mitchell made no effort to unify the ships under his command. Though the Louisiana gunboats agreed to follow his orders, those of the River Defense Fleet refused. Army commanders constantly questioned his decisions, especially over his reluctance to use the ironclad *Louisiana*. Thus, the Confederate fleet entered what looked like the final contest for New Orleans as a motley collection of individual ships instead of an organized squadron. There were no general orders issued and no coordinated plan for the employment of the vessels; each captain was left to fight as he saw fit. In fact, the only real direction issued by Mitchell was a series of naval signals for use at night, but it is unclear if all of the ships even had the signal book. This was in stark contrast to the previous leadership shown by George Hollins. Though disliked by some outside the navy, he entered battles with an organized plan of action. Without Hollins, each Confederate ship prepared as it saw best. Few sailors or gunners in the forts got any sleep that night as they awaited the largest ship-to-ship engagement of the war.[25]

The Battle of Forts Jackson and Saint Philip

At 2 am on the morning of April 24, 1862 Farragut ordered signal lights hoisted atop the mast of the USS *Hartford*. The run past Fort Jackson and Saint Philip began as 17 Federal warships weighed anchor and formed into three predetermined lines to steam upriver. It was a striking contrast to the uncoordinated Confederate naval deployment upriver. The Union ships moved

24 Kennon, "Fighting Farragut Below New Orleans," 79; Johnson K. Duncan to John K. Mitchell, Apr. 23, 1862, *Johnson K. Duncan Letters*, MSS 110, Williams Research Center, The Historic New Orleans Collection.

25 Thomas Arnold, "Night Signals for the Fleet," *Thomas Arnold Letters*, MSS 3220, Louisiana and Lower Mississippi Valley Collection, Louisiana State University Libraries, Baton Rouge, LA.

quietly in the darkness, not wanting to alert their opponents too soon. The USS *Cayuga* took the lead, under the command of Capt. Theodorus Bailey, a 43-year veteran sailor who previously commanded the USS *Lexington* in the Mexican War. Bailey led the first division of seven ships to sweep past Fort Saint Philip and engage the Confederate vessels known to be lying in wait. The *Cayuga* passed through the broken hulk barrier at 3:30 am. As the first division of ships moved through the Confederate obstructions, Cmdr. David Porter ordered his mortars to open fire on Fort Jackson, alerting all who remained ignorant that the fight was on.

The Confederate gunners and sailors were waiting, as prepared as they could be. For some unknown reason, Mitchell never gave the order to release fire rafts that General Duncan hoped would help illuminate the river. In the forts, gunners sprinted to their positions while the makeshift Confederate naval force waited along the riverbank to strike. The CSS *Louisiana* was moored just upriver from Fort Saint Philip. Some believed it was more formidable than the famous *Virginia* that fought the Union *Monitor*. Past the *Louisiana* was most of the Confederate naval force with only a couple of ships moored on the opposite bank at Fort Jackson.

Within five minutes of the first mortar shot, the guns of Fort Jackson responded in kind, targeting ships of Bailey's lead division. Sailors within the Confederate fleet likewise manned their posts, with the ironclad *Louisiana's* gunners opening fire along with the forts. Onboard the CSS *McRae*, it took but a matter of minutes for the crew to man battle stations and for steam pressure to build up in the boilers to get underway. The same was true on the *Louisiana* gunboat *Governor Moore*, which was underway within five minutes of the first alert. So many ships were steaming into the riverbank that it quickly became over crowded, so much so that Lt. Beverly Kennon angrily recalled having to wait "for the many vessels that were closely packed ahead of us to get out of the way."[26]

As the Confederate ships rushed to get underway, their Union counterparts pushed upriver as fast as possible. The first Union ships managed to get past the Confederate squadron before it could get underway and many of the Confederates chose to engage the middle of the Union column. "The space between the forts was filling up with the enemy's vessels," recalled one Confederate sailor, "which fired upon us as they approached, giving us grape, canister, and shell."[27]

---

26 "Report of Lieutenant Beverly Kennon," *ORN*, 18:305; "Report of Second Assistant Engineer James Tomb," *ORN*, 18:345.

27 Kennon, "Fighting Farragut Below New Orleans," 80.

With no overall leader such as Cmdre. Hollins to direct the Confederate ships, each captain fought as he saw fit. This resulted in a disorganized disaster; several captains among the River Defense Fleet chose to save themselves, abandoning their vessels and taking to the swamps. Lieutenant Beverly Kennon was aghast as he noticed these ships "set afire at their berths on the right bank, and deserted . . . burning brightly."[28]

Kennon pointed the *Governor Moore* upriver to chase the first Union ships to get through, believing that allowing any to escape could prove catastrophic. He caught up with the USS *Cayuga* and the USS *Oneida*. With no fire rafts, the river remained dark, except for brief flashes from cannon and shell explosions. Unable to discern the identity of the *Governor Moore*, both Union ships hailed the *Louisiana* gunboat. Seeking to gain an advantage, Kennon quickly grabbed a speaking trumpet and answered that his ship was the USS *Mississippi*, another ship in the Union squadron. Captain Bailey, knowing the *Mississippi* was further back in the line of ships, did not believe Kennon and ordered the guns on the *Oneida* and *Cayuga* to open fire at a distance of only 30 yards. The two ships of the first division were soon joined by a third, the USS *Pensacola*, whose shells wounded a dozen men manning the *Governor Moore's* bow cannon. Kennon ordered his vessel to increase speed to pass the three Union ships, with the intention of moving upriver to catch up to the lead Union ship.[29]

While three of Bailey's lead ships engaged the *Governor Moore*, 1Lt. Alexander Warley brought the little ironclad *Manassas* into the fray. Aiming at the USS *Mississippi*, its crew saw the iron turtle low in the water and maneuvered to avoid a blow from its ram. Warley was undaunted and the *Manassas* smashed into the *Mississippi*, simultaneously firing its gun, wrecking the Union ship's officers' quarters. The *Mississippi* returned fire, but the low freeboard of the *Manassas* saved it, and the shots missed. On its way upriver to engage the *Governor Moore*, the USS *Pensacola* added its cannon to the barrage, with several shots striking the ironclad, tearing away its flagstaff.[30]

Breaking free of the *Mississippi*, the *Manassas* steamed downriver looking for another target. At the same time, Lt. Kennon's increase in speed paid off when a sailor on the *Governor Moore* spotted a Union ship ahead, which was described as "a large, two-masted steamer rushing up-stream like a racer, belching 'black smoke,'

---

28 Ibid.

29 Ibid; "Report of Commander S. Phillips Lee," *ORN*, 18:208.

30 Warley, "The Ram Manassas at the Passage of the New Orleans Forts," 90.

firing on each burning vessel as she passed, and flying her distinguishing white light at the mast-head and red light at the peak."[31] This ship was the USS *Varuna*, which, thanks to the confusion of steaming upriver and fighting at night, passed the rest of Bailey's first division and became the forward-most vessel in the Union squadron; Kennon's ship raced to catch it.

The chase continued until first light when Kennon ordered his bow gun to open fire. Commander Charles S. Boggs, commander of the *Varuna*, returned fire. Kennon later wrote the Union cannon were "raking us with such guns as she could bring to bear, but not daring the risk of a sheer to deliver her broadside, as we were too close upon her."[32] About this time, the CSS *Jackson*, ordered upriver before the battle as a last defense should any Union ship pass the forts, sighted the two vessels and opened fire on both. After lobbing a few shots, the *Jackson* turned upriver to inform New Orleans that Union ships were past the two forts.

The *Governor Moore* now closed on the *Varuna* and there was barely any distance separating the two. They were so near that Kennon's bow gun could no longer fire directly at the Union ship. Undeterred, he ordered the gun depressed and fired through his own deck. The first shot fired in this manner "went through our deck all right but struck the hawse-pipe, was deflected and passed through the *Varuna's* smoke-stack. It was soon fired again through this hole in our bows, the shell striking the *Varuna's* pivot-gun, where it broke or burst." Three sailors on the *Varuna* were killed by this second shell, and a number more were wounded.[33]

The *Varuna* then sheered to starboard to fire its broadside guns. Kennon seized this opportunity and rammed his opponent. This blow disabled the engines of the Union ship and Kennon excitedly "backed clear, gathered headway again, and rammed her a second time." Sharpshooters on both ships exchanged fire at point blank range, with Cmdr. Boggs boasting that "the marines, although new recruits, more than maintained the reputation of that Corps. Their galling fire cleared the Morgan's [*Governor Moore*] rifled gun and prevented a repetition of her murderous fire."[34]

The *Governor Moore* backed off again and prepared to ram for a third time. The River Defense Fleet Ship *Stonewall Jackson* now appeared and rammed the *Varuna*

31 Kennon, "Fighting Farragut Below New Orleans," 81.

32 Ibid, 82.

33 Ibid, 83; "Report of Lieutenant C.H. Swasey," *ORN*, 18:212.

34 Kennon, 'Fighting Farragut Below New Orleans," 84; "Report of Commander Charles S. Boggs," *ORN*, 18:210.

The Louisiana State Navy Ship *Governor Moore* and River Defense Fleet Ship
General Stonewall Jackson engage the USS *Varuna.*

Naval History and Heritage Command and Frank Leslie's Illustrated Newspaper

for a third blow in the span of just a few minutes. The *Stonewall Jackson* then broke
off and steamed upriver, looking for more targets. The USS *Varuna* was in serious
condition and beginning to sink. Commander Boggs, even as his guns continued to
fire, ordered his ship "into the bank, let go the anchors, and tied up to the trees."[35]
Within 15 minutes, the ship sank. Eight Union sailors onboard the *Varuna* later
received the Medal of Honor for their actions.

The *Governor Moore* was also badly damaged and more was to soon come. The
remaining ships of Bailey's first division caught up with it and fired into the
Louisiana gunboat. Within minutes, "the wheel-ropes, the head of the rudder, the
slide of the engine, and a large piece of the walking-beam were shot away,"
releasing steam into the engine room. Sailors hurriedly evacuated the room to avoid
being scalded.[36] The additional damage proved fatal and Kennon ordered his
remaining crew to abandon ship. Many were then captured by Union boats
rescuing the crew of the *Varuna.* Of a crew of 93 men, 57 were killed and 17 more
wounded. Bailey's ships then targeted the *Stonewall Jackson*, disabling it as well.

While the first division was engaging the *Governor Moore* and *Stonewall Jackson*
further upriver, the remaining Union ships were having a rough time at the forts.

35 Ibid.

36 Kennon, "Fighting Farragut Below New Orleans," 84.

Several officers and men attached to the *Louisiana* were on the tender *W. Burto*n when the battle began and they "crawled one after another on a plank through a hole into the *Louisiana*."[37] The gunners on the ironclad had some difficulty getting their cannon ready to fire, preventing them from engaging any of the Federal ships in the first division. That changed as more Union ships steamed into range. The second division was led by the USS *Hartford*, Farragut's flagship, and it seemed that most of the Confederate efforts were directed to prevent those three ships from passing.

The ironclad *Louisiana* was in the thick of this fighting. Though immobile, the gunners fired at every enemy ship possible, even though only six of the ironclad's 16 guns were serviceable. Sharpshooters positioned themselves along the upper part of the casemate, adding their rifle fire to the deadly chaos. Commander Charles McIntosh joined the sharpshooters atop the casemate, looking to determine the effectiveness of his guns, and was mortally wounded. Command of the *Louisiana* passed to Lt. John Wilkinson, who passed the word to keep firing. The tenders alongside the *Louisiana* suffered damage in the exchange of shells. Wilkinson noted that "many of the mechanics, who were quartered onboard the tenders alongside of us, were killed or wounded."[38] Among the dead was the master of the tug *Belle Algrine*.

As the *Hartford* passed through the Confederate obstructions, she was fired on by both Forts Jackson and Saint Philip. The *Louisiana* added its guns to the din as well. It was at this critical moment that the *Hartford* encountered an unexpected eddy and ran aground, just off of Fort Saint Philip. To avoid hitting the *Hartford* the next ship in line, the USS *Brooklyn*, turned away which resulted in the *Brooklyn* ramming the USS *Kineo* of the first division. The two vessels quickly pulled apart and continued steaming upriver, leaving the *Hartford* to free itself.

The River Defense Fleet Ship *Warrior*, John Stevenson's personal command, then set its sights on the *Brooklyn*, just as it was clearing the scene. Stevenson wanted to ram the *Brooklyn*, but the Union ship opened fire before they could close. Captain Thomas Craven, the *Brooklyn's* commanding officer, remembered "the *Warrior* received our broadside of shells, and was soon in flames."[39] The lightly

---

37 Samuel C. Hyde Jr., ed., *A Wisconsin Yankee in Confederate Bayou Country: The Civil War Reminiscences of a Union General* (Baton Rouge, LA, 2009), 64.

38 Wilkinson, *Narrative of a Blockade Runner*, 46.

39 "Letter from Captain Thomas Craven to Mrs. Craven," ORN, 18:197.

Commander Charles F. McIntosh, CSN.

Naval History and Heritage Command

armed river steamer stood no chance against the powerful Union warship and was soon a burning, sinking wreck.

As the *Hartford* worked to get off the river bottom, it was approached by the unarmed tug *Mosher* pushing a blazing fire raft. In one of the most daring actions of the battle, the little tug pressed the fire raft against the *Hartford* and "in a moment the ship was one blaze all along the port side, halfway up to the main and mizzen tops."[40] The crew worked to put out the fire while one man dropped large shells onto the fire raft, creating several holes in the raft, which soon sank. The *Hartford's* gunners then fired on the *Mosher*, which likewise sank to the river bottom. After several tense minutes, the fires were under control and the *Hartford* was refloated. Farragut's flagship then continued upriver, firing broadsides into Fort Saint Philip.

The CSS *McRae* engaged the remainder of Farragut's second division. As the *McRae* got underway, 1Lt. Thomas Huger ordered the ship to present a broadside down the river and to cross to Fort Jackson, firing at any Union target in sight. The noise was so great that engineers below "could not hear the bell or gong at times" to indicate speed changes from the quarterdeck. After crossing the Mississippi, Huger saw a Union ship of the first division and he turned upriver to engage it. Just as he gave the order, "two large, full-rigged ships were discovered a short distance astern, one on each quarter, coming rapidly up"[41] These proved to be the USS *Brooklyn* of the second division and the USS *Iroquois* of the third division.

The *Brooklyn's* commanding officer, Capt. Thomas Craven, mistook the Confederate ship for the USS *Iroquois*. Craven's executive officer, hand on the lock string of a cannon, called out "It can't be the Iroquois! It is not one of our vessels,

---

40 "Report of Flag Officer David Farragut," Ibid, 154.

41 Campbell, *Engineer in Gray*, 38; "Report of Lieutenant Read," *ORN*, 18:332.

for her smoke-stack is abaft her mainmast!" Craven refused to believe him and withheld fire. Huger took advantage and let the two Union ships pass him. He then targeted the USS *Iroquois* with his guns, first firing his starboard broadside, then sheering his ship around quickly, firing the port guns as well. In Fort Jackson, Col. Higgins "observed the *McRae* gallantly fighting at terrible odds—contending at close quarters with two of the enemy's powerful ships." The fort's gunners likewise saw the *McRae's* double broadside. "When we saw her contending with two of the enemy's large Steam sloops," one volunteer recalled, "we gave her a rousing cheer by way of encouragement [and] applause."[42]

The *Iroquois* quickly responded in kind. One shell started a fire in the *McRae's* sail room while a second "exploded in the smoke stack just above the flames and filled the fire room with fire and ashes from the furnaces;" a third shell "passed through the fire room wounding a number of men by splinters." Huger dispatched his executive officer, Lt. Charles Read, below to deal with the fire. For a moment, it seemed as if the *McRae* would be overwhelmed by the two Union vessels when the CSS *Manassas* arrived, just having rammed the USS *Mississippi*. Warley targeted the *Brooklyn*, which fired at the armored turtle. The pair of Union ships then proceeded upriver, but not before the *Iroquois* fired one last parting shot at the *McRae*. It proved most disastrous as Lt. Read later wrote, it "mortally wounded our commander, wounded the pilot, carried away our wheel ropes and cut the signal halyards and took our flag overboard."[43]

Both the *Iroquois* and the *McRae* suffered heavy damage in their exchange of fire. One sailor onboard the *Iroquois* wrote home that the ship's "cutwater and bowsprit were carried away; just forward of the smoke stack a shell had struck and carried away her bulwark," and the vessel appeared "unseaworthy and wretched in the extreme." Lieutenant Warley believed that the *McRae* "was very badly used up."[44] The *Manassas* proceeded to move upriver against Farragut's main force, but two broadsides from the USS *Mississippi* disabled the ship. Warley ordered them crew to abandon ship as he set the ironclad afire. A boat of sailors from the *Mississippi* tried to salvage the ship, but could not, and the *Manassas* drifted

42 John Russell Barlett, "The Brooklyn at the Passage of the Forts," *B&L*, 2:67; "Report of Lieutenant Colonel Higgins," *OR*, 6:548; Jones, *Memoirs*, 27 – 28.

43 Charles W. Read to John H. Dent, Apr. 28, 1862, *John Horry Dent, Jr., Letters*; Read, "Reminiscences of the Confederate States Navy," 343.

44 Edward W. Bacon to Father, Apr. 30, 1862, *Bacon, Edward Woolsey Papers, 1861-1865*, Manuscript Collections, American Antiquarian Society; Warley, "The Ram Manassas at the Passage of the New Orleans Forts," 90.

downriver before exploding, the pieces of the ship going to the bottom. The ironclad's crew then made their way back to the forts.

Lieutenant Huger was taken below to his cabin and Read assumed command of the *McRae*. He ordered his wheel ropes repaired and steamed the ship upriver, looking for revenge for the wounding of his commander. Instead, Read rounded a bend in the river and found 11 Union ships and, as he later described, "not deeming it prudent to engage a force so vastly superior to my own, I determined to retire under the guns of the forts."[45] Spotting the *McRae* round the river bend, the USS *Kineo* exchanged a few shots with Read's gunners, which again tore away her wheel ropes. This time, the *McRae* uncontrollably slammed into the riverbank.

While repairing his ship's wheel ropes yet again, Read sighted another Confederate ship on the riverbank, flying a white flag. This was the *Resolute* of the River Defense Fleet, abandoned after Captain Isaac Hooper was mortally wounded. Read immediately dispatched Lt. Thomas Arnold and a detail of 10 men to the *Resolute*. Arriving onboard, Arnold found Captain Hooper lying on the deck with his leg blown off, his son comforting him. Arnold's men also found another sailor wounded on deck and discovered the ship's pilot dead in the pilothouse and the vessel's gunner dead at the entrance to the magazine. Furthermore, he found the purser, cook, and steward hiding below deck. The wounded and remaining crew was sent to the *McRae*. Surveying the *Resolute*, Arnold determined that the ship could be refloated with the assistance of a tow. Signals were sent to the nearby ship *Defiance* but the attempt snapped off a davit from that ship. By the time a second attempt could be made, the *Resolute* came under fire from Union gunners, who noticed the activity. Abandoning the effort to refloat the *Resolute*, Lt. Arnold ordered the ship's single gun manned and continued the fight. Two Union shells struck, one of which created a three-foot break in the hull below the waterline, causing still more flooding.[46]

It took some time for Farragut's third division to get past the river obstacles and engage the forts and it was not until the hints of first light that most of the third division was moving upriver. The gunners of Fort Jackson and onboard the ironclad *Louisiana* took advantage of the light and took careful aim at the remaining enemy ships. The last three ships in the Union third line, the USS *Itasca*, USS *Kennebec*, and USS *Winona*, all got entangled in the Confederate obstructions and, hit

---

45 "Report of Lieutenant Read," *ORN*, 18:332-333.

46 Thomas Arnold to John Mitchell, Apr. 26, 1862, *Thomas Arnold Letters*.

by destructive fire from Fort Jackson, withdrew downriver, abandoning their attempt to pass.

At dawn, Flag Officer Farragut anchored his ships at the Quarantine Station, several miles upriver from the forts and assessed the damage to his ships. While there, his crews received the surrender of the regiment of Louisiana militia stationed to guard against a landward attack on Fort Saint Philip. Thirteen of Farragut's ships anchored there after the battle. Three ships failed to make the passage and a fourth sank not far from where his ships were anchored. His gamble to steam past the Confederate forts worked, though one fourth of the ships failed to successfully pass the Confederate defenses. He pressed on to New Orleans.

By midmorning, the Confederates also took stock of their losses in the battle. It was a disaster. The ironclad ram *Manassas* was abandoned and sinking on the riverbank, the Louisiana gunboat *Governor Moore* was also sunk, and the River Defense Fleet ships *Stonewall Jackson* and *Warrior* were lost as well. The *McRae* was briefly stuck on the riverbank and towed back to Fort Saint Philip. Her commanding officer, however, lay mortally wounded. The unfinished ironclad *Louisiana* was still afloat, but her commander was likewise mortally wounded and her engines still not functional. The River Defense Fleet ship *Resolute* was aground on the riverbank, but still serviceable, as was the *Defiance*, whose captain was reportedly drunk during the fighting and had simply done nothing.

The remaining ships of the River Defense Fleet, the *General Lovell* and the *General Breckinridge*, along with the Louisiana gunboat *General Quitman*, took no part in the fighting. Instead, their captains ordered the vessels abandoned and burned as the first Union ships appeared past the Confederate obstructions. Casualties in the forts were low, but the forts likewise caused little damage against the bulk of Farragut's ships.

General Duncan surveyed the damage and prepared his garrisons for a renewed assault. He was not sure whether Farragut's ships would show themselves against his works again or if they would proceed upriver. Likewise, Cmdr. John Mitchell took stock of the remainder of his fleet, now consisting of the *Louisiana*, *McRae*, the grounded *Resolute*, and the poorly-handled *Defiance*, as well as the remaining few tugs and tenders.

Though the fighting was fierce, casualties were relatively light for both sides. Farragut reported some 184 casualties in the April 24 battle while Gen. Duncan reported 48 in the two forts. Casualties among the Confederate naval forces remained unreported, but the number likely lies somewhere between 100 and 150 men killed and wounded.

Farragut Moves Upriver and Confederate Reactions

Flag Officer Farragut knew that passing the two forts did not guarantee victory in this campaign; there were still fortifications further upriver at Chalmette blocking his advance. Additionally, his fleet was now divided with a limited amount of supplies for his isolated force operating behind Confederate lines. After leaving behind a few ships to watch the forts and guard against the remnants of the Confederate fleet, he led his dozen ships upriver to New Orleans.

Farragut's squadron encountered the second line of defenses for New Orleans at Chalmette on April 25. Brigadier General Martin L. Smith and Louisiana Militia Brig. Gen. Benjamin Buisson erected works on both sides of the river. The two batteries numbered only 14 guns and a couple of regiments and battalions of militia. Farragut expected another fierce battle, but the Confederate position was rather weak, with much of its defensive power shipped downriver earlier to support the ironclad *Louisiana* and forts.

The Chalmette battery had a limited supply of ammunition – only about 20 shells per cannon – and they waited until the leading ship was within a quarter of a mile before opening fire. The Confederates served their guns for close to a half hour until they ran out of ammunition. Smith then ordered his men to retreat into New Orleans, where Maj. Gen. Mansfield Lovell was already making preparations to evacuate his remaining men.

Lovell knew that the key to holding New Orleans was the two large forts downriver and that the city had nothing left to stop the enemy approach. Since he sent thousands of men north to Tennessee earlier in the year, all that remained in New Orleans were a few thousand untried and poorly trained militia. Upon receiving word that Farragut succeeded in getting ships past the forts, Lovell immediately contacted the mayor of New Orleans, John Monroe, and told him he planned to evacuate the city.[47]

General Lovell also abandoned the remainder of the forts in southern Louisiana. Their garrisons were ordered to march to Camp Moore, a large training camp north of Baton Rouge. Lovell's militia in New Orleans loaded onto trains and headed there as well. The evacuation of Forts Pike and Macomb were seen to by the small naval force operating in Lake Pontchartrain. The army gunboat *Oregon* was sunk in the Rigolets, the passage from Lake Borgne to Lake Pontchartrain

---

47 "Report of Brigadier General Martin Smith," *OR*, 6:553; David P. McCorkle to John M. Brooke, May 19, 1862, *Ironclads and Big Guns of the Confederacy*, 91.

protected by Fort Pike. This prevented Union forces from interfering in operations in Lake Pontchartrain for the time being. After blocking the Rigolets passage, the remaining four military ships on Lake Pontchartrain gathered at the terminus of the Lake Pontchartrain Railroad to assist in evacuating the city. The CSS *Pamlico*, CSS *Carondelet*, CSS *Bienville*, and the army transport *Arrow* began ferrying troops out of New Orleans on the night of April 24.

First Lieutenant Carter B. Poindexter, commander of the *Bienville* and senior naval officer present, oversaw the Lake Pontchartrain evacuations. The first move was to evacuate the 700 men garrisoning Forts Pike and Macomb. The next morning, Poindexter shifted to evacuating troops from New Orleans, ferrying two batteries of artillery and 2,000 soldiers to the city of Covington on the northern bank of Lake Pontchartrain. After assisting with the troop evacuation, Lovell recommended that the four ships attempt to make a run to Mobile, but the sunken *Oregon* blocked the channel and they were unable to escape.

Lieutenant Poindexter ordered the ships burned to prevent their capture by Union forces. The *Pamlico*, *Carondelet*, and *Bienville* all steamed to the north end of Lake Pontchartrain and their crews offloaded their cannon before setting the ships ablaze. Using a draft of money approved by William C. Whittle, 11 guns, along with ammunition, and the ships' crews were brought by rail first to Camp Moore, Louisiana, then to Vicksburg to add to the defense of that city. The army transport *Arrow* steamed into the West Pearl River in an attempt to escape but was burned on June 4, 1862 as Union forces closed in on it.[48]

Efforts continued on the river to get supplies out of the city as well. Many military stores were hastily thrown on trains overloaded with troops, while others were loaded onto civilian steamers lying at the city's wharves. The CSS *Saint Philip*, the navy's hospital and receiving ship, was loaded with specie from the New Orleans mint and proceeded upriver. The *Galveston*, *Magenta*, and *Pargoud* were likewise loaded with ordnance and commissary stores and escaped upriver, as did the speedy *W.H. Webb*. Besides supplies, the ships were filled with civilians attempting to escape Union occupation. The powder works were disassembled and sent north to Vicksburg.

The most important objective was to get the unfinished ironclad *Mississippi* to safety. Even as Farragut bombarded Fort Jackson, work continued on the *Mississippi*. On April 19, as Porter's mortars fired into Fort Jackson, the *Mississippi*

---

48 *Court of Inquiry*, 81; "Payment Receipt for CSS Bienville, CSS Carondelet, and CSS Pamlico," Jul. 21, 1862, *Subject File*, AX, NA.

was officially launched, though it was done so only after all of the shipbuilders of the city toured the hull and came to a consensus that it would float. Though still missing armor above her waterline and only "one of three propellers was in position, the others lying upon the wharf," the Tift brothers were confident that she could be ready by mid-May. Commander Arthur Sinclair was more pessimistic, believing it would take another three months of work to complete the vessel he was assigned to command. Work on the shafts and propellers continued until the last minute possible; unfortunately for the Confederacy, it was too late.[49]

Two tugs, the *Peytona* and *Saint Charles*, were dispatched to the *Mississippi* to tow the ship upriver, arriving alongside the unfinished ironclad on the evening of April 25. The *Peytona* was described as "of fine power" while the *Saint Charles* was considered "an old tow-boat." The masters of these tugs were not cooperative, instead desiring to quickly leave the city. "The captains of these boats," Sinclair recalled, "showed every disposition, in fact, determination, to thwart me in my wishes, and to accomplish my ends I had, with my own officers, to lash and secure them alongside, and furnished one of them, the steamer *St. Charles*, with an engineer." Unable to make way against the current after several hours of attempts, Sinclair steamed in the *Peytona* to Gen. Lovell, asking for more tugs to assist in the endeavor. While on the way, Sinclair sighted elements of the Farragut's squadron approaching and he immediately returned to the *Mississippi*, remembering his orders "not to let her fall into the hands of the enemy."[50] By the time he returned, Sinclair found that his executive officer, Lt. James I. Waddell, already applied the torch to the vessel. The ironclad originally hoped to defend New Orleans went up in smoke and Sinclair took his officers upriver to safety.

The citizens of New Orleans joined in the destruction, burning cotton on the riverbank and ships on the river to prevent Union forces from capturing them. No less than 13 vessels in the New Orleans area were destroyed before Farragut arrived; at least another seven fell into Union hands. Thousands of citizens gathered at the riverbank to protest against the arriving Union ships. Additionally, the CSS *Jackson* that brought word Farragut bypassed the forts, was burned on the levee at the Union squadron's approach. Joining the burning *Jackson* were the revenue cutters *Pickens* and *Washington*, likewise burned. As the *Pickens* burned, one

---

49 *Court of Inquiry*, 85. Francis W. Dawson, Reminiscences of Confederate Service: 1861-1865 (Charleston, SC, 1882), 42-43; "Payment Receipt for CSS Mississippi," Apr. 25, 1862, *Subject File*, AC, NA.

50 *Court of Inquiry*, 71, 86.

emotional sailor jumped onboard, located the ship's Confederate flag, as well as its old United States Revenue Marine flag, and "and wrapped them up and carried them off," away from the flames.[51] Military vessels under construction on the river and Lake Pontchartrain were all burned, including the nearly completed floating battery *Memphis*, gunboats under construction in several dry-docks, and the supplies gathered for the next wave of ironclads both in New Orleans and Lake Pontchartrain. It was a total loss.

Farragut's ships arrived at New Orleans on the afternoon of April 25 and Capt. Theodorus Bailey, along with Lt. George Perkins, walked to city hall to demand the surrender of the city. The men were surrounded by a mob of citizens, some of whom threatened harm against the officers. Upon reaching city hall, Mayor Monroe told them that he had no authority to surrender the city, as New Orleans was currently under martial law. Any talk of surrender must be with Gen. Lovell. Lovell soon joined the group at city hall and he also refused to surrender the city. Instead, he offered to withdraw his men and turn over control back to the mayor, leaving it open to occupation by Union forces.

Captain Bailey returned to Farragut, to report on what was discussed, having to sneak out of the back of city hall because of the mob forming outside. The next day, Union officers again went to see Mayor Monroe and demand surrender. This time, Monroe proclaimed that even though Lovell evacuated his men, the city could not be surrendered without first convening the city council, which would take some time to do. Meanwhile, Union sailors raised a U.S. flag over the mint. While his officers demanded the surrender of the city, Farragut dispatched several ships upriver where they took possession of Fort John Morgan, finding another set of obstructions to protect the city against an attack from upriver.[52]

As Farragut's officers argued with Mayor Monroe, Porter dispatched ships to cut off Forts Jackson and Saint Philip from any communications. Additionally, several hundred men from Maj. Gen. Benjamin Butler's infantry boarded transports and rowboats and moved through the swamps to isolate the two forts. In the forts, Gen. Duncan prepared for another fight as "an attack upon the Forts was hourly expected.[53]

---

51 "Statement of David Ritchie," *OR*, 15:499.

52 Theodorus Bailey to John T. Monroe, Apr. 26, 1866, *Miscellaneous Papers Related to the Confederacy, Confederate States of America Records, 1856-1915*, Dolph Briscoe Center for American History, The University of Texas at Austin.

53 Jones, *Memoirs*, 31.

On April 26, the CSS *McRae* was granted permission by Cmdr. Mitchell to steam to New Orleans with the injured from the battle. Wounded from the fleet and Fort Jackson crammed the ship's decks as it left the forts, first encountering the USS *Wissahickson*, which "with a white flag, dropped down from the Quarantine." Lieutenant Read on the *McRae*, acting in command after Thomas Huger was wounded, boarded the nearby USS *Mississippi*, whose captain was in command of the forces just upriver of the Confederate forts. Lieutenant George Dewey, the *Mississippi's* executive officer, remembered the encounter, recalling Read came "to get permission to take his dying captain and the other wounded of the *McRae* to New Orleans." With permission granted, the *McRae* continued upriver, doing so with great difficulty. The ship suffered severe damage in the battle on April 24, further weakening the engines, and Read was "frequently obliged to make fast to the bank" until steam pressure could build up in the overworked engines.[54]

The *McRae* anchored off of New Orleans on the morning of April 27 and Lt. Read boarded the Union flagship to ask permission to offload his wounded. The citizens of New Orleans did not wait for permission however, and Mayor Monroe "sent a request to one of the ferryboats to run along side" to offload the wounded. Farragut gave Read permission to offload his wounded, which was completed by mid-afternoon. That night, however, events turned against the *McRae* and its crew. At 8:30 pm, the ship began to drag its anchor and Read ordered his crew to start the engines "and sheered over to the point near the second district ferry landing," which was more shallow water. On the way, the ship hit a snag, veered around in a circle, and began taking on water. The crew worked alongside a detachment of police officers dispatched to help man the pumps, but it proved of no use. By dawn of April 28, "the water was six feet in the hold and gaining on us, the vessel was settling rapidly, and the water on the outside was only 2 inches below the shot holes in the ship's sides." Read ordered the vessel abandoned and the *McRae* slipped beneath the river at 7 am. The next day, the *New Orleans Daily Crescent* published a story of what happened, writing a small epitaph for the ship boasting that it "was a fine little steamer, and has done good service."[55] With no way to return to the forts, the crew joined in the evacuation of the city.

54 "Report of Brigadier General Duncan," *OR*, 6:550; George Dewey, *Autobiography of George Dewey: Admiral of the Navy* (New York, 1913), 75; "Report of Lieutenant Read," *ORN*, 18:334.

55 "Arrival of the Wounded," *The New Orleans* [LA] *Daily True Delta*, Apr. 29, 1862; "Report of Lieutenant Read," *ORN*, 18:334; "Sinking of the Confederate Steamer McRae," *New Orleans* [LA] *Daily Crescent*, April 29, 1862.

Surrender and Final Collapse

Back at Forts Jackson and Saint Philip, the remnants of the Confederate fleet organized for the continued struggle. Following the April 24 battle, and with the *McRae* sent upriver to deliver the wounded to New Orleans, all that remained afloat at the forts was the ironclad *Louisiana* and the River Defense Fleet vessels *Defiance* and *Resolute*, the latter of which was still aground on the riverbank. Besides these warships were the few tenders and tugs that housed workers and handled the fire rafts.

Even this small force continued to dwindle. Lieutenant Thomas Arnold, sent from the *McRae* to take command of the grounded *Resolute* in the battle, worked hard to repair the vessel. The day after the fighting, Union ships from upriver noticed the work on deck during the day of April 25, the *Resolute* was "attacked by one of the gunboats from above, which succeeded in putting several shots through her hull at the water line." After inspecting the damage done, with the assistance of a carpenter sent from the *Louisiana*, Arnold determined that the vessel could not be saved and, after receiving confirmation from Mitchell, he set it on fire it, bringing his detachment to the tug *Landis*.[56]

Many of the personnel of the River Defense Fleet deserted. Besides the grounded and abandoned *Resolute*, the *General Lovell* and *General Breckinridge* were both abandoned and burned at the start of the battle. The crews made their way into the Louisiana swamps, with several taking refuge in the homes of locals while the rest worked their way to New Orleans. The remainder of the naval personnel moved onto the *Louisiana* to help complete and man the ironclad. If it could be made fully operational, then the *Louisiana* might steam upriver and destroy Farragut's force while the forts held back Porter's mortars. Others believed that more drastic action should be taken, to steam the *Louisiana* downriver into the Gulf and somehow make it to Mobile. Mitchell ignored these requests, knowing how incomplete and vulnerable his ironclad was.[57]

With so many ships lost and their crews looking for a place to go, the decks of the *Louisiana* were crowded with officers, sailors, workers, and soldiers all striving to get the ship fully operational. With the wounding of its commander on April 24,

---

56 Wilkinson, *Narrative of a Blockade Runner*, 47; Thomas Arnold to John Mitchell, Apr. 26, 1862, *Thomas Arnold Letters*.

57 Anonymous, "Originator of the Ironclad," *Marine Review and Marine Record* (July 1903), No. 2, 28:67.

Cmdr. Mitchell assumed personal command of the ironclad. Before the *McRae* left upriver, Lt. Read transferred several officers, most of his engineers, and all of his marines to the ironclad to further assist. Lieutenant Alexander Warley led his remaining crew from the *Manassas* onboard as well, along with Lt. Beverly Kennon and the surviving crew from the *Governor Moore*.

April 27 was the decisive day both in New Orleans and at the forts. While negotiations continued at city hall, William B. Munford, a resident of the city, climbed the mint building and tore down and desecrated the United States flag hoisted there, an action for which he was later executed. Mobs grew through the city and Mayor Monroe activated the remaining state militia under Brig. Gen. Paul Juge, consisting mostly of foreign nationals exempt from Confederate military service, to reestablish order. In the afternoon, Gen. Lovell left the city for Camp Moore, north of Baton Rouge, Louisiana with the remainder of his troops, leaving New Orleans at the mercy of the Union squadron.

At the forts downriver, rumors were rampant that New Orleans surrendered. In the afternoon, the wife of a Confederate soldier who was stationed at the Quarantine Station emerged outside of Fort Jackson and "managed to inform one of our pickets that the City had certainly surrendered." The garrison of Fort Jackson took this news to heart and at 11 pm, a large portion of the garrison mutinied against their officers. General Duncan's aide wrote "every effort was made by the officers to induce the mutineers to return to duty" to no avail, and several of the fort's guns were spiked.[58] Mutineers came from every company in the fort except the Saint Mary's Cannoneers light artillery company. Some 300 Confederates marched out of Fort Jackson and surrendered to Benjamin Butler's Union infantry opposite Quarantine. With many of his guns spiked and half of his garrison deserted, Gen. Duncan informed Cmdr. David Porter that he was willing to discuss surrender terms for the two forts.

Just as the mutiny was taking hold, work on the *Louisiana* was completed. Lieutenant Wilkinson noted that "after unremitting labor, our machinery was at last completed, as we prepared to make the attempt to go up the river in pursuit of the [Union] fleet."[59] Instead, as daylight broke on April 28, Cmdr. Mitchell and Lt. Wilkinson found Fort Jackson preparing to surrender. The CSS *Louisiana* was ready, but too late to fight. Mitchell held a council of war to determine what should be done. The consensus was that the ironclad, though finally complete, could not

58 Jones, *Memoirs*, 32.

59 Wilkinson, *Narrative of a Blockade Runner*, 52-53.

operate without the forts as a base of supply. The decision was made to destroy the ironclad. First the gunboat *Defiance* was burned and the remaining sailors, workers, soldiers, and officers loaded onto the tugs, which made their way to Fort Jackson to lay down their arms.

A few of the officers refused to surrender and received permission to escape into the swamps to try and to reach Confederate lines. A total of 13 officers made the attempt, dividing themselves into at least two groups. Lieutenant George W. Gift, Lt. Thomas Fister, Master James Baker, Acting Master Dennis Bremond, Second Assistant Engineer James Durning, and Third Assistant Engineers James Nolan and James H. Riley all made good their escape and rejoined Confederate naval forces at Vicksburg, Mississippi. Six men, Lt. Robert Bowen, Acting Master John Glass, Acting Master Albert Hulse, Master Sidney Smith Lee Jr., Passed Midn. Edward McDermett, and Acting Midn. Francis Chew were all captured in the swamps by Union infantry and brought north as prisoners.[60]

The ironclad *Louisiana* was set afire by a group of seven officers who did not leave the vessel until "the flames were ascending the forward hatchway." The mooring lines burned and the vessel broke free, drifting downriver, an imposing but abandoned mass. At 10:45 on the morning of April 28, the flames hit the magazine and the ironclad *Louisiana* blew up. "The spectacle was magnificent," recalled one Union officer, "as if an immense balloon 500 feet high and 100 feet in diameter made of fire of all hues and smoke and shattered timbers around majestically, followed by a roar as of the loudest thunder."[61] The naval officers captured were sent north as prisoners while the garrisons of the forts were paroled. Resistance below New Orleans ended. General Butler's men provided garrisons for the two forts while Porter sent word upriver to Farragut.

By April 29, Farragut received word of the surrender of the two forts and the destruction of the remaining Confederate naval forces. He grew impatient to have the city officially surrender. The flag officer gathered a full battalion of marines who marched to the customhouse and raised a United States flag. There they remained until May 1, when Gen. Butler's troops arrived. He immediately ordered 1,400 men ashore to garrison the customhouse and other prominent government buildings, placing New Orleans under martial law and making his headquarters at

60 "Report of Commander Mitchell," *ORN*, 18:299; Booth, *Military Records*, 1:108 & 734, 2:35, 3:324.

61 "Report of Commander Mitchell," *ORN*, 18:299; Hyde, *A Wisconsin Yankee in Confederate Bayou Country*, 44.

the Saint Charles Hotel. Farragut was pleased that Butler's men arrived. He ordered his sailors and marines to return onboard their ships. As Butler's troops were garrisoning the city of New Orleans, Farragut ordered a detachment of ships to steam upriver to capture the Louisiana capital of Baton Rouge.

"The hour is dark and gloomy for our beloved South" was what Stephen Mallory penned following the loss of New Orleans; adding that the city's fall "was a sad, sad blow, and has affected us bitterly, bitterly, bitterly."[62] The largest port and city of the new nation, as well as the gateway to the Mississippi River, was now under U.S. control and many in the Confederacy wanted answers. A court of inquiry was convened in 1863 to determine why the city fell.

New Orleans was lost for several reasons, chief among them being a lack of coordination at the top levels of command. Army officers failed to work closely with naval officers to coordinate a defense and ensure adequate preparations were undertaken. There was too much confidence in the improvised naval forces that proved unfounded. The ironclads were seen as the critical weapons needed to defeat Union naval forces, but everything from worker strikes to lack of materials caused serious delays. Many of the limited resources and funds available were spent acquiring and converting civilian riverboats into makeshift gunboats that accomplished little. In the end, the CSS *Louisiana* was completed, but a few days too late. The *Mississippi*, on the other hand, was still weeks away from being finished when it was burned. The loss of New Orleans likewise doomed the construction efforts to make a second wave of such ironclads.

The comparison with the Union efforts to build armored river vessels shows the superior resources and manufacturing capability of the North. Starting in August 1861, seven ironclad river gunboats were constructed in St. Louis from the keel up. The first of these went into combat in just five months. Each ironclad was armed with 13 large cannon and fully crewed, commanded by U.S. Navy officers when commissioned in early January 1862. These seven craft absorbed 240,000 pounds of iron armor and were soon joined by three more within the next couple of months. They participated in the capture of Forts Henry, Donelson, Island Number Ten, Columbus, and Memphis from February through April while the only functional Confederate ironclad on the river was the tiny ram *Manassas*.

Unlike the U.S. river forces, there was a lack of Confederate naval coordination on the river as well as disjointed naval command at New Orleans. One of the Confederacy's most capable officers, Commodore George Hollins, was relieved

---

62 Diary of Stephen R Mallory, May 15, 1862, Vol. 1.

Destruction of the CSS *Louisiana*. *Battles and Leaders of the Civil War*

when he showed initiative and went to help defend New Orleans. Hollins's sacking left William Whittle in command of the New Orleans naval station, but not over ships already in commission. Commander John Mitchell held command over Confederate forces afloat there, but he needed to coordinate with the gunboats of Louisiana's state navy and the River Defense Fleet, as well as with the army. Farragut's more powerful warships were crewed by experienced sailors and officers. Losing only one vessel, they steamed past the forts guarding New Orleans and inflicted a stunning defeat on the sometimes bravely led, but much weaker Confederate naval forces that were poorly coordinated.

There also was no overall commander at Forts Jackson and Saint Philip. General Duncan controlled army forces in the area and Cmdr. Mitchell held command over some of the naval forces. Duncan asked him to bring the CSS *Louisiana* downriver but Cmdr. Mitchell refused to move the unfinished ship to where the army wanted it. The result of this lack of cooperation and confusing command structure was the loss of the Confederacy's most important port and largest city, as well as hundreds of miles of the Mississippi River. Confederate forces were now retreating along the river from both the north and the south. Whether they could reorganize and mount another defense was yet to be seen.

CHAPTER SEVEN

The First Campaign for Vicksburg

Operations on the White River

CONFEDERATE control over the Mississippi River was reduced to the waters between Baton Rouge, Louisiana, and Vicksburg, Mississippi. This area was under imminent threat by Union naval and land forces. Following the capture of New Orleans, Farragut began preparations to capture Baton Rouge.

Upriver, Flag Officer Charles Davis used his squadron to keep pressure against the Confederates in the waterways of Arkansas. Davis, who replaced the wounded Foote, wanted to clear the Mississippi River and its tributaries of any remaining Confederate gunboats that escaped destruction at Island Number Ten and Memphis. Another task was to send much-needed supplies to Gen. Samuel Curtis's army forces in northern Arkansas. To do this, Davis gathered the ironclads *Mound City*—refloated and repaired since its sinking at Plum Point bend in May—and *Saint Louis*, along with the timberclad gunboats *Lexington* and *Conestoga* and a few transports carrying supplies and the 46th Indiana Regiment. The expedition, under Cmdr. Augustus H. Kilty of the *Mound City*, was to advance up the White River, a tributary of the Mississippi leading into northern Arkansas, and resupply Curtis's forces while clearing any Confederate naval opposition in his path.

Confederates in Arkansas were spread thin—most army forces were deployed against Gen. Curtis in the northern portions of the state. Only the navy could oppose Cmdr. Kilty's advance up the White River. After the loss of Island Number Ten, Cmdr. Hollins ordered two ships, the CSS *Maurepas* and the CSS *Pontchartrain*, to travel up the White River and locate a defensive position. They were soon joined by the transports *Eliza G.* and *Mary Patterson*, seeking safe waters. First Lieutenant Joseph Fry of the *Maurepas* was the senior officer present. He was assisted by 1Lt. John Dunnington of the *Pontchartrain*. With only 100 or so sailors and their two gunboats, they prepared fortifications just outside of Saint Charles, Arkansas, in May 1862. The *Pontchartrain* unloaded two 32-pounder guns ashore and, without Lt. Fry, left for the Arkansas River to defend Little Rock, the state capital. Lieutenant Dunnington and most of his crew remained behind to man the guns at Saint Charles.

Work continued slowly until the Confederates received word that Kilty's expedition was ascending the White River. Three guns on the *Maurepas* were removed and joined the two guns already ashore, as well as two more cannon sent overland from Little Rock. The total of seven guns were positioned in two batteries a short distance from one another. To block the river, the now unarmed *Maurepas*, *Eliza G.*, and *Mary Patterson* were all sunk as river obstructions.[1]

Joining the sailors were 100 soldiers from the 29th Arkansas Regiment, but most of these were sent upriver to Little Rock because of a lack of available muskets. All told, there were some 114 sailors and soldiers at the small fortification to resist Kilty's advance, which closed to within a few miles of the Confederate position by the evening of June 16.

Colonel G. N. Fitch's Union infantry disembarked their transports and marched toward Saint Charles at first light the next morning. At 7 am, Kilty's ships advanced upriver as well. It took an hour and a half for the ships to get in range when Lt. Fry's men opened fire on the ironclads. Union gunners returned fire while the ships slowly closed the distance until, by 10:30 am, they were at nearly point-blank range.

A lucky Confederate shell struck the USS *Mound City*, pierced its armor, and exploded. This forced the steam drum of the ironclad to explode, scalding a good portion of the crew. Many jumped overboard in an attempt to escape, but it was too late for the majority of the crew. Of the 175-man crew, 105 were killed and 45 more were wounded, including Cmdr. Kilty. The *Mound City* drifted helplessly back down the White River, smashing into the riverbank not far from the Confederate earthworks. There were accusations that some Confederates fired at the Union sailors as they tried to escape. Lieutenant Dunnington adds credence to the claim,

---

1 Alexander Miller Diary, Jun. 17, 1862.

noting that they did so because the *Mound City* refused to strike her flag in surrender.[2]

While Lt. Fry's gunners fought against the ironclads, Colonel Fitch's nearly 1,000 infantrymen marched to get behind the Confederate batteries. When the *Mound City's* steam drum exploded, Fitch's men were nearly at the Confederate works. The colonel signaled the Union sailors to hold their fire so he could launch an attack on the Southern position.[3]

The Union ironclads and gunboats acquiesced and Col. Fitch's men charged the batteries. Hopelessly outnumbered, Lt. Fry ordered his men to retreat, "the officers bringing up the rear, until scattered in the woods."[4] Some 30 Confederates were captured in the retreat, among them Lt. Fry, who was wounded in his bid to escape. The *Mound City*, badly damaged for the second time in as many months, was towed to recently captured Memphis for repairs.

The skirmish at Saint Charles ended as another defeat for the Confederacy in the western waters. The *Maurepas* was sunk, along with two transports, all of the artillery at Saint Charles fell into Union hands, and Lt. Fry and many of his trained sailors were prisoners. Worse still, despite the damage inflicted on the USS *Mound City*, the Union force continued its advance upriver. It took the better part of a day for sailors to clear a gap in the sunken ships, but once breeched, Kilty's expedition moved on.

Low water level, not Confederate efforts prevented them from reaching Gen. Curtis. Falling waters forced the Union ships back to Saint Charles, eventually joining with Davis's squadron on the Mississippi River. Once reunited, the squadron moved downriver to meet Farragut's ships as they advanced upriver from New Orleans. Back on the White River, Lt. John Dunnington assumed command over the remaining Confederate sailors and marched them to the Arkansas River, where they crewed the *Pontchartrain*. He then took the ship to Fort Hindman, being constructed to defend approaches to Little Rock.[5]

2 "Report of Lieutenant McGunnegle," *ORN*, 23:166.

3 "Report of Colonel Fitch," Ibid, 172; Alexander Miller Diary, Jun. 17, 1862.

4 "Report of Lieutenant Dunnington," *ORN*, 23:201.

5 Alexander Miller Diary, Jun. 18 and 20, 1862.

Farragut Continues Upriver

With New Orleans occupied by Gen. Benjamin Butler, Flag Officer David Farragut turned his fleet to the next task. Farragut did not want to move up the river, instead wishing to assault Mobile, but his superiors in Washington deemed gaining control over the rest of the Mississippi River as more important than the capture of the last major Confederate port in the Gulf of Mexico. After a few days at New Orleans to repair damage to his ships and resupply, Farragut continued upriver to join with Union naval forces steaming down from Memphis. The goal was for the two fleets to unite and capture the final main stronghold of the Confederate Mississippi River: Vicksburg.

On May 6, 1862, Farragut dispatched the USS *Iroquois* and USS *Brooklyn* upriver to capture Baton Rouge, the capital of Louisiana. When the ships arrived at the city the next day, they found it abandoned by Confederate government and military officials; Union sailors landed and raised United States flag over government buildings. A second force of ships was sent further upriver to seize the town of Natchez, Mississippi, which was likewise accomplished without incident. Sailors occupied both towns until Butler sent soldiers for permanent garrisons.

The only Confederate defense left along the Mississippi River in May was the city of Vicksburg, Mississippi as gun emplacements were not installed at Port Hudson until August. Vicksburg was called the Gibraltar of the West. Its steep and high bluffs allowed cannon to shoot directly down into the river while enemy ships could not reach the land defenses with their guns. Additionally, the town was situated at a bend in the river where passing ships must slow down making them easier targets.

Vicksburg's naturally strong position was fortified. By April 1862, there was "active work going on above the hills" outside of town.[6] Major General Earl Van Dorn, a Mississippi native and professional soldier, commanded the city. At the start of the war, he fought in Missouri and Arkansas before crossing the Mississippi River in the late spring of 1862 to bolster the defenses of western Tennessee and northern Mississippi. By the summer of 1862, Vicksburg deployed 30 cannon garrisoned by a few-thousand men. They were soon augmented by the remains of Mansfield Lovell's command and sailors from the New Orleans area.

Farragut began the first attempt against Vicksburg in late June of 1862. With him were most of his wooden gunboats, several of Porter's mortar boats, and 3,000

---

6 Campbell, *Engineer in Gray*, 24.

of Butler's men under the command of Brig. Gen. Thomas Williams. Once there, Porter's mortars commenced a two-day bombardment, supplemented by a few of Farragut's warships that could reach some Confederate positions with their cannon. Just as at the forts protecting New Orleans, two days of mortar bombardment did little damage to the Confederate earthworks and Farragut determined to run his gunboats past Vicksburg, just as he did at Forts Jackson and Saint Philip.

However, Vicksburg was unlike New Orleans in several key aspects. First, the main Confederate defenses were around the town, not miles away as Forts Jackson and Saint Philip were from New Orleans. Most of Gen. Earl Van Dorn's men were also in the city. In addition, Vicksburg enjoyed a secure line of supply through railroads east into the rest of Mississippi. Finally, the bluffs of Vicksburg were a greater defensive barrier than the lowlands and swamps of southern Louisiana.

Farragut pushed his squadron past Vicksburg in the early morning of June 28. The Confederate gunners were ready. "Shot flew briskly all around us," observed a sailor on the USS *Iroquois*, "cutting the rigging close above our heads."[7] Just as at the forts guarding New Orleans, three Union ships, the USS *Brooklyn*, USS *Kennebec*, and USS *Katahdin*, failed to get past the batteries of Vicksburg. However, Farragut succeeded in bypassing the heavily fortified city, steaming the majority of his ships upriver to unite with the advance guard of Flag Officer Charles Davis's squadron moving downriver from Memphis.

Farragut wrote to Davis that the guns of Vicksburg were temporarily silenced after passing them, but "the moment we passed out of our range they would up again and rake us with the guns that were intended for your fleet."[8] Farragut proposed that Maj. Gen. Henry Halleck's army at Corinth, Mississippi, march south to help invest Vicksburg, which he deemed was too strong for his ships and for Williams's 3,000 soldiers to assault alone. Porter's mortars continued their bombardment while Farragut and Davis discussed further action. Time was not on their side. The water level on the Mississippi River that summer began to drop; Farragut could not take his deep-draft gunboats more than 10 or 15 miles upriver from Vicksburg. General Williams started construction of a canal to bypass the defenses of Vicksburg. They utilized several hundred slaves from Jefferson Davis's plantation, located a few miles away, in the effort, but the project halted after little progress.

---

7 Edward W. Bacon to Isham, Jun. 30, 1862, *Bacon, Edward Woolsey Papers, 1861-1865*.

8 "Letter from Flag Officer Farragut to Flag Officer Davis," ORN, 18:589.

The Confederate Navy Reorganizes on the Yazoo River

Just as the *Maurepas* and *Pontchartrain* retreated up the White River, the last ship of the River Defense Fleet, the *General Earl Van Dorn*, did likewise up the Yazoo River. There it rendezvoused with the CSS *General Polk* and the CSS *Livingston* near Liverpool Landing. These three ships were lightly armed. The *General Earl Van Dorn* mounted a single cannon. As for the other two, they originally mounted 13 guns between them, but now had a combined total of just two.

When stationed below Fort Pillow, the guns of the *Polk* and *Livingston* were offloaded and mounted in earthen batteries at Fort Randolph, a smaller bastion below Fort Pillow. The removal of the guns to Fort Randolph was questioned because, as one naval officer put it, "Randolph could not hold out if Fort Pillow fell, and as Pinckney had no infantry supports, he was at the mercy of the Yankee raiders by land."[9] Thus, when Fort Pillow was abandoned, Cmdr. Pinckney ordered his ships to retreat to the Yazoo River. Before doing so, Lt. Sardine G. Stone, executive officer of the *General Polk*, ordered his guns in Fort Randolph to be removed, but the crew only succeeded doing so for two cannon before the ship got underway. The two ships made their way up the Yazoo, joined by the *Earl Van Dorn*. They protected the Yazoo River while workers struggled to complete the unfinished ironclad *Arkansas*.

Overseeing the operations on the Yazoo River was Capt. William F. Lynch, dispatched to Mississippi as the official replacement for Cmdre. Hollins who commanded forces afloat on the Mississippi River. Like Hollins, Lynch was an older man. Born in 1801 and at sea since 1819, he commanded ships in the United States Navy since 1839 and operated extensively in Africa and the Middle East. At the start of the war, he resigned and served in Virginia and North Carolina before being sent to Vicksburg. Lynch planned to use his three ships to protect the Arkansas until it was completed and then lead the small squadron against the growing Union flotilla. For the time being, Lynch kept Cmdr. Pinckney, commander of the naval forces at Fort Pillow, in nominal command of the three wooden gunboats anchored at Liverpool Landing.

The unfinished *Arkansas* was towed away from Memphis after the fall of Island Number Ten. It was brought to Greenwood, Mississippi, which lies some 200 miles up the Yazoo River and empties into the Mississippi a few miles upriver from

---

9 Read, "Reminiscences of the Confederate Navy," 348.

First Lieutenant Isaac N. Brown, CSN.

Naval History and Heritage Command

Vicksburg. The Yazoo River and its tributaries formed the Mississippi Delta, an area of western Mississippi that was rich in soil and featured numerous plantations.

When the *Arkansas* arrived at Greenwood in April, there were no shipbuilding facilities in the town or the surrounding area. It was not until the end of May that work recommenced. On May 29, 1862, Lt. Isaac N. Brown assumed command of the *Arkansas* and he worked with a passion to get the ship ready for battle. Brown previously served in the Mexican and Seminole Wars, as well as the coast survey department. He spent the first year of the war working on constructing gunboats and fortifications on the Mississippi River and its tributaries and was eager to prove himself in command of a ship.

Brown found the *Arkansas* in a sad state: "the vessel was a mere hull, without armor" Brown observed, and "the engines were apart; guns without carriages were lying about the deck; a portion of the railroad iron intended as armor was at the bottom of the river, and the other and far greater part was to be sought for in the interior of the country."[10] The iron intended to armor the ship was in a barge carelessly sunk in the river the month before. Added to this was the ironclad's location. Due to recent rains, the Yazoo River flooded the surrounding area, leaving the ship stranded four miles from dry land.

Brown ordered the ship towed to Yazoo City, where there were proper facilities. Once there, he "issued orders to press all the blacksmiths and mechanics in the country for a hundred miles around." Divers began the process of raising the

---

10 Isaac N. Brown, "The Confederate Gun-Boat 'Arkansas,'" *B&L*, 3:572; "Isaac Brown to Daniel Ruggles," Jun. 7, 1862, *Subject File*, AC, NA.

sunken barge of iron and orders sent to transport cannon and supplies from across the state.[11]

Laborers were housed on nearby steamers. Secretary Stephen Mallory pleaded with President Davis for the release of soldiers with special skills that could assist in construction efforts. Once Davis approved, 200 men from the garrison in Vicksburg were dispatched to augment the workers. Men were divided into two 12-hour shifts so that work progressed around the clock. Fourteen local forges were removed from nearby plantations and brought to Yazoo City so that the blacksmiths could clad the ship in iron as quickly as possible.[12]

To protect the construction workers, Brown ordered a barrier of logs placed across the Yazoo River at Liverpool Landing. Just below the obstructions the *General Earl Van Dorn*, *Livingston*, and *General Polk* were posted. The two guns saved onboard the *General Polk* were again sent ashore and mounted in a small battery guarding the position. Lacking any other cannon, Lynch decided to use the wooden vessels as sacrificial craft with orders "to moor their head down stream, to keep steam up, and be prepared to ram any boats of the enemy that might venture up."[13] Several other gunboats, escaping the debacle at New Orleans, likewise made their way up the Yazoo, taking station above the barrier and serving as transports further up the river. These included the CSS *Saint Philip*, CSS *Ivy*, CSS *Mobile*, and the lightly armed transport *Saint Mary*.

Brown contracted with two men in Jackson, Mississippi to assemble the 10 gun carriages needed to mount his artillery. The iron recovered from the sunken barge was insufficient and Brown requisitioned iron from all across the state of Mississippi to be carted for miles to military forges. After five weeks the work was complete. The 165-foot vessel required a crew of 250 men to man its 10 guns. Officers came from the destroyed naval vessels at New Orleans and Memphis. Several sailors were with the hull since it left Memphis and still more obtained from the gunboat *Mobile*. More crewmen arrived from Gen. M. Jeff Thompson, who volunteered 60 of his Missourians to serve as gunners. The remainder of the crew

11 Read, "Reminiscences of the Confederate Navy," 349; "Payment Acknowledgement for CSS Arkansas," Jun. 2, 1862, *Subject File*, BG, NA.

12 Brown, "The Confederate Gun-Boat 'Arkansas,'" 572; Stephen Mallory to Jefferson Davis, June 11, 1862, *Letters Received by the Confederate Secretary of War, 1861-1865*.

13 Read, "Reminiscences of the Confederate States Navy," 350; Thomas Weldon, "Contract by Thomas Weldon," October 15, 1862. *Thomas Weldon Papers*. (National Archives Microfilm Publication M346, Records Group 109), National Archives Building, Washington DC.

Confederate forces strive to complete the CSS *Arkansas*. *Naval History and Heritage Command*

was made up of Louisiana and Kentucky volunteers from General Van Dorn's garrison at Vicksburg.[14]

On June 25, 1862, Lt. Brown ordered the mechanics and craftsmen ashore. The newly commissioned CSS *Arkansas* then made a trial run from Yazoo City, anchoring at Liverpool Landing just above the log obstructions. On the way, they learned that two Union rams were ascending the Yazoo River on a patrol to locate Confederate ships in the area. Ignoring his orders to ram approaching enemy ships, Cmdr. Pinckney did not let his three wooden gunboats at the obstructions fall into Union hands; by the time the *Arkansas* reached Liverpool Landing, they were already ablaze. Brown sent small boats filled with men to extinguish the flames. They were too late. Instead of being the flagship of a small squadron, the *Arkansas* was now alone. In a rage, Captain Lynch travelled to Vicksburg, leaving Lt. Brown to handle his ship as he saw fit.[15]

14 "Isaac Brown to Daniel Ruggles," Jun. 7, 1862, *Subject File*, AC, NA.

15 Read, "Reminiscences of the Confederate States Navy," 350-351.

Pinckney and his executive officer, Lt. Carter Poindexter, both faced court martial by Lynch. The charge was dereliction of duty. Convening in August 1862 at Jackson, Mississippi, three officers heard testimony about the burning of the ships at Liverpool Landing. The court concluded by September. The three officers exonerated Cmdr. Pinckney, who was reassigned to Savanna, Georgia; Poindexter was found guilty and suspended from duty for six months.[16]

The *Arkansas* remained at Liverpool Landing for several days conducting trials on its engines. Additionally, Brown ordered Lt. Charles Read, formerly of the CSS *McRae*, to survey the log obstructions. Read, who was born and raised in the Mississippi Delta, determined that the obstructions could be easily removed and that there was enough water for the *Arkansas* to safely pass. When it was ready, the ironclad returned to Yazoo City for final adjustments and repairs.

The Run to Vicksburg

The *Arkansas* slipped below the obstructions at Liverpool Landing on July 14. The passage down the Yazoo was not without problems. The first delay occurred when it was discovered that engine steam penetrated the magazine, wetting the ship's supply of gunpowder. The rest of the day was spent drying the powder and sealing the magazine, with Brown nervously expecting to sight Union ships approaching at any moment. The Confederate ironclad anchored at Hayne's Bluff that night, just a few miles from where the Yazoo entered the Mississippi, and prepared for battle.

Brown was ordered by Gen. Earl Van Dorn to leave the Yazoo River and make his way to Vicksburg past the combined Union fleets of Farragut and Davis. Brown instead wished to use the *Arkansas* to defend the Yazoo River as a supply line for Vicksburg and central Mississippi. Van Dorn was adamant, however, and at 3 am on July 15, the *Arkansas* weighed anchor to proceed into the Mississippi. The ironclad grounded on a sandbar soon after getting underway, with the crew spending an hour getting free.

Union ships advanced up the Yazoo just as Brown's armored warship was working off the sandbar. Farragut, who assumed command over the combined Union squadrons, sent the ironclad *Carondelet*, the gunboat *Tyler*, and the ram *Queen of the West* up the Yazoo River to meet the *Arkansas*. Spotting the Union vessels as

16 "Order to Convene Court Martial," Aug. 1, 1862, *Subject File*, NO, NA; "French Forrest to C.B. Poindexter," Sep. 10, 1862, *Subject File*, NO, NA.

his ironclad broke free, Brown decided to ram the *Carondelet* and ordered the engines to full power. Before he could close, the Union ships came about and headed back down the Yazoo toward the Mississippi River to rejoin the Union fleet, firing their stern guns and tempting the *Arkansas* to give chase.

The *Arkansas* returned fire at the *Carondelet*. In the pilothouse, Brown observed, "our shot seemed always to hit his stern and disappear, his missiles, striking our inclined shield, were deflected over my head and lost in air." Brown's luck did not last. One shot struck the pilothouse, wounding Lt. Brown and two Yazoo River pilots. The pilots were taken below, but Brown refused to leave; one of the pilots, as he was being carried away, yelled out to "keep in the middle of the river."[17]

Brown was anxious to finish off the *Carondelet*, ordering the helmsman to close with the enemy ironclad. Commander Henry Walke, commanding the *Carondelet*, steered his ship to shallow water, forcing Brown to stop his ramming attempt for fear of running aground. Instead, he moved the *Arkansas* as close as he dared and ordered his gunners to keep up their fire. The Confederate guns cut away the wheel ropes of the *Carondelet*, which slammed uncontrollably into the riverbank. Additionally, Walke reported "very extensive damages in our hull and machinery."[18] Thirty of the *Carondelet's* sailors were killed and wounded. To halt the bloodshed, Walke ordered his flag lowered in surrender.

Ecstatic at his success, Brown later noted the *Carondelet* "ran ashore with his colors down, giving us no more trouble."[19] With his pilots wounded, Brown refused to stop to collect prisoners, continuing to the Mississippi River and giving chase to the *Tyler* and the *Queen of the West*. After the *Arkansas* moved away, Walke raised his flag and moved to rejoin his squadron, reasoning that no one took possession of his vessel and thus, his ship and crew were not prisoners.

The crew onboard the *Arkansas* did not have time to celebrate their success. The two Federal ships they were chasing made it to the Mississippi River and raised the alarm. The combined Union squadron was not expecting a fight, believing that the three ships sent into the Yazoo could handle one Confederate gunboat. When only two returned in a hasty retreat, Farragut and Davis ordered their men to battle stations. One Union sailor was angry, having been "turned out of a very

17 Brown, "The Confederate Gun-Boat 'Arkansas,'" 574; Read, "Reminiscences of the Confederate Navy," 354.

18 "Report of Commander Henry Walke," *ORN*, 19:41.

19 "Report of Lieutenant Brown," Ibid, 68.

comfortable snooze, much to my disgust, to go into a fight on an empty stomach."[20]

The battle was a tough one for the Confederates. Several shots pierced the ironclad's smokestack, reducing the speed of the *Arkansas* and building heat in the engine room, where temperatures rose to 130 degrees. Lieutenant Henry Stevens, the executive officer, "organized a relief party from the men at the guns, who went down into the fire-room every fifteen minutes, the others coming up or being, in many instances, hauled up, exhausted in that time."[21] Brown's vessel had to run a twelve-mile gauntlet to reach the safety of Vicksburg's land batteries.

At about 8:45 am, the *Arkansas* entered the Mississippi River to face the bulk of the Union fleet. Though anchored and with no steam built up, the Federal warships still presented a dangerous challenge. Lieutenant Charles Read, in command of the *Arkansas's* two stern guns, later wrote that "Yankee tars were soon at their guns, and shot and shell came quick and fast upon our single little ship." Brown described the Union fleet as "a forest of masts and smoke-stacks—ships, rams, iron-clads, and other gun-boats on the left side, and ordinary river steamers and bomb-vessels along the right." A third Confederate sailor was more pessimistic and, after observing the Union fleet through a gun port, yelled out "Holy mother, have mercy on us; we'll never get through there!"[22]

The *Arkansas* steamed on, steering very close to Union gunboats to discourage Union rams from approaching and hitting their own ships. Nonetheless, the ram *Lancaster* made the attempt. Lieutenant George Gift fired one of the *Arkansas* bow guns directly at the ram, which exploded its boiler, killing 18 men and scalding another 10. The remainder of the crew jumped overboard as the Union ram drifted into the riverbank. The *Lancaster* did not sink but was so damaged that it took months of work in repair yards to make it serviceable.

The *Arkansas* got past Davis's ships, but then contended with Farragut's. With enemy ships now both up and downriver, Lt. Brown felt that "the line of fire seemed to grow into a circle constantly closing. The shock of missiles striking our sides was literally continuous, and as we were now surrounded." The gunfire from so many Union ships was having an effect. Lieutenant Gift witnessed a horrifying

---

20 Edward W. Bacon to Skid, July 16, 1862, *Bacon, Edward Woolsey Papers, 1861-1865.*

21 Brown, "The Confederate Gun-Boat 'Arkansas,'" 575.

22 Read, "Reminiscences of the Confederate Navy," 354; Brown, "The Confederate Gun-Boat 'Arkansas,'" 575; George W. Gift, "The Story of the Arkansas," *Southern Historical Society Papers* (1887), 12:115.

CSS *Arkansas* runs past the Union squadrons, July 15, 1862.

Naval History and Heritage Command

scene when "an 11-inch shell broke through immediately above the port, bringing with it a shower of iron and wooden splinters," killing or wounding an entire gun crew.[23] Gift was wounded by the shell when a splinter broke his arm, but he refused to leave his position commanding the forward guns.

The USS *Benton*, Davis's flagship, managed to raise steam and moved downriver to block the *Arkansas* from reaching Vicksburg. Both ships moved to ram the other, but the *Benton* turned away at the last minute, the two ironclads barely missing one another. After passing, Lt. Read gave the *Benton* one last shot from his stern guns.

One of the Union mortar boats, the *Sidney C. Jones*, was aground for several days and unable to move. Learning that the *Arkansas* was approaching, Porter's sailors made preparations to destroy the vessel. As Brown moored the ironclad at Vicksburg, the *Sidney C. Jones* was blown up, adding to the embarrassment of the Union commanders. The *Arkansas* arrived at the docks of Vicksburg without further incident.

---

23 Brown, "The Confederate Gun-Boat 'Arkansas,'" 576; Gift, "The Story of the Arkansas," 117.

The townspeople and Van Dorn's soldiers lined the riverbank in celebration. Generals Earl Van Dorn and John Breckinridge boarded to congratulate Brown on his achievement. After offloading the wounded and the army gunners on loan from Vicksburg's defenses, Brown repositioned the *Arkansas* to a coaling pier to make hasty repairs, refuel, and assess damage. Ten men were killed with another 15 wounded in passing the Union squadrons, which suffered 111 casualties. To make up for the Confederate casualties and replace the army volunteers onboard the ironclad, General Van Dorn ordered more soldiers sent onboard.

Farragut Targets the *Arkansas*

The Union shelling continued throughout the rest of the day. Cmdr. Porter's mortars below Vicksburg opened a sporadic fire at the *Arkansas*, causing no damage but offering no respite for the sailors and soldiers onboard who struggled to complete makeshift repairs amidst the shells. Brown contemplated taking his ship down the river that afternoon to engage Porter's mortars directly, but repairs could not be completed that day.

Embarrassed by the Confederate achievement and worried about his vulnerable mortar craft, *Farragut* planned to make a run past the Vicksburg batteries in an attempt to both destroy the *Arkansas* and reach the mortar boats. "No one will do wrong who lays his vessel alongside of the enemy or tackles with the ram," he declared to his wardroom, emphasizing that "the ram must be destroyed."[24] Flag Officer Davis agreed and provided three of his ironclads to cover Farragut's passage.

It was not until the evening that Farragut's ships built up steam and started to move. By then, the Confederates in Vicksburg "noticed a range light on the opposite bank abreast of us, evidently intended to point out our position" and, expecting an assault, determined to move the *Arkansas*, using the coming darkness and an approaching thunderstorm to mask the shift.[25] As Davis's ships distracted Vicksburg's land batteries, Farragut's warships steamed downriver. When they came abreast of the range light marker, the Union ships fired their broadsides where the *Arkansas* was supposed to be. Undamaged, Brown ordered his guns to return fire and gave orders to get the ironclad underway to engage the Union fleet.

---

24 "General Order of Flag Officer Farragut," *ORN*, 19:8.

25 Read, "Reminiscences of the Confederate States Navy," 355.

When the *Arkansas* opened fire, it gave away its new location and Union gunners redirected their fire. A shell from the USS *Richmond* found its mark, piercing the ironclad's armor, disabling the engines, tearing through the medical supplies, and causing a leak in the hull. With no engines, the ironclad could only respond with its guns. "We could hear our shot crashing through their sides," Brown recalled, "and the groans of their wounded."[26]

Confederate gunners worked furiously "as though the fate of the nation hung on their individual efforts" and they met with success.[27] The USS *Winona* was damaged so heavily that it ran ground to prevent it from sinking. Some 27 Union sailors were killed or wounded among the squadron. The last of Farragut's ships passed, and though damaged, the *Arkansas* remained afloat. Ten more Confederates onboard were killed and wounded and it took days to get the engines serviceable again. July 15 was an exhausting and exhilarating day for the CSS *Arkansas*. The combined Union fleet under Farragut suffered serious damage and was embarrassed by one Confederate ironclad. The USS *Carondelet* was disabled and struck her colors, though she was repaired and rejoined the Union fleet; the USS *Winona* was damaged so heavily that she ran aground to avoid sinking; and the USS *Sidney C. Jones* was blown up to prevent its capture.

Farragut was not finished with the *Arkansas*. He brought forward Porter's mortars to open fire. Lieutenant Charles Read feared a direct hit on the ironclad. To protect against this, "her moorings were changed frequently to impair the enemy's range; but the enterprising Yankees shelled us continually, their shell often exploding a few feet above decks and sending their fragments into the decks."[28]

It took three days for the engines of the *Arkansas* to be repaired. Not wanting a repeat of the July 15 embarrassment, Union commanders kept steam up on all of their ships through the day and night, burning large quantities of coal. Porter's mortars continued their bombardment for a week but failed to score a single hit. The crew of the *Arkansas* was diminished, not by enemy shells, but through sickness and exhaustion. Additionally, many of the army volunteers returned to their commands. By July 22, only 28 enlisted men and a few of the officers remained onboard able to fight. Farragut, who just received word of his promotion to the new rank of rear admiral for his capture of New Orleans, devised another plan to eliminate the lethal armored ship.

---

26 Brown, "The Confederate Gun-Boat 'Arkansas,'" 577.

27 Gift, "The Story of the Arkansas," 164-165.

28 Read, "Reminiscences of the Confederate States Navy," 356.

Farragut convinced Flag Officer Davis to send two of his ships, the ironclad *Essex* and the ram *Queen of the West*, downriver. The *Essex* provided a distraction, engaging the *Arkansas*, while the ram then drove in for a killing blow. Seeing enemy ships approach in the early morning of July 22, the few men onboard the *Arkansas* were roused at 4 am for yet another battle. Lieutenant Brown observed the passion of his crew, writing that his ship was "at anchor and with only enough men to fight two of our guns; but by the zeal of our officers, who mixed in with these men, as part of the guns' crews, we were able to train at the right moment and fire all the guns which could be brought to bear upon our cautiously coming assailants."[29]

The *Essex* and *Queen of the West* ignored Vicksburg's batteries and aimed straight at the *Arkansas*. First came the *Essex* which, as Lt. Read described, "swung alongside of us, when we gave him our port broadside with guns depressed—which apparently disabled him, for he ceased firing and drifted down the river."[30] Before disengaging, the *Essex* fired a broadside into the *Arkansas*. One shell penetrated the armor, killing six men and wounding another six. The *Essex* crashed into the riverbank, where it lay under fire from shore batteries for 10 minutes until its engineers could build steam pressure to move the ship downriver.

The Union ram was approaching, too fast for the *Arkansas* get out of the way. However, it struck at an odd angle and "'butted' us so gently that we hardly felt the shock." The *Queen of the West* then turned upriver to rejoin Davis's squadron above Vicksburg, chased by shots from the *Arkansas*. One sailor in the Union fleet wrote home "we may write down more defeat for our poor Union cause."[31]

This attempt to destroy the *Arkansas* failed, though the ship suffered damage and its crew was reduced by illness, fatigue, and casualties to a mere score. It remained afloat and defiant. General Earl Van Dorn, observing the failure of the *Queen of the West*, sent a telegram to Jefferson Davis that "an attempt was made this morning by two ironclad rams to sink the *Arkansas*. The failure so complete that it was almost ridiculous."[32] Every day that passed gave renewed vigor to Confederates along the Mississippi River as the CSS *Arkansas* and its small crew continued to defy two Union naval squadrons almost single-handedly.

---

29 Brown, "The Confederate Gun-Boat 'Arkansas,'" 577.

30 Read, "Reminiscences of the Confederate Navy," 358.

31 Brown, "The Confederate Gun-Boat 'Arkansas,'" 578; Edward W. Bacon to Father, Jul. 22, 1862, *Bacon, Edward Woolsey Papers, 1861-1865*.

32 "Telegram from Major General Van Dorn to President Davis," ORN, 19:74.

Admiral Farragut was faced with a predicament. His ships were far from their base of supply, his coal was running low, and the water level of the Mississippi river continued falling. After the unsuccessful attempt on July 22, Farragut withdrew his squadron and the 3,000 infantry under Gen. Williams downriver to New Orleans. His ships left on July 25; Flag Officer Davis's squadron withdrew upriver to Memphis six days later. One daring, audacious and bravely led ironclad forced two Union squadrons to retreat and saved Vicksburg.

Counterattack at Baton Rouge

The first Union naval campaign to capture Vicksburg ended in a resounding Confederate success, thanks to the actions of the CSS *Arkansas*. It embarrassed two Union squadrons and helped the Confederacy retain control of several hundred miles of the Mississippi River. It was a testament to what might have been possible defending New Orleans if the CSS *Louisiana* and CSS *Mississippi* were completed in time. But Confederate commanders did not dwell on what might have been. Instead, they were planning a counteroffensive to regain part of the Mississippi River Valley.

Following the retreat of the two Union squadrons from Vicksburg, Gen. Van Dorn planned two offensives, one to the north and the other to the south. Van Dorn moved the bulk of Vicksburg's soldiers into northern Mississippi. From there, he intended to unite with Confederates under Gen. Sterling Price, moving east from Arkansas, and advance to recapture the important railroad junction of Corinth, Mississippi. This might extend Confederate control into western Tennessee, possibly recapture Memphis, and provide support for Confederate advances into eastern Kentucky by the armies of Generals Braxton Bragg and Edmund Kirby Smith.

While Van Dorn was marching north, he detailed Maj. Gen. John C. Breckinridge to head south. Breckinridge was seen by some as the perfect southerner. As a Kentuckian, he gave legitimacy to the Confederate claim of that state. As a former vice president, he gave authority to the Confederate cause. Some considered him the best statesman that the new nation possessed.

Generals Van Dorn and Breckinridge planned a two-part campaign. A small force under Breckinridge left Vicksburg and traveled by rail to Camp Moore, the large training camp in Louisiana that Lovell's forces moved to after their evacuation from New Orleans. Once there, Gen. Daniel Ruggles, commanding a small division of troops, joined that army. The combined force, numbering perhaps as many as 5,000 men, marched to liberate Union held Baton Rouge, the capital of Louisiana.

Breckinridge's combined army was deemed large enough to defeat the small Union garrison at Baton Rouge. Most of the Union's forces in Louisiana were sent back to New Orleans due to supply constraints and less than 3,000 troops garrisoned Baton Rouge. A victory might even enable the Confederates to begin a campaign to recapture New Orleans.[33]

Breckinridge left Vicksburg on July 27, 1862, with perhaps 4,000 men, arriving at Camp Moore the next day. Due to a shortage of railroad cars, "nothing could be transported except the troops, with their arms and ammunition."[34] Without rail support, large amounts of supplies needed to be foraged in Louisiana. Upon arriving at Camp Moore, Breckinridge organized his army, dividing it into two divisions. The first was commanded by Brig. Gen. Charles Clark, a Mexican War veteran who fought at the Battle of Shiloh; it consisted of two brigades under Brig. Gen. Benjamin Helm and Col. Thomas Smith. General Ruggles commanded the second division, with two brigades under Col. A. P. Thompson and Col. Henry W. Allen; the latter was the same man who served as the garrison commander of Ship Island in 1861.

Breckinridge's small army left Camp Moore on July 30, marching south to Baton Rouge. On the way, intelligence reports arrived that there were Union gunboats at the Louisiana capital and Breckinridge determined "not to make the attack unless we could be relieved from the fire of the fleet." He telegraphed Gen. Van Dorn in Vicksburg for assistance from the CSS *Arkansas*. Van Dorn went onboard the ironclad to order it downriver, but there was a problem. Lieutenant Brown took ill and was recovering at Grenada, Mississippi. This left Lt. Henry K. Stevens, the ship's executive officer, in command. Furthermore, the ship's chief engineer was also incapacitated with illness and was ashore. Nonetheless, Van Dorn ordered Stevens to get underway. Stevens sent a note to Brown explaining the situation and Brown quickly replied "with a positive order to remain in Vicksburg" until he could rejoin the ironclad.[35] Brown made his way to Vicksburg as quickly as possible but was too late. The *Arkansas* got underway on the early morning of August 4.

---

33 Log Entry, Sept. 1, 1862, *U.S. Ship Portsmouth Log.*

34 "Report of Major General Breckinridge," *OR*, 15:76.

35 Ibid; Brown, "The Confederate Gun-Boat 'Arkansas,'" 579.

The small Confederate army continued its march and on August 4, 1862 it arrived at the Comite River, 10 miles from Baton Rouge. There, Breckinridge planned for the coming battle. Word reached him that *Arkansas* was steaming downriver and should arrive at Baton Rouge the next day. The Confederate soldiers, however, were in poor health. It was estimated that only about half of the men were capable of bearing arms and Breckinridge estimated that he had only about 2,500 men that could fight. The opposing army in Baton Rouge was of comparable size. Union Brigadier General Thomas Williams fielded only seven regiments of infantry and four batteries of light artillery, none of which was previously involved in a major battle. Conversely, virtually all of Breckinridge's men were veterans of campaigns since early 1862 in Kentucky, Tennessee, and Mississippi.

Breckinridge's force left the Comite River at 11 pm on August 4 and commenced a night march to Baton Rouge with the hope of achieving surprise against Williams's men. The Union commander knew the Confederates were approaching but was unaware of the night march. Leading the Confederates was the 30th Louisiana Regiment, under Lt. Col. Shields, and the First Confederate Light Artillery Battery. They were to scout ahead and locate Union forces before Breckinridge's main body arrived.

The Confederates arrived before dawn on August 5 and organized into a line of battle. Breckinridge formed up east of the city, planning to advance into Baton Rouge and drive the Union forces toward the Mississippi River. With luck, the *Arkansas* might then arrive and sweep away the Union gunboats, leaving the defeated Union soldiers in Baton Rouge cut off and isolated, with no choice but to surrender.

Breckinridge ordered all of his units into a single line facing west. Ruggles's division was on the southern wing of the line while Gen. Clark's men comprised the northern section. At first light, Breckinridge ordered his men forward. Ruggles engaged Union forces first as they marched forward a few hundred yards when his division encountered "a brisk fire from the enemy's skirmishers, strongly posted on our extreme right, in some houses surrounded by trees and picket fences." The Sixth Battery of Massachusetts Light Artillery also opened fire on Ruggles's men. The First Confederate Light Artillery Battery was ordered into the fray, to deal with the Union guns and soon the Confederates "moved forward with great impetuosity, driving the enemy before them."[36] Two Union lines formed up, one behind the other, and Breckinridge's men began pushing back the first line, made up of the 14th Maine, 21st Indiana, and 6th Michigan Regiments, with little effort. The second Union line formed in the town. General Clark's men also advanced, driving back the first line of Union soldiers. It was about 8 am and Breckinridge ordered his men to halt for a moment to reorganize their lines.

General Williams rushed his reserves forward and stabilized a line in the city of Baton Rouge. The Confederates, after reforming, marched ahead piecemeal. Colonel Allen's Louisiana brigade pushed forward, making "as gallant a charge as was ever witnessed."[37] Union artillery and infantry returned fire. One canister round slammed into the Confederate line, striking Col. Allen, "shattering one leg—just above the ankle—and passing through the other."[38] Allen's attack lost momentum without its commander as Col. Gustavus Breaux of the 30th Louisiana Regiment struggled to control the brigade.

As Col. Allen's brigade stalled, Hunt's brigade, being led by one of Breckinridge's staff officers, moved forward. The brigade approached the Union line and exchanged several volleys. Realizing that they could not break the Union line, Gen. Clark ordered them to fall back. As the withdrawal began, Clark was wounded and was taken from the field. Breckinridge then ordered Col. Smith's brigade forward. Smith's men, too, stalled in their attack and Col. Thompson's Kentucky brigade then advanced. The 21st Indiana engaged the Kentuckians in a fierce firefight. Soon, all of the Union regiment's field officers were incapacitated. General Williams arrived on the scene and, seeing the situation, yelled out to the Union regiment: "Boys, your field officers are all gone; I will lead you."[39] Moments later, at around 10 am, Williams fell mortally wounded. Command of Union forces devolved to Col. Thomas Cahill.

Cahill ordered his men to withdraw under the pressure of the renewed Confederate assaults. Breckinridge described this last fight, noting that "the contest at and around this last encampment was bloody, but at the end of it the enemy were completely routed." As the Union forces withdrew closer to the riverbank, their naval support joined in the contest. As Breckinridge began his attacks, a naval party

---

36 "Report of Brigadier General Ruggles," OR, 15:91; "Report of Major General Breckinridge," OR, 15:77.

37 "Report of Colonel Allen," Ibid, 100.

38 Sarah A. Dorsey, Recollections of Henry W. Allen (New Orleans, 1866), 138.

39 "Report of Colonel Cahill," OR, 15:57.

of spotters was sent ashore into the tower of the statehouse. From there, they directed fire from the Union ships anchored at Baton Rouge. As the Union soldiers withdrew close to the riverbank, four gunboats opened fire "with a fine effect, throwing their shells directly in the midst of the enemy, producing great dismay and confusion."[40]

The Confederates halted their advance again and waited for the *Arkansas* to show itself and drive away the Union ships. The Confederate ironclad failed to make an appearance and Breckinridge ordered his men to withdraw out of the town, destroying the Union campsites they overran earlier in the process. By the late afternoon, it was clear that the *Arkansas* was not going to appear and Breckinridge's men began marching back to the Comite River. The battle was bloody for the few thousand men involved, particularly among the leaders on both sides. General Williams was mortally wounded and Gen. Clark wounded, along with Col. Allen and several regimental commanders on both sides. The Union lost nearly 400 of the 2,500-man garrison while Breckinridge counted his losses at about 450. Nearly 20 percent of the soldiers that fought at Baton Rouge were casualties.

Tragedy and Loss of the *Arkansas*

As Breckinridge advanced his men into Baton Rouge, the CSS *Arkansas* underwent an odyssey in its attempt to join the battle. Without the ironclad, the state capital could not be reclaimed. The ironclad left Vicksburg at 2 am on August 4, steaming downriver. Stevens's goal was to arrive at Baton Rouge the next morning and destroy the four Union wooden gunboats there to help Breckinridge trap the Union garrison. The ill Lt. Brown arrived in Jackson, Mississippi just hours after the *Arkansas* weighed anchor. Brown, determined to meet the ironclad before it gave battle, immediately travelled south in an attempt to rendezvous with the ship outside of Baton Rouge.

As the *Arkansas* steamed downriver at about 15 knots, people crowded the riverbank and, as one officer onboard noted, "hailed with exclamations of delight the sight of their country's flag, and the gallant little '*Arkansas*' moving down to

---

40 "Report of Major General Breckinridge," Ibid, 79; "Report of Flag Officer Farragut," *ORN*, 19:116.

chastise the savage foe."[41] The ironclad's good fortune held up to this point, but soon changed.

At 1 am on August 5, the engines suddenly broke down and refused to restart. Lieutenant Charles Read, on watch as officer of the deck, immediately "rounded the vessel to, and let go the anchor," before passing word down to Stevens.[42] They were less than 10 miles from Baton Rouge and sailors were already making the final preparations to join in the morning battle. Lieutenant Stevens immediately came on deck and ordered the engineers to begin repairs. It took hours of continuous work, but at 8 am Stevens was told that the engines were ready; they could hear artillery off in the distance as Breckinridge's attack went forward.

While making the repairs, Stevens dispatched several officers ashore to meet with locals and militia to confirm the strength of the Union naval forces at Baton Rouge. They learned there were three wooden gunboats present, supported by the ironclad *Essex*. Once he received word that his engines were repaired, Stevens ordered the ship to get underway and "in feverish haste our lines were cast off and hauled aboard" and the crew manned battle stations.[43] The wooden gunboats did not concern Stevens very much. Likewise, the *Essex* was built identical to the *Carondelet*, the ironclad that Lt. Brown defeated on the Yazoo in July. Skilled handling of the *Arkansas* should again bring victory.

Unfortunately, the ironclad's "engine again broke down, and the ship drifted ashore, where she was secured." Lieutenant Read described this in more detail, writing that "the starboard engine stopped; the port engine continuing to go ahead at full speed, turned the vessel quickly towards the bank, when, an eddy catching her bow and the swift current sweeping her stern down stream, she was irresistibly shoved ashore."[44] The ship was wedged between several cypress trees. Once again, the engineers were mustered to repair the overworked and malfunctioning engines.

The repairs were again completed after several hours and the ship brought off the riverbank near dark. All afternoon, Lt. Stevens kept a watch downriver, waiting for Union ships to appear. With darkness upon them, Stevens ordered the *Arkansas* upriver for a few miles to a wharf where his ship could moor and re-coal in the night. As the ironclad arrived at the wharf "the unfortunate engine became disabled

---

41 Read, "Reminiscences of the Confederate Navy," 359.

42 Ibid.

43 Gift, "The Story of the Arkansas," 207.

44 "Notes of Acting Master's Mate Wilson," *ORN*, 19:135: Read, "Reminiscences of the Confederate Navy," 360.

Destruction of the CSS *Arkansas*. Naval History and Heritage Command

a third time."[45] After on loading the coal, it took the rest of the night to repair the engines, which needed a new wrist pin to be manufactured on the spot.

The USS *Essex* got underway early in the morning of August 6 and proceeded upriver in search of the *Arkansas*. The two ships spotted one another at 10 am and began to close. The port engine again failed after the ship travelled only a few hundred yards. Again, the *Arkansas* crashed into the riverbank, this time with its bow facing upriver. The *Essex* opened fire on the Confederate ironclad, which could only reply with its two stern guns. Unable to move and with more Union ships approaching, the *Arkansas* was doomed. Stevens ordered his crew to abandon ship. Years later, one of Stevens's officers recalled "the look of anguish he gave me, and the scalding tears running down his cheeks when he announced his determination."[46]

The crew was rushed ashore while officers prepared the ship for destruction, loading the guns, smashing equipment, and preparing combustibles. They then set the ironclad afire. The crew made its way away from the riverbank, encountering civilian refugees from Baton Rouge. One civilian described the Confederate sailors as "they came, dirty, half dressed, some with only their guns, a few with bundles

45 "Notes of Acting Master's Mate Wilson," *ORN*, 19:135.

46 Gift, "The Story of the Arkansas," 210.

and knapsacks on their backs, grimy and tired."[47] The *Arkansas* continued to burn as the crew watched alongside the river. Without the crew onboard, the ship was lighter and drifted downriver, firing its preloaded guns as flames reached each cannon. At last the fire reached the ship's magazine and the *Arkansas* exploded, sinking into the Mississippi.

The campaign for Baton Rouge was another defeat for the Confederacy, made especially bitter by the loss of its last ironclad on the Mississippi River. The campaign, however, did briefly achieve its initial objective. Shortly after the battle, Gen. Benjamin Butler ordered the evacuation of Baton Rouge by Union forces, taking them back to New Orleans. Baton Rouge remained unoccupied by either army for several months. This gave the Confederacy time to prepare adequate fortifications at Port Hudson, which was a strong position to emplace guns.

Fortifying Port Hudson

The *Arkansas'* sailors marched north and made their way to Port Hudson, Louisiana. Elements of Breckinridge's army were also ordered there to fortify the position. Though the battle for Baton Rouge ended in failure, fortifying Port Hudson, several miles upriver from the state capital, solidified Confederate control of the Mississippi between Baton Rouge and Vicksburg, as well as control of the entrance to the Red River.

The *Arkansas* sailors, having no ship and no orders for the moment, helped fortify the town at Port Hudson. Located 20 miles northwest of Baton Rouge, Port Hudson stood atop a bluff overlooking the Mississippi River at a hairpin turn in the river. With Port Hudson in Confederate hands, the Confederacy controlled the 100-mile stretch of the Mississippi River from there to Vicksburg. Both the Red and Atchafalaya Rivers connected to the Mississippi within this region, providing waterways deep into sections of Louisiana. Moreover, these rivers were key supply arteries, particularly for beef, travelling from Texas and western Louisiana to both Vicksburg and Port Hudson where they could be sent further east to support the Confederate war effort.

By the end of August 1862, Brig. Gen. William Beall, a Kentucky native and West Point graduate, was placed in command at Port Hudson. He strengthened his position against river assault and by September, Beall could muster 1,000 men, over half of them artillerists. This garrison prepared positions for defense against Union

---

47 Sarah Morgan Dawson, *A Confederate Girl's Diary* (Boston, 1913), 194.

ships while the sailors from the *Arkansas* manned the five siege cannon and "kept a sharp lookout" for Union gunboats.[48] They did not have long to wait.

The Union gunboat USS *Essex* steamed upriver to blockade the Red River. It grew low on coal and steamed down the Mississippi River to Farragut's lines. It approached Port Hudson on September 7, 1862, intending to pass the fortifications before dawn. At 4:15 am, Cmdr. William Porter, commander of the *Essex*, reported that the Confederates "opened on us with a vigorous fire with heavy siege guns."[49]

The Confederate sailors, seeking retribution against the ship that forced the destruction of their ironclad off Baton Rouge, "pounded away in fine style" into the *Essex*. The Union ironclad was struck 16 times by shells, four of which breached both the iron and wood protection of the vessel. One shell exploded in the dispensary onboard and afterwards "fragments of small field artillery shells were picked up inside the vessel."[50]

After a fight that lasted over an hour, the *Essex* continued downriver to report to Farragut of the Confederate batteries at Port Hudson. The fast and accurate fire by the Confederate sailors, manning just a few guns, convinced the *Essex* that there were more guns there than in reality. Farragut received reports that Port Hudson consisted of batteries mounting as many as 50 cannon. From then on, Union ships were cautious of the Confederate fortification.

Port Hudson continued to grow in strength into 1863. In addition, the Confederates began experimenting with a new weapon, lining the area near Port Hudson with underwater mines, called torpedoes. In January 1863, the USS *Essex* encountered and defused one such torpedo near Port Hudson. Another torpedo was found and disabled near the USS *Mississippi* in February near Baton Rouge. In March 1863, Adm. Farragut steamed his squadron past the Port Hudson batteries, and one of the new torpedoes struck and damaged the USS *Richmond*.[51] Union naval operations on the river in 1863 became much more dangerous.

---

48 Read, "Reminiscences of the Confederate Navy," 361.

49 "Report of Commodore William Porter," *ORN*, 19:182.

50 Read, "Reminiscences of the Confederate Navy," 361; "Report of Commander Caldwell," *ORN*, 19:320.

51 "Report of Commander Caldwell," *ORN*, 19:543-544; "Report of Captain Smith," *ORN*, 19:640-641; "Report of Captain Alden," *ORN*, 19:673.

CHAPTER EIGHT

Shift to the Unconventional

Birth of Torpedo Warfare

AFTER Adm. Farragut and Flag Officer Davis withdrew their squadrons, Maj. Gen. Ulysses Grant prepared for a campaign against Vicksburg through a combination land and river approach. Half of his army marched south through Mississippi while naval transports carried the other half down to Vicksburg, protected by Davis's ironclads. If things turned out according to plan, Vicksburg could be cut off from supplies and then assaulted by both naval and ground forces—solidifying Union control over the entire Mississippi River as well as central Mississippi.

The loss of the ironclad *Arkansas* eliminated Confederate naval power on the Mississippi River. Furthermore, Union leadership on the river changed. David D. Porter, commander of Farragut's mortar boats, received a promotion to rear admiral and succeeded Charles Davis as commander of the Federal northern squadron. His role was to expand control of the river with his ships while supporting Grant's movements. With no warships to counter Porter's forays, the Confederate Navy turned to alternative ways to fight.

While Lt. Isaac Brown was outfitting the *Arkansas* at Yazoo City, he spoke with several men about the idea of using torpedoes to protect the Yazoo River. Brown, now without a command, returned to Yazoo City to see if torpedoes could make an effective weapon. He experimented with such devices previously at Columbus, Kentucky, and with Brown's encouragement, torpedoes soon lined the Yazoo River. These devices were tied along the banks or to floating logs and rested a few

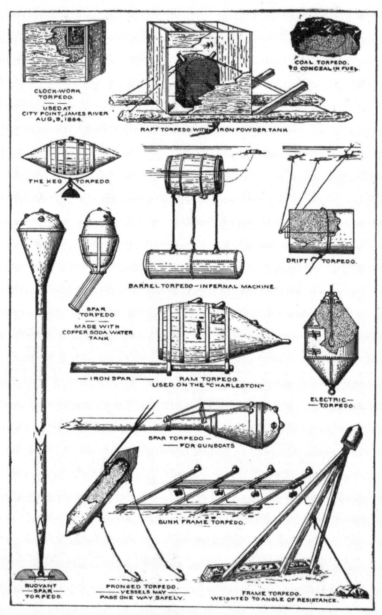

Torpedoes used by the South.

The Confederacy experimented with numerous types of torpedoes.

Our Navy in Time of War

feet under the surface of the river. An electric wire was connected to each, enabling an operator on shore to detonate them when enemy ships approached.

These Confederate underwater explosive devices were soon tested against the enemy. In conjunction with Grant's plan, Gen. William T. Sherman advanced his command from Memphis to Vicksburg. To assist, Adm. Porter moved his ships up the Yazoo River to ensure that it was both safe to land troops along its banks and that no Confederate ships were hidden, lying in wait to attack a Union landing force.

On December 11, 1862, two Union ships, the USS *Signal* and the USS *Marmora*, steamed up the Yazoo River to draw out Confederate riflemen that lined the shores and to scout up the river. There were no Confederate riflemen nearby but Acting Master Zedekiah McDaniel and a small team of torpedo operators were lying in wait. The scouting mission brought the gunboats 20 miles up the Yazoo, where they spotted objects floating in the water, described as "small scows and stationary floats of various kinds along the channel of the river."[1] Before they could investigate, McDaniel's men took action and two explosions ruptured the river, about 50 feet from the Union ships. Union sailors immediately began shelling the riverbanks with both cannon and rifles, failing to hit anything, while the Federal ships hastily withdrew downriver to report the incident to R. Adm. Porter.

The next day, Porter sent a larger contingent of his squadron up the Yazoo River to clear the waterway. The *Signal* and *Marmora* returned, accompanied by the ram *Queen of the West* and the ironclads *Cairo* and *Pittsburgh*. Union sharpshooters on loan from the army augmented gunners and their cannon.

The five ships proceeded up the Yazoo River at 7:30 am on December 12. The Confederate torpedo-men were again lying in wait. The USS *Marmora* was in the advance and proceeded forward around a bend in the river and out of sight of the rest of the Union ships. Her crew sighted a block of wood floating in the water, near where the torpedoes were discovered the day before. Men on the *Marmora* fired a volley at the block of wood, both as a signal to the rest of the Union ships and in an attempt to detonate the device. Lieutenant Commander Thomas Selfridge Jr., son of the Captain Selfridge who previously commanded the USS *Mississippi*, heard this volley and believed the *Marmora* was under attack. He immediately ordered his ship, the USS *Cairo*, to proceed up the river. Arriving on the scene, Selfridge learned that the volley was a signal, not an attack. He then

---

1 "Report of Captain Walke," *ORN*, 23:546; Alexander Miller Diary, Dec. 11, 1862.

lowered a boat to investigate the flotsam, finding that it was "a portion of a torpedo which exploded the day before."[2]

McDaniel's men struck, detonating two torpedoes near the *Cairo*. Her commanding officer remembered "two sudden explosions in quick succession occurred, one close to my port quarter, the other apparently under my port bow—the latter so severe as to raise the guns under it some distance from the deck." Sailors from the *Marmora* "saw her anchor thrown up several feet in the air."[3] The *Cairo* began to settle and Lt. Cmdr. Selfridge ran his ship to the riverbank, where it sank. The rest of the Union flotilla closed with the *Cairo*. The USS *Pittsburgh* covered the rescue by firing at both sides of the riverbank. It took 12 minutes for the *Cairo* to sink. Surprisingly, only a few sailors were wounded in the explosion and all of the ironclad's sailors were rescued.

Though the *Cairo* was lost, the Union sailors continued their expedition, finding and disabling another 10 torpedoes. Confederate pickets opened a sporadic fire on the ships, but retreated after Union sharpshooters and gunners returned fire. The flotilla made its way back to the Mississippi River to report the incident to Adm. Porter, who described the sinking of the *Cairo* as "a great loss to us"[4] For the Confederacy, it was proof that they could still challenge the United States on the western waters, even if it was through unconventional and immobile means. Torpedo operations expanded along the Yazoo River and Red River to deny Union naval forces access to these inland waters. The same defensive apparatus soon appeared in most of the Confederacy's remaining ports and harbors. The torpedo was the young Confederate Navy's most successful weapon, eventually sinking or seriously damaging over 40 Union ships.

The laying of torpedoes in the Yazoo River continued. To counter them, Union ships regularly patrolled the waterway. On Christmas Eve, a force of nine Union vessels, including two ironclads, began such a patrol, sighting several torpedoes alongside the Johnson Plantation. The torpedoes were brought onboard for inspection, but Confederate sharpshooters in a house on the plantation opened fire. The Union ships suppressed the Confederate pickets before steaming back downriver with the captured torpedoes. These provided Union sailors with

---

2 "Report of Lieutenant Commander Selfridge," *ORN*, 23:549.

3 Ibid, 549-550; "Report of Acting Ensign Fentress," Ibid, 548.

4 "Report of Acting Rear Admiral Porter," Ibid, 545.

USS *Cairo*. *Naval History and Heritage Command*

information on the workings of the torpedoes, helping them to devise future countermeasures.[5]

Though the USS *Cairo* was lost, operations against Vicksburg continued. In late-December, Gen. William T. Sherman landed soldiers opposite the town. His troops, backed up by Adm. Porter's squadron, made an attack against Confederate fortifications at Chickasaw Bayou. The defending Confederates were well-entrenched and defeated Sherman's advancing columns. Additionally, Gen. Grant's supply depot at Holly Springs was captured, forcing Grant to abandon his advance from northern Mississippi as well. As January 1863 dawned, Union commanders began planning their next moves to capture Vicksburg.

Collapse of Naval Forces in Arkansas

A few days after Sherman was defeated, another general arrived on the scene, Maj. Gen. John McClernand. McClernand was a political appointee who promised President Abraham Lincoln that he could raise an army and use it to capture

5 Alexander Miller Diary, Dec. 24, 1862.

Vicksburg. Lincoln, desperate for victories and to gain control over the entirety of the Mississippi River, agreed to McClernand's proposal to raise his army.

Within a few months, McClernand raised 10,000 men and was anxious to put them to use. McClernand originally promised Lincoln that he would use them in an attack against Vicksburg, but the general had other ideas. He arrived at Sherman's camp at Milliken's Bend, Louisiana on January 4, 1863, just a few days after Sherman's defeat at Chickasaw Bayou. Being senior to Sherman in date of rank, McClernand assumed command of both Sherman's men and his own, making his makeshift army consist of two corps totaling some 35,000 men.

McClernand's plan was to ascend the Arkansas River and capture Fort Hindman, an important Confederate position that protected supply vessels moving on the Arkansas River and the Mississippi River and a key defense to the approaches to Little Rock, the capital of Arkansas. He reasoned that Vicksburg could not be taken until its supply lines were cut and that Fort Hindman was the first step. The problem with McClernand's plan was that no one knew about it. Lincoln approved an assault on Vicksburg, not an advance into Arkansas. Furthermore, Sherman's corps was part of Grant's army and McClernand simply demanded that Sherman follow his orders. No dispatches were sent to Grant, still on his campaign in central Mississippi, to inform him of the situation. Surprisingly, this lack of coordination and communication did not result in disaster.

Fort Hindman was constructed just on the edge of Arkansas Post, Arkansas. It was situated on a bluff about 25 feet above the Arkansas River. Named after Confederate Gen. Thomas Hindman, it was a key Confederate position in Arkansas, defended by a full quarter of the Confederate soldiers in the state. Brigadier General Thomas J. Churchill, a Kentucky lawyer and Arkansas planter who served in the Mexican War, was in command of the installation.

By the start of 1863, Churchill's force consisted of 5,500 men in three brigades, led by Col. Robert Garland, Col. James Deshler, and Col. John Dunnington. The fort's garrison was a mixture of two regiments of Arkansas infantry, several detachments of Louisiana cavalry, six regiments of Texas infantry and dismounted cavalry, the 2nd Arkansas Field Artillery Battery, and sailors. The fort mounted 13 heavy cannon.

The most diverse unit was Col. Dunnington's brigade, made up of Arkansas infantry, assorted cavalry, and a detachment of 37 sailors from the navy. Dunnington himself held a dual commission as a colonel in the army and as a first lieutenant in the navy. He was captured in the Battle of Saint Charles on the White River in 1862. After being exchanged, he rejoined his ship, the CSS *Pontchartrain*, at Little Rock. From there, he, and elements of his crew, journeyed to Fort Hindman to assist in preparing defenses.

McClernand loaded his men onto Porter's transports and moved into the Arkansas River. They were accompanied by nine warships, both ironclads and wooden gunboats, for protection. The Confederates received word of the approaching Union force and manned a line of entrenchments a little more than a mile north of their main fortification. Unlike at Chickasaw Bayou, Gen. Churchill's men were seriously outnumbered by McClernand's force.

The Union fleet arrived at the mouth of the Arkansas River on January 9, 1863 and began to slowly ascend the 50 miles of the river to Fort Hindman, keeping on the lookout for Confederate torpedoes and warships. McClernand's men offloaded the next day, three miles from the fort, all under the observation of Confederate cavalry pickets. General William T. Sherman was ordered to take his corps on a wide sweep to approach Arkansas Post from the northwest while Gen. George Morgan's corps of McClernand's army approached from the north on a direct route from the landing site.

As Sherman's corps marched to get into the Confederate rear, Porter's gunboats moved up the Arkansas River to bombard Fort Hindman. General Churchill did not want the gunboats to bombard his men in their makeshift trenches and once he received word of Sherman's flanking move, he ordered his garrison back to a second line of breastworks just outside of the fort itself. Morgan's Union corps advanced unopposed through the first line of Confederate trenches while Sherman's men spent most of the day getting lost in the backwoods and swamps surrounding Arkansas Post. Meanwhile, Porter's gunboats exchanged shots with Churchill's heavy guns in Fort Hindman.

During the night, Churchill received a dispatch from his superior, Lt. Gen. Theophilus Holmes in Little Rock, to "hold out till help arrived or until all dead."[6] Believing that a Confederate force was marching to their relief, Churchill positioned his men to resist a Union attack the next day. He placed Col. Deschler's brigade of dismounted Texas cavalry on the left of his line. Colonel Garland's brigade held the right flank of the entrenchments and ended on the Arkansas River. Colonel Dunnington's mixed brigade of Arkansas troops and sailors manned Fort Hindman's heavy cannon to support the line. Unknown to Churchill, there was no relief force coming.

The Union gunboats continued their bombardment on January 11. Their gunfire proved increasingly effective, and all but one small cannon was disabled in the Southern works. Meanwhile, Sherman's corps advanced against the

6 "Report of Brigadier General Churchill," *OR*, 17, Part 1:781.

Confederate left. Colonel Deshler's brigade tried to meet them, but its flank was exposed. Sherman's men moved to outflank the position and Deshler "was forced to weaken my line by detaching two companies from each regiment" to lengthen his position to meet the Union advance.[7]

Sherman's first division made an advance against the 10th Texas Infantry and the 15th Texas Dismounted Cavalry, which "did not fire upon this column with small-arms until its head was within 80 to 100 yards from our line."[8] The Union charges on the Confederate left were repulsed with Sherman losing over 400 men. General Morgan however, had more luck with his attack on the Confederate right.

Morgan advanced Gen. Andrew Smith's division against Col. Garland's brigade. As the Union forces approached the Confederate position, "the front line was hotly engaged for some minutes, driving the enemy before us." The Confederate right flank collapsed and retreated into Fort Hindman. As McClernand prepared to assault the main fortification, white flags began to appear all across the line. Fort Hindman surrendered and soon the rest of the Confederate position gave up as well. General McClernand's army suffered 1,061 casualties in its attacks. What they captured was substantial. McClernand sent a note to Gen. Grant annotating his spoils of war as "5,000 prisoners, 17 pieces of cannon, large and small; 10 gun carriages and 11 limbers, 3,000 stand of small-arms."[9]

The loss of Fort Hindman was another disaster for the Confederacy. The 5,000 men captured were fully one third of all of the Confederate soldiers in Arkansas. The CSS *Pontchartrain*, now without a full crew, made its way to Little Rock where it sat idle. Efforts were made to overhaul the ship and reform a crew, with advertisements calling for local carpenters and mechanics to assist. Manpower shortages were so prevalent that requests went out for local plantation owners to supply 50 slaves to augment the limited crew. Attempts to outfit and man the *Pontchartrain* continued until October 1863 when the vessel was burned to prevent its capture when Little Rock fell to Union forces.[10]

McClernand's army gathered its prisoners and made its way back to Milliken's Bend, Louisiana, following orders from Gen. Grant to prepare to resume the campaign against Vicksburg. By the end of January, Grant arrived at Milliken's

---

7 "Report of Colonel Deshler," Ibid, 792; "Report of Brigadier General Churchill," Ibid, 781.

8 "Report of Colonel Deshler," Ibid, 793.

9 "Report of Brigadier General Smith," Ibid, 726; "Report of Major General McClernand," Ibid, 708.

10 "Advertising Receipt for CSS Pontchartrain," August 8, 1863, *Subject File*, AR, NA.

Bend and assumed personal command of the forces there, superseding McClernand.

Southern Success on the Red River

With Fort Hindman secured, the Arkansas River was closed to the Confederacy. Combined with Union control of the mouth of the Yazoo River, only the Red River remained under Confederate control among the major tributaries of the Mississippi River. Located upriver from Port Hudson, the Red River carried supplies from Texas and western Louisiana to Vicksburg where they were offloaded and sent to the rest of the Confederacy. Blockading the Red River could stop Confederate transports from moving these much-needed supplies to feed Confederate armies further east.

The Red River lay deep in the Confederate held portion of the Mississippi River between Port Hudson and Vicksburg. Any Union effort to blockade the Red River forced gunboats to pass these strongholds. Furthermore, Federal supplies must run past the Confederate fortifications to keep the gunboats on station. Although risky, Adm. David Porter thought it worthwhile to make an attempt. He turned to Col. Charles R. Ellet, son of Col. Charles Ellet, Jr., who organized the United States Ram Fleet, now commanding the ram *Queen of the West*. Porter directed Ellet to take his ram in a run past the Vicksburg batteries. As the ship passed, it was supposed to ram and sink the *City of Vicksburg*, a transport then docked at Vicksburg known for transferring men and supplies from Louisiana to Mississippi. After ramming the *City of Vicksburg*, the *Queen of the West* would then proceed to the mouth of the Red River and set up a guard. Other ships would join Ellet soon afterward, solidifying the blockade.

Ellet got the *Queen of the West* underway before dawn on February 2, 1863, and steamed downriver. Vicksburg's gunners quickly spotted the single ship and opened fire. The shore batteries hit the ram three times but failed to cause significant damage. Ellet targeted the *City of Vicksburg*, which was moored at the same spot as the *Arkansas* the previous fall. Just as then, the Union ram did not cause much damage because a "very strong and rapid" current twisted *Queen of the West*, diminishing the force of the blow."[11]

Ellet was prepared for such a contingency and ordered a cannon filled with incendiary shot to rake the transport. The gun fired just as the *Queen of the West*

---

11 "Report of Colonel Ellet," *ORN*, 24:219.

rammed, setting the Confederate transport on fire. The Union ram was also in flames as several bales of cotton used as protection caught fire. Confederate gunners hit Ellet's ram another twelve times before she continued downriver out of range. The *City of Vicksburg* sustained serious damage and could no longer serve as a transport. Instead, it remained moored at Vicksburg, still afloat but no longer serving a purpose. The *Queen of the West* then continued downriver to set up its blockade of the Red River.[12]

Once on station, Ellet's ram immediately produced results. Throughout the next day, February 3, the *Queen of the West* captured three Confederate transports, the *A. W. Baker*, *Moro*, and *Berwick Bay*. The *Moro* was empty of cargo, having just dropped off supplies at Port Hudson, and was returning to the Red River to pick up more. The other two were full of supplies moving down the Red River destined for Vicksburg, including over 70 tons of pork, salt, molasses, sugar, flour, and 500 hogs.[13]

On February 14, the Confederate transport *Era Number 5* was captured on the Red River filled with 4,500 bushels of corn. After interrogating its captain, Col. Ellet determined that there were several more transports about 30 miles further up the Red River and he moved to intercept. Before Ellet located the transports, he encountered a battery of four Confederate 32-pounder guns set ashore in a position known locally as Fort Taylor—later to be renamed Fort DeRussy. It was about 5 pm when men in the fort's garrison opened fire on the *Queen of the West*.

Ellet ordered a withdrawal, but his ship ran aground. Efforts to get the ship refloated were soon dismissed as Ellet heard "an explosion below and a rush of steam around the boat told me that the steam pipe had been shot in two."[14] Ellet ordered his men to abandon the ship. He left without burning the ram because 13 wounded, who could not be moved, were left behind. Confederate soldiers boarded the ram and captured the wounded.

Ellet and his men made their way down the Red River, where they boarded the captured *Era Number 5*. From there, they left the Red River and proceeded up the Mississippi to reach Porter's squadron. In the early morning of February 13, the USS *Indianola* ran past the Vicksburg batteries. The ironclad carried with it two barges filled with coal meant to supply the *Queen of the West* and to assist in the blockade of the Red River. After passing Vicksburg, the *Indianola* met with Ellet's

---

12 Alexander Miller Diary, Feb. 2, 1863.

13 "Report of Colonel Ellet," *ORN*, 24:224.

14 Ibid, 384.

men onboard the *Era Number 5*. It was determined that the blockade of the Red River must continue and the *Indianola* moved upriver, believing that its iron armor protected it from Confederate cannon.

The Confederates towed the *Queen of the West* to Alexandria, Louisiana, for repairs. The steam valve was fixed and an improvised crew of soldiers boarded the ram. Meanwhile, the *W. H. Webb*, a speedy transport that evacuated from New Orleans before Farragut seized the city, steamed down the Red River in search of the *Era Number 5* and Ellet's men that escaped. The *Webb* was under the command of Lt. Col. William S. Lovell, the brother of Gen. Mansfield Lovell and U.S. Naval Academy graduate who organized and outfitted both the River Defense Fleet and Louisiana State Navy. Lt. Col. Lovell was on temporary assignment in Louisiana from the staff of John Pemberton, commander at Vicksburg. He prepared his vessel for active service as a ram, drafting local smiths, carpenters, and slaves to outfit his vessel. He further impressed a detachment of Louisiana militia to man the ship. His past experiences and expertise soon provided great fortune for the Confederates on the Red River.

As the *Queen of the West* engaged Fort Taylor on the evening of February 14, Lt. Col. Lovell led the *Webb* from Alexandria to the fort's assistance. Upon arriving at the fort, Lovell discovered that the Union ram was disabled and abandoned. Ironically, Lt. Col. Lovell captured the *Queen of the West*, the very ship that rammed and sank the *Colonel Lovell* of the River Defense Fleet at Memphis, named in his honor. He immediately set off in search of the *Era Number 5*, capturing several stragglers from Ellet's ram and moved into the Mississippi River that night. One of the prisoners informed Lovell that the *Indianola* was expected to arrive to continue the blockade of the Red River.

The next morning, in a heavy fog, the *Webb* sighted smokestacks. Cautiously making an approach, the *Webb* was fired upon by the USS *Indianola*. The ironclad successfully ran past the Vicksburg batteries and took on Ellet's survivors from the *Era Number 5*. Lieutenant Colonel Lovell tried to return fire, but his supply of friction primers was faulty and he ordered a retreat, steaming upriver through the fog to give warning to Fort Taylor of the Union ship.[15]

The USS *Indianola* returned to the mouth of the Red River to re-assume the blockade against Confederate transports. Word reached the vessel's commander, Lt. Cmdr. George Brown, that Confederates were preparing to attack. Brown, cut off from support and supply due to Vicksburg's batteries, determined to steam

---

15 "Report of Lieutenant Colonel Lovell," Ibid, 399.

back up the Mississippi River past the batteries again and establish communications with Adm. Porter.

Brown's intelligence proved accurate. Besides the *Webb* at Fort Taylor, the *Queen of the West* was repaired with the steamer *Grand Era* serving as a tender. The two vessels, both outfitted as rams and armed with a few light guns each, were readied for action. Maj. Gen. Richard Taylor, in command of western Louisiana, ordered them to steam down the Red River and attack the USS *Indianola*. Furthermore, the *Dr. Beatty*, a river transport sent from Port Hudson, was loaded with 250 soldiers for use in boarding enemy ships. Volunteers from the garrison at Fort Taylor joined as well, consisting of a mixed battalion of Texas sharpshooters, the 3rd Maryland Artillery Battery, the Crescent Artillery Battery, and the 21st Tennessee Infantry Regiment. There were 75 volunteers on the *Queen of the West* and another 60 on the *Webb*, plus those from Port Hudson on the *Dr. Beatty* and the *Grand Era*. After a day of test firing the cannon onboard each ship, the improvised four-vessel flotilla left Fort Taylor and proceeded into the Mississippi River, on the hunt for the Union ironclad.[16]

The *Indianola* left the Red River two days before and moved north to link up with Porter. The Confederate ships raced upriver to catch the Union ironclad before it could reach the safety of the Porter's fleet. Fortunately for the Confederates, the *Queen of the West* and the *Webb* were both swift vessels and quickly closed the gap, steaming at twice the speed of the *Indianola*, which had a barge tied on either side full of coal.

Natchez, Mississippi, was back in Confederate hands after its brief occupation in mid-1862. Stopping for coal there on February 23, which was provided free of charge by the locals, the Confederate flotilla learned that they were just 24 hours behind the Union gunboat. An odd scene occurred here when four escaped slaves waved down the *Dr. Beatty*. They boarded the vessel from a small boat and upon arriving on deck they "set up a shout and Hurrah for Marse Linkum [sic]."[17] Their happiness soon turned to anguish once they realized they boarded a ship flying the Confederate flag. They were immediately brought ashore under guard for return to their masters. The white population of Natchez lined the riverbank, waving handkerchiefs as a welcome to the makeshift Confederate flotilla.

16 Linn Tanner, "The Capture of the Indianola," *Miscellaneous Papers Related to the Confederacy*; Bartlett, *Military Records*, 46-47.

17 Linn Tanner, "The Capture of the Indianola," *Miscellaneous Papers Related to the Confederacy*; Bartlett, *Military Records*, 48.

The chase continued into February 24. The confident Confederates slowed their pursuit to ensure that they overtook the Union ironclad that night instead of during the day. At 9 pm, it was spotted ahead. Major J.L. Brent, in command of the *Queen of the West*, described the evening, writing, "the moon was partially obscured by a veil of white clouds, and gave and permitted just sufficient light for us to see where to strike with our rams, and just sufficient obscurity to render uncertain the aim of the formidable artillery of the enemy." The *Queen of the West* was in front of the Confederate formation with the *Webb* about 500 yards behind.

The steamers *Grand Era* and *Dr. Beatty* were two miles further downriver, steaming to catch up and join in the action. The *Dr. Beatty* was an old cattle transport that was used primarily because it was felt that the vessel was of no use as a river transport for the military and thus expendable. To prepare it for the coming boarding attempt, "the Pilot house was cut away, and the rudder attachments were placed on cabin deck and cotton bales piled in front and on every side" to afford protection; furthermore, the men loaded onboard "stowed themselves like rats where ever they found space enough to stretch their limbs."[18]

The Confederate rams got to within 150 yards of the *Indianola* before they opened fire. Lieutenant Commander Brown immediately turned the *Indianola* and used the coal barge lashed to his port side as a shield against ramming. The *Queen of the West* crashed "clear through the barge, and was not arrested until it shattered some of his timbers amidships and deeply indenting the iron plating of his hull." The two vessels became stuck for several minutes, unable to break free. Sharpshooters from the *Queen of the West* swept the Union decks while Sgt. Edward Langley fired the vessel's 30-pounder Parrot Rifle at the *Indianola* to little effect. Soon afterwards, the *Webb*, while under the fire of two of the ironclad's guns, also rammed the *Indianola*, but failed to cause any significant damage. A coal barge broke free and began drifting downriver in a sinking condition. On the barge was one recently escaped slave who was heard crying out in anguish. Soldiers onboard the *Dr. Beatty* heard the noise and fired at the barge, killing the frightened runaway slave before letting the barge sink.[19]

The darkness of the night caused confusion on both sides. The Union ironclad broke free and moved upstream before turning back down to engage the two

---

18 "Report of Major Brent," *ORN*, 24:403; Linn Tanner, "The Capture of the Indianola," *Miscellaneous Papers Related to the Confederacy*.

19 "Report of Major Brent," *ORN*, 24:403; Linn Tanner, "The Capture of the Indianola," *Miscellaneous Papers Related to the Confederacy*; Bartlett, *Military Records*, 49-50.

Confederate ships. Major Brent moved the *Queen of the West* to ram again, but the two vessels struck nearly bow on, again causing little damage. The *Indianola's* gunners fired point-blank at the Confederate ram, one shell disabling a gun and wounding six men while a second round knocked several cotton bales overboard that were being utilized for protection, causing the *Queen of the West* to list considerably. The *Grand Era* and *Dr. Beatty* looked on from a distance, waiting to be called in to board.[20]

The *Webb* rammed the *Indianola* once again. This time, it was to good effect as "the sharp bow of the *Webb* penetrated as if it were going to pass entirely through the ship." This final ramming "crushed in the starboard wheel, disabled the starboard rudder, and started a number of leaks abaft the shaft" of the Union ironclad. Lieutenant Commander Brown, despite damage to his ship, continued to fight on. The *Webb* backed off and slammed again into the *Indianola*, this time "so that the water poured in in large volumes." The *Dr. Beatty* advanced to close and board the *Indianola* at this time, but there were problems connecting grappling hooks. The *Dr. Beatty* then moved to reposition itself, but before grappling hooks could be thrown again, the boarding was called off because the ironclad began to sink.[21]

Lieutenant Commander Brown steered the *Indianola* to the riverbank and beached the bow of the vessel to prevent it from sinking before he could get his crew off. Additionally, he struck his flag so that his men could escape without the Confederate ships firing on them. One man was killed onboard the *Indianola* in the fighting with another wounded. Seven men were reported as missing after the battle and likely drowned as the ship sank. The Confederates suffered two men killed and five wounded on the two rams. As Brown evacuated the *Indianola*, the *Grand Era* arrived and moved to board it. Before doing it, however, they received word that the Union ship surrendered. Lieutenant Colonel Frederick Brand, in command of the *Grand Era* and its load of boarders, took on survivors and accepted the surrender of Lt. Cmdr. Brown and his remaining crew.

The Confederate ships landed the prisoners on the Mississippi shore and turned them over to members of the Vicksburg garrison. Believing that the *Indianola* could be salvaged, they took on mechanics from Vicksburg and brought them, via the government-owned side-wheel steamer *Paul Jones*, to the wreck to

20 Bartlett, *Military Records*, 50.

21 "Report of Major Brent," *ORN*, 24:403; "Report of Lieutenant Commander Brown," Ibid, 381; Linn Tanner, "The Capture of the Indianola," *Miscellaneous Papers Related to the Confederacy*.

Destruction of the Indianola. *Naval History and Heritage Command*

begin work. After a few days, they made progress on refloating the sunken ironclad. The *Dr. Beatty*, which remained in the area, impressed 30 local slaves as well to assist in the work. The remaining Confederate ships returned to Alexandria to refit and make needed repairs.[22]

Admiral Porter was incensed at the loss of the *Queen of the West* and *Indianola*, but thanks to other operations beginning along the Tallahatchie River and Yazoo Pass, and the need to guard Ulysses Grant's army near Milliken's Bend as it tried digging a canal around the Confederate fortifications, he did not have any other ships available to send past the Vicksburg batteries to halt the Confederate efforts at raising the sunken ship. Instead, he turned to subterfuge. Taking a large barge, he disguised it to look like a powerful Union ironclad, complete with fake guns and a large American flag at its stern. He released the barge to float past the Vicksburg batteries in the night. Word reached the salvaging crew that an enemy ironclad was approaching. The *Indianola* was nearly completely raised by this point but was unable to move. Rather than let it be recaptured, the *Indianola* was put to the torch.

The first Federal attempt to blockade the Red River ended in humiliation.

22 Ibid.

CHAPTER NINE

River Operations in
Southern Louisiana

The Bayou Lafourche Campaign and the *Cotton*

FOLLOWING

the Battle of Baton Rouge, Maj. Gen. Benjamin Butler withdrew all of his soldiers back to New Orleans to ensure they were well supplied and to plan his next campaign in Louisiana. As summer shifted to fall, Butler developed a plan to consolidate Union control in southeastern Louisiana by marching soldiers west from New Orleans to capture Donaldsonville and Thibodaux. From there he would advance on Brashear City, where the New Orleans & Opelousas Railroad ended on the Atchafalaya River, a small distributary of the Mississippi River that fed into the Red River, Gulf of Mexico, and several bayous and swamps in the surrounding area.[1] Butler correctly reasoned that taking Brashear City, the largest port in Louisiana besides New Orleans, was tantamount to controlling southern Louisiana and for creating a staging point to advance into the central portion of the state.

Butler moved in two columns. One brigade under Brig. Gen. Godfrey Weitzel advanced up the Mississippi River to Donaldsonville and sought out Confederate forces while a second column of two regiments moved directly toward Thibodaux

---

1 A distributary is a waterway that flows out of a river where a tributary is a body of water feeding into a river. The Atchafalaya River is a distributary as it flows from the Mississippi River into the Gulf of Mexico.

and Brashear City. Once there, supplies could be forwarded to Weitzel's men – and cut off supplies from the area to the Confederate fortifications at Port Hudson. Admiral David Farragut supported the mission, providing several small gunboats to achieve control of the Atchafalaya River.

Weitzel's men loaded onto transports and left New Orleans on October 24, 1862, traveling toward Donaldsonville. Simultaneously, a makeshift Union flotilla entered the Atchafalaya River from the Gulf of Mexico. Farragut detached crews to man four gunboats converted from captured Confederate steamers. Lieutenant Commander Thomas M. Buchannan led the four-ship detachment, consisting of the USS *Diana*, USS *Kinsman*, USS *Estrella*, and USS *Calhoun*.

Weitzel's column made good time and landed a few miles outside of Donaldsonville the next day. By midmorning, his 4,000 men occupied the town and established a defensive perimeter. From Donaldsonville, they marched directly to Thibodaux along Bayou Lafourche, a shallow distributary of the Mississippi River. Major General Richard Taylor, in command of Confederate forces west of the Mississippi River, had few men to resist Butler's incursion after most Confederate soldiers were sent north to Port Hudson and Vicksburg.

Brigadier General Jeanne Jacques Alfred Alexandre Mouton was the local field commander in the Lafourche region. Mouton, the son of former Louisiana Governor Alexandre Mouton, was a graduate of West Point, and engineer for the New Orleans & Opelousas Railroad. When the war started, he raised his own company and rose to the rank of colonel, was wounded at Shiloh, and returned to help organize defenses in Louisiana. Mouton ordered his few men, amounting to perhaps 1,500 total, to an improvised line defending Bayou Lafourche.

Mouton positioned his men at the Winn Plantation, two miles above Labadieville, midway between Donaldsonville and Thibodaux. As he advanced south, Weitzel divided his Union brigade with one regiment on the western bank and his remaining three on the eastern bank supported by artillery. To ensure he was not outflanked, Mouton also divided his force. Weitzel met Mouton outside Labadieville early on October 27 and deployed to face Mouton's smaller force.

The Union soldiers on the eastern bank of Bayou Lafourche advanced. Mouton's skirmishers opened fire and "though much inferior in numbers, resisted their onward march and effectually succeeded in checking them."[2] Weitzel knew there were Confederates on both sides of the bayou and he did not want to fall into

2 "Report of Brigadier General Mouton," *OR*, 15:177; William G. Vincent, "Reminiscence by Commander of Second Louisiana Cavalry of Teche Campaign in Louisiana, 1862," *Miscellaneous Papers Related to the Confederacy*.

a trap. Instead, he ordered his men on the eastern bank to fall back and act on the defensive; the Union attack occurred on the western bank of the bayou.

The Union forces advanced on the western bank where the Confederates were positioned "in a ditch on the lower side of a plantation road in the edge of woods at Georgia Landing," and opened fire.[3] They pressed the attack and as the Confederate line began to falter, Mouton ordered his men to retreat toward Labadieville. Weitzel's men advanced into the woods that were behind the Confederate line and captured 166 prisoners. The Louisianans suffered another 33 casualties as compared to 97 in Weitzel's brigade. Though the skirmish at Georgia Landing was small, it was the first time, for the most part, that either force saw serious combat.

Mouton withdrew his men to Thibodaux, where he learned that Weitzel's brigade was not the only Federal force moving against him. Two more Union regiments marched directly to Thibodaux from New Orleans through thick swamps and forests. Besides this, the Union squadron moving up the Atchafalaya River approached Brashear City from the Gulf of Mexico. With the army coming from two directions and the navy moving in his rear, Mouton evacuated Thibodaux and marched his men to Brashear City to regroup and resupply. During the retreat, most of his militia melted away, returning to their plantations and homes in the surrounding area. Upon reaching Brashear City, Mouton spoke with Gen. Taylor and the two agreed to retreat from that town before they were cut off by the Union gunboats.

Taylor and Mouton rallied west of Pattersonville, Louisiana, where soldiers and teams of slaves began erecting fortifications along Bayou Teche. They chose the Bisland Plantation as their site, 18 miles by road west of Brashear City. It was a well-sited position with only 1,000 yards of dry land on either side of the bayou before swampland rose. On the southern bank behind the breastworks they also constructed an earth fortification named Fort Bisland.

Also present at Fort Bisland was the *J. A. Cotton*, an armed steamer and former transport that escaped from New Orleans when that city fell to Farragut. It made its way up the Mississippi River and down the Atchafalaya until reaching Berwick Bay. Her captain, a civilian named E.W. Fuller, earlier commanded the privateer *Music* operating at New Orleans. He now suggested that his vessel be armed and partially protected with railroad iron taken from the New Orleans & Opelousas Railroad.

---

3 "Report of Brigadier General Weitzel," *OR*, 15:169.

General Taylor had a high opinion of Fuller, writing that he was "a western steamboat man, and one of the bravest of a bold, daring class."[4]

Over the summer and fall of 1862, the small steamer was loaded with railroad iron and cotton bales for protection and three small cannon were installed. The Saint Martin's Independent Louisiana Ranger Company, specifically recruited to crew and operate the privateer *Music*, was transferred to man the guns. Though it was not commissioned into the navy, naval officer Lieutenant Henry Stevens agreed to serve as Captain Fuller's executive officer on the *J. A. Cotton*.[5] Stevens, who briefly commanded the CSS *Arkansas*, was detailed to Brashear City after his ironclad's destruction to train the crew of this makeshift iron-cotton-clad.

Accompanying the *Cotton* was the *Hart*, another transport towing a barge of sugar, the *A. B. Segar*, a third transport commanded by Acting Master I. C. Coons, and *Launch Number One*. As Brashear City was evacuated, these ships retreated with Mouton's men. The steam launch was ordered into Grand Lake where it could avoid Union ships by staying in shallow water near Island Bend. The *A. B. Segar*, which at one time mounted two light artillery pieces in an attempt to convert it to a gunboat, turned up the Atchafalaya River where it was deserted with the claim that Coons "abandoned his men and proceeded as fast as possible to Saint Martinsville." As the other ships escaped, Fuller exchanged a few shots with the Union ships, scoring a hit against the USS *Kinsman* in Berwick Bay. The *Cotton* then turned around and back up into Bayou Teche "keeping our teeth towards the enemy," it being too narrow of a waterway for the vessel to turn around.[6]

The *Hart*, commanded by army Lt. E. Montague, steamed up Bayou Teche to the town of New Iberia. Built in 1860 in Kentucky, the ship escaped from New Orleans, making its way to Brashear City alongside the *Cotton*. Upon its arrival at New Iberia, the vessel was officially taken into the Confederate Navy with the goal of converting it into an ironclad gunboat. Navy Lt. Joshua Humphreys, a Virginian, was entrusted to oversee the conversion and assumed command from Lt. Montague. New Iberia was a good city to oversee a conversion. It had easy access

---

4 Richard Taylor, *Destruction and Reconstruction: Personal Experiences of the Late War* (New York, 1879), 119; Sources conflict over Fuller's first name, with some listing it as Edward and others listing it as Emelius.

5 "Report of Captain Fuller," *ORN*, 19:337.

6 Ibid, 335.

to Bayou Teche and a Confederate iron foundry that manufactured shells, which was hoped could convert to producing iron plate.[7] At some point, the vessel was referred to as the CSS *Stevens*, after Lt. Henry K. Stevens, though most records refer to the vessel's original name. The design included four cannon, most likely the standard naval 32-pounders such as were on the *Cotton*. Several sources claim that at least three inches of railway iron plate were installed. Blacksmiths were taken from Taylor's command and sent to New Iberia to help with the conversion process. The first task was finding the best location for the transformation to take place and in December 1862 the *Hart* was brought down the bayou about three miles below New Iberia to the Oliver Plantation.[8]

The day after evacuating Brashear City, the *Cotton* received orders to Cornay's Bridge, a small bridge in front of the Confederate lines at Fort Bisland. At the bridge, two small ships were sunk to serve as an obstruction. Mouton's brigade continued building trenches and fortifications to extend the defenses of the fort. Meanwhile, two field artillery batteries, one on each side of the bayou, positioned themselves to give fire support to the *Cotton*.

Lieutenant Commander Buchannan, in command of the Union naval forces cooperating with Gen. Weitzel, did not wait long to pursue the *Cotton*. He took his four ships up Bayou Teche on November 3, steaming single file due to the narrow width of the waterway. Captain Fuller remembered that the Union ships "came up in full confidence of overpowering numbers."[9] The Union ships deployed 27 guns where the *Cotton* had only two old 32-pounders and a single 9-pounder rifle, supported by the 10 lighter field pieces ashore. As Lt. Cmdr. Buchannan's ships approached, Fuller ordered his men to open fire.

The battle was one of the most lopsided naval engagements of the war. First came the USS *Calhoun*, Buchannan's flagship and the former Confederate privateer that was captured in early 1862. It opened fire on the *Cotton* with its forward Parrot gun. Within 15 minutes, the gun broke free of its carriage and the *Calhoun* made fast to the bank of Bayou Teche to allow the other Union ships to bypass it while her sailors worked to repair the carriage. Next in line was the USS *Estrella*. The *Cotton's* gunners, along with the shore batteries, focused their fire on the second ship and

---

7 *New Orleans Ship Register*, 5:74; "New York, April 26," *The Maysville* [KY] *Dollar Weekly Bulletin*, Apr. 30, 1863.

8 Booth, *Military Records*, 3:535; "Daily Memorandum for Adjutant General's Office," *OR*, 26:380.

9 "Report of E.W. Fuller," *ORN*, 19:335-336.

were quickly rewarded. Lieutenant Commander Buchannan observed that "the second or third shot struck the *Estrella* on her port rail," killing two gunners and cutting away the vessel's wheel ropes.[10] Like the *Calhoun*, the *Estrella* then ran into the bank of Bayou Teche to allow the remaining two Union ships to press on.

The USS *Diana* was next to engage the Confederates. She, too, soon had her bow gun's carriage fouled and stopped to make repairs. The *Cotton's* gunners then focused their fire on the last of the Union ships, the USS *Kinsman*. The *Kinsman*, however, did not give up so easily. It continued up the bayou as far as the obstructions. From there, the *Kinsman* engaged and drove off the Confederate shore batteries, leaving the *Cotton* on her own. The two ships then exchanged fire at 1,000 yards. Captain Fuller recorded the efforts of the Union ship, writing "the shot and shell literally rained on and about our boat." As the *Kinsman* approached the obstructions, the *Cotton's* gunners "gave her a plunging shot from each of her guns, which all struck near the water on the starboard quarter." This plunging fire proved devastating as the *Kinsman* "received 54 shots through his hull and upper works and had three through his flag" in addition to one shot penetrating the shell room and nearly igniting the magazine.[11]

The *Kinsman* retreated back down Bayou Teche. Lieutenant Commander Buchannan then brought the *Calhoun* back into the fight, presenting his broadside to the Confederates. Fuller ordered his gunners to retarget but was told that they ran out of powder bags to load into his cannon. Undeterred, Fuller ordered powder bags improvised "by cutting off the legs from the pantaloons of some of our men."[12] The *Cotton* then withdrew with its guns firing.

As the *Cotton* withdrew, Buchannan ordered his ships to attempt to break through the obstructions. It was to no avail, as the sunken ships could not be moved. When darkness approached, he ordered the squadron back to Brashear City to resupply. The Confederates lost two men killed and another two wounded through the entire day. No Union shots caused any serious damage to their ship. On the other hand, the Union squadron was handily discomfited. The *Calhoun* was struck eight times, and one sailor remembered, "one shot carried our sour tureen and our roast beef into the paddle wheel."[13] The *Estrella* and *Diana* were each struck

---

10 "Report of Lieutenant Commander Buchannan," Ibid, 327.

11 Ibid; "Report of E.W. Fuller," Ibid, 336.

12 "Report of E.W. Fuller," Ibid, 336.

13 "Diary of Assistant Engineer Baird," Ibid, 332.

three times and the *Kinsman*, receiving the focus of Confederate efforts, was struck 54 times.

Two days later on November 5, the USS *Calhoun* and the USS *Estrella* again steamed up Bayou Teche to test the Confederate positions. Again, the *Cotton* fired accurately, striking the Union ships and killing two men before forcing their withdrawal again. The naval skirmish was repeated again on November 12 and 13, with similar results. The obstructions on Bayou Teche remained and the Union ships could not advance without help from the army, which was currently intent on fortifying Brashear City, instead of advancing against Fort Bisland.

The Lafourche campaign concluded at the end of November 1862. Despite the successful Confederate defense on Bayou Teche, it was a complete Union victory in that Donaldsonville, Thibodaux, and Brashear City all now lay in Union hands. The J. *A. Cotton's* excellent gunnery bolstered the morale of Generals Taylor and Mouton, along with their men. Additionally, the victory of this makeshift iron-cotton-clad transport enabled Mouton to fortify Fort Bisland while Taylor gathered reinforcements in preparation for the next Union push.

Mouton and Taylor both recognized Captain Fuller's achievement and wrote to the Confederate secretary of war. "Something must be done for Fuller," exclaimed Richard Taylor; "He certainly deserves it."[14] The request was forwarded to Stephen Mallory, the secretary of the navy, with the request that Fuller be commissioned a lieutenant. He was nominated for the position, but it was determined in December 1862 that there was no open commission that could be offered him. Instead he was awarded a congratulatory letter, with the promise of a future commission when an opening was found.

Weitzel was not ready to launch a ground offensive, so the navy continued to skirmish with its Confederate nemesis. In mid-January, 1863, Lt. Cmdr. Buchannan, with the approval of Adm. David Farragut, planned a joint army-navy attack to eliminate the *J. A. Cotton*. This time, Buchannan's four ships were accompanied by Union cavalry, five regiments of infantry, and three batteries of artillery to drive back the Confederate field artillery and provide small arms fire against the Confederate semi-ironclad.

In the early morning of January 14, 1863, the Union infantry advanced and engaged Confederate skirmishers outside of Fort Bisland. Moments later, the naval squadron moved in, this time with the USS *Kinsman* in the lead, followed by the *Estrella*, *Calhoun*, and *Diana*. The *Kinsman*, commanded by Lt. George Wiggin, was

14 "Letter from Major General Taylor," Ibid, 337.

The *J.A. Cotton* engages the Union squadron, January 14, 1863.

Naval History and Heritage Command and Harper's Weekly

fired upon by Confederate skirmishers and the *Cotton*, striking it five times and wounding the ship's executive officer. A team ashore detonated an underwater torpedo, dislodging the *Kinsman's* rudder. It did not sink, as Union sailors contained the damage and withdrew the ship from the battle for repairs.

The *Estrella* next moved toward the obstructions. There its crew found a second torpedo but managed to disarm it before it could be detonated. Meanwhile, Confederate riflemen continued to engage the Union ships and the approaching Union infantry. They paid particular attention to the USS *Calhoun*, flagship of the Union squadron, firing into the pilothouse, killing Lt. Cmdr. Buchannan and two sailors, and wounding two quartermasters and four bluejackets.

After driving the skirmishers back, the Union infantry fired on the *Cotton*. Captain Fuller withdrew his iron-cotton-clad. The retreat was slow and the Union infantry "were soon upon the very banks of the bayou, firing volley after volley."[15]

---

15 "C.S. Gunboat *J.A. Cotton* Burned," *Houston* [TX] *Tri-Weekly Telegraph*, February 2, 1863; E.W. Fuller to Mary B. Fuller, Apr. 18, 1863, *Earl Blake Cox Family Papers*, Washington State University Libraries.

Lieutenant Henry Stevens was killed while leading the gun crews and Captain Fuller was wounded, shot through both arms. Despite his wounds, Fuller refused to relinquish command until the *Cotton* was safely moored behind a bend in the bayou and under the protection of Fort Bisland. He was then carried off the ship to receive medical care. Lieutenant E. T. King, an army artillery officer that led the men manning the *Cotton's* cannon, assumed command. Five men were killed and another nine wounded onboard the Confederate gunboat. Another 10 Confederates were casualties ashore. Union losses amounted to 43 total. It was likely after Stevens's death that it was determined to rename the *Hart* in his honor.

After the *Cotton* withdrew, the Union squadron began clearing the obstructions in the bayou. General Godfrey Weitzel, in command of the land forces, made preparations to attack Fort Bisland the next day.

While Union forces planned their assault, Gen. Mouton assessed his situation. Fort Bisland had cannon, but his earthen fortifications were not fully completed. He also saw the Union sailors removing the obstructions in the bayou. Mouton ordered Lt. King to sink the *Cotton* in the bayou to provide another obstruction and remove its cannon for placement in Fort Bisland. King brought the ship into the middle of the bayou and set it afire. Mouton then braced to receive the Union attack. There was, however, no renewed attack on January 15. Upon learning that the *Cotton* was destroyed, Weitzel cancelled his assault, satisfied with "the object of the expedition having been accomplished," and he withdrew his brigade back to Brashear City.[16]

The Bayou Teche Campaign and Ships on the Atchafalaya River

As winter turned into spring in 1863, Union forces in southern Louisiana began preparing for a campaign to move up Bayou Teche. This waterway was important; it connected to both Brashear City and the Atchafalaya River, as well as provided a water route into southwestern Louisiana. Thus, it could connect ships in the Gulf of Mexico to the Mississippi River.

Rumors began circulating among the Union forces in Brashear City that Taylor was preparing to mount an attack. It was true that Taylor was collecting Confederate soldiers from Texas and he hoped to reclaim New Orleans. Additionally, he moved gunboats from the Red River down into the Atchafalaya River to help him accomplish this goal. The Confederate river flotilla steamed in

---

16 "Report of Brigadier General Weitzel," *ORN*, 19:521.

two groups of two ships each: the *Queen of the West* and *Nina Sims* advanced first with the *Grand Duke* and *Mary T* following behind. Such a force might, once reinforced with a completed and partially armored *Hart*, support a Confederate offensive to New Orleans.

The rumors of naval reinforcements moving to assist Gen. Taylor proved too serious of a threat to be ignored, and Gen. Nathanial Banks, who replaced Benjamin Butler, ordered the Union ships in Brashear City to begin patrols of the Atchafalaya River. To get there, Union ships must steam from Brashear City into Grand Lake, an expansive waterway formed by the Atchafalaya River north of the positions along Bayou Teche. Grand Lake's other feeder met in Bayou Teche just north of the town of Pattersonville. Union ships left Brashear City and steamed into Grand Lake. They could then enter the Atchafalaya River and advance on the river until it met Bayou Teche. From that point, the patrol could reverse its course and make its way back to Brashear City via Grand Lake. Orders were issued preventing ships from entering Bayou Teche alone; there was no room for maneuver and any ship becoming disabled in the bayou had no means of escape.

These patrols frequently took on secondary objectives, often in an attempt to make a profit off of the local residents. In one instance, Union sailors approached the Cochrane Plantation, a few miles up Bayou Teche from Pattersonville, and began confiscating the sugar, loading it onboard their ship. Mrs. Cochrane gave "resolute protestations" but it was only when Confederate scouts began approaching that the Union ship left the scene.[17]

Another such patrol was made by the USS *Diana* on March 28, 1863. The *Diana* was operating in southern Louisiana and took part in the campaign against the *Cotton*. She mounted five cannon and was under the command of Acting Master Thomas L. Peterson. Peterson was determined to make the most of his mission.

On March 28, Peterson took onboard several army engineers and a staff officer of Gen. Weitzel. For added protection, Weitzel also provided 60 soldiers, detachments each from the 116th New York and 12th Connecticut Regiments, to serve as sharpshooters. The *Diana's* reconnaissance began as it made its way into Grand Lake. It was at this point that things went astray. Acting Master Peterson, who apparently "wanted to be wiser than his instructions," ordered his ship into Bayou Teche in the early afternoon to continue the patrol.[18]

---

17 "Another Splendid Victory," *Memphis* [TN] *Daily Appeal*, April 10, 1863.

18 John William De Forest, *A Volunteer's Adventures: A Union Captain's Record of the Civil War* (New Haven, CT, 1946), 83.

Confederate forces commanded by Maj. Hannibal H. Boone were lying in wait. Boone had perhaps 500 men from his own 13th Battalion of Texas Cavalry, elements of the 28th Louisiana Infantry, along with a detachment from the 1st Arizona Infantry Regiment and the Val Verde Battery of field artillery, both of which took part in the failed Confederate invasion of New Mexico and Arizona in 1862. Major Boone was waiting for Union naval commanders to make a mistake and he was all too happy to oblige Master Peterson and the USS *Diana*. The Confederates were arrayed along Bayou Teche waiting behind embankments, hidden from view. Peterson steamed the *Diana* into Bayou Teche with the intention of using that route to get back to Brashear City instead of retracing his steps through Grand Lake as ordered.

Once the *Diana* passed their positions, the Val Verde Battery opened fire at the stern of the vessel, whose machinery was exposed from that angle. After the first salvo from the field artillery, Boone's cavalry, who were "lying down upon the ground and leveling their rifles over the bank," swarmed the banks of the Teche firing wildly from both sides. Several Union soldiers returned fire, but to little effect. The rest "were swept away as if by lightning" or hid within the ship. Acting Master Peterson was killed instantly by a Confederate cavalryman in the first moments of the attack and moments later his executive officer was mortally wounded from a bullet shot though his lungs. Command of the vessel devolved to Acting Master's Mate Henry Weston who immediately passed orders to turn the ship around and steam back into the Atchafalaya while simultaneously "urging his men to deeds of prowess and valor."[19]

Back in Brashear City, Lt. Cmdr. A. P. Cooke anxiously awaited news. As commander of Union naval forces in the area, he oversaw two operations. Besides the *Diana's* reconnaissance, Cooke earlier dispatched the USS *Estrella* down the Atchafalaya River with a pilot in anticipation of reinforcements arriving. This left him with only the USS *Calhoun* at Brashear City for the day. At about 2 pm, Cooke began hearing the sound of artillery up Bayou Teche and he wanted to know what was going on; perhaps the *Diana* found and engaged a Confederate gunboat. Orders were issued and the USS *Calhoun* got underway "to ascertain the cause."[20]

19 "Report of Acting Master's Mate Weston," *ORN*, 20:111; "Another Splendid Victory," *Memphis* [TN] *Daily Appeal*, Apr. 10, 1863; "The Capture of the Yankee Gunboat Diana," *Wilmington* [NC] *Journal*, Apr. 23, 1863.

20 "Report of Lieutenant Commander Cooke," *ORN*, 20:108.

Back in Bayou Teche, the ship's crew managed to turn the *Diana* around in the narrow waters through herculean efforts and it began moving back toward the Atchafalaya River and relative safety. Just then, a volley of field artillery struck the ship. "Our wheel ropes were cut by the shot," recalled Acting Master's Mate Henry Weston, and "the wheel itself was partially shot away."[21] This made steering all but impossible, but Weston attempted to maneuvering using the paddle wheels.

The Confederate battery divided itself into two groups, with one section firing on the Union ship and the second repositioning. This way, the *Diana* remained under continuous artillery fire. Shells struck the *Diana*, with one entering the engine room, killing an engineer, wounding a fireman, and cutting the engines escape pipes. To prevent scalding, the remaining engineers abandoned their equipment. With no steering and no one manning the engine room, the *Diana* ran aground.

As Boone's Confederates concentrated their fire on the disabled ship, the Union sailors spent 30 minutes working to get back into the engine room and get the *Diana* refloated, but it was to no avail. Weston held a quick meeting with his chief engineer and Gen. Weitzel's staff officer. The three agreed that the situation looked hopeless and at 4:30 pm the *Diana* struck its colors in surrender. Nine sailors were killed or wounded and the Union soldiers attached to the vessel suffered another 24 casualties. On the banks of the bayou, Maj. Boone suffered about 40 casualties altogether. About 150 men on the *Diana* became prisoners; the soldiers and sailors were immediately paroled but the officers were held in prison camps until the end of the war.

The USS *Calhoun*, steaming to aid the *Diana*, was not aware of the surrender. Arriving at the Atchafalaya River, they found no sign of the *Diana*. Acting Master M. Jordan determined to return to Brashear City to report this and as his ship was turning around in Grand Lake, it too ran aground. Hours were spent attempting to refloat the *Calhoun*. At dark, three sailors in a skiff approached the ship; they were members of the *Diana's* crew who escaped "through the plantation and the swamps to the lake," bringing word of the day's unfortunate events.[22] Not wishing to become prisoners as well, the *Calhoun's* crew threw overboard all they could, including coal, ammunition, and food, to lighten the vessel. At midnight, the *Calhoun* was refloated and slowly worked its way back to Brashear City, spreading word of the day's debacle.

---

21 "Report of Acting Master's Mate Weston," Ibid, 112.

22 "Extract of Diary of Acting Third Assistant Engineer Baird, Ibid, 113.

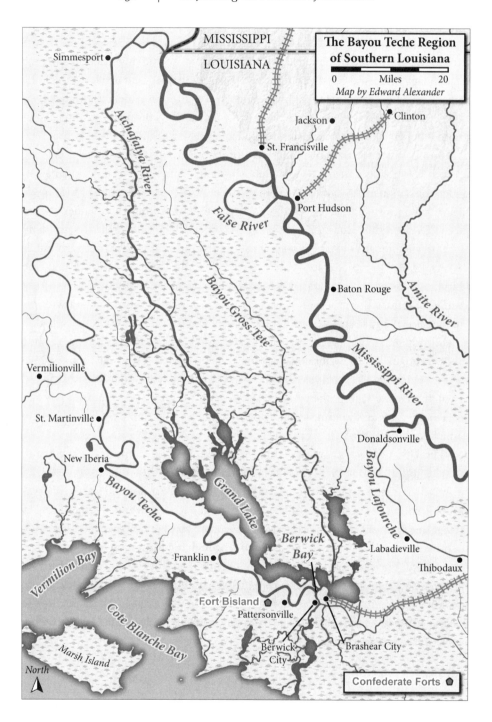

The *Diana* was refloated by Maj. Boone's men and brought, with the assistance of captured Union engineers, up Bayou Teche to the camp at Bisland. Damage to the superstructure was extensive: "Doors, windows, looking-glasses, tables, chairs, sofas, trunks, crockeryware, the contents of feather beds, the pantry, store rooms and the surgeon's shelves looked as though they had been struck by lightning, and then given up to the tender mercies of a hurricane."[23] The vessel itself however was structurally intact. Furthermore, the steering system was repaired and once the engines cooled, men entered the engine room to commence repairs there. It was a formidable addition to Gen. Taylor's defenses: mounting five guns including one 32-pounder rifled Parrott gun, two 32-pounder smoothbores, and two smaller 12-pounders. The ship, now flying a Confederate flag, was moved beyond the sunken *Cotton*, moored at a turn in Bayou Teche and kept out of sight of Union soldiers.

First Lieutenant Timothy D. Nettles, the second in command of the Val Verde Battery, was placed in command of the *Diana* and a detachment of Company K, 28th Louisiana Infantry Regiment was sent aboard as gunners. Weitzel's men, backed by the Union forces in Louisiana under Gen. Nathanial Banks prepared to advance up Bayou Teche and clear southern Louisiana from Confederate opposition once and for all.

Nathanial Banks moved up Bayou Teche in early April 1863 and encountered the Confederate positions at Camp Bisland. Taylor's Louisiana and Texas troops were outnumbered. Banks was determined to avoid a costly frontal assault against the Southern position. Instead, he divided his force. Two divisions, most of his soldiers, remained in front of Camp Bisland, threatening an assault and occupying Taylor's attention. Meanwhile, a third division was carried via Grand Lake to another entrance into Bayou Teche behind the Confederate lines near Franklin, Louisiana. Banks hoped that this force could cut off and perhaps surround Taylor's Bisland fortifications, forcing either their surrender or hasty evacuation.

The advanced guard of Banks's column arrived in front of Bisland on April 11, 1863 and immediately began preparing as if for an attack. Skirmishing took place the next afternoon with both sides maintaining a 1,000-yard separation. Throughout this skirmishing, the *Diana* maintained a constant and accurate fire, which "added to the universal din." Union officers observed the *Diana* firing its five guns and then disappearing down the bayou. Lieutenant Nettles developed an ingenious firing arrangement where the Confederate ship was tied to a large tree

---

23 "Another Splendid Victory," *Memphis* [TN] *Daily Appeal*, April 10, 1863.

when his gunners were loading their cannon. When ready to fire, soldiers ashore released the ship from its tether to drift down the bayou far enough to a clear line of fire. After discharging the cannon, the soldiers along the bayou used lines to reel the ship back behind the turn in Bayou Teche and out of sight once again. One Union officer noted the effectiveness of the *Diana's* fire, describing it as "very singular" and that "ahead and behind us, the shells were exploding every instant." General Taylor agreed, believing that Nettles handled the *Diana* "with great skill."[24] The artillery exchange and skirmishing continued until nightfall when Banks's troops withdrew out of range, keeping Taylor's attention focused on the enemy soldiers in front of him.

While the skirmishing continued in front of Fort Bisland that Sunday, Banks's flanking column, commanded by Brig. Gen. Cuvier Grover, continued its advance across Grand Lake. At dusk, Richard Taylor became aware of this threat and detached a small force to keep Grover's men in check; Taylor himself travelled north to determine if this detachment could delay the Union flanking force. Meanwhile, Taylor's subordinates were preparing an offensive of their own. Brigadier General Henry Sibley, commanding a brigade of Texans, organized an attack against the Union forces on the western bank of Bayou Teche, set to commence at dawn. Taylor believed that Sibley's force, backed by the *Diana*, might push back the Union main force, thwarting Banks's plan for moving up Bayou Teche altogether.

The morning attack never fully materialized as Sibley failed to coordinate his movements in time. Furthermore, Lt. Nettles, commanding the *Diana*, became seriously ill overnight and relinquished command of the ship to Capt. Oliver J. Semmes, commander of the 1st Confederate Artillery Battery, a Regular Army unit.

Oliver Semmes was the son of Raphael Semmes, the former commander of the CSS *Sumter* who was then roaming the high seas in command of the CSS *Alabama*. It took time for the younger Semmes to assume command of the ship and it was not until after dawn that he took stock of the situation. He did manage, however, to move the vessel in preparation for the proposed attack, taking the *Diana* from behind the bend in the bayou to abreast of Fort Bisland, where it could fire on Union positions but likewise was more exposed to their fire.

24 "The Late Battles Above New Orleans," *The Daily Green Mountain* [VT] *Freeman*, Apr. 30, 1863; Frank M. Flinn, *Campaigning with Banks in '63 and '64, and with Sheridan in the Shenandoah Valley in '64 and '65* (Lynn, MA, 1887), 42; W. Randolph Howell Diary, Apr. 11 and 12, 1863, *W. Randolph Howell Papers, 1861-1879*, Dolph Briscoe Center for American History, The University of Texas at Austin; "Report of Major General Taylor," *OR*, 15:390.

To announce its new position, the *Diana* fired on a group of Union scouts with its 32-pounder rifled Parrot gun. "The shell passing in dangerous proximity to our little force" recalled a member of the party, which promptly retreated to the main Union line. After the scouts retreated, Semmes noticed a group of soldiers crossing Bayou Teche behind the Union lines on a pontoon bridge. Taking aim with his 32-pounder rifled Parrot, Semmes threw several shells at the troops as they crossed. The shots failed to hit anyone, but two fell close to the pontoons "splashing water on two or three companies" of the 38th Massachusetts Regiment.[25]

With the Confederate counterattack over before it even began, the initiative was held by Banks, who ordered his men to advance midmorning. The *Diana* fired on Union forces on the western bank of the bayou, hoping to slow their advance. A heavy morning fog prevented Union gunners from seeing the *Diana* in its new position. The ship's position was further obscured from Union soldiers on the western bank of the Teche by several slave cabins of the nearby plantation. Brigadier General Halbert E. Paine, commanding a Union brigade, ordered the cabins burned "so that the smoke might cover and conceal the puffs of our guns and impair the accuracy of the enemy's fire."[26] As the cabins burned and the morning fog dissipated, the *Diana* became visible. Elements of two Union infantry regiments were ordered to the banks of the bayou to fire into the *Diana*, but they were quickly recalled to the main Union line because they were exposed there.

Several Parrot guns from Capt. Albert Mack's 18th New York Light Artillery Battery, the "black horse battery," advanced with the infantry with the mission of firing on and silencing the *Diana*. Experiencing combat for the first time, the New Yorkers handled themselves well as Confederate guns opened fire. "The shot and shell bursted [sic] in front and all around us" recalled Corp. Charles F. Nichols, "but we paid them back in their own coin, with interest added."[27] Captain Semmes ignored the Union battery, letting Taylor's field artillery try and silence the Union gunners at a range of 800 yards. The Union gunners continued their bombardment of the *Diana*, hoping to silence the ship's guns and allow the Union infantry to close on Taylor's fortifications.

---

25 Flinn, *Campaigning with Banks*, 44; "Report of Lieutenant Colonel Rodman," *OR*, 15:351.

26 "Report of Colonel Paine," Ibid, 340.

27 "Mack's Battery in Action," *Manchester* [NH] *Democrat and American*, June 27, 1863.

This exchange of artillery fire continued for two hours with little result, though Gen. Taylor proclaimed that the bayou was "boiling like a kettle."[28] The *Diana's* guns continued to hold back the Union soldiers with little hindrance from the New York gunners, who emptied two caissons of ammunition in two hours of firing. More Union guns were sent forward, a section of two 32-pounder rifled Parrot guns from Capt. McLaflin's Battery G, 1st Indiana Artillery. Captain McLaflin unlimbered his cannon much closer to the *Diana* to ensure better accuracy but this left his men more exposed as well. His two guns opened fire at 9:30 am.

Federal persistence was rewarded when the first Indiana shell slammed into the *Diana*, shattering plates protecting the boilers, before entering the engine room and exploding. The chief engineer and one of his assistants were killed and five more crewmen were wounded. Quickly, the *Diana's* gunners were redirected to fire on the Indiana battery. "A 32-pound shot passed over my head and buried itself in the ground but a few feet behind me," recalled one Union gun captain, and "at another time, one came bounding down the road . . . and just missed my gun."[29] The Indiana artillerists fired 20 shots from their Parrot guns to great effect, tearing away the large Confederate flag flying above the ship and smashing a boiler which scalded several more engineers. Captain Semmes realized that his ship was partially disabled and he dispatched a note to Gen. Taylor informing him of the vessel's condition.

Richard Taylor immediately made his way to the bayou to speak with Semmes personally. As he approached, one man appeared on deck to speak with him, but was immediately struck by a Union shell and "he disappeared as suddenly as Harlequin in a pantomime." Semmes then appeared and he yelled the ship's condition to the general ashore. Both agreed to withdraw the *Diana* up Bayou Teche to keep the safe the ship from further damage. As the vessel withdrew, Union soldiers "applauded with cheers" of the accuracy of the Northern gunners.[30]

General Taylor's forces at Camp Bisland managed to hold off the Union advances for the rest of the day, but Banks was just waiting to spring his trap. Gen. Grover's division landed up Bayou Teche with little opposition as Banks's troops were skirmishing with the Confederates further down the bayou. Taylor, aware of the Union flanking force, ordered his men to withdraw from Camp Bisland that

---

28 Taylor, *Destruction and Reconstruction*, 131.

29 "Mack's Battery in Action," Manchester [NH] *Democrat and American*, June 27, 1863.

30 Taylor, *Destruction and Reconstruction*, 131; Harris H. Beecher, *Record of the 114th Regiment, NYSV* (Norwich, NY, 1866), 143.

night and make their way to Franklin, Louisiana. There was no time to alert the Confederate ships on the Atchafalaya River steaming at that very moment for a rendezvous to support the aborted offensive operation.[31]

Repairs to the *Diana* were made that night. Semmes was under orders to withdraw the vessel up Bayou Teche to Franklin as soon as possible to rendezvous with the rest of Taylor's army. The retreating Confederates marched through the night in a heavy rain, arriving in Franklin on April 14 to block Grover's flanking column. The *Diana* joined them in the morning, positioned just up the bayou from the town on the flank of the Confederate defensive force "so that her guns could sweep the fields and woods which the enemy had held."[32]

Grover was determined to block the retreating Confederates and he urged his men to advance against the small group of defenders in their way; most of the Confederates were on the road marching to move past Grover's troops. In midmorning, his Union division advanced against Taylor's skirmishers, commanded by Gen. Alfred Mouton, but did so at a leisurely pace. Captain Semmes used the *Diana's* guns to good effect in keeping the Union column at bay. One Union artillery officer became "annoyed by the fire of the gunboat, several of her shells (30 pounders) falling among the teams of the section, but fortunately not exploding."[33]

With the assistance of Semmes's gunners, Mouton's small force managed to delay Grover's flanking column long enough for Taylor's army to successfully escape. However, the *Diana* was now trapped between the two Union forces as Banks's main column approached Franklin from below. Semmes kept the ship pinned against the banks of Bayou Teche just north of the town of Franklin with orders to work his artillery "to the last moment," firing into the two Union columns approaching his ship on either side. This final act by Semmes, who was described as "an officer of high merit," assured the escape of the smaller Confederate army.[34] As the last of Taylor's soldiers reached safety, Semmes set the *Diana* afire and it quickly sank, obstructing the bayou. In covering Taylor's retreat, Semmes and his men

---

31 William G. Vincent, "Reminiscence by Commander of Second Louisiana Cavalry of Teche Campaign in Louisiana, 1862," *Miscellaneous Papers Related to the Confederacy,* W. Randolph Howell Diary, Apr. 13, 1863, *W. Randolph Howell Papers, 1861-1879.*

32 "Report of Major General Taylor," *OR,* 15:392.

33 "Report of Lieutenant Rodgers," Ibid, 367.

34 Taylor, *Destruction and Reconstruction,* 134; "Report of Brigadier General Mouton," *OR,* 15:399.

were cut off and many fell into the hands of Union cavalry, including Capt. Semmes, who remained behind to ensure that the *Diana* burned.

With Bayou Teche now open to Union naval forces, Gen. Taylor ordered his men to retreat as far as Vermillionville, modern day Lafayette, Louisiana. Even as the *Diana* burned, he sent an inquiry to New Iberia, asking Lt. Joshua Humphreys whether the *Hart* was completed in its conversion. Humphreys responded that same day "she was in an unfinished condition and unfit for action with the enemy." With nothing now between the unfinished ironclad and the Union Navy, Taylor ordered the ship sunk to obstruct Bayou Teche. Thus, Confederate aspirations of an ironclad fleet in Louisiana's bayous ended.[35]

The Confederates ships steaming down the Atchafalaya River were not aware of the Union movements against Camp Bisland or Franklin. The *Queen of the West* and the *Nina Sims* were in the lead while the *Mary T* and *Grand Duke*, due to their slower speeds, followed behind. This Confederate attack took on the aspect of a personal score to be settled: The *Mary T* was regarded as the *Cotton Number Two*. Additionally, the *Queen of the West* was commanded by none other than Captain E.W. Fuller, who was partially recovered from the wound he received when commanding the *J.A. Cotton* earlier in January.

In the early morning of April 14, the column of Confederate ships approached the entrance to Grand Lake and the squadron of Union ships supporting the landing at Irish Bayou to flank Taylor's main force at Bisland. Captain Fuller did not expect to encounter Union ships in Grand Lake and when he saw them, he immediately knew that Taylor's planned offensive was undone.

The Union sailors noticed the approach of the two ships for some time, as each was shining one light to alert Taylor to their presence. At 5 am, the Union ships manned battle stations and got underway to face Fuller's approaching two vessels, described as a "large black steamer and a white river boat."[36] Lieutenant Commander A. P. Cooke, commanding the small Federal flotilla, ordered his three ships to form into a crescent, with the *Estrella* on the left, the *Calhoun* in the center, and the *Arizona* on the right.

"There is that damned *Calhoun*," barked Captain Fuller; "I would rather see the devil than that boat." Recognizing that he could not face three enemy gunships with his fewer cannon, Fuller ordered his two ships to turn and escape, but in the

---

35 "Report of Major General Taylor," *OR*, 15:393; W. Randolph Howell Diary, Apr. 14, 1863, *W. Randolph Howell Papers, 1861-1879*.

36 "Report of Lieutenant Commander Cooke," *ORN*, 20:134.

process the *Queen of the West* ran aground.[37] The *Nina Sims* continued back up the Atchafalaya River to safety. Cooke saw the grounded vessel and ordered his ships to close on it. They opened fire at a range of three miles with 30-pounder Parrots mounted on each ship's bow. One of the first shots fired struck the grounded *Queen of the West*, smashing into the superstructure and causing cotton protecting the engineering machinery to catch fire. Among the damage was a cut steam pipe filling the engine room with steam that scalded many. The ship was afire and Captain Fuller, wounded once again in the bombardment, ordered the vessel abandoned.

The surviving crewmen, 90 in all, were taken prisoner from the *Queen of the West*, including Captain Fuller. The ship continued to burn uncontrollably for hours until it drifted into Grand Lake. After several miles, the *Queen of the West* grounded once again at 10 am and "shortly afterwards exploded with a tremendous report." Captain Fuller and his surviving crewmen were taken first to New Orleans, then north. The wounds proved fatal for Fuller and the captain of the *Cotton* and *Queen of the West* eventually died in June 1863 while in the Johnson's Island prison camp in Ohio. Interestingly, Fuller was later listed as a naval lieutenant in Stephen Mallory's records; though he did not survive the war, he eventually received the commission that many thought he deserved.[38]

April 14 was a disaster for the Confederacy's control of southern Louisiana. The *Queen of the West*, the *Diana*, and the incomplete *Hart* were all destroyed within hours of one another. Confederates in southern Louisiana were "much disturbed by the intelligence of these events." They, like the defenders of Vicksburg, placed their hopes on armored ships augmenting land forces. One newspaperman editorialized that "one after another disappears the prizes won by our gallant partisans."[39] Just like the fate of New Orleans, Memphis, and the *Arkansas*, the small Confederate naval force in southern Louisiana proved that even if it could offer a spirited and temporarily effective defense, it could not withstand the larger and well-led Union army and navy. General Taylor's army retreated to Vermillionville, Louisiana, and from there into the central part of the state. With all

37 "Extract of Diary of Acting Third Assistant Engineer Baird," Ibid, 138; "From the West," *Raleigh* [NC] *Weekly Standard*, Apr. 29, 1863.

38 "Report of Lieutenant Commander Cooke," ORN, 20:135; "Telegraphic News," *The Redwing* [MN] *Goodhue Volunteer*, Apr. 29, 1863; "Obituary," *New York Times*, August 16, 1863; Register of the Commissioned and Warrant Officers of the Navy of the Confederate States to January 1, 1864," *Subject File*, NA, NA; E.W. Fuller to Mary B. Fuller, No. 3, Jun., 1863, *Earl Blake Cox Family Papers*.

39 Taylor, *Destruction and Reconstruction*, 121; "More of Mallory's Successes," *Raleigh* [NC] *Semi-Weekly Standard*, May 1, 1863.

of southern Louisiana in Union control, Union forces in the state turned to invest Port Hudson and complete their conquest of the Mississippi River.

The wrecks of the *Cotton*, near Bisland, and the *Hart*, near New Iberia, continued to obstruct Bayou Teche for the rest of 1863. In late July, Confederates began to raise the *Hart*, but at the approach of the USS *Clifton*, the ship was, in the words of one Union officer, "immediately sunk again and now lies under water." In October, efforts were made to clear the two ships and open the bayou to navigation. The *Cotton's* stern was removed, but this caused the rest of the sunken hull to destabilize. Union surveyors realized more efforts to remove the wreck would shatter the sunken hull, permanently obstructing the channel. They settled for the partial opening already cleared by removing the *Cotton's* stern, which allowed smaller ships to navigate past.

The *Hart* took more efforts to clear. One engineer inspected its hull and found that it "had her machinery on board and three large boilers which were under water, securely bolted to her hull and connected with large boiler-iron pipes." Union soldiers remained encamped at New Iberia for two days in early October 1863 while engineers laid charges to the ship. First, they blew up the boilers, which were observed to be thrown "clear of the bed and nearly on shore" before laying a second set of charges to split the hull to allow it to be cleared away. The United States was once again in full control of the waters of southern Louisiana.

Richard Taylor's ground forces recaptured much of the Bayou Teche region later in 1863 while Union forces were investing Port Hudson and Vicksburg. A highlight of this effort was the temporary reclaiming of Brashear City for the Confederacy, done so through a nighttime assault by Confederate infantrymen riding boats, pirogues, sugar coolers, and whatever else they could get to float into Berwick Bay.[40] This success proved temporary. The end of 1863 saw Confederate land forces pushed out of southern Louisiana and no Southern naval forces remained in the area.

---

40 "Report of Acting Volunteer Lieutenant Crocker," *ORN*, 20:380; "Report of Captain Bulkley," *OR*, Ser. 3, 3:979; Beecher, *Record of the 114th Regiment, NYSV*, 258; "Daily Memorandum for Adjutant General's Office," *OR*, 26:380; L. Boyd Fitch, "Surprise at Brashear City: Sherod Hunter's Sugar Cooler Cavalry," *Louisiana History* (Fall 1984), No. 4, 25:403-434.

CHAPTER TEN

The Loss of Vicksburg
and the Yazoo River

Rebuilding a Naval Squadron on the Yazoo

W HILE events unfolded in southern Louisiana, Isaac N. Brown, promoted to commander for his performance at Vicksburg, worked diligently on the Yazoo River to rebuild a viable naval force to contest Adm. David Porter's squadron of ironclads and wooden steamers supporting Union operations against Vicksburg.

Besides the Atchafalaya River, most ships that escaped from New Orleans when that city fell to Farragut's forces in 1862 retreated to the relative safety of the Yazoo. After the CSS *Arkansas* left the tributary to operate at Vicksburg, the river was for a time vulnerable. Only the sinking of the USS *Cairo* in December 1862 by an underwater torpedo kept Union naval forces at bay. It was hoped that the torpedo threat could buy enough time for the Confederacy to build more ships for battle.

After the *Arkansas* was lost at the Battle of Baton Rouge, Cmdr. Brown assumed control from Capt. William F. Lynch of all naval forces on the Yazoo. Besides the detachment of men laying and detonating torpedoes, the Confederate naval presence was negligible. Most of the vessels at Brown's disposal were merchants or lightly armed government vessels that escaped from New Orleans. The receiving ship *Saint Philip* was one of the first to arrive after transferring gold from the New Orleans mint to safety upriver. Lieutenant William Comstock brought the ship up the Yazoo with some difficulty, suffering a major accident

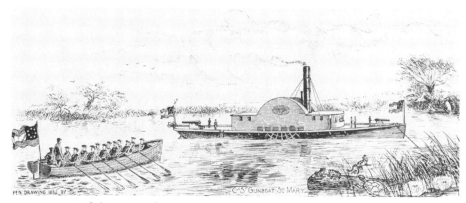

Confederate armed transport *Saint Mary*. *Naval History and Heritage Command*

when three sailors drowned on the way. Though a commissioned ship of the navy, it was barely armed.

Other Confederate gunboats made their way up the Yazoo as well. The transport *Saint Mary*, a small river steamer built in Plaquemine, Louisiana that mounted two light pieces of artillery, neared its completion when Farragut's forces entered the Mississippi River. Too small to be a viable gunboat, the 60-ton vessel served as a transport supporting Vicksburg. Added to these two was Lt. Francis E. Shepperd's command, the CSS *Mobile*. This vessel was converted into a gunboat on the Atchafalaya River before being ordered to the Yazoo after the loss of New Orleans. Finally, the small but battle-tested CSS *Ivy* made the journey as well. After bringing Cmdre. Hollins to New Orleans against orders, the little *Ivy* steamed back upriver to rendezvous with Cmdr. Pinckney's forces defending Memphis. After arriving in Tennessee waters, 1Lt. William L. Bradford was ordered to bring the ship to the Yazoo River.[1]

These four gunboats formed the core of Cmdr. Brown's defenses, which were concentrated first at Liverpool Landing before continuing further up the Yazoo after the chain of logs was installed to protect Yazoo City. Once there, most of the crews were transferred to the CSS *Arkansas*. After the chain barrier at Liverpool Landing was put in place, the remainder of Cmdr. Pinckney's squadron and the River Defense Fleet were trapped below. The forces up the Yazoo, however, were relatively safe as the summer of 1862 began. Besides the three small gunboats and the armed transport, a host of civilian and unarmed government steamers

---

1 *DANFS*, 2:550, 563.

amounting to at least 23 ships were up the Yazoo. As 1862 turned to 1863, Cmdr. Brown began formulating plans to use this growing collection to resurrect a Confederate naval squadron to contest the Mississippi River.

Confederate efforts focused on wooden ships converted to ironclad warships. Since the ironclad *Arkansas* was completed at Yazoo City, the area was advantageous for future naval construction and conversions. Commander Brown, who oversaw most of the *Arkansas'* completion, supervised these new projects. At first, Brown looked for vessels that could be converted and decided to use two of the strongest hulls available. The CSS *Mobile*, displacing 283 tons and propelled by a screw propeller was selected because it appeared well suited for the mounting of iron. In addition, the merchant steamer and troop transport *Republic* was selected for conversion because of its structurally sound hull and larger size. A third ironclad was planned as well, though this one began from the keel up. Described as "a monster," the unnamed craft was 310 feet long and 70 feet wide, possessing as many as six engines, four paddle wheels, and iron plating laid four inches thick. Predictions circulated that if the vessel was completed, it could provide "much trouble" for Union control of the waters around Vicksburg.[2]

Assisting Brown with the workload was Thomas Weldon, a local shipwright. The two initially hoped their ironclads could be ready for battle by autumn of 1863. Backed up by several smaller wooden steamer transports and gunboats, the reconstituted squadron could be an imposing force to challenge the Union Navy's control of the Mississippi River. Just like the *Arkansas*, the ironclads were protected by railroad iron brought in from other parts of the Confederacy. The local machine shops, blacksmiths, and mechanics brought to Yazoo County by Brown to finish the *Arkansas* were kept in place to facilitate the conversion processes. Additionally, Brown formally established a navy yard at Yazoo City, building five saw mills, a machine shop, plus more blacksmith and carpenter shops.

Despite all of this support and the navy department spending nearly $300,000—90% of the naval budget in the Yazoo River area—in a few months on the ships, the three conversions soon ran into delays due to lack of materials and ongoing military operations, just as happened with the *Arkansas*. Furthermore, a

---

2 Ibid, 550, 561; "Report of Lieutenant Commander Walker," *ORN*, 25:8; "Report of Rear Admiral Porter," *ORN*, 25:8.

lack of available skilled laborers caused more delays. Requests by Weldon to release local soldiers with carpentry and caulking skills obtained few workers.[3]

Other construction efforts were ordered by Secretary Stephen Mallory, these along the Tennessee River. As conversion efforts of the *Mobile* began on the Yazoo, Capt. Samuel Barron was dispatched to evaluate the feasibility of potential construction efforts on the Tennessee River in Alabama. Chief Constructor John L. Porter designed a side-wheeler ironclad converted from river steamers found there. The town of Florence, Alabama was suggested as a suitable location for such conversions and John T. Shirley, the same shipbuilder who constructed the ironclad *Louisiana* at New Orleans, expressed interest in joining the project. Barron made his way to Florence and conducted his survey, but army operations soon made the efforts moot.

Confederate offensives against Corinth, Mississippi and into Kentucky failed and as a result, the safety of the Tennessee River for construction sites could not be guaranteed. Furthermore, Barron determined that the only suitable machinery available for use on these ironclads must be obtained from ships on the Yazoo River, interfering with efforts there. As a result, Mallory abandoned the idea of building an ironclad squadron on the Tennessee River.[4]

Yazoo River Ships Support the Vicksburg Campaigns

After the sinking of the USS *Cairo* by one of Brown's underwater torpedoes and the Union defeat at the Battle of Chickasaw Bluff in December 1862, Gen. Ulysses Grant and Adm. David Porter looked for alternate ways of seizing the Confederate stronghold at Vicksburg. This gave the Confederates a two-month respite on the Yazoo River to solidify their positions unhindered by Union operations.

---

3 "Payment Receipts for Yazoo City Naval Station," Aug. 15, Aug. 28, Oct. 17, Nov. 13, Dec. 16, 1862, Jan. 23, 1863, *Subject File*, AC, NA; "Payment Receipt for Yazoo City Naval Station," Apr. 2, 21, 1863, *Subject File*, PB, NA; "Payment Summary for Yazoo City, 1862-1863," *Subject* File, PI, NA; "Report of Lieutenant Commander Walker," *ORN*, 25:8; Thomas Weldon to John C. Pemberton, Feb. 14, 1863. *Thomas Weldon Papers*; Alexander Gardner to John C. Pemberton, Feb. 6, 1863. *General John C. Pemberton Papers*. (National Archives Identifier 599432, Records Group 109), National Archives Building, Washington DC; Thomas Ware to Nixon, Aug. 26 and Dec. 2, 1862. *Correspondence and Political Records of the Confederate States Navy Paymaster at Mobile, Alabama*. (National Archives Identifier 1848930, Records Group 45), National Archives Building, Washington DC.

4 "Order of Secretary Mallory," *ORN*, 23:703-704; "Letter of Captain Barron," *ORN*, 23:705.

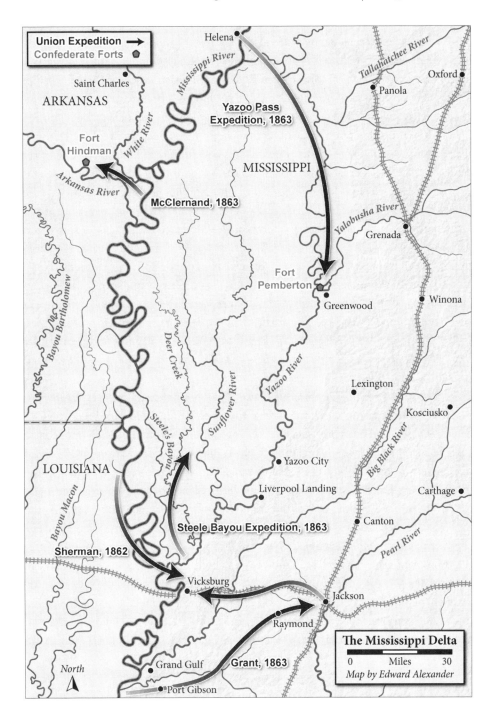

Union Expedition →
Confederate Forts ⬠

Helena

Tallahatchee River

Mississippi River

Saint Charles

Oxford

Panola

ARKANSAS

Yazoo Pass
Expedition, 1863

MISSISSIPPI

Fort
Hindman

White River

Arkansas River

McClernand, 1863

Yalobusha River

Grenada

Fort
Pemberton

Greenwood

Winona

Bayou Bartholomew

Deer Creek

Sunflower River

Yazoo River

Lexington

Kosciusko

Steele's Bayou

LOUISIANA

Yazoo City

Liverpool Landing

Big Black River

Bayou Macon

Steele Bayou Expedition, 1863

Canton

Sherman, 1862

Carthage

Pearl River

Vicksburg

Jackson

Raymond

The Mississippi Delta

North

Grand Gulf

Grant, 1863

0   Miles   30

Map by Edward Alexander

Port Gibson

Grant's next move swung wide to the north into the Mississippi Delta in the hope of moving down the Yazoo River. He sent 4,500 men who, on February 3, 1863, broke a levee on the Mississippi River and flooded much of the Mississippi Delta, allowing passage through Yazoo Pass into the Tallahatchie River. From there, the goal was to move south accompanied by Union gunboats and get into the Yazoo River, outflanking the Confederate positions held along Chickasaw Bayou. The Union soldiers were loaded onto barges and protected by Lt. Cmdr. Watson Smith's squadron consisting of two ironclads, six gunboats, and two rams.

Lieutenant General John Pemberton, commanding the overall defenses of the Vicksburg area, did not sit idly by, directing Maj. Gen. William Loring, a former United States Army colonel and veteran of the Mexican War, to take his division and block this advance from the north. Loring placed obstructions in Yazoo Pass, conscripting local slaves, but these proved ineffective and were rebuilt. Next, Loring fortified the banks of the river at Yazoo City using more slaves who constructed a fort where the Tallahatchie River joined the Yazoo, three miles north of Greenwood, Mississippi. The fortification, named Fort Pemberton, mounted eight cannon and was well placed at bends in the rivers, offering no approach by land. The Confederate position must be silenced before the Union Navy continued into the Yazoo River.[5]

Lieutenant Commander Smith's Union squadron approached Fort Pemberton on March 11. To try to block passage of the river, Cmdr. Brown ordered the CSS *Saint Philip* scuttled beam into the river. Fort Pemberton's gunners then opened fire on the USS *Chillicothe*, the leading Union ship, at 10 am. After an hour of exchanging fire, the Union vessel withdrew. The *Chillicothe* returned again in the afternoon, exchanging shots for two hours before it again withdrew after receiving "a shot in one of her port-holes" that killed or wounded sixteen sailors.[6] Using the ship's fire as cover, Union soldiers attempted an amphibious landing via barges, but the Confederate defenders drove them away.

March 12 was spent by the Union forces erecting a land battery that could fire on Fort Pemberton. Due to their limited stock of ammunition, the Confederate gunners held their fire. Lieutenant Commander Smith renewed his attacks against Fort Pemberton on the morning of March 13, this time by the land battery, two gunboats, and one mortar boat. The Union gunners scored one fortunate hit

---

5 J. McFarland to Jacob Thompson, Apr. 14, 1863. *Thomas Weldon Papers.*

6 "Report of Brigadier General Ross," *OR*, Part 1, 24:395.

against the fort when a shell "passed through the parapet, displaced a cotton bale, and ignited a tub of cartridges," killing one Confederate.[7]

Both sides then spent several days receiving reinforcements. Union ground troops arrived while Confederate transports made their way to Fort Pemberton during the night of March 14, bringing ammunition and food for a protracted siege. Another attack was made against the fort on the morning of March 16 under the covering fire of the USS *Chillicothe* and USS *Baron De Kalb*, formerly the ironclad *Saint Louis*, veterans of several river battles. The Union plan was to "arrange for a short and brisk fight at close quarters, and, if successful in silencing their batteries, to make a descent upon the fort with infantry, loaded on the light-draught gunboats, and storm it."[8] After 15 minutes, Confederate shots struck the *Chillicothe*, forcing her gun ports shut. The ship withdrew, unable to fight and the *Baron De Kalb* also retreated, unwilling to face the fort alone. The Union land battery continued firing through the day, but to no avail. When the ironclads withdrew, the infantry attack never materialized.

Grant grew concerned about the stymied operations against Fort Pemberton, knowing there was little dry land for infantry maneuver, making reinforcements and resupply difficult. Additionally, Fort Pemberton was well supplied by Brown's naval transports. As a result, Grant formulated a plan "to get into the Yazoo below Fort Pemberton."[9] This second expedition was under the overall command of Maj. Gen. William T. Sherman, whose instructions were to proceed up Steele's Bayou into Deer Creek. From there, he could advance into the rear of Fort Pemberton and cut it off from Vicksburg and the naval supply line of transports.

Rear Admiral David D. Porter took command of the naval contingent consisting of five ironclads, four mortar rafts pulled by tugs, and two transports packed with Sherman's men. The advanced group proceeded into Steele's Bayou on March 14 and immediately ran into complications. The swamps were overgrown and the water was "obstructed by overhanging oaks, and filled with cypress and cotton-wood trees" cut to impede passage.[10] On March 20, Confederates skirmished with sailors working to clear the obstructions.

---

7 "Report of Major General Loring," Ibid, 416.

8 "Report of Brigadier General Ross," Ibid, 396; Alexander Miller Diary, Mar. 14, 1863.

9 Ulysses S. Grant, *The Personal Memoirs of Ulysses S. Grant*, 2 Vols. (New York, 1885), 1:268.

10 William T. Sherman, *Memoirs of General William T. Sherman*, 2 Vols. (New York, 1875), 1:307.

Porter realized the Confederate delaying tactic was to enable reinforcements to arrive from Vicksburg. He ordered his ships to withdraw from Bear Creek. By then it was too late as over 40 trees were blocking his withdrawal. Only the Union 8th Missouri Infantry was present to remove the trees, as the remainder of Sherman's force was a day's march away. When they received word that Porter's ships were trapped, Sherman ordered his men to their rescue. They arrived just in time and the Confederates pulled back, allowing Porter to clear the obstructions. By March 27, the expedition withdrew from Bear Creek and Steele's Bayou back to the Mississippi River. Back at Fort Pemberton, Union forces continued to skirmish with, but not assault the fort. With little accomplished, Grant ordered the expedition abandoned on April 12, 1863.

Vicksburg proved a conundrum for Grant. The navy failed to take the city on its own. Grant's marches across Mississippi to attack Vicksburg from the northeast, and attempts to maneuver through swamps and bayous just north of Vicksburg in the Mississippi Delta also all failed. The Confederate defense skillfully used a coordinated use of interior lines to meet threats while supplying those defenses with naval transports, and using the topography of the Mississippi Delta to its advantage. Grant needed to take a different approach to capture Vicksburg.

Loss of Vicksburg and the Yazoo River

Grant began his final campaign against Vicksburg in late April 1863 by crossing the Mississippi River south of the city. His land forces then marched to Jackson, the capital of Mississippi, capturing it on May 14. His army then turned westward and began a siege of the city's fortifications, trapping Pemberton's defenders in Vicksburg. To assist Grant, Adm. David Porter's squadron divided in two, with part covering Grant's crossing the Mississippi while the remainder invaded the Yazoo River. Porter personally stayed with the Yazoo force, hoping to end the Confederate presence on the tributary, and keep Vicksburg's defenders occupied while Grant flanked them from the south.

Porter led his northern squadron, which included the ironclads *Baron De Kalb* and *Choctaw*, as well as two wooden gunboats that were "boarded up on the sides and covered with iron plates, loopholed for small arms," into the Confederate Yazoo country on May 19, 1863. His first obstacle was the Confederate guns atop Hayne's Bluff, which supported the Confederate line along Chickasaw Bluff the previous winter. These cannon protected the Yazoo approaches and supported Vicksburg's northern flank. The Confederate position mounted 14 heavy siege

Rear Admiral David D. Porter, USN.

Library of Congress

cannon and held enough supplies to maintain their position against a siege for a considerable time.

Fortunately for the Union sailors, the defenders of Hayne's Bluff were not eager to fight. Upon Porter's approach, the Confederates "ran and left everything in good order—guns, forts, tents, and equipage, of all kinds." Porter distributed the fort's captured ammunition and gunpowder through his squadron and burned a nearby mill, before continuing up the Yazoo and anchoring near the mouth of the Sunflower River, where it met and joined the Yazoo 42 miles down the river from Yazoo City.[11]

Commander Isaac Brown was aware of Porter's division of forces and advance up the Yazoo. The defensive tactic Brown employed was used previously by the Confederacy when in dire need: sacrifice some ships to save the rest. To block the Sunflower River, Brown ordered four vessels sunk as obstructions: the *Dew Drop*, *Argony*, *Argo*, and *Sharp*. At the town of Greenwood, Brown ordered four more transports "sunk on a bar, completely blocking it up," to prevent further Union encroachment up the Yazoo as well: the *Scotland*, *R.J. Lockland*, *John Walsh*, and *Golden Age*. Finally, at Liverpool Landing, Brown ordered 1Lt. William L. Bradford to scuttle the CSS *Ivy* as another obstruction, the *Ivy* being too small and lightly armed to fight Porter's forces alone. The remainder of Brown's supply transports and government vessels retreated upriver past Yazoo City in an effort to escape.[12]

---

11 "Report of Colonel Wirt Adams," *ORN*, 25:13; "Report of Acting Rear Admiral Porter," *ORN*, 25:5; Alexander Miller Diary, May 20, 1863.

12 "Report of Lieutenant Commander Walker," *ORN*, 25:183; "Report of Major General Sherman," *ORN*, 25:136.

On May 20, a detachment of Confederate soldiers commanded by Col. Wirt Adams briefly engaged Porter's squadron as it approached Liverpool Landing. Adams had a small field battery and some infantry and cavalry with him, troops assigned to Fort Pemberton, and hoped to delay the Union squadron. The brief skirmish resulted in one sailor killed and seven wounded and delayed Porter's ships by about one hour. Additionally, Union sailors onboard the USS *Forest Rose*, while steaming toward Yazoo City, discovered, recovered, and disabled at least four underwater torpedoes that Brown's underwater submarine battery service laid.[13] The Union ships then found the sunken obstructions at Greenwood and prepared to move the scuttled ships out of the way.

There was now nothing left to protect Yazoo City and its ironclad navy yard except for Brown's improvised sunken obstructions. The ironclads undergoing conversion were too large to move further up the Yazoo River and the monster ram was barely started. Furthermore, they could not fight. The *Mobile* was ready for its iron plating, but some of the required iron was sent to ships being built in Selma, Alabama, to defend Mobile. The *Republic* was still without a ram, iron, or guns.[14] With no other choice, the commander of the Yazoo River naval defenses ordered the navy yard abandoned and the three ironclads burned on the night of May 20. The fires continued into the next morning, signaling the final end of a reconstituted naval squadron to challenge Union hegemony on the Mississippi.

The obstructions near Greenwood were cleared by Porter's sailors by setting them afire. The burned hulks were then cleared from the channel. Porter continued up as far as Yazoo City. Arriving at the abandoned navy yard, Porter inspected the three burned ironclads and surveyed what he styled the "fine navy yard." Among the spoils captured was "a large quantity of bar, round, and flat iron" painstakingly stockpiled for installation on the *Mobile*.[15] The Union ships proceeded no further than Yazoo City. As many as 13 Confederate transports were spared, though they had no guns and no crews. Even if they could move supplies, that was now impossible since Vicksburg was completely surrounded by Grant's soldiers and ships.

With Yazoo City eliminated as a Confederate naval resource, Porter took his ships back into the Mississippi River to assist in the final siege of Vicksburg.

---

13 "Abstract Log of USS Forest Rose," Ibid, 135.

14 "Report of Acting Read Admiral Porter," Ibid, 8.

15 Ibid; "Report of Lieutenant Commander Walker," Ibid. 134; Alexander Miller Diary, May 21, 1863.

Commander Brown and his few remaining transports could only watch as the city's garrison wasted away. Brown tried to form a relief force with Gen. Joseph E. Johnston to march to the city's rescue. However, it gathered too late and Gen. Pemberton surrendered his army and the city of Vicksburg on July 4, 1863. Within a week the Confederate defenses at Port Hudson, in Louisiana, similarly surrendered. The "great artery of the Confederacy" as Jefferson Davis styled it, was now completely under Union control.[16]

With Vicksburg again flying the United States flag, Adm. Porter made it his immediate goal to completely clear the Yazoo River of Confederates. General Ulysses Grant approved, knowing that the operation could weaken the small army under Gen. Joseph Johnston, which, though it failed to relieve the Vicksburg garrison, was still a threat to his forces in Mississippi. Furthermore, Johnston's forces were assisted by over 1,000 local slaves who were busy building fortifications along the Yazoo River; Grant wanted to break up resistance along the tributary before it became too fortified and require another costly siege. In mid-July Porter steamed back into the Yazoo River.[17]

This expedition, under the command of Lt. Cmdr. John G. Walker, consisted of his own ironclad USS *Baron De Kalb* and the wooden gunboats *New National*, *Kenwood*, and *Signal*; they were backed up by 5,000 troops. Leaving Vicksburg on July 12, the squadron arrived opposite Yazoo City the next day. As they approached the town, Confederate skirmishers opened fire on the ships from along the riverbank and a detachment of the Union infantry deployed and cleared them.[18]

Commander Isaac Brown coordinated with elements of Johnston's Confederate infantry operating near Yazoo City. His few remaining sailors were mostly small detachments of the submarine battery service, but Brown was still determined to resist Union occupation of the Yazoo River. After the Confederate infantry detachment was driven out of Yazoo City, Brown was forced to abandon his position manning a small battery of guns overlooking the town. He determined to leave nothing for the Federal forces to take. "If the cotton is left for the enemy it will more than pay their expenses in taking Vicksburg," he penned to the army leadership nearby. Hundreds of bales were set to the torch, though Union forces later boasted of capturing 3,000 bales, done to compensate the United States for the treachery of the local Confederate civilians. Furthermore, Brown's sailors

16 "Address of President Davis," *Memphis* [TN] *Daily Appeal*, Dec. 29, 1862.

17 "Letter from Major General Grant," *ORN*, 25:280-281.

18 "Report of Lieutenant Commander Walker," Ibid, 283.

USS *Baron De Kalb. Naval History and Heritage Command*

burned what few transports remained; by the end of July, Brown scuttled 13 vessels. Only the *Saint Mary* fell into Union hands. After seeing to the destruction, Brown ordered his men to Mobile Bay to commence laying torpedoes there.[19]

The Union conquerors suffered one last significant casualty. As the *Baron De Kalb* approached Yazoo City's navy yard on the evening of July 13, the ironclad was struck by a contact torpedo. The vessel took on water and Lt. Cmdr. John Walker ordered it made fast to the riverbank to allow for the offloading of the crew and equipment. Within 15 minutes, the ironclad sank, but all of the crew was able escape with their baggage and small arms. No one was injured in the torpedo explosion and the sailors transferred to the USS *Kenwood*. While the squadron was alongside Yazoo City that night, another torpedo exploded, this one near the USS *Kenwood*, but it failed to cause any damage. Lieutenant Commander Walker spent the next week consolidating his hold of the Yazoo River, removing the remaining torpedoes, fortifying his position at Yazoo City, and recovering the cannon from the sunken *De Kalb*.[20]

The United States Navy remained in control of the Yazoo River for the rest of the war. Yazoo City was briefly occupied by Confederates in early 1864, but another Union naval force was dispatched to the town to clear it once again. This

---

19 "Report of Commander Brown," Ibid, 290; "Report of Acting Rear Admiral Porter," Ibid, 284; "Report of Lieutenant Commander Walker," Ibid, 283; "Telegram from Commander Brown," Ibid, 290.

20 "Report of Lieutenant Commander Walker," Ibid, 283; "Report of Rear Admiral Porter," Ibid, 284; "Report of Rear Admiral Porter," Ibid, 285; "Abstract Log of USS Kenwood," Ibid, 286.

time the lightly armored "tinclad" gunboats USS *Petrel* and the USS *Prairie Bird* protected the Union expedition. Accompanied by a small force of Union infantry and one unarmed transport, Acting Master Thomas McElroy, the senior naval officer present and commander of the *Petrel*, was in command. The Union squadron drove away a small body of Confederate skirmishers below Yazoo City on April 21, 1864. After clearing the area, McElroy brought his ships to the docks of Yazoo City where the sailors encountered women and children. That afternoon, Confederate soldiers from the 11th and 17th Arkansas Consolidated Mounted Infantry Regiment, opened fire on the Union flotilla with several small fieldpieces. The USS *Prairie Bird* was partially disabled and McElroy steamed his vessel past Yazoo City to engage the Confederates. Additionally, he sent a note to Union infantry to help him clear the area.

McElroy kept the *Petrel* north of Yazoo City, fighting the Confederates into the next morning. As the exchange continued on April 22, the *Petrel* lost numerous crew members killed and wounded, including the ship's gunner and his mates. Confederate shells struck the stern and magazine of the *Petrel*, and the ship was doomed when a shell entered the boilers, causing them to explode. Most of the remaining crew abandoned ship, swimming for the *Prairie Bird*, while McElroy and a few of his officers and senior enlisted men remained behind to burn the ship. Those that remained behind were captured when the Arkansas soldiers boarded the *Petrel* to extinguish the fires.

The *Prairie Bird* fled down the Yazoo to report the disaster. Wirt Adams, now a brigadier general and commander of Confederate forces in the Yazoo area, ordered the cannon from the captured *Petrel*, consisting of eight 24-pounders, offloaded. The ship was then burned and sunk to obstruct the river.[21]

The capture and destruction of the USS *Petrel* was the last Confederate success in the Yazoo City area. Within a month, the Union army marched a force up the river and occupied the city once again. Several prominent buildings were then burned on May 19 by the Union soldiers, including the Yazoo City courthouse. Thus ended the final major military action along the Yazoo River. Sporadic, limited fighting continued in the region for about a year after Vicksburg surrendered. Once considered a possible refuge and major naval construction area and supply route, the Confederacy was unable to transform the river into an important defensive zone before the Union's larger and well-led forces destroyed that hope.

---

21 "Report of Acting Master McElroy," Ibid, 26:246-249; "Report of Acting Ensign Flanigan," Ibid, 26:252; "Report of Lieutenant General Polk," Ibid, 26:260.

Chapter Eleven

Defending the Red River

Operations in 1863

T HE fall of Vicksburg and Port Hudson left the Confederacy divided geographically. The loss of control over the Mississippi River split the Confederacy into two parts. Texas, the Indian Territory, Arkansas, western Louisiana, and the claimed territory of Arizona were isolated from the central Confederate government; military leaders and the state and territorial governments managed their own affairs with only limited support from Richmond. The flow of men, horses, cattle, and other food and supplies from the western Confederacy into the eastern states was reduced to a trickle.

Lieutenant General Edmund Kirby Smith, commander of the Confederate Trans-Mississippi department, was responsible for the defense of this collection of states, headquartered in Shreveport, Louisiana. His task was enormous: he possessed only a fraction of the number of soldiers that were available for use east of the river, there were no major transportation centers such as Atlanta and Richmond to ship supplies by rail, the Federal blockade prevented supplies from reaching his armies, and aggressive Union forces threatened to seize what remained of the Confederacy's Trans-Mississippi territory. Assisting Smith in Shreveport were the Confederate governors of Louisiana and Missouri, both exiled from their capitals due to advancing Union forces.[1]

---

1 Arthur Fremantle. *Three Months in the Southern States: The 1863 War Diary of an English Soldier April-June 1863* (Edinburgh, 1863), 82.

The major transportation network that did exist in Smith's Confederacy was the series of rivers that wound through Arkansas and Louisiana. These, all tributaries of the Mississippi River, were key to maintaining control of the area. The largest of these tributaries was the Red River, which cuts northwest from the Mississippi River in central Louisiana and extends to Shreveport before continuing into Arkansas and later forming the border between Texas and the Indian Territory (modern day Oklahoma). Control of the Red River meant control over what remained of Confederate Louisiana and eastern Texas.

The Confederate defense of the Red River was among the most effective employed during the Civil War. Just as on other rivers, it involved cooperation between the army, navy, and civilian forces. General Kirby Smith, however, took that cooperation to a new level, combining an innovative management of the Red River with tactics already employed by other Southern naval forces in the Mississippi River Valley. Ships and land-based fortifications were just two of his weapons; he resorted to many more including underwater torpedoes, obstructions, and even the river's water level to keep northwestern Louisiana in Confederate control.

Before the fall of Vicksburg and Port Hudson, a Confederate naval buildup commenced at Shreveport. A town of 2,000 inhabitants before the war, refugees and government officials swelled the town's population past 3,000. The wharves along the Red River marked Shreveport as the largest trade center in northwestern Louisiana and the only suitable location in that part of the state capable of servicing gunboats.

The Bayou Teche campaign was a Confederate disaster: the unfinished ironclad *Stevens* was scuttled near Vermillionville; the *Diana* and *J.A. Cotton* gunboats were both lost on Bayou Teche; the *Queen of the West* was destroyed in April 1863 on the Atchafalaya River; and the captured ironclad *Indianola* was burned to prevent its return to Union control. Only three warships remained to defend the Red River, along with several unarmed supply and civilian vessels: the *Mary T*, renamed as the *Cotton Number Two* was a lightly armed gunboat manned by a combination of naval officers and artillerymen from the army; the *Grand Duke* was pressed into service earlier in the year; and the *W. H. Webb*, involved in the capture of the *Queen of the West*, was at Shreveport. These three ships represented the entire Confederate Navy in the Trans-Mississippi.[2]

---

2 Ibid.

As Union forces surrounded Vicksburg and Port Hudson, Adm. David Porter planned to advance up the Red River. Only Fort Taylor—renamed Fort DeRussy—about four miles from the town of Marksville, stood as a physical barrier to Union incursions up the river. It was lightly defended with only two companies of Louisiana artillery to hold the position, the Saint Martin's Company of Louisiana Artillery and Company A of the Crescent Artillery. The fort consisted of two positions, a small fortification along the river and a larger one unmanned about 900 yards further inland guarding the main road. A collection of obstructions was chained together to keep enemy ships from ascending the river.

Admiral Porter was aware of the fort, having unsuccessfully fought it in early 1863. As his ships bombarded Vicksburg in May 1863, he planned a separate operation to capture the fort and the city of Alexandria beyond. Securing Alexandria provided an avenue for a joint river-land advance against Shreveport. It also offered Porter an opportunity of personal revenge if he could capture or destroy the *W. H. Webb*, rumored to be at Alexandria. On May 5, Admiral Porter led the expedition up the Red River, taking the ironclads *Benton*, *Lafayette*, and *Pittsburgh*, along with the wooden gunboats *General Sterling Price*, *Switzerland*, *Estrella*, *Arizona*, *Albatross*, and the tug *Ivy*.[3]

With so many Union ships approaching, it was decided to abandon Fort DeRussy. Rising spring floodwaters in the lower fort, built along the riverbank, already submerged several guns, just as happened at Fort Henry on the Tennessee River in 1862, though the main fortification sited on a hill remained dry. The *Grand Duke*, *Mary* T, and the unarmed transport *Countess* were dispatched to remove the fort's garrison, supplies, and artillery. The evacuation began on May 2, 1863, with the collection of supplies. The next day, the supplies, along with a 32-pounder which was under the rising water, were loaded onto a barge.[4]

Admiral Porter's ships approached just as Fort DeRussy was evacuating. Three Union ships, *Albatross*, *Estrella*, and *Arizona*, were in the lead on May 4. Seeing their approach, Capt. J. Kelso, commanding the Confederate transports, ordered the steamer *Countess* upriver to Alexandria with a supply barge in tow. The fort's garrison then boarded, the Saint Martin's Battery of Louisiana Artillery on the *Mary* T, and Company A of the Crescent Artillery on the *Grand Duke*. They moved and manned the artillery pieces onboard, provided small arms support, and augmented the small crews of the ships, hoping to escape.

---

3 "Report of Acting Rear Admiral Porter," *ORN*, 24:647.

4 "Report of Captain Kelso," Ibid, 20:91.

Captain Kelso ordered the two Confederate ships, with their small cannon, to open fire on the lead Union vessel. The USS *Albatross* approached the river's obstructions to within 500 yards of the Confederate ships before returning fire; the *Estrella* and *Arizona* remained behind at a distance lobbing shells inaccurately at both the fort and opposing ships. Twenty minutes into the skirmish a steam pipe was cut onboard the *Mary T*, scalding several soldiers and disabling the vessel. The *Grand Duke's* wheel ropes were shot away and all internal communication equipment disabled. Five separate fires engulfed the ship, but the quick actions of the Crescent artillerymen extinguished the flames. Despite the damage, both Southern ships continued firing. Captain Kelso praised Lt. E. T. King, commanding the *Mary T*, for his "unflinching coolness" while under fire.[5] During the action, the towline on the escaping *Countess* was cut and the barge full of supplies drifted downriver and settled against the barrier of obstructions. This forced Capt. Kelso to remain in place until he could recover the supplies.

The Confederates continued to focus their fire on the USS *Albatross*. The wheel ropes of the *Albatross* were shot away and the vessel began drifting downriver. Quartermaster James Brown steered the ship to safety, earning the Medal of Honor in the process of saving the ship. The damaged *Albatross* managed to rejoin the supporting ships. The battle lasted an hour. Once clear of the fort, Capt. Kelso ordered the *Grand Duke* to take the *Mary T* and the supply barge in tow, steaming for Alexandria and leaving only the obstructions in place to slow the Union ships. The Confederate forces suffered several casualties onboard the two ships: 17 artillerymen and sailors were wounded and another four declared missing.[6]

The *General Sterling Price* breeched the obstructions for the remainder of the Union flotilla to pass but Porter ordered his ships to anchor for the night alongside the fort. He determined "it would take too much time to destroy it effectually." The next morning, Porter pressed on to Alexandria in the hope of seizing the Confederate ships that withdrew, but he found no ships upon his arrival; they retreated further to Shreveport in the night, leaving only the town, which "submitted without a dissenting voice" as Union ships approached.[7] Alexandria was occupied by an advance guard of Gen. Nathanial Banks's infantry, on their way

5 "Monroe, 11," *Dallas* [TX] *Herald*, May 20, 1863; Ibid.

6 "Report of Captain Kelso," *ORN*, 24:685; "Report of Lieutenant E.T. King," *OR*, Part 1, 24:686; "Report of Lieutenant W. Hervey," *OR*, Part 1, 24:686.

7 "Report of Acting Rear Admiral Porter," *ORN*, 24:645; Alexander Miller Diary, May 6, 1863; Porter, *Naval History*, 318.

from the bayous of southern Louisiana to besiege Port Hudson. Porter's ships blockaded the river. While the city and lower portion of the Red River were now in Union control, Gen. Kirby Smith gathered his remaining naval forces at Shreveport to defend the upper river.

The fall of Fort DeRussy and Alexandria left central Louisiana open to Union incursion. Combined with the loss of the Bayou Teche region, thousands of refugees travelled the roads looking for the relative safety of Confederate territory. Included among the refugees were rich owners fleeing their plantations, bringing their slaves to Shreveport or Texas. One observer commented, "the road to-day was alive with negroes, who are being 'run' into Texas ... we have met hundreds of them."[8] The envelopment of Vicksburg and Port Hudson only increased the number of refugee plantation owners and their slaves fleeing central Louisiana ahead of Porter's gunboats and Banks's troops, choking the roads more.

After helping to capture Alexandria, Admiral Porter's squadron supported the siege of Vicksburg into July 1863 and following its capture by Federal forces on July 4, Porter consolidated his control over the Yazoo River. This left only token forces to ensure the Confederate ships remained bottled up at Shreveport.

The most serious Confederate campaign occurred in October as Gen. Richard Taylor relocated his forces to the Shreveport area following his operations in the Bayou Teche region. He was looking for ways to expand his reach from the Red River into the Atchafalaya. Both waterways merge into the Mississippi River just a few miles from each other and if Union ships vacated their hold on the Red River near Alexandria, as they did occasionally to resupply, then it might be possible for Confederate ships to move from the Red River into the Atchafalaya with troops and supplies.

The attempt was made in October, when Gen. Taylor dispatched his aide, Lt. John M. Avery, to oversee the movement of the troop transport *Robert Fulton* into the Atchafalaya River. The ship was near the mouth of the Red River on October 6, waiting for the right time to make the dash into the Atchafalaya. Another supply steamer, the *Argus*, was already anchored there waiting for the opportunity to move as well. The *Argus* served as General Smith's "chief dependence for supplies of groceries and provisions" from the Atchafalaya up to Shreveport[9]

---

8 Fremantle, *Three Months in the Southern States*, 85.

9 "Order of Major General Taylor," *ORN*, 25:459; "Report of Acting Volunteer Lieutenant Couthouy," *ORN*, 25:454.

A nearby encampment of escaped slaves learned of these movements and a few trekked down the Red River to inform Union naval authorities of the Confederate ships. The former slaves encountered the USS *Osage* at the mouth of the Red River and provided their intelligence. Twenty sailors were dispatched to seize the Southern ships. Led by Acting Chief Engineer Thomas Doughty, the scratch force included a collection of engineers and pilots to steam the ships into Union lines. One of the escaped slaves, Benjamin Williams, volunteered to guide the sailors.

The sailors arrived just as the *Robert Fulton* met the *Argus*. Both vessels, unarmed and lightly manned, were surprised by Doughty's contingent. Unable to escape, the two Confederate ships were burned and their small crews taken prisoner. Engineer Doughty praised Benjamin Williams "for his intimate knowledge of all the short cuts to the Red River" that enabled the destruction of both ships. This was the last attempt by Confederate ships on the Red River to escape into the Atchafalaya. To thwart possible future breakthroughs by Confederate ships, Adm. Porter worked with Gen. Banks to fortify the mouth of the Red River.[10]

Losing access out of the Red River limited Kirby Smith's options. The next anticipated Union move was an advance up the Red to capture Shreveport, the headquarters of the Confederate Trans-Mississippi. Smith needed both ground and naval forces to oppose such an advance, but he possessed a limited number of ships that steadily shrank. In the fall, the *Grand Duke* caught fire by accident and was lost, leaving only the *W. H. Webb* and *Mary T* serviceable at the wharves of Shreveport.

Forming a Naval Squadron at Shreveport

Though Shreveport lay hundreds of miles inland, it was still an active port vital to commerce in northern Louisiana. As early as the fall of 1862, Confederate Secretary of the Navy Stephen Mallory ordered a survey of potential facilities for naval yards for shipbuilding. As the hulls of the proposed ironclads at Yazoo City and along Bayou Teche were laid down for conversion, two more were contracted for at Shreveport. Mallory gave the task to 1Lt. Jonathan H. Carter. A veteran naval officer who commanded the CSS *General Polk* in the battles for control of

10 "Report of Acting Volunteer Lieutenant Couthouy," Ibid, 456; "Letter from Rear Admiral Porter," Ibid, 523.

Memphis, he helped to reorganize Confederate forces on the Yazoo River after the destruction of the *General Polk* in June 1862. Carter was also experienced outfitting a warship and by October was reassigned to Shreveport, where he set to work.[11]

Carter surveyed the docks of Shreveport and determined that there was enough material on hand and in the vicinity to complete an ironclad vessel. He interviewed potential shipbuilders, determining that two men, Thomas Moore and John Smoker, were the only experts available west of the Mississippi "who could or would undertake the construction of iron-clad vessels with any reasonable probability of success." Smoker was a riverboat captain before the war and enlisted in the Confederate Guards Regiment for the defense of New Orleans in March 1862, assigned to Gen. Mansfield Lovell as a special aide. After the fall of the city, Smoker was discharged from the army and made his way to Shreveport. A contract between Carter, Moore, and Smoker was signed on November 1, 1862, for delivery of one ironclad ship at Shreveport within six months for a cost of $336,500. Another contract was signed for a second ship with George Fitch, though the navy department decided to hold off construction of the Fitch ironclad until work on the Moore and Smoker ironclad was completed. A lack of resources for a second ironclad also influenced the navy's decision.[12]

The Moore-Smoker ironclad was as a three-rudder sternwheeler with a draft of eight feet for service on the rivers of Louisiana. It was protected by a 30-degree sloped casemate of iron, over four inches thick backed by two feet thick pine. A small pilothouse was situated forward atop the casemate. No full blueprint of the ship remains, but speculation is the vessel was designed by Chief Constructor John L. Porter.[13]

The contractors acquired land along the river and laid the keel of the ironclad in December 1862. Carter, Moore, and Smoker immediately ran into problems. Shreveport contained few skilled craftsmen that worked on the construction of vessels. Carter asked both Secretary Mallory and Gen. Kirby Smith to send specialists from other naval facilities and local army garrisons to beef up the number of men needed for construction, but this was not always possible;

11 *Confederate Navy Register*, 31.

12 Booth, *Records*, 3:638; Confederate States of America Congress, *Report of Evidence Taken Before a Joint Special Committee of Both Houses of the Confederate Congress to Investigate the Affairs of the Navy Department* (Richmond, VA, 1863), 464-465; Jonathan H. Carter to Stephen Mallory, Feb. 1 & 20, 1863, *Jonathan H. Carter Letter Book*.

13 *DANFS*, 2:549.

Confederate laws now required that all soldiers detailed to naval service must have able substitutes to replace them. Another concern was building materials. Lumber remained in ready supply, but both nails and iron were needed. Regarding the iron, Carter seized collections of rail iron from stockpiles in Alexandria and collections of rails and spikes from the Vicksburg, Shreveport, and Texas Railroad.[14]

For heavy engineering machinery, Moore and Smoker purchased the Confederate supply vessel *Paul Jones*, which was involved in the salvage of the USS *Indianola* before being sent up the Red River to safety. The navy department also lent its assistance in this matter. John W. Parks, a civilian engineer, was sent to Shreveport to oversee the transfer of machinery from the *Paul Jones* to the ironclad. Another matter was the name of the vessel. Carter, in a note to Secretary Mallory, proposed to name the ship *Caddo*, in honor of a local Native American tribe. Instead, the ship was christened *Missouri* in honor of the state that many believed was unlawfully prevented from being a state of the Confederacy.[15]

Work on the *Missouri* progressed and by the end of March much of the planking was installed, inside work was progressing, and caulking was well underway. On April 14, 1863 Carter proudly wrote to Mallory about "the successful launching of the gun-boat" with reassurances that "the cladding [caulking] and placing the machinery will commence immediately and be pushed forward as rapidly as possible."

After being launched, the iron was installed, bit by bit using railroad ties confiscated throughout Louisiana. Since there was no iron rolling mill in northwest Louisiana, the railroad ties were attached directly. They were laid "diagonally along the sides of the casemate, with the crowns placed alternately in and out, and locked into each other" while on the bow and stern they were laid vertically.[16] The ties, though not perfectly interconnected, provided four and a half inches of iron armor, backed by 23 inches of pine.

14 Jonathan H. Carter to Waskam, Feb. 11, 1863, *Jonathan H. Carter Letter Book*; A.T. Bledsoe to Stephen Mallory, Dec. 19 and 28, 1861. *General Orders and Circulars of the Confederate War Department 1861-1865.* (National Archives Microfilm Publication M901, Records Group 109), National Archives Building, Washington DC.

15 *DANFS*, 2:555; Jonathan H. Carter to John C. Pemberton, Feb. 15, 1863, *Jonathan H. Carter Letter Book*; Jonathan H. Carter to Stephen Mallory, Feb. 15, 1863, *Jonathan H. Carter Letter Book*; Jonathan H. Carter to Stephen Mallory, Feb. 1, 1863, *Jonathan H. Carter Letter Book*.

16 Jonathan H. Carter to Stephen Mallory, Apr. 14, 1863, *Jonathan H. Carter Letter Book*; "Report of Lieutenant Commander Lull, Acting Chief Engineer Tate, and Acting Volunteer Lieutenant Swaney," *ORN*, 27:241.

Acquiring a trained crew was more problematic. By the time the *Missouri* was launched and ready to receive a crew, the final campaign for Vicksburg began and the Trans-Mississippi was effectively cut off from the government in Richmond. Carter therefore turned to other sources for crewmen. His first request was sent to Galveston, Texas, where the CSS *Harriet Lane* was anchored. After being captured on New Year's Day 1863, the former Union revenue cutter *Harriet Lane* sat idle, fully manned, but trapped by the blockade. It was currently undergoing conversion to a government owned blockade-runner on which less crew was needed. Carter asked for the bulk of the *Lane's* crew, which was duly dispatched to Shreveport in May. The remainder of the crew needed for the ironclad was drafted from local army garrisons and from the other ships in the Shreveport area. The need was so great that sailors on the *Mary T* were transferred and slaves impressed to serve on the *Mary T* in their place.[17]

By mid-June, the machinery was installed and a trial run conducted. The ship, partially clad in its railroad iron, only managed to steam at six miles per hour, half the speed promised by its builders. Further work finalized the machinery, completed the armored casemate, and installed the vessel's armament. The CSS *Missouri* was officially commissioned on September 19, 1863. Final engine trials revealed slight leaks in the hull, and a partial dry-dock was built around the hull to allow for repairs.[18]

Selected to command the Missouri was 1Lt. Charles M. Fauntleroy, a Virginian who previously served onboard the CSS *Nashville* and commanded the blockade-runner *Economist*. Since then he was on special assignment in Louisiana coordinating with local army forces. Fauntleroy was not happy with his assignment, preferring instead to be as sea. He complained that this assignment was a punishment by the navy department and his complaints about the *Missouri* began before he even laid eyes on the ship, desiring to "condemn her." He spoke with Lt. Carter, expressing the opinion that "the damned boat would sink." Recognizing that such a man could not properly command a ship he did not believe in, Fauntleroy was reassigned in July 1863, ordered to make his way to Mexico where

17 Jonathan H. Carter to Brent, Apr. 19, 1863, *Jonathan H. Carter Letter Book*; Jonathan H. Carter, to Stephen Mallory, May 18, 1863, *Jonathan H. Carter Letter Book*; Jonathan H. Carter to John K. Mitchell, Dec. 2, 1863, *Jonathan H. Carter Letter Book*; J. Ramsey to W.W. Hunter, Apr. 18, 1863, *William W. Hunter Papers*.

18 Jonathan H. Carter to Stephen Mallory, Jun. 20, 1863," *Jonathan H. Carter Letter Book*; Jonathan H. Carter to Stephen Mallory, Sept. 19, 1863," *Jonathan H. Carter Letter Book*; Jonathan H. Carter to Stephen Mallory, Oct. 24, 1863," *Jonathan H. Carter Letter Book*.

he assumed command of another blockade-runner. In his place, 1Lt. Jonathan H. Carter was ordered to assume direct command of the *Missouri*.

Assigned as Carter's executive officer was Lt. Alexander Grant, last seen in command of the Louisiana State Navy gunboat *General Quitman* during the 1862 campaign for New Orleans. Confederate officials in Texas and Louisiana suspected that the *Missouri* was not constructed with the best of materials and Gen. John Magruder in Texas constantly asked for the return of the sailors he dispatched, believing they were better used in Texas waters. The men were retained at Shreveport as Gen. Smith and Lt. Carter believed the Red River's defense was more important.[19]

Carter next turned his attention to armament. Cannon were requested from Mobile and dispatched under the care of Acting Master Linus Musgrave, but the guns were confiscated by Gen. John Pemberton to add to his fortifications at Vicksburg and Grand Gulf. Musgrave arrived to join the *Missouri's* crew, but the guns came from elsewhere. Designed to carry six heavy naval cannon, the ship only mounted half as many. Two guns salvaged from the wreck of the USS *Indianola*, one 11-inch Dahlgren smoothbore and one 9-inch Dahlgren smoothbore, were detailed by General Kirby Smith for the vessel and Carter ordered gun carriages prepared for their use. A third cannon, a standard naval 32-pounder, was also added. Gun carriages were manufactured locally despite limited equipment to carry the weight of each cannon while mounting. Carter scoured the decks of all ships in Shreveport for enough line and blocks to lift the guns.[20]

With the first ironclad now nearing completion, the Fitch contract for a second armored gunboat was cancelled due to both a lack of materials and a loss of faith in the builder. The navy department asked Lt. Carter to approach Moore and Smoker about the feasibility of them constructing another vessel, but they refused, citing the lack of materials and rising prices of scarce resources. They agreed to consider another contract if the government was willing to forward $100,000, which never occurred. The state of Louisiana also passed an act calling for the construction of two ironclad vessels to reconstitute its own naval forces, but this too was abandoned due to lack of funds and materials. Carter received orders from the navy

19 *Confederate Navy Register*, 58; "Report of Lieutenant Commander Greer," *ORN*, 25:395; Jonathan H. Carter to Stephen Mallory, Jul. 1 & Oct. 24, 1863, *Jonathan H. Carter Letter Book*; *Confederate Navy Register*, 74; "Report of Major General Magruder," *OR*, Part 2, 26:261.

20 "Payment Receipt to L. Musgrove," Apr. 3, 1863, *Subject File*, BG, NA; Jonathan H. Carter to Richard Taylor, Apr. 15, 1863," *Jonathan H. Carter Letter Book*; Jonathan H. Carter to Larmour, Nov. 11, 1863," Jonathan H. Carter Letter Book.

department to begin construction another ironclad on his own, but the project never got started. The intended small flotilla of ironclads on the Red River resulted in only the *Missouri*, another case of limited resources preventing Southern naval ambitions from becoming realized.[21]

The *Missouri* was the backbone of Carter's Red River defense, with its improvised rail iron armor hopefully able to protect it against enemy shells. The *W. H. Webb*, transferred to control of the navy and now under the command of 1Lt. John L. Philips, reinforced the ironclad with its own guns and its ram, which was successfully used against the USS *Indianola*. The *Mary T*, also now under the navy's control, acted as a supply ship, troop transport, and support vessel, its soldiers able to act as boarding parties.[22]

Other smaller vessels underwent construction in Shreveport in 1864. These were unconventional craft that proved themselves on the Yazoo River and along the Atlantic seaboard defending the harbor of Charleston, South Carolina. Lieutenant Carter received orders from the navy department and developed a two-fold plan: lay a series of underwater torpedoes as a static defense; and build torpedo boats for active operations against enemy ships. The underwater torpedoes were similar to those employed on the Yazoo River beginning in 1862; Carter was perhaps guided and advised by Cmdr. Isaac N. Brown, who was performing the same task in the Mississippi Delta. At least 30 torpedoes were either constructed at or delivered to Shreveport and emplaced by officers and men assigned to the *Missouri* on the Red River near the town of Grand Ecore.[23]

The matter of the torpedo boats was another issue altogether. Indeed, whether there were such vessels built at Shreveport remains shrouded in controversy and contradictions. Confederate Navy scholar R. Thomas Campbell documents Shreveport as a city that constructed at least one torpedo boat. Historian Gary Joiner says no torpedo boats were constructed there, but five submarines were. There is actual evidence that small craft of some sort were constructed or assembled in Shreveport with the purpose of offensive torpedo warfare. Shreveport historian and archaeologist Marty Loschen believes he recently uncovered the remains of four such craft, with initial imagery and documentation

21 Jonathan H. Carter to Stephen Mallory, Apr. 9, 1863," *Jonathan H. Carter Letter Book*; Jonathan H. Carter to Halsey, Jul. 16, 1863," *Jonathan H. Carter Letter Book*; Jonathan H. Carter to Franklin Buchanan, Jul. 14, 1863," *Jonathan H. Carter Letter Book*.

22 Jonathan H. Carter to Stephen Mallory, Jan. 5, 1864," Ibid; *Confederate Navy Register*, 153.

23 "Order of Lieutenant General Smith," *ORN*, 26:165.

supporting they could be either torpedo boats or submarines, but a full analysis has yet to be completed to determine the exact makeup of these vessels.[24]

Lieutenant Jonathan H. Carter left one major clue as to these boats. Three of his letters mention torpedo boats in some fashion, both in Shreveport and ascertaining the feasibility of constructing them in Texas. In one letter, written in March of 1864, Carter orders Naval Constructor R. P. Meads to "ascertain if it is practicable to build, at or near Houston, one or more Small Torpedo Boats similar to those now being used in Charleston Harbor." Another letter in January 1865 stated "a torpedo boat is now in course of construction near Houston." These references to torpedo boats might refer to both semi-submersible boats and submarines, as both the torpedo boat *David* and the submarine *H.L. Hunley* were employed in Charleston: the *David* damaged the ironclad USS *New Ironsides* in October 1863 and the *Hunley* sank the USS *Housatonic* in February 1864. Both vessels used a torpedo explosive mounted at the end of a long spar.

In April 1864, Carter wrote another letter, this one to Secretary of the Navy Stephen Mallory, noting that Naval Constructor Meads was sent to Texas to examine feasibility of "building the iron clad Torpedo boats. According to the plans and specification sent me." A final letter at the end of April forwards Meads's recommendations regarding "the construction of an iron clad Torpedo boat at, or near Galveston, Texas," noting that there are not enough materials on hand locally to construct such a vessel in Texas.[25] Thanks to better coastal defenses and access to resources, four ironclad ships were constructed in Charleston, South Carolina and they mounted spar torpedoes attached to their bows. Perhaps Carter's letters reference an attempt to build a full-size ironclad in Galveston Bay, which also included a spar torpedo mounted in place. Nonetheless, no ironclads were ever constructed in Texas waters.

In the case of Shreveport there is one more piece of evidence to consider. A Union officer, Major A. M. Jackson, wrote a report at the end of the war outlining what he heard rumored about such vessels in Shreveport. He described a letter he intercepted between a Confederate scout and an agent in New Orleans that detailed Confederate plans to use boat-mounted torpedoes to attack Union ironclads.

24 Gary D. Joiner, *One Damn Blunder from Beginning to End: The Red River Campaign of 1864* (London, 2003), 18; R. Thomas Campbell, *Hunters of the Night: Confederate Torpedo Boats in the War Between the States* (Shippensburg, PA, 2000), 68; John Andrew Prime, "Civil War subs: Lost no more?" *Shreveport* [LA] *Times*, Jan. 24, 2015.

25 Jonathan H. Carter to Stephen Mallory, Jan. 17, Apr. 4, & Apr. 25 1864, Jonathan H. Carter to Meads, Mar. 22, 1864," *Jonathan H. Carter Letter Book*.

Jackson's report explained that four vessels were built at Shreveport and a fifth in Houston, each designed and constructed by the same men who built the semi-submersible *David* in Charleston Harbor that crippled the USS *New Ironsides*.

These craft were 40 feet long, 40 inches wide, shaped like a steam boiler with pointed ends, and powered by hand cranks to turn a small propeller. Two torpedoes, one mounted on a spar on the bow and another mounted on the stern, served as offensive armament. The vessels used "two iron flanges (called fins) for the purpose of raising or lowering the boat in the water." Jackson further noted that "the boat is usually worked 7 feet under the water" and that "the air arrangements are so constructed as to retain sufficient air for four men at work and four idle two or three hours."[26]

Jackson's report mentions secondhand information of questionable reliability. The portions of the report speaking about air regulation hinted at a true submersible. Fins along the hull could support either a full submersible or a semi-submersible that could be lowered to show a smaller freeboard above the waterline. Both types of vessels used spar torpedoes. A clue supporting a semi-submersible is the mention of the builders who constructed the *David*, a semi-submersible torpedo boat.

There was almost certainly some type of small craft created at Shreveport. Modern archaeology uncovered potential evidence for these craft, but their details are not certain. Being on the Red River, subject to a strong current, a full submersible was not as likely as a partially submerged torpedo boat, which was safer and better able to manage river current. Whatever the type of small spar torpedo mounted craft was constructed at Shreveport, they were never employed in action against Union forces. Admiral David D. Porter, commanding Union naval forces on the Mississippi River, however, was aware of their potential threat. "The rebels are fitting out at Shreveport, four torpedo boats," he wrote to the commander of one of his ironclads, ordering him to construct obstructions that could block their passage down the Red River.[27] These possible torpedo boats, along with the ironclad *Missouri*, meant that any Union naval advance toward Shreveport must move with caution to avoid being surprised or unprepared.

---

26 "Report of Major Jackson," *ORN*, 22:104.

27 "Order of Rear Admiral Porter," *ORN*, 26:438.

The Red River Campaign of 1864

Major General Nathanial Banks, commanding Union armies in Louisiana, wanted to launch a campaign to capture Shreveport, place the Red River in Union hands, and threaten Texas. This was a dual-purpose campaign to deprive the Confederate Trans-Mississippi Theater of its main city-headquarters and its last major river, and send a diplomatic message to French officials to get out of Mexico. In 1861, Spain, Britain and France occupied Veracruz to protect their interests. In 1862 France stayed and sent reinforcements. In 1863 France sent Maximilian to be the Mexican emperor. A guerilla war ensued and in 1865 the United States demanded French withdrawal. The 1864 Red River campaign can be seen as the preliminary U.S. move against French occupation of Mexico.

Banks's Red River campaign began in March 1864, with 30,000 soldiers marching toward Shreveport, backed up by the bulk of Adm. Porter's Mississippi River Squadron. The Union operation involved land forces marching along the Red River and the outlying areas, steadily advancing toward Shreveport while Porter's gunships concurrently steamed up the river, followed by a flotilla of supply ships and troop transports.

Generals Edmund Kirby Smith and Richard Taylor gathered ground forces while 1Lt. Jonathan Carter readied his torpedoes and 3-vessel navy to defend the river. The ironclad *Missouri*, ram *W. H. Webb*, and steamer *Mary T* were manned, armed, and prepared to fight as much as they could be. The primary naval issue was river water depth, which needed to be a certain level to allow the *Missouri* to float safely down the river. Carter's underwater torpedoes were deployed further downriver, along with a series of log obstructions "driven deep into the muddy bottom." Proposals were made for a collection of fire rafts, just as were used in the 1862 defense of New Orleans. Though no torpedo boats were completed as yet, the idea of potential torpedo boats also posed a concern to Porter's advance.[28]

One last obstruction was put in place. The steamer *New Falls City*, a large side-wheeler moored at Coushatta, Louisiana was confiscated by the government. The vessel was brought to the mouth of Scorpion's Cutoff, about 30 miles downriver from Springfield Landing. Using a team of local slaves, the ship was raised out of the river, with both bow and stern carried onto either riverbank. It then broke in half and settled in the river, filled with mud and silt, blocking passage. If Union ships made it past the torpedoes and obstructions on the lower portions

---

28 Porter, *Naval History*, 496; "Report of Major General Taylor," *ORN*, 26:166.

of the Red River, this wreck might delay the Federal ships long enough to enable Carter's small flotilla to prepare for battle.[29]

Porter proceeded slowly and with caution. He commanded 13 ironclad warships, a collection of tinclad and wooden gunboats, and scores of supply ships. The largest ironclad at Porter's disposal, the USS *Eastport*, took the vanguard of the advance upriver. This was the same ironclad that the Confederacy attempted to convert in 1862 before it was captured by Union forces.

The first Confederate position encountered was Fort DeRussy, reoccupied after the brief skirmish the previous fall and manned with many of the same artillerymen that garrisoned the position in 1863. On March 14, the lightly manned fortification fell again. The river obstructions alongside the fort were also cleared and Porter continued upriver, seizing Alexandria, Louisiana, again on March 15. Continued movement beyond the falls above the town took time and it was not until March 31 that Porter's ships passed that natural barrier, some with only inches to spare between their hulls and the mud bottom of the waterway.[30]

Porter did not know it, but he was steaming into a trap. The reason that Porter's ironclads were able to steam up the Red River was because the river's water level was high at the start of the campaign, high because of a Confederate ruse. Before the campaign commenced, Gen. Kirby Smith ordered a dam constructed. Known as the Hotchkiss dam, it diverted river water from Tone's Bayou, a distributary near Shreveport, into the river. This caused the Red River to rise several feet above normal level, deceiving Adm. Porter into steaming his larger ironclads further upriver. After Union ships passed Alexandria and approached Grand Ecore, Gen. Smith ordered the Hotchkiss dam blown up. Water once again flooded into Tone's Bayou and the Red River slowly began falling, eventually trapping many of Porter's ships above the Alexandria falls.[31]

Despite observing the river water begin to fall, Porter steamed further toward Shreveport. Upon reaching Springfield Landing, he encountered the next obstacle left by the Confederates: the broken wreck of *New Falls City*, the use of which Porter described as "the smartest thing I ever knew the rebels to do."[32] Attached to

29 W. Craig Gaines, *Encyclopedia of Civil War Shipwrecks* (Baton Rouge, LA, 2008), 71; "Report of Lieutenant Cunningham," Ibid, 164.

30 "Particulars of the Capture of Fort De Russy," *Memphis* [TN] *Daily Appeal*, Apr. 8, 1864; J. Fuller to J.L. Brent," Feb. 2, 1864, *William W. Hunter Papers*.

31 Joiner, *One Damn Blunder from Beginning to End*, 25, 67.

32 "Report of Rear Admiral Porter," *OR*, Part 3, 34:172.

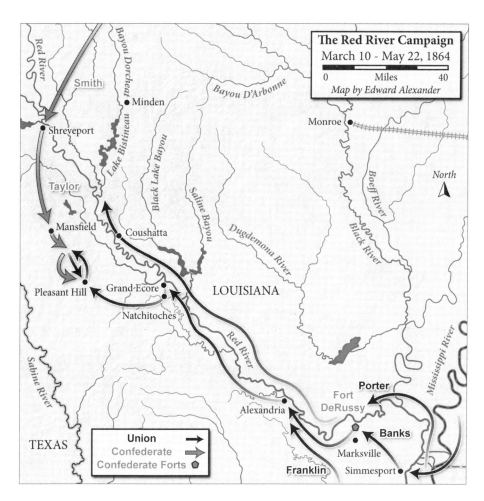

The Red River Campaign
March 10 - May 22, 1864
0   Miles   40
Map by Edward Alexander

the hull was an invitation, left mockingly for Porter and Banks, to attend a ball in Shreveport. As Porter's sailors began work to clear the obstruction, the admiral received word of another setback. Richard Taylor's land forces attacked the Union column at Mansfield on April 8. The battle continued the next day at Pleasant Hill, resulting in a halt to the Union advance and withdrawal back to Alexandria to regroup.

Not wanting his ships to be isolated, Porter likewise began withdrawing to Alexandria. There was just one problem: the river's level was now falling quickly. A very narrow deep channel remained in the Red River and Porter managed to get his ships back to just upriver from Grand Ecore. Then his ships began to run aground as they neared the Alexandria river falls. There the ships remained until another dam, this one constructed by U.S. Army engineers and known as Bailey's Dam,

Admiral Porter's squadron at Alexandria, Louisiana. *Naval History and Heritage Command*

managed to raise the water level enough for ships to steam away, though it would take at least two weeks to construct.

However, it was too late for the USS *Eastport*, which struck an underwater torpedo on April 15. Sunk to her gun decks and with a large hole in the hull, Porter initially managed to refloat the ship, but it kept running aground. He therefore ordered the ship destroyed. Meanwhile, further down the river in the line of support vessels, Confederate cavalry opened fire on the USS *Signal*, USS *Covington*, and *Champion Number Three*, a tug transporting 172 escaped slaves. All three sank after their pilots and officers were killed, and four cannon from the lost *Signal* were salvaged by the Confederates. The slaves that managed to reach the riverbank scattered as best they could. At least another seven military transports were lost either to Confederate artillery or in an unsuccessful attempt to get over the river falls.[33]

Thanks to Bailey's Dam, completed by May 13, Porter's remaining ships managed to get back to Alexandria and relative safety, effectively ending the offensive campaign. For the moment, Union naval activity on the Red River ceased. The same falling water that forced Porter to turn back also kept the Confederate ships at bay. Carter knew this, writing to Stephen Mallory that

---

33 Porter, *Naval History*, 518-519, 521, 523; "Report of Rear Admiral Porter," Ibid, 449; "Later," *Alexandria* [VA] *Gazette*, May 7, 1864; "List of Gunboats," *Shreveport* [LA] *News*, May 24, 1864; Thomas O. Selfridge, "The Navy in the Red River," *B&L*, 4:364; R.L. Robertson to J.L. Brent," July 5, 1864, *William W. Hunter Papers*; W. Randolph Howell Diary, May 2 and 3, 1863, *W. Randolph Howell Papers*, 1861-1879.

operations of his squadron "will depend entirely on the river."[34] A rise in water level could permit a pursuit by the Confederate flotilla; until then, they remained at Shreveport. Banks's expedition turned back, including Adm. Porter's embarrassed squadron. Once the Union ships retreated, Smith cleared the wrecked *New Falls City* to allow for the Confederate ships to pass. Once the river was at sufficient depth, they could strike.

Attack Against the USS *Rattler*

Though action on the Red River halted, 1Lt. Jonathan Carter kept his sailors busy, training and performing needed maintenance on the few ships he possessed while also overseeing all naval matters in Texas by mail. Such discourse and upkeep did not prevent active operations when the opportunity presented itself. In August 1864, Gen. Kirby Smith received word regarding the USS *Rattler*, a gunboat patrolling the Mississippi River. The captain of the gunboat, Acting Master D.W. Glenney, apparently desired to defect to the Confederates, turning over his ship and crew as well. With "arrangements having been made," Carter took a special detail of 20 officers and sailors with the object of boarding and seizing the vessel.[35] They left in mid-August, moving toward the Mississippi River by land.

The USS *Rattler* was assigned to patrol a portion of the Mississippi River near Vicksburg, which it did since that city's capture. Glenney, in exchange for payment, determined to let his ship fall into Confederate hands, weakening Union control over that stretch of the Mississippi River long enough to allow the Confederates to swim 2,000 cattle across for Southern armies further east. Glenney arranged to have his ship devoid of officers and most of its crew ashore, creating an enticing opportunity for any Confederate force that laid in wait.

By the beginning of September, Carter's detail of sailors reached the Louisiana shore off the Mississippi River. There they rendezvoused with a detachment of soldiers and waited. Acting Master Glenney received word that local civilians were aiding Confederate forces and offering sanctuary to deserting Union officers, and he decided that this was his moment to act. A cutter with 22 sailors from the *Rattler* was dispatched at sunset on September 4 with orders to land, capture the civilians,

---

34 Jonathan H. Carter to Stephen Mallory, Apr. 18, 1864, *Jonathan H. Carter Letter Book*.

35 "Report of Acting Master Glenney," *ORN*, 26:545; "Payment Receipt for CSS Missouri," Jun. 30, 1864, *Subject File*, PI, NA; Jonathan H. Carter to Stephen Mallory, Oct. 1, 1864, *Jonathan H. Carter Letter Book*.

and bring them back to the ship for questioning. The party of sailors landed and left their cutter in the charge of two runaway slaves, making their way inland to find and capture the civilians.[36]

As the Union sailors moved to find the suspected civilians, 1Lt. Carter took his party of men and captured the Northern cutter, killing the two runaway slaves. Boarding the cutter, the Confederates began rowing toward the *Rattler*. Glenney, hearing the gunfire, ordered another boat, commanded by his executive officer, lowered to determine the cause of the firing. The Union boat hailed and challenged the cutter filled with Carter's Confederates. Receiving no reply, they opened fire. The Confederates quickly retreated back to the riverbank and ran into the woods to escape, abandoning their attempt to seize the *Rattler*. The treacherous activity of Acting Master Glenney was soon discovered. He was relieved of his command and placed under arrest, but before a formal court martial was convened, Glenney escaped the ship and deserted to Confederate lines.[37]

Lieutenant Carter returned to Shreveport, where he remained for the rest of 1864. His most pressing issue from that point was the increasing desertions that plagued his department. Letters were dispatched weekly to Richmond noting another collection of deserters or sailors absent without leave. Carter repeatedly asked for special permission to convene courts martial, usually a matter reserved for a more senior officer, to provide suitable punishment for those caught in the act. Though desertions increased, they did not impair Confederate naval operations on the Red River, thanks in part to the impressments of nearby soldiers.

1865 dawned upon the Red River with the opposing sides in largely the same positions they occupied the previous year. Once the river began to rise, it was Carter's intention to steam his small flotilla down to Alexandria to await the next spring campaign to begin.[38]

---

36 "Report of Acting Master Willets," *ORN*, 26:537; "M.N. Lynn and L. Beatty to Phelps," *ORN*, 26:548-549.

37 Ibid, 538; "Report of Acting Master Glenney," Ibid, 542; "Gideon Welles to S.P. Lee," Ibid, 548; Jonathan H. Carter to Stephen Mallory, Oct. 1, 1864, *Jonathan H. Carter Letter Book*.

38 Jonathan H. Carter to Stephen Mallory, Oct. 1, 1864, *Jonathan H. Carter Letter Book*; Jonathan H. Carter to Stephen Mallory, Jan. 17, 1865, *Jonathan H. Carter Letter Book*.

CHAPTER TWELVE

Denouement on the Tributaries

Confederate Cavalry
Versus Union Ships on the White River

DUE to the capture of Vicksburg, Confederate military efforts in western Tennessee, eastern Arkansas, and northern Mississippi stopped. Union military advances up the Red River and toward Atlanta necessitated concentration of Confederate forces to meet these threats. After the Red River campaign ended in a Union setback, and, ironically, with the loss of Atlanta, Confederate military forces were free to maneuver in the west in 1864. Slowly, Confederate forces began to contest Union control of Tennessee. Part of this effort focused on the internal waterways of Tennessee: the Mississippi River, the Tennessee River, and the Cumberland River. For the first time since 1862, these rivers once again saw the Confederate flag.

Following the defeat of Gen. Banks in Louisiana and Gen. Frederick Steele in Arkansas, Confederate cavalry swept into central Arkansas on raids against Union supply depots and fortifications. One of these cavalry raids, occurring in June 1864, is worthy of note for this study because it brought about the capture and burning of the USS *Queen City*, a tinclad gunboat mounting eight small guns with a crew of 65 sailors. This vessel was one of several that patrolled the White River after it fell to Union forces following the 1862 campaign for control of the Tennessee and Arkansas riverbanks of the Mississippi.

Brigadier General Jo Shelby raided central Arkansas, taking one brigade of cavalry and one battery of artillery. The raiders reached the White River in mid-June and made camp. While there, Shelby learned of the *Queen City*, lying near the town of Clarendon. He took two of his regiments and his artillery, entering Clarendon at midnight and quietly secured the town. His men then slowly advanced toward the gunboat, anchored beside the town and oblivious to the Confederates. Cavalrymen crawled to within 200 yards of the ship and laid in wait, ready to strike at first light.[1]

At 4 am on the morning of June 24, Shelby's troopers opened fire. Acting Master Michael Hickey ordered his sailors to man their guns and return fire. The exchange did not last long. The tinclad was disabled by hits in its two engines from the Confederate field artillery. Hickey was wounded by a rifle bullet in his leg. After 10 minutes, the ship raised a white flag, which Shelby was "gratified by the sight of." With the assistance of several horsemen, the ship was brought to the riverbank so a formal surrender could take place. Before being boarded by Confederates, Hickey mustered the crew and told them "they could choose between becoming prisoners or jumping into the water to escape."[2] Twenty-five sailors surrendered, with the remainder swimming to safety. Two of those fleeing, however, drowned in the attempt.

With the ship in Confederate hands, Shelby ordered the guns offloaded. He was able to remove only two cannon before he learned that three Union gunboats were on the way. As they approached, Shelby ordered the *Queen City* burned to prevent it from falling back into Union hands, and his artillery briefly engaged the approaching ships. After a few shots to keep the Union ships at a distance, Shelby took his prisoners and retreated back to his encampment. This action was the last time that the Confederate flag, if ever so briefly, stood triumphant on Arkansas waters.[3]

Nathan Bedford Forrest's Navy in Tennessee

As Gen. Jo Shelby raided through Arkansas, another cavalry commander did the same in Tennessee. Major General Nathan Bedford Forrest earned a reputation as one of the toughest fighters in the Confederacy. He led an escape from the siege of Fort Donelson in early 1862 and then commanded cavalry in Tennessee and Mississippi. By 1864, Forrest commanded a division of horsemen that disrupted the supply lines of Union armies advancing toward Atlanta. Forrest did this by

---

1　"Report of Brigadier General Shelby," *ORN*, 26:431.

2　Ibid; "Report of Acting Assistant Surgeon Westfall", Ibid, 428.

3　"Report of Brigadier General Shelby," Ibid, 433; "Report of Acting Master Rogers," Ibid, 425.

invading western Tennessee, a raid that included his infamous capture of Fort Pillow where 300 black soldiers were massacred in April 1864. He also directed a daring nighttime raid into Memphis in August to capture two Union generals and free Confederate prisoners. With only 1,500 cavalry against 6,000 Union soldiers, Forrest left without the generals or any liberated Confederates.

Following these raids, Forrest's cavalry rendezvoused in central Tennessee with Gen. John B. Hood's Confederate army marching from Georgia and Alabama. Hood hoped to force Gen. Sherman's Union columns advancing through central Georgia to turn around, or retake Tennessee for the Confederacy. Forrest was instructed to raid Union supply lines until Hood's army arrived, and then to merge and augment the Confederate Army of Tennessee.

Forrest's cavalry advanced into central Tennessee in October 1864 to strike Union supply centers. The largest of these was located at Johnsonville, lying on the Tennessee River, connecting larger depots in Ohio and Illinois with Federal armies in Tennessee. This position was defended with numerous light gunboats and a garrison of infantry.

The Confederate cavalrymen reached the Tennessee River on October 28, near Paris Landing in northern Tennessee. There they captured the steamer *Mazeppa*, a 700-ton supply ship en-route from Cincinnati, which was towing two barges filled with more supplies. The ship surrendered after the third shot from Forrest's artillerymen, hidden along the bank, hit their mark. The supplies on the ship and barges were then taken ashore and loaded onto the Confederate's wagons. During this activity, three small Union gunboats arrived and began shelling the woods. The *Mazeppa* was burned to prevent her being recaptured, but the supplies were successfully removed. Forrest eventually returned with his men and artillery to line the riverbank in anticipation of more action to come, effectively cutting the Union river supply line into central Tennessee.[4]

The next day, more Union supply ships moved up the Tennessee River, steaming from the depot at Johnsonville to refill with supplies further north. The supply steamer *Anna* was first to cross the hidden Confederate batteries. Once again, Forrest's gunners shot accurately; the *Anna* managed to get past the hidden guns but sustained so much damage that it sank before reaching the safety of Union lines. Now warned, Union supply steamers waited for gunboats to silence the woods. The USS *Undine*, mounting eight 24-pound howitzers, was sent from

---

4 "Report of Lieutenant Colonel Sinclair," *OR*, Part 1, 39:860; "Report of Brigadier General Donaldson," *OR*, Part 1, 39:863-864; "Report of Major General Forrest," *OR*, Part 1, 39:870.

Lieutenant General Nathan B. Forrest, CSA.

Library of Congress

Johnsonville and escorted two transports, the *J. W. Cheesman* and *Venus*, each towing a barge.

Forrest's men sprang the trap again. One enterprising cavalryman called out "Halloo there, gunboat," which caused the commander of the *Undine*, Acting Master J.L. Bryant, to stop his engines.[5] The cavalrymen and artillerymen then commenced fire on all three ships. Bryant returned fire and continued steaming the convoy past the batteries, but Forrest's guns were spread along several miles of river and kept the enemy ships under sustained fire. After an hour, a Confederate shell cut a steam pipe while another smashed into a furnace. More shells killed two sailors and mortally wounded another two on deck. Bryant steamed past these guns and halted to assess damage to his gunship, when suddenly another hidden battery commenced firing.

The transport *Venus* continued, staying close to the *Undine* for protection. Her captain was killed in the fight and the transport, "riddled by shells and musketry," anchored in the river near the Union gunboat as the *Undine* shelled the woods. The other transport, the *Cheesman*, lagged behind the two ships. While passing the first set of batteries, her steam pipe was cut. The second transport crashed into the riverbank and surrendered to the cavalrymen in the woods, in full view of the USS *Undine*, which continued to fire on the Confederates. Acting Master Bryant lost another six men wounded when another Confederate shell crashed into his engine room, cutting another steam pipe and forcing the engineers to evacuate the lower decks. With no engine power Bryant ordered his crew to abandon ship and he raised the white flag. Another Union gunboat observing the battle and firing at a distance retreated after seeing the fate of the convoy.[6]

---

5 "Evidence of Acting Master Bryant," *ORN*, 26:602.

6 "Interesting from the Mississippi," The *Wyandot* [OH] *Pioneer*, Nov. 11, 1864; "Evidence of Acting Master Bryant," *ORN*, 26:602.

The three barges and the disabled *Cheesman*, empty of any valuable supplies, were burned, just as the *Mazeppa* was the previous day. The commander of the 26th Tennessee Cavalry Battalion, Lt. Col. David C. Kelley, boarded the *Venus*, bringing her alongside the riverbank. His men also boarded the *Undine*. At the cost of one cavalryman wounded, Forrest's men captured a gunboat and a transport and sank several barges and two supply ships. Cavalrymen now crewed the two ships. For the first time in two years, the Confederate flag flew on the Tennessee River.[7]

Now in possession of two ships, Forrest determined to press his advantage and strike the supply depot at Johnsonville by land and water. Colonel W. A. Dawson was given command of the vessels with instructions to keep pace with the cavalry during their march. On November 2, after becoming familiar with their ships, Col. Dawson's improvised sailors steamed out of support range of the cavalrymen. It was then that two Union gunboats closed and opened fire on them. Ill prepared and inexperienced at naval warfare, Dawson ordered the *Undine* abandoned and burned, and the men escaped back to Confederate lines in the *Venus*. Union sailors boarded the burning *Undine* and extinguished the flames, bringing the ship back to Johnsonville for repairs.[8]

Undeterred, Forrest continued his cavalry march to Johnsonville. On November 3, the *Venus* was once again pushed ahead in an attempt to lure Union gunboats into range of hidden batteries. The ploy did not work, however, and the *Venus* was disabled and abandoned by Col. Dawson, whose men escaped. Union gunboats then towed the *Venus* back to Johnsonville. A collection of five small gunboats attempted to run past the Confederate batteries in an effort to reach Johnsonville, but they were all held back by the accuracy of the Confederate artillerists. Forrest's troopers reached Johnsonville that night and the general prepared to sack the largest supply depot in Tennessee the next day.[9]

Forrest later recalled what he saw, closely examining the position in preparation for the following day's assault. Besides a wharf filled with supply ships and gunboats, "an immense warehouse presented itself filled and was represented as being stored with the most valuable supplies, while several acres of the shore were covered with every description of army stores."[10] The depot was lightly

7 "Report of Brigadier General Chalmers," *OR*, Part 1, 39:873-874.

8 John A. Wyeth, *That Devil Forrest: Life of General Nathan Bedford Forrest* (Baton Rouge, LA, 1989), 462.

9 Ibid, 462-463.

10 "Report of Major General Forrest," *OR*, Part 1, 39:870-871.

United States Colored Troops at Johnsonville, Tennessee. *Library of Congress*

defended by just a few hundred inexperienced men of 13th and 100th Regiments of the United States Colored Troops, soldiers who were aware of Forrest's reputation and his massacre at Fort Pillow of hundreds of United States Colored Troops earlier in 1864.

Forrest ordered his artillery to commence firing at 3 pm on November 4. Their initial targets were two gunboats, lashed together in the river. Union gunners, afloat and ashore, quickly returned fire, but the men began to panic. The gunboats were set afire fifteen minutes after the action started and were abandoned. Forrest next targeted the supply ships, which burned along the riverbank. "The immense amount of stores," Forrest reported, "were also set on fire, together with the huge warehouse." The Colored Troops took refuge in their small but well sited fortification nearby, hoping to avoid a repeat of the Fort Pillow massacre. Forrest left them alone; his goal was the supplies. All told, four gunboats, the USS *Key West*, USS *Undine*, USS *Elfin*, and USS *Tawah* were destroyed. Another eight transports and 28 barges also burned along the riverbank. Forrest's cavalry retreated, having caused over $6,000,000 in damages at a cost of eleven casualties.[11]

11 Ibid, 871; "We Learn," The *Daily Nashville* [TN] *Union*, Nov. 8, 1864.

Final Naval Activity in Tennessee

The cavalry of Nathan Bedford Forrest continued riding through Tennessee, eventually uniting with the Confederate Army of Tennessee on November 16. Hood's bloody attack at Franklin and repulse at Nashville sealed the fate of his army and ended Confederate army operations in Tennessee. One final action on that river occurred in 1865. A party of Confederate sailors was captured in March 1865 by a group of local militia near Kingston, Tennessee, in the eastern part of the state. The sailors were dispatched from Richmond, Virginia, with a small boat full of supplies. Their objective was to move down the Tennessee River and destroy any Union ships encountered. Among the captured items were several boxes, each containing an underwater torpedo [12]

The last operation by Confederate forces on the western waters of the northern Confederacy took place on April 10, 1865. The steamer *Saint Paul* was docked at Brownsville Landing on the Hatchie River, a tributary of the Mississippi. A Lt. Joseph Luxton boarded the steamer with a band of guerillas, claiming to be part of Nathan Bedford Forrest's cavalry. They took possession of the vessel and got underway. For reasons unknown, Luxton shot a deckhand and threw him overboard. Two days later, the guerrillas rendezvoused with a contingent of Quantrill's Rangers and burned the *Saint Paul* before escaping into the woods. Luxton was captured a few days later under the name of Wilcox. After confessing to having shot the deckhand and burning the steamer, he was hung. Thus, the Civil War ended in Tennessee waters.[13]

Final Efforts and Surrender in Louisiana

As the *Saint Paul* burned on the Hatchie River, Confederate Gen. Robert E. Lee's army prepared to stack its arms for the last time, having surrendered the previous day at Appomattox Court House. After retreating from the trenches at Petersburg and abandoning Richmond, Lee's army was cut off from supplies and trapped by Grant's vastly larger force. By the end of April, the remnants of the Confederate Army of Tennessee also surrendered in North Carolina. On April 12, Mobile, Alabama surrendered, the last Confederate controlled port city. Richard Taylor surrendered the last major force east of the Mississippi River on May 4, and

12 "General Order of Acting Rear Admiral Lee," *ORN*, 27:87-88.

13 "Report of Acting Master Fitzpatrick," *ORN*, 27:148-149.

President Jefferson Davis was captured in Georgia on May 10. Nathan Bedford Forrest disbanded his small command later that month.

Word of the Confederacy's collapse was slow to reach Confederate forces in the Trans-Mississippi region, and actions by Gen. Kirby Smith and 1Lt. Jonathan Carter continued on the Red River well into 1865. Despite scant resources, surveys were conducted in Texas to determine again the feasibility of constructing an ironclad near Galveston. Plans and drawings of the ironclad *Missouri* were forwarded by Lt. Carter to commanders in Galveston to use for construction of another ironclad there. Before construction or conversion could commence, word reached Texas of the collapse of the rest of the Confederacy and the project was abandoned.[14]

Water levels on the Red River began to rise in March 1865 with the spring thaws and Carter ordered the ironclad CSS *Missouri* to get underway, leaving Shreveport for the first time. The steamer *Mary T*, unarmed but filled with supplies, accompanied the ironclad, as did the gunboat *W. H. Webb*. Steaming down the Red River, Carter was pleased with the performance of his ironclad, noting that the vessel "equals my expectations." He was not pleased however, with the lack of coal in Shreveport. His ships were forced to stop at plantations along the river and requisition wood to keep their engines operating. The ironclad reached Coushatta on March 30 and passed Grand Ecore the next day. On April 4, Carter docked at Alexandria, just above the river falls, ready to face any Union threat.[15]

There was no enemy opposition. Union commanders in Louisiana sent much of their forces east to the Confederate port city of Mobile. Though Mobile Bay was in Union hands, the city itself continued to resist until it surrendered on April 12 rather than face destruction. With Federal focus on the final capture of Mobile, there was no planned spring campaign to move against Confederates on the Red River. Carter's ironclad *Missouri* waited in vain for a battle that never came.

As 1Lt. Carter steamed the *Missouri* down the Red River, another Confederate naval officer arrived. First Lieutenant Charles W. Read was one of the Confederacy's most daring officers. Read was no stranger to river operations, assuming command of the CSS *McRae* after her captain was wounded in the battle for New Orleans in 1862 and then serving onboard the ironclad *Arkansas* in its

---

14 Jonathan H. Carter to Hawes, Mar. 6, 1865," *Jonathan H. Carter Letter Book*; Jonathan H. Carter to Roy, Apr. 3, 1865," *Jonathan H. Carter Letter Book*.

15 Jonathan H. Carter to Edmund K. Smith, Mar. 31, 1865," Ibid; Jonathan H. Carter to Simon B. Buckner, Mar. 30, 1865," Ibid; Jonathan H. Carter to Stephen Mallory, Apr. 5, 1865," Ibid; "Report of Major Jackson," *ORN*, 27:142.

operations at Vicksburg and Baton Rouge. Afterwards, Read spent a year of commerce raiding, even cutting out a Union revenue cutter in Maine before being captured and held prisoner for a year. He was exchanged in October 1864 and assumed command of a small squadron of torpedo boats operating on the James River in Virginia, protecting the Confederate capital.

Just before Richmond was evacuated, Read was sent by his own request to assume command of the *W. H. Webb*. He wanted to make a bold escape with the *Webb* out of the Red River and into the Mississippi, steaming past New Orleans and the Union fortification below. Once clear of the Mississippi, Read planned attacks against Union commerce in the Gulf of Mexico, even possibly threatening the Atlantic seaboard of the United States, just as he did in 1863.

Reaching Alexandria just as 1Lt. Carter's small squadron was arriving, Read boarded and assumed command of the *Webb*, relieving Lt. J. L. Philips. Read performed a quick survey of his vessel: the best supplies available were already issued to the *Missouri*; the weapons onboard were limited in effectiveness; the crew of the *Webb* was unprepared; and there were only two engineers Read felt he could trust with his engines. Finding the ship ill equipped for a dash down the Mississippi and ocean voyage, the *Webb* was detached from Carter's squadron. Read carried a letter of introduction from Carter for Gen. Kirby Smith and steamed back upriver to Shreveport.[16]

At Shreveport, 1Lt. Read made his way to Smith's headquarters. After providing the introduction and outline of his mission, Smith put his scant resources at Read's disposal, offering to support however he could. One 30-pound Parrot cannon and two 12-pound howitzers from army stores were loaded onto the *Webb*, with the Parrot mounted on the bow. The 12-pounders should be enough to intimidate and halt any merchant ships encountered and the 30-pounder could provide some protection if facing a warship. Additionally, five torpedoes were loaded on the *Webb*, ready to be equipped on the bow with a spar.[17]

For 1Lt. Carter, the biggest concern about Read's mission was the water level of the Red River. Though the river level was higher than it was in the past two years, it could fall anytime and if it reached a level too low, then the *Webb* could not transit the falls that impeded Union ships the previous spring. Carter dispatched notes to 1Lt. Read urging quick action. The *Webb* steamed back to Alexandria as soon as the artillery was loaded and secured. The crew was ignorant of their mission; Read kept

16 Jonathan H. Carter to Edmund K. Smith, Mar. 31, 1865," Ibid.

17 "Report of Lieutenant Read," *ORN*, 22, 168-169.

First Lieutenant Charles W. Read, CSN.

Naval History and Heritage Command

everyone in the dark to prevent leaks to Union sympathizers. Rumors circulated that Read intended to attack Union ships at the mouth of the Red River.[18]

Getting past the numerous Union gunboats constantly on patrol in the Mississippi River was going to require more than cannon. 190 bales of cotton, acquired from local army stores, were loaded onto the deck to provide protection for the machinery and sailors, as well as potentially disguise the ship as a civilian transport at first glance. Additionally, the ship's hull was whitewashed to make it more difficult to see from a distance in fog, and a rough bulwark was constructed on the bow to provide protection against heavy waves once at sea.

1Lt. Carter authorized Read to fill the complement of the *Webb's* crew, taking most of the sailors assigned to both the *Missouri* and *Mary T.* The *Webb* needed power to steam down the river and the limited coal available left only a one-day supply for the vessel. Read scoured the local plantations, just as Carter did previously, and found a supply of wood that, when distributed with the coal, provided a fuel supply for five days of steaming.[19]

Read's plan required careful timing for any chance of success. Three Union ironclads and two gunboats were stationed at the mouth of the Red River. Additional gunboats regularly patrolled the Mississippi River between New Orleans and the Red River. Furthermore, Union telegraph lines along the

18 Jonathan H. Carter to Charles W. Read, Apr. 7, 1865," *Jonathan H. Carter Letter Book*; "Report of Allan Pinkerton," Ibid, 152.

19 "Report of Lieutenant Read," *ORN*, 22:168; "Order of Brigadier General Sherman," *ORN*, 22:146; Clarence Jeffries, "Running the Blockade on the Mississippi," *Confederate Veteran* (1914), 12:22; Scharf, *History of the Confederate States Navy*, 365.

riverbanks connected coaling and supply stations with the cities. Knowing this, Read ordered Confederate guerillas to sever these communication lines as the *Webb* made its journey. Read also ordered the lines cut below New Orleans to further confuse enemy ships.

It took a fortnight to prepare the *Webb* and its crew for the ship's dash downriver. Once ready, Read kept the ship in a state of heightened alert to slip out when the weather was fortuitous and the night dark. Just before getting underway in the predawn hours of April 23, 1865, Read learned of the assassination of President Abraham Lincoln. The information was kept from the crew, as they were in the final preparations to steam downriver and Read did not want the crew to question their orders. Before the sun rose on April 23, 1865, Read ordered the *Webb* underway. The first obstacles to overcome were formidable. The ironclad monitor *Manhattan* and the ironclads *Tennessee*—formerly the Confederate ironclad that protected Mobile Bay—and *Lafayette* lay in wait at the mouth of the Red River, along with the wooden gunboats *Lexington* and *Vindicator*.

Weighing anchor at Alexandria at 4 am on April 23, the *Webb* steamed downriver. Once clear of the town, Read ordered the *Webb* to increase speed for the approach to the Mississippi. Union sentinels onboard the monitor *Manhattan* did not sight the *Webb* until it was nearly upon them. Acting Master Charles W. Adams, the monitor's executive officer, sounded two whistle blasts, indicating for the approaching *Webb* to heave to. Read ignored the signal and by the time the monitor was cleared for battle, the *Webb* slipped past. Believing the *Webb* as just the first in a full-scale attack by the entire Confederate fleet in Alexandria, Adams kept his ship in place "to be in readiness for the rebel ironclad *Missouri*." The ironclad *Lafayette* and gunboat *Vindicator* gave chase for about 40 miles, pushing their engineering machinery to the point of "serious and dangerous conditions," before turning around and abandoning the chase. The Union ships attempted to notify officials in New Orleans about the Confederate ship's passing, but the Confederate guerillas succeeded in cutting the telegraph lines. Lieutenant Read moved into the Mississippi River; now he needed to get out of it and into the Gulf of Mexico.[20]

Each time that 1Lt. Read encountered a ship on the river, he ordered a light raised on the mast as a signal. This successfully deceived any passing ships long enough for the *Webb* to steam past at its top speed of 25 miles per hour. In between these ruses, Read ordered sailors ashore briefly to cut more telegraph lines down to

---

20 "Report of Acting Master Adams," *ORN*, 22:162; "Report of Acting Master Slattery," *ORN*, 22:151; "Report of Lieutenant Commander Foster," *ORN*, 22:163.

New Orleans. This plan worked well except when one party encountered a detachment of soldiers of United States Colored Troops, which forced the sailors to hastily return to the *Webb*. So far his plan was working, and April 23 saw the *Webb* steaming downriver toward New Orleans.[21]

Sunrise on April 24 found the *Webb* near Donaldsonville, where 1Lt. Read continued with his deception by flying signal flags to confuse the Union fort there. Reaching New Orleans at lunchtime, Read and his men raised the flag of the United States, putting it at half mast, just as all other flags in the city, to mourn President Abraham Lincoln's recent assassination. He also dressed several sailors in Union army overcoats to roam the decks and mask their identity. Confident, the Confederates steamed past the city in view of numerous Union gunboats that mistook the vessel for an army transport.

The deception however, was finally unmasked. Pursuing Union warships reached Donaldsonville, and explained the situation to the Union garrison there. Hasty telegraphs were sent south to Thibodaux, and then to New Orleans via a wide arc of telegraph lines the *Webb's* sailors could not reach to cut. Word arrived in the Crescent City that the *Webb* moved into the Mississippi River just a couple of hours after it passed Donaldsonville. Alarms were sent to the ships lying at New Orleans, to the forts further downriver, and to the army garrisons within the city, and even to Mobile and along the Texas coast.[22]

Along the city docks were a collection of Union gunboats. Among these were the USS *Quaker City*, USS *Florida*, USS *Port Royal*, USS *Ossipee*, USS *Lackawanna*, USS *Hollyhock*, and USS *Pembina*, all wooden gunboats mounting several guns each. They received warning of the *Webb's* approach about the same time that Read's ship made its appearance. The ships were prepared for imminent action, raising steam, loading their cannon, and training them into the river as the *Webb*, still steaming at her top speed of 25 miles an hour, was "almost flying by." As the Confederates crossed the gunboats abreast of New Orleans, the guns of the *Lackawanna* opened first, followed by the rest.[23]

The *Webb* continued past, "so close that a rock could have been thrown from one boat to the other." It was impossible to miss and the first shot of the *Lackawanna* struck the *Webb*, smashing into the hull. Read refused to return fire,

---

21 Jeffries, "Running the Blockade on the Mississippi," 22; "Report of Allan Pinkerton," Ibid, 153.

22 "Report of Major Hoffman," *ORN*, 22:146; Scharf, *History of the Confederate States Navy*, 365.

23 Charles A. Earp, ed., *Yellow Flag: The Civil War Journal of Surgeon's Steward C. Marion Dodson*, (Baltimore, MD, 2002), 121; "Report of Commander Le Roy," *ORN*, 22:148.

instead ordering the Confederate flag hoisted as a sign of defiance. He even ordered the Confederate flag dipped in salute as his ship passed abreast of a docked French man-of-war. The *Webb* moved so quickly with the current that there was only time for each Union gunboat to fire one broadside.

Read sighted one vessel that looked as if ready to get underway and he ordered the *Webb* to steam at the approaching ship, ready to strike it with his bow spar torpedo. However, determining that the enemy vessel was going to leave the Confederates alone, Read steamed quickly past it, with the safety valves tied off in the engine room. This was fortunate for the Confederate sailors, as they were not aware of how close they came to blowing themselves up. It was not a Union gunboat; it was the ammunition transport *Fear Not*, which was fully loaded with gunpowder and shells. If the torpedo struck and detonated, it might have created a huge fireball that engulfed both ships and likely parts of the city.

As the *Webb* continued down the riverfront, the captain of the USS *Ossipee* ordered his gunners to fire, but half of the cannon misfired. The *Pembina* and *Port Royal* added their guns to the battle and scored several hits. One shell smashed into a cotton bale protecting the *Webb's* pilothouse while another struck near the smokestack. Another hit smashed the supporting fixtures of the bow spar torpedo and Read ordered it cut away.[24]

The people of New Orleans heard the cannonading and hundreds filled the riverbank to observe the exchange. Rumors quickly spread through the crowds, who had not seen the Confederate military in action for three years. Some speculated that the ship carried Confederate President Jefferson Davis while others believed that it was full of Confederate bullion and government documents seeking safety abroad. One man in the crowd even claimed that Lincoln's assassin, John Wilkes Booth, was at the helm.[25]

The gunboats *Hollyhock*, *Quaker City*, and *Florida* were the first to raise steam and chase the *Webb* downriver, their orders to either "run her down or press her to the forts below."[26] By the time they were in the channel, the *Webb* was clear of the city, steaming downriver at maximum speed, burning everything combustible in the boilers to gain more speed.

24 Jeffries, "Running the Blockade on the Mississippi," 23; "Abstract Log of USS Lackawanna," *ORN*, 22:166; Scharf, *History of the Confederate States Navy*, 365-366.

25 Scharf, *History of the Confederate States Navy*, 366.

26 Earp, *Yellow Flag*, 122.

Only two obstacles remained: Forts Jackson and Saint Philip below New Orleans. Read knew them well, having taken part in their defense exactly three years prior while onboard the CSS *McRae*.

Read's good fortune, however, was about to end. Unbeknownst to Read, lying below the city was the USS *Richmond*, a wooden gunboat that Read faced in the 1862 campaign for New Orleans. The *Webb* rounded a bend at 2 pm some 24 miles below the city and Read caught a quick glimpse of the *Richmond*, immediately recognizing the warship. He ordered the *Webb* to reverse course behind a river bend, but it was too late; Union sailors caught sight of the Confederate ship and began to weigh anchor in pursuit with its crew at general quarters. Seeing the *Richmond* approaching, Read ordered his gunners to fire the bow Parrott three times to keep the Union sailors at bay momentarily. He then called his officers together for a quick counsel of war.[27]

By then, the Union ships giving chase saw the *Webb* turn around toward them. The men of the USS *Hollyhock* believed that the "tug of war ad [sic] come." The final battle did not happen. As the Confederate officers listened, Read said "It's no use; it's a failure," adding "the *Richmond* will drown us all."[28] The *Webb* was steered toward the riverbank, grounding about 50 yards from land.

Read did not allow the *Webb* to fall into enemy hands. He gave orders to destroy the ship. While sailors put the torch to the vessel, a slow match was lit leading to the magazine. The crew threw lines to shore and made haste to abandon the vessel. Others jumped overboard and swam for safety. Both the USS *Richmond* and USS *Hollyhock* closed in an attempt to extinguish the flames; it was observed earlier that the *Webb* was laden with a great amount of cotton, which made a rich prize to the captain and crew that managed to capture it intact.

An engineer from the *Hollyhock* boarded the *Webb*, releasing the steam pressure in the boilers while other sailors set to work at the pumps to put out the flames. While attempting to clear the flames, several Confederates fell into Union hands. The prisoners were yelling to clear the area and that the magazine was set to blow. Hearing this, the Union ships beat a hasty retreat, moving to a safe distance. They steamed away so quickly that several Union sailors were left onboard the *Webb*.

27 "Abstract Log of USS Richmond," *ORN*, 22:167.

28 Earp, *Yellow Flag*, 124; Jeffries, "Running the Blockade on the Mississippi," 23.

Destruction of the CSS *Webb.*

Naval History and Heritage Command and Harper's Weekly

They lowered a cutter from the burning ship to row themselves, along with several more prisoners, to safety.[29]

Most of the *Webb's* crew regrouped on the riverbank where 1Lt. Read divided them into three groups. Each group was ordered to make their way through the Louisiana swamps back to Confederate lines; the same attempt was made successfully by numerous naval officers in 1862 following the destruction of the ironclad *Louisiana* and Read thought it might work again. This time, however, the enemy was ready for an attempted escape. Union cavalry was dispatched from New Orleans with orders to hunt down the sailors. Read saw flight was futile and returned to the riverbank, preferring to surrender to fellow sailors. One group continued but was captured by Union cavalry shortly afterward.[30]

Fire consumed the *Webb* into the afternoon. At 4:30 pm, the flames reached the magazine and the ship blew up with a terrific explosion. All that was saved of the cargo was 11 bales of cotton, picked up by the USS *Richmond*. Lieutenant Read and his captured crew were brought onboard the *Richmond* as well, before being taken to New Orleans. The Confederates were declared prisoners of war and brought north for imprisonment in Fort Warren in Boston Harbor—the same prison Read spent the better part of 1863 in after being captured while commerce raiding on the Atlantic coast.[31]

---

29 Earp, *Yellow Flag*, 124.

30 "Report of Allan Pinkerton," *ORN*, 22:154; Scharf, *History of the Confederate States Navy*, 367; Jeffries, "Running the Blockade on the Mississippi," 23.

31 "Abstract Log of USS Richmond," *ORN*, 22:167.

The attempted escape by the *W.H. Webb* was the last major operation by Confederate naval forces on the Mississippi River and its tributaries. The very day that Shreveport learned of Read's failure to escape the Mississippi River, word also arrived regarding General Robert E. Lee's surrender. More bad news continued arriving throughout April and May. Mobile, the last Confederate port on the Gulf of Mexico, surrendered on April 12. Two days after the *Webb* burned, another Confederate army, commanded by Gen. Joseph Johnston, surrendered in North Carolina. In early May, Confederate forces in Alabama and Mississippi likewise surrendered. The only active Confederate military now was Gen. Kirby Smith's ground forces and 1Lt. Jonathan Carter's small flotilla at Alexandria.

General Smith opened communications with Union commanders in New Orleans to negotiate his own surrender, following the same terms granted to Generals Lee and Johnston. Union envoys were dispatched to Alexandria and Shreveport to oversee the surrender.

A squadron of Union ships steamed to Alexandria for the final capitulation. First Lieutenant Jonathan H Carter surrendered the ironclad CSS *Missouri* to Lt. Cmdr. W. E. Fitzhugh on June 3, 1865. Carter, along with 41 officers and men, were paroled and allowed to return home. The *Mary T*, Carter claimed, was never fully paid for by the Confederate government and he turned the ship over to its owners. Fitzhugh however, confiscated that steamer as a prize of war. The Union ships then continued to Shreveport, with Carter onboard the confiscated *Mary T* preceding them to prevent potential misunderstandings. Upon arriving at Shreveport on June 7, 16 more sailors received their parole and the remaining naval stores fell into Union hands, along with two army-owned steamers, the *Beauregard* and *New Champion*. The torpedo boats built there were scuttled before Union forces arrived.[32]

The *Missouri* and the *Mary T* were examined and taken to New Orleans and sold. With the loss of these vessels and the surrender of 1Lt. Carter and his sailors, Confederate naval forces on the Red River ceased to exist. It took over four years, but the United States finally reclaimed sovereignty over all of the Mississippi River and its numerous tributaries. Of the remaining Confederate naval forces, only a couple of small ships were in Texas waters and the commerce raider *Shenandoah* was currently at sea in the Pacific Ocean. These, too, soon surrendered, ending what was the Confederacy's short-lived navy.

---

32 "Report of Lieutenant Commander Fitzhugh," Ibid, 27:229-231; "Report of Acting Rear Admiral Lee," Ibid, 27:235; "Report of Lieutenant Commander Fitzhugh," Ibid, 27:239.

CHAPTER THIRTEEN

Confederate Riverine Ambitions, Armament, and Innovations

Confederate Strategic Planning

A fully functioning riverine force capable of maintaining control over the Mississippi River Valley was one of Confederate Secretary of the Navy Stephen Mallory's most important goals. His plan was to utilize a fleet of ironclad warships, backed by gunboats converted from civilian river steamers, to keep the supply lines of the internal Confederacy open while denying the southern waterways to the United States. Ultimately, that objective failed and the Confederacy's riverine navy never matched its Union counterpart. Despite winning several hard-fought tactical victories, the Confederates could never capitalize on them to alter the North's strategic advantages.

Mallory's ambitions and efforts show just how closely contested the Mississippi River Valley became. Although the Battle of Hampton Roads in Virginia saw the most well-known employment of a Confederate ironclad, the Mississippi River was where the Confederate Navy made the greatest attempt to use ironclad warships. As the Confederacy rapidly organized for war, Mallory contracted to produce ironclads across his nascent country.

The numbers tell the story. In 1861, the famed *Virginia* began its conversion from the USS *Merrimack* in Norfolk, Virginia and fought the Union ironclad *Monitor* to a draw in March of 1862. Late in the year, the ironclad *Atlanta* was converted from a one-run blockade runner in Savannah, Georgia but was not commissioned until November of 1862. Other projects were in the planning phase but had not yet begun construction. By comparison, in 1861 Mallory ordered the conversion of the

Eastport into an ironclad on the Tennessee River, acquired the converted armored privateer *Manassas* in New Orleans, ordered the construction of the ironclads *Tennessee* and *Arkansas* at Memphis, and arranged for the construction of the ironclads *Louisiana* and *Mississippi* at New Orleans. Three-fourths of the Confederacy's 1861 ironclad programs were in the Mississippi River Valley. Mallory's primary focus was obvious.

In 1862, the Confederacy's naval strategy included a second wave of construction that spring, aiming to operate nine ironclads on the Mississippi River by fall. Even after these initial hulls were destroyed due to the spring 1862 Union river campaigns, the Confederate Navy finished the *Arkansas*, the only survivor of those campaigns, and planned to add eight new ironclads built on tributary waters: three on the Yazoo River; two on the Tennessee River; the *Missouri* on the Red River at Shreveport (with hopes for a second project there); and the partial ironclad *J.A. Cotton* and the conversion project known as the *Stevens* in Bayou Teche.

Obtaining Naval Artillery

Although their armored casemates were intended to help them survive combat, the key to the potential offensive success of these ironclads was their armament. The Southern navy department intended to utilize the most modern artillery and ordnance for its vessels. The question was how to do that when the South had so few iron foundries that might be able to produce cannon, compared to numerous active gun foundries in Pennsylvania, Ohio, New York, and New England. The easiest and quickest expedient was seizing cannon in U.S. armories and forts located in the South. The Confederacy's ability to equip its navy and expand its fortifications might have been impossible without the hundreds of heavy naval and siege guns captured at the U.S. Gosport Navy Yard in Norfolk, Virginia in 1861.

Civil War artillery firing procedures were complex, relying on algebra, physics, and geometry to determine what cannon, projectile, and powder charge was appropriate for different targets at different ranges. In fact, the Union's *Elementary Instructions in Naval Ordnance and Gunnery*, published in 1861 and used by naval officers on both sides, spent an entire chapter introducing the reader to principles of physics related to motion, inertia, density, and resistance.[1]

---

1 James H. Ward, *Elementary Instructions in Naval Ordnance and Gunnery* (New York, 1861), 14-25.

There were two ways to measure Civil War artillery, diameter of the bore of a gun barrel or the weight of the projectile being fired. For example, an 8-inch cannon had a barrel diameter of eight inches while a 12-pounder fired a shell or solid cannonball that weighed 12 pounds. Essential to the effectiveness of the round fired was the charge of gunpowder used to launch the projectile from the cannon. A bigger charge—more powder—resulted in greater force and range. Elevation of a cannon's barrel also affected range and the arc of the shot fired.

Additionally, the barrel weight must be considered. Barrel weight is measured in hundredweights, shortened to cwt in ordnance texts, where one cwt is equal to 100 pounds. The heavier the barrel, or greater the cwt, the more powerful gunpowder charge that can be placed safely in the barrel, enabling a heavier projectile to be fired at a longer range. An increased cwt is created by lengthening or thickening a barrel. Furthermore, the consideration of whether an artillery barrel is smoothbore or rifled must likewise be considered. Rifling can shoot projectiles at a greater range with more accuracy. The majority of naval cannon were muzzle-loading types: the powder and projectile were loaded at the front—the same end of the cannon where the projectile would exit when fired.

The most commonly used Confederate naval cannon of the Civil War era was the 32-pounder. Fortunately for the Confederacy, dozens of these were captured at the U.S. Gosport Navy Yard in Norfolk, Virginia in 1861. Using them required specialized knowledge; there were twelve different version of the gun, with six different cwt measurements, ranging from 27 cwt to 57 cwt, plus variants for smoothbore and rifled barrels for each. The lighter 27 cwt 32-pounder used a gunpowder charge of four pounds, whose smoothbore variant could fire a shell out to 1,600 yards (nearly a mile). The heavier 57 cwt version of the same gun could absorb an explosive powder charge of up to nine pounds; its smoothbore variant had a range out to 2,700 yards.[2]

In the decade before the Civil War, artillery capable of firing explosive shells was developed. In the United States, naval officer John A. Dahlgren established the U.S. Navy's Ordnance Department. He explored better scientific processes for creating more reliable and more effective artillery used from the mid-1850's through the Civil War. Navy guns originally fired only solid iron cannon balls. Under Dahlgren's direction, these "shot-guns" were supplemented by "shell-guns" using hollow projectiles filled with gunpowder that exploded at pre-set ranges using timing fuses.

2 John A. Dahlgren, *Shells and Shell Guns* (Philadelphia, PA: 1856), 29, 32.

6.4-Inch Brooke Cannon, with Banding Around the Barrel. *Library of Congress*

While both navies utilized the 32-pounder gun, artillery of larger sizes was common. Dahlgren used bore diameter as a standard measurement, making cannon as large as 20-inches; these larger pieces could handle gunpowder charges as heavy as 100 pounds and fired shells weighing over 1,000 pounds. A 32-pounder, by comparison, had a 6.4-inch bore diameter and fired a 32-pound shell.

The Confederacy tried to match Dahlgren's cannon with its own designs. John M. Brooke, the Confederate Navy's ordnance expert, developed his own series of cannon. These were measured by bore diameter and ranged in size from 6.4-inches (the Brooke version of the standard navy 32-pounder) to 11-inch guns. He created both smoothbore and rifled versions of the guns, which are easily identified by their banding, rings of reinforced iron wrapped around the base of the barrel to add strength for containing heavier gunpowder charges. Most of Brooke's artillery was used on the Atlantic coast, but one 6.4-inch rifled cannon was placed on the Lake

Pontchartrain gunboat *Florida* early in the war and other Brooke guns might have made their way to the Mississippi River.[3]

Just as important as the gun was the ammunition used. Naval cannon used several types of ammunition, including shot, shells, and grapeshot. Shot were solid iron, either shaped into a traditional round cannonball or molded into a conical projectile. Shells were hollow and filled with explosives. Grapeshot were small solid metal balls packaged together; when fired, they spread out, turning the cannon into a large shotgun. Each type of ammunition had its advantages in certain situations. Exploding shells could easily damage wooden steamers, but generally were not as effective against ironclads. Grapeshot could sweep decks of personnel. Shot was used to smash into and fracture the protective plating of ironclad warships. All three types of ammunition were utilized by Confederate naval forces to defend the Mississippi River. John M. Brooke, the Confederacy's cannon designer, also created ammunition, including an armor-piercing variant of shot with an iron bolt tip used to focus its the energy into one point, maximizing potential penetration against Union ironclad casemates.[4]

Ultimately, the Confederacy was not able to employ as many modern pieces of artillery as it desired. The South did produce reliable naval cannon later in the war, but most of these were created in the east and utilized on the Atlantic seaboard. New Orleans foundries started experimenting with cannon manufacture, but the city fell to the Union before mass production could commence.

Most of the artillery utilized on the Mississippi River by Confederate naval forces came from three avenues: the huge supply at the U.S. Gosport Navy Yard, Union heavy guns seized in state armories and U.S. forts, or lighter field guns in armories or captured from Union armies that were modified for naval use. The Gosport Navy Yard at Norfolk, Virginia, contained the largest collection of naval ordnance in the United States in 1861. Much of this was older cannon or artillery tubes without carriages, but was still a huge windfall for the Confederacy. Most of the guns placed onto Confederate warships used throughout the Mississippi River Valley came from Norfolk, such as ten 32-pounders that armed the raider *Sumter* and gunboat *McRae* at New Orleans in 1861. One historian catalogued that by the

3 *DANFS*, 2:554.

4 John M. Brooke Diary," Mar. 10, 1862, *Ironclads and Big Guns of the Confederacy*, 74.

end of 1861, 155 heavy artillery pieces, 113 of which were naval 32-pounders, were dispatched to New Orleans; the vast majority of these were from Gosport.[5]

Whenever Confederates destroyed or captured a Union warship, they tried to salvage the vessel's artillery for their own use. Such was the case when Confederate General Wirt Adams offloaded eight 24-pounders before burning the captured USS *Petrel* on the Yazoo River in 1864. The same type of recovery occurred two months later when Confederate General Jo Shelby captured the USS *Queen City*, armed with another eight cannon, several of which were removed before the ship was burned. The case of the ironclad CSS *Missouri's* armament highlights the importance of reusing Union guns. It was armed with only three cannon, a standard naval 32-pounder, likely from the Gosport Navy Yard, and two Dahlgren smoothbores, one 11-inch and one 9-inch, both salvaged from the sunken Union ironclad *Indianola*.[6]

When heavy naval artillery was not available, lighter field guns in army depots were substituted. The New Orleans privateer *Calhoun* captured numerous prizes using cannon smaller than the army 24-pounder. The privateer *Music* did the same with just a pair of 6-pounder field pieces. The army gunboat *Grampus* utilized a pair of army 12-pounder field pieces when it took part in the defense of Island Number Ten. One of the three cannon on the *J.A. Cotton* as it defended Bayou Teche in early 1863 was a light 9-pounder (the other two were 32-pounders). The entire armament of the CSS *Bienville* and CSS *Carondelet* on Lake Pontchartrain were army guns supplied by General Mansfield Lovell. Though Secretary Mallory wished for the most modern naval cannon possible, clearly, Confederate manufacturing and supply limitations meant that often ships were outfitted with whatever was available.[7]

Confederate Innovations

Despite initially having no navy and no warships, forced to rely on older, captured cannon, and lacking military shipyards and few skilled ship builders, the Confederacy's improvised efforts in the Mississippi River Valley saw innovations

---

5 Semmes, *Memoirs of Service Afloat*, 99; James M. Merrill, "Confederate Shipbuilding at New Orleans," *Journal of Southern History* (Spring 1962). No. 1. 28:92.

6 "Report of Lieutenant General Polk," *ORN*, 26:260; "Report of Brigadier General Shelby," *ORN*, 26:433; Jonathan H. Carter to Richard Taylor, Apr. 15, 1863," *Jonathan H. Carter Letter Book*.

7 *DANFS*, 2:505, 529, 536, 551.

that revolutionized naval warfare. The most important of these was the enthusiastic adoption of the ironclad warship. Secretary Mallory envisioned a fleet of ironclads prowling the Mississippi River. True, the Confederacy's press and public attention focused on the CSS *Virginia* in Norfolk. But the first ironclad warship used in combat, and privately built, was the iron turtle ram *Manassas*. Even before the *Manassas* was tested at the Battle of the Head of Passes in October 1861, Mallory realized that more armored vessels were needed and construction programs began at New Orleans, Memphis, and along the Confederate Atlantic coastline.

Directly tied to the technologically advanced ironclads was an ancient weapon: the ram. The Union paid no attention to rams until the winter of 1861 and spring of 1862. The little *Manassas* again was first, using its iron-tipped ram to smash a hole in the USS *Richmond* at the Battle of the Head of Passes. Though it did not inflict crippling damage, Confederate naval officials in Richmond were convinced of the ram's offensive potential. In January 1862 the River Defense Fleet was born, with each of these army organized and civilian manned ships armed with a ram.

Initially the U.S. Navy discounted the ram as a potential weapon. However, when the CSS *Virginia* rammed and sank the Union sailing frigate *Cumberland* in March 1862, that same month the United States Ram Fleet was born on the Mississippi River, becoming a Union counter to the Confederacy's River Defense Fleet.

The ram remained a viable and formidable weapon of the Confederacy's river forces throughout the war. The *Manassas* rammed, but did not sink, ships at the Head of Passes in October 1861 and again at the Battle of Forts Jackson and Saint Philip in April 1862. Also at Fort Jackson, the USS *Varuna* sank after being rammed by the Louisiana Navy gunboat *Governor Moore* and the Confederate Army River Defense Fleet Ship *Stonewall Jackson*. The River Defense Fleet struck again at the Battle of Plum Point Bend in May 1862, ramming and sinking the Union ironclads *Cincinnati* and *Mound City*, and in February 1863, the *W.H. Webb* rammed and sank the Union ironclad *Indianola*. Mallory's ancient but effective naval weapon sank three enemy ironclads after it was introduced in the Mississippi River Valley. For the remainder of the war some Union naval officers suffered from "ram fever" believing all Confederate ships might strike at any moment.[8]

8 "The Battle of the Passes: The Enemy's Account," *New Orleans* [LA] *Daily Picayune*, Oct. 15, 1861; "The Wrought Iron Prow," *Charleston* [SC] *Mercury*, Apr 9, 1862; *Court of Inquiry*, 68; Scharf, *History of the Confederate Navy*, 254; "Report of Major Brent," *ORN*, 24:403.

The third major innovation of Confederate naval forces on the western waterways was the torpedo. Known as mines today, Confederate torpedoes were moored to an anchor or allowed to drift with the river current. Different designs were developed, ranging from contact mines set to explode when they struck an object, to wire detonated torpedoes that exploded when men on a riverbank connected wires to complete the circuit of electricity feeding the device.

This unconventional weapon was first tried in the American Revolution unsuccessfully and a few other nations experimented with it before the Civil War. The Confederacy employed torpedoes on an unprecedented level, the first examples appearing on the upper Mississippi River in late 1861. It was one of the most feared weapons by Union naval officers. Torpedoes could strike without warning, were cheap and relatively easy to produce, and saturating a waterway with them could deny its use or at least significantly delay Union ships passage. Three Union ironclads were sunk by Confederate torpedoes in this theater, the *Cairo* in 1862, the *Baron De Kalb* in 1863, and the *Eastport* in 1864. Three wooden gunboats, USS *Richmond*, USS *Kinsman*, and USS *Kenwood*, were also struck by river torpedoes, but did not sink and were later repaired.

Beyond the physical destruction inflicted by torpedoes was the psychological fear they caused. Droves of torpedoes guarded Confederate positions on the Yazoo and Red Rivers, and Union fleets proceeding into them were required to delay their operations to remove them. When Union warships advanced against Fort Hindman in Arkansas in early 1863, scouting ships were sent ahead to detect and disable Southern torpedoes. Perhaps the most famous occurrence of "torpedo fever" was at the Battle of Mobile Bay in 1864, when the monitor *Tecumseh* sank in just minutes after striking a torpedo. Admiral David Farragut urged his lines of ships to continue the attack, allegedly shouting to his officers "damn the torpedoes!"[9]

Though commerce raiding was a key part of Confederate naval strategy, it was not employed on the Mississippi River. However, some of the Confederacy's most successful privateers operated out of New Orleans in 1861, and many of those ended up in the Confederate Navy. The first commissioned raider, the CSS *Sumter*, was outfitted for sea at the Crescent City.

A final Confederate innovation pioneered in the Mississippi River Valley was submarine warfare. Though the Confederate submarine *H.L. Hunley*, the first to

---

9 "Abstract Log of USS Forest Rose," *ORN*, 25:135; "Order of Rear Admiral Porter," *ORN*, 26:438.

sink an enemy ship in battle, was constructed and operated in Charleston, South Carolina, its predecessor, the *Pioneer*, was fabricated and tested in Lake Pontchartrain, at New Orleans. The same team that eventually built the *Hunley* developed their design ideas with the *Pioneer*, even sinking a test target in early 1862.

Effectiveness of Naval Weapons

The Confederacy defended the Mississippi River through a combination of mobile warships, torpedoes, fire rafts chained together, and static fortifications that sometimes-included floating batteries.

Fire ships were used for centuries in naval warfare. Although they created temporary anxiety among Union sailors, in the Civil War fire rafts failed to achieve any notable successes.

The forts were a traditional form of defense, but they provided only an illusion of strength. They were supposed to hold Union forces at bay while Confederate vessels supplied them and gunboats provided combat support, attacking any Union ships that slipped past. In several instances, Confederate fortifications disabled or seriously damaged Union warships (ironclads *Essex* at Fort Henry, *St. Louis* and *Pittsburgh* at Fort Donelson, and *Mound* City at St. Charles, Arkansas, and the wooden *Queen of the West* at Fort DeRussy), but in almost all of these instances, the Union ships were repaired and returned to service. Although some Union vessels were damaged running by forts, individual gunboats and entire squadrons repeatedly steamed past these forts with only one mortar boat sunk by a fort's artillery fire (*Maria J. Carleton* at Fort Jackson south of New Orleans) and one wooden ship so disabled by gunfire it was destroyed to prevent capture (*Mississippi* at Port Hudson).

Inexperience with gunnery, the slow reloading process, the difficulty of hitting moving targets at night, and spotting enemy vessels through smoke hampered Confederate gun fire. In some places these static fortifications offered weak defenses easily overcome, while others saw dynamic battles. In addition to their garrisons of artillerymen, the fortifications needed mobile armies to protect them on the land side, as in the case of Island Number Ten and Vicksburg. Tied to these forts, an army lost its mobility; thousands of Confederate soldiers were eventually trapped and captured as occurred at Fort Donelson and Vicksburg.

Forts had better success at blocking Union navigation on narrow and shallower waterways such as Fort DeRussy on the Red River, Fort Hindman in Arkansas, Fort Bisland on Bayou Teche, and Fort Pemberton in the Mississippi

Delta. These positions were often augmented with sunken obstructions and torpedoes.

A combination of old and new static fortifications supported by naval ships was a fairly sound strategy that bought the South time to transfer men, animals, and supplies across the Mississippi to its eastern armies. Fortifications in the upper Confederacy included those at Columbus, Island Number Ten, New Madrid, and Fort Pillow; those at the Mississippi's mouth included Forts Jackson and Saint Philip backed by Batteries Chalmette and McGehee at New Orleans. Vicksburg and Port Hudson fortifications provided last-ditch defenses of the middle Mississippi.

Overwhelming Federal numbers on the waterways, well led by aggressive officers, steadily gained control of the Mississippi River and its tributaries despite Confederate heroics. By late 1864, only Confederate defenses on the Red River continued to defy Union gunboats.

Although much hope was placed in Confederate river ironclads, their combat record was disappointing. The small one-gun ram *Manassas* damaged a few Union warships but sank none. Of the others, only the *Arkansas* defeated a Union ironclad warship. In July 1862 in a running battle, it forced the armored river gunboat *Carondelet* to surrender, nearly sank the wooden ram *Lancaster*, and forced the mortar boat *Sidney C. Jones* to be scuttled. Over the following days the *Arkansas* nearly sank the wooden gunboat *Winona* and seriously damaged the ironclad *Essex* before the Confederate ironclad was scuttled to prevent capture. It was the single most successful C.S. Navy armored warship in the war.

By comparison, the revived ram and unconventional torpedo were the Confederacy's most effective river weapons Wooden naval surface vessels armed with rams destroyed or captured four Union warships. In the spring 1862 New Orleans campaign, the wooden gunboat *Varuna* sank after being struck numerous times by Confederate rams. In May 1862 at Plum Point Bend, rams of the River Defense Fleet sank the ironclads *Cincinnati* and *Mound City*, and in February 1863 the *W.H. Webb* drove the ironclad *Indianola* aground and captured it.[10]

By far, an unconventional weapon—the torpedo—proved the most effective against the U.S. Navy on the South's coastline and internal waterways. Three ironclads, the *Cairo*, *Baron De Kalb*, and *Eastport* were sunk by torpedoes on western rivers. Though this is comparable to destruction by rams or damage by

---

10 John Hart Diary, Apr. 20, 1862, MSS 134, Williams Research Center, The Historic New Orleans Collection.

fortifications, torpedoes caused permanent destruction, with sunken ships that were not recovered and returned to service. Another four Monitor style vessels (*Tecumseh*, *Osage*, *Milwaukee*, and *Patapsco*) were sunk by torpedoes in Mobile or off Charleston, South Carolina, and an estimated 33-51 Union wooden gunboats and supply ships were lost or damaged to them in all theaters of war.[11]

In summary, unconventional methods of defense were the most effective: ironclads; rams; torpedoes. Of these, torpedoes were the fastest to produce and the cheapest. Throughout all theaters of the Civil War, dozens of them damaged or sank Union ships and delayed or denied navigation on the rivers or coastlines of the South. If torpedoes were made sooner and in greater numbers, could they have changed the strategic riverine situation in favor of the Confederacy?

In addition to the military impact of torpedoes, a massive saturation of them in the Mississippi River Valley could have meant serious political problems for the Lincoln administration. After the Union capture of Vicksburg and Port Hudson in July 1863, the use of massive numbers of torpedoes might have slowed or even stopped commercial shipping for periods of time. President Lincoln was under pressure to open the Mississippi to trade and export for midwestern farmers and factories. However, this was a strategy of denying the Union free use of the rivers, not of establishing Confederate control over its waterways. Also, such a strategy made more sense after the 1862 Union spring campaigns that destroyed the Confederacy's conventional naval forces.

In order to use its rivers to transport men, animals, raw materials, vital equipment, and supplies, the Confederacy needed a conventional river fleet. Torpedoes were also most effective when used in conjunction with Confederate fortifications and ships. If Union naval officers were more cautious or less aggressive, like army Major General McClellan in the east, the South might have gained the time required to complete more ironclads and convert more civilian riverboats into gunboat rams.

The Confederate Navy's failure to control the Mississippi River Valley can be condensed to three factors: a disorganized chain of command, scarcity of all types of resources, and lack of time. The ships operated by the Confederacy to protect its inland waters were funded, built, equipped, crewed, and operated by several organizations. Entrepreneurs operated privateers with little or no government or

---

11 For incomplete lists and figures related to torpedo damage, see Scharf, 768; G.J. Rains, "Torpedoes," *Southern Historical Society Papers* (1877), 3:256.; Herbert M. Schiller, ed., *Confederate Torpedoes: Two Illustrated 19th Century Works with New Appendices and Photographs*, (Jefferson, NC, 2011), 139-167.

military oversight. The C.S. Navy tried, unsuccessfully, to control construction, training, and riverine operations at the start of the war. The C.S. Army purchased, converted, and operated its own ships, which took part in the defense of Columbus, Kentucky in the first year of the war, as well as later on Lake Pontchartrain and the Mississippi Sound. Most notable was the establishment of the River Defense Fleet: these were ships owned by the army, but operated by civilian contractors who sometimes cooperated with other ships and sometimes obeyed military officials. To confuse matters more, the state of Louisiana organized and operated its own naval force in 1862, technically independent of Confederate authority and the Confederate Revenue Service maintained a pair of ships on the Mississippi in the war's first year.

The result was an inefficient and dysfunctional chain of command for Confederate riverine forces. One naval commander who did make a difference was Cmdre. George N. Hollins, but his control was limited to maybe half the Southern warships on the Mississippi River. Hollins worked well with army commander Gen. Mansfield Lovell to arm ships protecting approaches to New Orleans and in the defense of Island Number Ten. This cooperation did not last long. When New Orleans was threatened in April 1862, Hollins steamed downriver to assist in its defense. He was promptly relieved for not waiting for approval from Richmond even though he showed initiative. Individual Confederate ship captains later scored tactical victories, but there was never again a western naval commander like Hollins with as much authority to direct Confederate riverine operations.

After the loss of New Orleans, the Confederate Army gained hegemony regarding river operations. Though naval officers maintained certain autonomy in how they operated their vessels, they still obeyed the orders of senior army commanders. The government recognized that the loss of New Orleans and most of the river fleet required better army-navy cooperation. Army officers were all senior in rank and controlled resources vital to the navy: army volunteers filled out crew complements on the ironclads *Arkansas* and *Missouri*; army fort garrisons provided guns and supplies as well as assigned personnel to crew ships, such as on the *J.A. Cotton* and *Diana* in Bayou Teche and the *Grand Duke* on the Red River. On the other hand, some ships were disarmed to strengthen land fortifications, and the army sometimes refused to detach soldiers who were skilled laborers to help build and convert ships. An army running a navy was not an ideal situation, but Richmond's decision was a necessary if desperate one.

The Confederate Navy fought bravely on the western rivers even as its number of warships steadily shrank. It aggressively employed the few ironclads that became operational, and the rams on converted civilian steamships gave a good account of themselves. The C.S. Navy was supplemented by sunken obstructions, torpedoes, and fortifications that delayed but rarely defeated the larger Union riverine navy. Contracted civilians, cavalry raiders, field artillery, and infantry forces also participated, sometimes with spectacular results, in waterway battles.

Ultimately, however, these efforts were not enough to stave off Confederate defeat.

Analysis and Conclusions

SENIOR Confederate naval officers arrived in New Orleans in the war's opening days to acquire or construct suitable ships. In the first year of the conflict, an impressive ship building program saw as many as nine ironclads being developed in New Orleans and Tennessee and dozens of wooden steamers converted into warships. By the campaign for New Orleans in late April 1862, only the small, veteran one-gun armored ram *Manassas* and unfinished 16-gun ironclad *Louisiana* were available to defend the forts guarding the city.

By comparison, the United States launched ten riverine ironclads, with 124 heavy cannon total by February of 1862. Six of these fought at Forts Henry and Donelson in February—just six months from when the construction contract was signed.

Confederate Secretary of the Navy Stephen Mallory did everything he could to match the Union effort. How then did the Confederacy fail in its goal to control its internal waterways?

First, time was never a Confederate ally. Union campaigns along the Mississippi River in the spring of 1862 destroyed the Confederate ad hoc wooden warship fleet and erased the initial Confederate ironclad building program. Of the nine planned ironclads, only the *Manassas, Louisiana* and *Arkansas* saw combat in 1862; the remainder were captured by the United States or destroyed before their completion due to advancing enemy forces. Even these three were lost by the end of the year. Second, when New Orleans and Memphis fell to Union forces, the fate of the Mississippi River was sealed, and with it the end of the Confederacy's hope for large-scale naval riverine operations. Though a second round of ironclad construction began in the fall of 1862 on the Yazoo River, Red River, and Bayou Teche for another six ironclads, nearly all of these efforts once again proved futile. The lack of suitable construction facilities, scarcity of supplies, and a variety of delays forced the self-destruction of all but one of these ironclads; only the *Missouri* was completed in this second wave. Likewise, it was the only ironclad produced on the western waters that still flew the Confederate flag at the war's end.

Third, a significant amount of the Confederacy's limited money, ship building resources, and skilled laborers went into converting civilian river steamships into dubious warships usually armed with few and small cannon, and crewed with non-military sailors or borrowed soldiers. Most fought bravely if ineffectively. Some simply fled as soon as they faced the reality of large, purpose-built Union multi-gun warships operated by trained and experienced officers and crew. The attempt to organize a traditional wooden naval river squadron in the war's first year resulted in improvised and disorganized efforts that failed to keep Union forces at bay and drew resources away from ironclad building.

Fourth, the United States exploited its superior manufacturing capabilities, its established professional navy, and a much larger labor pool to create and activate its river squadron more quickly. Though these city-class Union ironclads built in late 1861 and early 1862 were powerful, they were not invincible. Of these ten initial Union ironclads, two (*Cairo* and *Baron De Kalb*) were sunk by torpedoes, two (*Cincinnati* and *Mound City*) were rammed by the River Defense Fleet and sunk at the Battle of Plum Point Bend (both later salvaged and repaired), another (*Indianola*) sank after being rammed by the *W.H. Webb* in early 1863, and one (*Carondelet*) struck her colors while fighting the CSS *Arkansas* (but later withdrew its surrender when the *Arkansas* failed to take possession of it). This is a 60% loss rate, leading to what-if speculation that perhaps even just a few more of the Confederate ironclads becoming operational might have seriously hampered Union naval efforts in the Mississippi River Valley.[1]

These Union ironclad losses were replaced by a second wave of seven more Union ironclads that entered service by early 1863. One of these, the *Eastport*, built on the captured hull of an unfinished Confederate ironclad begun in early 1862, sank when struck by a Confederate torpedo in 1864. The Confederacy could never counter or sink as many Union warships that were built.

This begs the question of whether the Confederacy should have tried to build a conventional wooden naval river fleet at all instead of focusing all resources on launching ironclad vessels as quickly as possible. Most cost effective were

---

1 "Report of Commander Henry Walke," Ibid., 19:41; "Report of Second Master Gregory," Ibid., 23:16; "Report of Lieutenant Commander Selfridge," Ibid., 23:549-550; "Report of Lieutenant Commander Walker," Ibid., 25:283; Thompson, *The Civil War Reminiscences of M. Jeff Thompson*, 157; Linn Tanner, "The Capture of the Indianola," Miscellaneous Papers Related to the Confederacy.

Confederate torpedoes: not only cheaper and easier to make, they delayed, stopped, sank or damaged more Union gunboats than the ironclads. Such radical decisions might have required a clairvoyance or strategic understanding beyond either side's leaders at the start of the war.

What Southern leaders did understand early was their limited railroad infrastructure. Compared to the Union, the South had fewer railroad lines, fewer miles of rails, and most of those lines were not connected due to incompatible gauges (width of the rails). Taking steel rails from railroads to build ironclads was a necessary expedient, but a poor strategic decision. Much of the railroad iron used on the CSS *Missouri*, which never fought an enemy vessel, and the railroad iron stockpiled then lost at Yazoo City for unfinished ironclads, might have been better utilized keeping a railroad operating.

The Confederate Navy was often downplayed in Civil War military histories. Most casual students of the war are aware of the ironclad CSS *Virginia* and its famous duel with the Union armored *Monitor,* and are likely familiar with Confederate blockade-runners, commerce raiders, and perhaps the submarine *H.L. Hunley.* Southern naval efforts, if mentioned, are often presented as reactions to the Union blockade and other naval operations.

Secretary Mallory's efforts to control the Mississippi River Valley were not always simply defensive reactions to Union movements and attacks such as relying on fixed fortifications, sunken obstructions, and torpedoes. Quickly embracing the latest ironclad technology and improvising the ancient ram before the Union deployed it were pro-active aggressive actions.

Mallory and his naval officers did not lack for ideas. These included the Confederate joint operations in the Island Number Ten campaign in early 1862, the attempt to use the ironclad CSS *Arkansas* before it was scuttled to help launch a counterattack with land forces to liberate Baton Rouge, Louisiana in the fall of 1862, and efforts to shift gunboats on the Red River to the Atchafalaya to support Confederate armies on Bayou Teche in early 1863.

Ultimately, lack of resources, time, and trained personnel resulted in a Confederate Navy too weak to do anything but play a supporting role to the static fortifications and mobile armies protecting the western waterways. However, its doomed efforts were daring and inventive, and hopefully this book provides the Confederacy's riverine forces with a better epitaph.

BIBLIOGRAPHY

Primary Sources

Unpublished Manuscript Collections

Alabama Textual Materials Collection, Alabama Department of Archives and History, Montgomery, AL
    Baker, Alpheus Address and Diary
American Antiquarian Society, Worcester, MA
    Bacon, Edward Woolsey Papers, 1861-1865
Confederate States of American. Medical Records, University of Southern Mississippi, Hattiesburg, MS
    Freeman, Robert J. "Journal of Medical and Surgical Practice on board the CS Steamer Genl Polk"
Dolph Briscoe Center for American History, The University of Texas, Austin TX
    Howell, W. Randolph Papers, 1861-1879
    Hunter, William W. Papers
    Miscellaneous Papers Related to the Confederacy
Louisiana and Lower Mississippi Valley Collections, Louisiana State University, Baton Rouge, LA
    Anonymous Confederate Letter
    Arnold, Thomas Letters
    Miller, Alexander Diary
    Oliver, Adolphus Letters
Louisiana Historical Association Collection, Tulane University, New Orleans, LA
    Foster Jr., Freeman Letters
    Roy, John Diary
    Van Benthuysen, A. C. Papers
Manuscripts, Archives, and Special Collections, Washington State University Libraries, Pullman, WA
    Cox, Earl Blake Family Papers
National Archives, Washington, DC
    Records Group 45, Carter, Jonathan H. Letter Book
    Records Group 45, Correspondence and Political Records of the Confederate States Navy Paymaster at Mobile, AL
    Records Group 45, Subject File of the Confederate States Navy, 1861-1865
    Records Group 109, Confederate Vessel Papers: Papers Pertaining to Vessels Involved with the Confederate States of America
    Records Group 109, General Orders and Circulars of the Confederate War Department 1861-1865
    Records Group 109, Jackson and Company Papers
    Records Group 109, John Hughes and Company Papers
    Records Group 109, Leeds and Company Papers
    Records Group 109, Letters received by the Confederate Secretary of War 1861-1865
    Records Group 109, Pemberton, John C. Papers
    Records Group 109, Weldon, Thomas Papers
    Records Group 365, Letters received by the Confederate Secretary of the Treasury 1861-1865

Southern Historical Collection, University of North Carolina, Chapel Hill, NC
      Mallory, Steven R. Diary and Reminiscences
The Historic New Orleans Collection, New Orleans, LA
      Caldwell, Charles H. B. Papers
      Duncan, Johnson K. Letters
      Hart, John Diary
      US Ship Portsmouth Log
United States Naval Academy, Special Collections and Archives, Annapolis MD
      Hart, John E. Letters
University of Alabama, University Libraries Division of Special Collections, Tuscaloosa, AL
      Dent Jr., John Horry Letters

Published Books

Ashkenazi, Elliott ed. *The Civil War Diary of Clara Solomon: Growing Up In New Orleans 1861-1862*. Baton Rouge, LA: LSU Press, 1995.

Barlett, John Russell. "The *Brooklyn* at the Passage of the Forts" in *Battles and Leaders of the Civil War*, 4 Vols. New York: The Century Co, 1887.

Beecher, Harris H. *Record of the 114th Regiment, NYSV*. Norwich, NY: J.F. Hubbard, 1866.

Brooke Jr., George M. ed. *Ironclads and Big Guns of the Confederacy: The Journal and Letters of John M. Brooke*. Columbia, SC: University of South Carolina Press, 2003.

Brown, Isaac N. Brown. "The Confederate Gun-Boat 'Arkansas'" in *Battles and Leaders of the Civil War*, 4 Vols. New York: The Century Co, 1887.

Campbell, R. Thomas ed. *Engineer in Gray: Memoirs of Chief Engineer James H. Tomb*. Jefferson, NC: McFarland and Co., 2005.

Cotham Jr., Edward T. ed. *The Southern Journey of a Civil War Marine: The Illustrated Note-Book of Henry O. Gusley*. Austin, TX: University of Texas Press, 2006.

Davis, Jefferson. *The Papers of Jefferson Davis*. 14 Vols. Baton Rouge, LA: Louisiana State University Press, 2003.

Davis, Jefferson. *The Rise and Fall of the Confederate Government*. 2 Vols. New York: Appleton and Co., 1881.

Dawson, Francis W. *Reminiscences of Confederate Service: 1861-1865*. Charleston, SC: News and Courier Book Presses, 1882.

Dawson, Sarah Morgan. *A Confederate Girl's Diary*. Boston: Riverside Press, 1913.

De Forest, John Williams. *A Volunteer's Adventures: A Union Captain's Record of the Civil War*. New Haven, CT: Yale University Press, 1946.

Dewey, George. *Autobiography of George Dewey: Admiral of the Navy*. New York: Charles Scribner's Sons, 1913.

Dix, John A. *Memoirs of John Adams Dix*. 2 Vols. New York: Harper and Brothers, 1883.

Earp, Charles A. ed. *Yellow Flag: The Civil War Journal of Surgeon's Steward C. Marion Dodson*. Baltimore, MD: Maryland Historical Society, 2002.

Ellet, Alfred W. "Ellet and His Steam-Rams at Memphis" in *Battles and Leaders of the Civil War*. 4 Vols. New York: The Century Co, 1887.

Dorsey, Sarah A. *Recollections of Henry Watkins Allen*. New Orleans, LA: Doolady, 1866.

Flinn, Frank M. *Campaigning with Banks in '63 and '64, and with Sheridan in the Shenandoah Valley in '64 and '65*. Lynn, MA: T.P. Nichols, 1887.

Fremantle, Arthur. *Three Months in the Southern States: The 1863 War Diary of an English Soldier April-June 1863*. Edinburgh: William Blackwood and Sons, 1863.

Grant, Ulysses S. *The Personal Memoirs of Ulysses S. Grant.* 2 Vols. New York: Charles L. Webster and Co., 1885.

Gunther, Charles F. *Two Years Before the Paddlewheel: Charles F. Gunther, Mississippi River Confederate.* Edited by Bruce S. Allardice and Wayne L. Wolf, Buffalo Gap, TX: State House Press, 2012.

Hermann, E. C. ed. *Battle-Fields of the South.* New York: John Bradburn, 1864.

Hermann, E.C. ed. *Yeoman in Farragut's Fleet: The Civil War Diary of Josiah Parker Higgins.* Monterey, CA: Guy Victor Publications, 1999.

Jackson, Oscar L. *The Colonel's Diary.* Sharon, PA: David P. Jackson, 1922.

Kell, John M. *Recollections of a Naval Life: Including the Cruises of the Confederate States Steamers, "Sumter" and "Alabama".* Washington, DC: Neale Co, 1900.

Kennon, Beverly. "Fighting Farragut Below New Orleans," in *Battles and Leaders of the Civil War.* 4 Vols. New York: The Century Co, 1887.

McGuire, Judith W. *Diary of a Southern Refugee, During the War.* New York: E.G. Hale and Son, 1867.

Mahan, Alfred T. *The Gulf and Inland Waters.* New York: Charles Scribner's Sons, 1883.

Morgan, James Morris. *Recollections of a Rebel Reefer.* New York: Houghton Mifflin Co, 1917.

Order of the Regimental Association. *History of the Forty-Sixth Regiment Indiana Volunteer Infantry: September, 1861-September, 1865.* Logansport, IN: William Humphreys & Co, 1888.

Hyde Jr., Samuel C. ed. *A Wisconsin Yankee in Confederate Bayou Country: The Civil War Reminiscences of a Union General.* Baton Rouge, LA: LSU Press, 2009.

Poe, J. C. ed. *The Raving Foe: The Civil War Diary of Major James T. Poe, C.S.A. and the 11th Arkansas Volunteers and a Complete List of Prisoners.* Eastland, TX: Longhorn Press, 1967.

Pope, John. *The Military Memoirs of General John Pope.* Edited by Peter Cozzens and Robert I. Girardi. Chapel Hill, NC: University of North Carolina Press, 1998.

Porter, David D. *The Naval History of the Civil War.* New York: Sherman Publishing Company, 1886.

Porter, David D. "The Opening of the Lower Mississippi" in *Battles and Leaders of the Civil War* 4 Vols. New York: The Century Co, 1887.

Rains, Gabriel J. and Michie, Peter S. *Confederate Torpedoes.* Edited by Herbert M. Schiller. Jefferson, NC: McFarland Press, 2011.

Scharf, J. Thomas. *History of the Confederate States Navy from its Organization to the Surrender of its Last Vessel.* New York: Roger and Sherwood, 1887.

Schiller, Herbert M. ed. *Confederate Torpedoes: Two Illustrated 19th Century Works with New Appendices and Photographs.* Jefferson, NC: McFarlane Press, 2011.

Selfridge, Thomas O. "The Navy in the Red River" in *Battles and Leaders of the Civil War.* 4 Vols. New York: The Century Co, 1887.

Semmes, Raphael. *Memoirs of Service Afloat: During the War Between the States.* Baltimore, MD: Kelly Piet & Co, 1868.

Jones, Terry L. ed. *The Civil War Memoirs of Captain William J. Seymour: Reminiscences of a Louisiana Tiger.* Baton Rouge, LA: LSU Press, 1991.

Sherman, William T. *Memoirs of General William T. Sherman.* 2 Vols. New York: D. Appleton and Co., 1875.

Taylor, Richard. *Destruction and Reconstruction: Personal Experiences of the Late War.* New York: D. Appleton and Co, 1879.

Thompson, M. Jeff. *The Civil War Reminiscences of General M. Jeff Thompson.* Edited by Donald J. Stanton, Goodwin F. Berquist, and Paul C. Bowers. Dayton, OH: Morningside Press, 1988.

Twain, Mark. *Life on the Mississippi.* Boston: James R. Osgood and Co, 1883.

Walke, Henry. "The Western Flotilla at Fort Donelson, Island Number Ten, Fort Pillow and Memphis" in *Battles and Leaders of the Civil War.* 4 Vols. New York: The Century Co, 1887.

Walker, Jeanie Mort. *Life of Captain Fry: The Cuban Martyr.* Hartford, CT: J.B. Burr's Publishing Company, 1875.

Warley, A.F. "The Ram *Manassas* at the Passage of the New Orleans Forts" in *Battles and Leaders of the Civil War* 4 Vols. New York: The Century Co, 1887.

Wilkinson, John. *The Narrative of a Blockade Runner*. New York: Sheldon & Co, 1877.

Published Government Documents

Booth, Andrew B. *Military Records of Louisiana Confederate Soldiers and Louisiana Confederate Commands*. 3 Vols. New Orleans: Louisiana Military Records, 1920.

Confederate States of America, *Journal of the Congress of the Confederate States of America*. 7 Volumes. Washington D.C., 1904-1905.

Confederate States of America Congress, *Report of Evidence Taken Before a Joint Special Committee of Both Houses of the Confederate Congress to Investigate the Affairs of the Navy Department*. Richmond, VA, G.P. Evans & Co., 1863.

Confederate States of America Navy Department. *Regulations for the Navy of the Confederate States. 1862*. Richmond, Virginia: Macfarlane and Fergusson, 1862.

Confederate States of America War Department, *Proceedings of the Court of Inquiry Relative to the Fall of New Orleans*. Richmond, VA, R.M. Smith, 1864, 206 pp.

Dahlgren, John A. *Shells and Shell Guns*. Philadelphia, PA: Kind and Baird, 1856.

Dictionary of American Naval Fighting Ships. 8 Vols. Navy Department, Office of the Chief of Naval Operations, Naval History Division, 1959-1981.

Official Records of the Union and Confederate Navies in the War of the Rebellion. 31 Vols. Washington, D.C.: Government Printing Office, 1894 – 1922.

Ship Register and Enrollments of New Orleans, Louisiana. 6 Vols. Baton Rouge, Louisiana: LSU Press, 1941-1942.

The War of the Rebellion: A Compilation of the Official Records of the Union and Confederate Armies. 128 Vols. Washington, D.C.: Government Printing Office, 1880 – 1901.

United States Naval War Records Office. *Officers of the Confederate States Navy, 1861 – 1865*. Washington D.C. Government Printing Office, 1898.

United States Naval War Records Office. *Register of Officers of the Confederate States Navy 1861 – 1865*. Washington D.C. Government Printing Office, 1931.

Ward, James H. *Elementary Instructions in Naval Ordnance and Gunnery*. New York: D. Van Nostrand, 1861.

Published Periodical Articles

Anonymous, "Originator of the Ironclad," *Marine Review and Marine Record* (July 1903), No. 2. 28:67.

Cunningham, S.A. "The Last Roll, Commodore J.E. Montgomery". *Confederate Veteran* (1902), 10:416-417.

Gift, George W., "The Story of the Arkansas," in *Southern Historical Society Papers* (1887), 12:116.

Hollins, George N. "Autobiography of Commodore George Nicholas Hollins, C.S.A." in *Maryland Historical Magazine* (1939), No. 3. 34:228-243.

Jeffries, Clarence. "Running the Blockade on the Mississippi" in *Confederate Veteran* (1914), 12:22-23.

Morgan, James M. "The Pioneer Ironclad," in *United States Naval Institute Proceedings*. No. 10. 43:2277.

Rains, G.J., "Torpedoes," in *Southern Historical Society Papers* (1877), 3:255-260.

Read, Charles W., "Reminisces of the Confederate States Navy" in *Southern Historical Society Papers* (1876), 1:331-362.

"The Declaration of Paris, 1856". *The American Journal of International Law* (1907). No. 2 1:89-90.

Contemporary Newspapers

Athens [TN] *Post*, December 20, 1861.
Alexandria [VA] *Gazette*, May 7, 1864.
Baltimore [MD} *Daily Exchange*, May 24, 1861.
Baltimore [MD] *Sun*, July 1861-March 1862.
Belmont [OH] *Chronicle*, March 20, 1862.
Carrolton [LA] *Sun*, May 29, 1861.
Charleston [SC] *Mercury*, April 9, 1862.
Clarkesville [TN] *Chronicle*, February 14, 1862.
Daily Green Mountain [VT] *Freeman*, April 30, 1863.
Daily Nashville [TN] *Patriot*, December 11, 1861.
Daily Nashville [TN] *Union*, June 1862-November 1864.
Dallas [TX] *Herald*, May 22, 1861.
Gallipolis [OH] *Journal*, October 1861-March 1862.
Galveston [TX] *Tri-Weekly News*, October 1, 1863.
Harper's Weekly, November 1861-June 1862.
Hartford [CT] *Daily Courant*, June 1861-March 1862.
Houston [TX] *Tri-Weekly Telegraph*, February 2, 1863.
Keowee [SC] *Courier*, May 18, 1861.
Manchester [NH] *Democrat and American*, June 27, 1863.
Maysville [KY] *Dollar Weekly Bulletin*, April 30, 1863.
Memphis [TN] *Daily Appeal*, March 1862-April 1864.
Nashville [TN] *Union and American*, November-December, 1861.
New Berne [NC] *Weekly Progress*, October 29, 1861.
New Orleans [LA] *Bulletin*, October 3, 1861.
New Orleans [LA] *Daily Crescent*, March 1861-April 1862.
New Orleans [LA] *Daily Picayune*, October, 1861.
New Orleans [LA] *Daily True Delta*, June 1861-April 1862.
New York Herald, April 24, 1862.
New York Times, January 1862-August 1863.
Raleigh [NC] *Semi-Weekly Standard*, May 1, 1863.
Raleigh [NC] *Weekly Standard*, April 29, 1863.
Redwing [MN] *Goodhue Volunteer*, April 29, 1863.
Richmond [VA] *Daily Dispatch*, December 1861-January 1862.
Semi-Weekly Shreveport [LA] *News*, March-April, 1862.
Shreveport [LA] *Daily News*, May-October, 1861.
Shreveport [LA] *News*, May 24, 1864.
Shreveport [LA] *Times*, January 24, 2015.
Shreveport [LA] *Weekly News*, May-July 1861.
Washington Evening Star, November 6, 1861.
White Cloud [KS] Chief, October 31, 1861.
Wilmington [NC] *Journal*, October 1861-April 1863.
Wyandot [OH] *Pioneer*, November 11, 1864.
Yorkville [SC] *Enquirer*, December 5, 1861.

Secondary Sources

Books

Bartlett, Napier. *Military Records of Louisiana*. Baton Rouge, LA: LSU Press, 1962.

Bergeron, Arthur W. *Guide to Louisiana Confederate Military Units 1861-1865*. Baton Rouge, LA: LSU Press, 1989.

Burns, Zed H. *Ship Island and the Confederacy*. Hattiesburg, MS: University and College Press of Mississippi, 1971.

Campbell, R. Thomas. *Confederate Naval Forces on Western Waters*. Jefferson, NC: McFarland & Co., 2005.

Campbell, R. Thomas. *Hunters of the Night: Confederate Torpedo Boats in the War Between the States*. Shippensburg, PA: Burd Street Press, 2000.

Campbell, R. Thomas. *Sea Hawk of the Confederacy: Lt. Charles W. Read and the Confederate Navy*. Shippensburg, PA: Burd Street Press, 2000.

Chatelain, Neil P. *Fought Like Devils: The Confederate Gunboat McRae*. Bloomington, IN: Authorhouse, 2014.

Daniel, Larry J. and Bock, Lynn N. *Island No. 10: Struggle for the Mississippi Valley*. Tuscaloosa, AL: University of Alabama Press, 1996.

Donnelly, Ralph W. *The Confederate States Marine Corps: The Rebel Leathernecks*. Shippensburg, PA: White Main, 1989.

Durkin, Joseph T. *Stephen R. Mallory: Confederate Navy Chief*. Chapel Hill, NC: University of North Carolina Press, 1954.

Frazier, Donald S. *Blood on the Bayou: Vicksburg, Port Hudson, and the Trans-Mississippi*. Buffalo Gap, TX: State House Press, 2015.

Frazier, Donald S. *Thunder Across the Swamp: The Fight for the Lower Mississippi February 1863-May 1863*. Buffalo Gap, TX: State House Press, 2011.

Gaines, W. Craig. *Encyclopedia of Civil War Shipwrecks*. Baton Rouge, LA: LSU Press, 2008.

Greene, Jack and Massignani, Alessandro. *Ironclads at War: The Origin and Development of the Armored Warship, 1854-1891*. Da Capo Press, 1998.

Hearn, Chester. *Admiral David Dixon Porter: The Civil War Years*. Annapolis, MD: Naval Institute Press, 1996.

Hearn, Chester. *The Capture of New Orleans 1862*. Baton Rouge, LA: Louisiana State University Press, 1995.

Joiner, Gary D. *One Damn Blunder from Beginning to End: The Red River Campaign of 1864*. London: SR Books, 2003.

Luraghi, Raimondo. *A History of the Confederate Navy*. Translated by Paolo E. Coletta, Annapolis, MD: Naval Institute Press, 1996.

McCaul Jr., Edward B. *To Retain Command of the Mississippi: The Civil War Naval Campaign for Memphis*. Knoxville, TN: University of Tennessee Press, 2014.

Parkerson, Codman. *New Orleans: America's Most Fortified City*. New Orleans, LA: The Quest, 1990.

Pratt, Fletcher. *Civil War on the Western Waters*. New York: Henry Holt and Company, 1956.

Raphael, Morris. *The Battle in the Bayou Country*. Detroit, MI: Harlo Press, 1994.

Richey, Thomas H. *The Battle of Baton Rouge*. College Station, Texas: VirtualBookworm, 2005.

Robinson, William M. *The Confederate Privateers*. New Haven, Connecticut: Yale University Press, 1928.

Seymour, William H. *The Story of Algiers: Now Fifth District of New Orleans, The Past and the Present*. Algiers, Louisiana: Algiers Democrat Publishing Company, 1896.

Simpson, Jay W. *Naval Strategies of the Civil War: Confederate Innovations and Federal Opportunism*. Nashville, Tennessee: Cumberland House Press, 2001.

Smith, Myron J. Jr. *Civil War Biographies from the Western Waters: 956 Confederate and union Naval and Military Personnel, Contractors, Politicians, Officials, Steamboat Pilots and Others*. Jefferson, North Carolina: McFarland and Co., 2015.

Still Jr., William N. *Confederate Shipbuilding*. Columbia, South Carolina: University of South Carolina Press, 1969.

Still Jr., William N. *Iron Afloat: The Story of the Confederate Armorclads*. Nashville, Tennessee: Vanderbilt University Press, 1971.

Tenney, W.J. *The Military and Naval History of the Rebellion in the United States*. New York: Appleton and Co., 1866.

Winters, John D. *The Civil War in Louisiana*. Baton Rouge, LA: Louisiana State University Press, 1991.

Wyeth, John A. *That Devil Forrest: Life of General Nathan Bedford Forrest*. Baton Rouge, LA: LSU Press, 1989.

Periodical Articles

Bogle, Robert V. "Defeat Through Default: Confederate Naval Strategy for the Upper Mississippi River and its Tributaries, 1861-1862," *Tennessee Historical Quarterly* (Spring 1968). No. 1. 27:62-71.

Brittan, A. Angelo. "Samuel Bryan Brittan Jr., U.S.N.," *Brittan's Journal: Spiritual, Science, Literature, Art, and Inspiration* (1874). No. 3. 2:307-322.

Chatelain, Neil P. "Pelican Gunboats: The Louisiana State Navy and the Defense of Confederate New Orleans," *Journal of America's Military Past* (Spring/Summer 2015). No. 2. 40:5-24.

Chatelain, Neil P. "The Confederacy's Lake Pontchartrain Naval Squadron: A Cooperative Defense of the Coastal Approaches to New Orleans, 1861-1862," *Louisiana History* (Spring 2018). No. 2. 59:167-195.

Chatelain, Neil P. "William S. Lovell: Confederate Army Riverine Expert," *Civil War Navy – The Magazine* (Winter 2019). No. 3. 6:16-26.

Christ, Mark K. "'The Awful Scenes That met My Eyes': Union and Confederate Accounts of the Battle of St. Charles, June 17, 1862," *The Arkansas Historical Quarterly* (Winter 2012). No. 4. 71:407-423.

Donnelly, Ralph W. "Battle Honors and Services of Confederate Marines," *Military Affairs* (Spring 1959). No.1. 23:37-40.

Fitch, L. Boyd. "Surprise at Brashear City: Sherod Hunter's Sugar Cooler Cavalry," *Louisiana History* (Fall 1984), No. 4. 25:403-434.

Krivdo, Michael E. "Confederate Marine Corps Recruiting in New Orleans and Marine Activities in the First Year of the Civil War," *Louisiana History* (Fall 2007). No.4. 48:441-466.

Long, E.B. "The Paducah Affair: Bloodless Action that Altered the Civil War in the Mississippi Valley," *The Register of the Kentucky Historical Society* (October 1972). No. 4. 70:253-276.

Merrill, James M. "Confederate Shipbuilding at New Orleans," *Journal of Southern History* (Spring 1962). No. 1. 28:87-93.

Oxley, Robert M. "The Civil War Gulf Blockade: The Unpublished Journal of a U.S. Navy Warrant Officer Aboard the USS Vincennes, 1861-1864," *International Journal of Naval History* (April 2002). No. 1. 1:1-13.

Roca, Steven Louis. "Presence and Precedents: The USS *Red Rover* During the American Civil War, 1861-1865," *Civil War History* (June 1998). No. 2. 44:91-110.

Whitesell, Robert D. "Military and Naval Activity Between Cairo and Columbus," *The Register of the Kentucky Historical Society* (April 1963). No. 2. 61:107-121.

Index

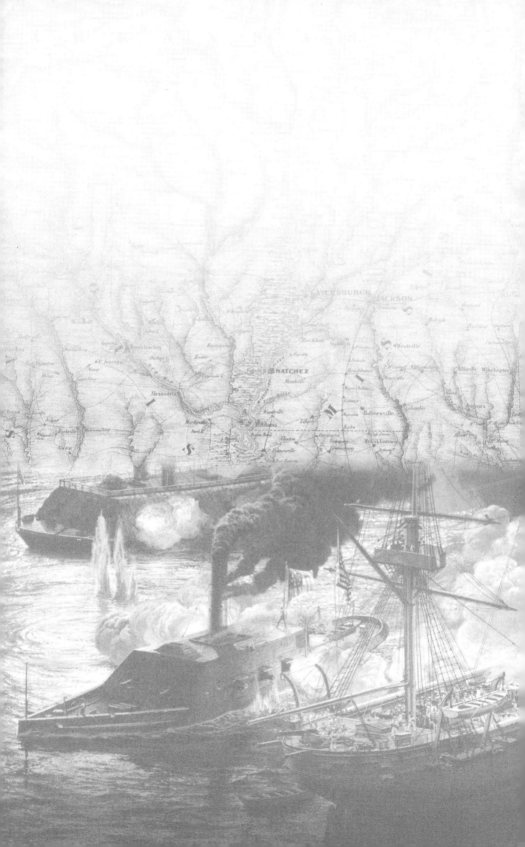

NEIL P. CHATELAIN IS AN ADJUNCT PROFESSOR OF HISTORY at Lone Star College-North Harris and a social studies instructor at Carl Wunsche Sr. High School in Spring, Texas. The former U.S. Navy Surface Warfare Officer is a graduate of the University of New Orleans, the University of Houston, and the University of Louisiana-Monroe. Neil researches U.S. Naval History with a focus on Confederate naval operations. He is the author of *Fought Like Devils: The Confederate Gunboat McRae* (2014), and many magazine, journal, and online articles. He lives with his wife Brittany in Humble, Texas.